STUDIES IN BAPTIST HISTORY AND THOUGHT
VOLUME 12

'Redeeming Love Proclaim'

John Rippon and the Baptists

STUDIES IN BAPTIST HISTORY AND THOUGHT

A full listing of all titles in this series
appears at the close of this book

Christians Magazine.

THE REV? JOHN RIPPON A.M.

John Rippon (1751-1836)
Picture courtesy of Michael A.G. Haykin

STUDIES IN BAPTIST HISTORY AND THOUGHT
VOLUME 12

'Redeeming Love Proclaim'

John Rippon and the Baptists

Ken R. Manley

Foreword by B.R. White

Paternoster:
thinking faith

British Library Cataloguing in Publication Data
A catalogue record for this book is available from the British Library

ISBN-10 1–84227–193–8
ISBN-13 978–1–84227–193–3

Typeset by K.R. Manley and A.R. Cross
Printed and bound in Great Britain
for Paternoster
by Nottingham Alpha Graphics

Series Preface

Baptists form one of the largest Christian communities in the world, and while they hold the historic faith in common with other mainstream Christian traditions, they nevertheless have important insights which they can offer to the worldwide church. *Studies in Baptist History and Thought* will be one means towards this end. It is an international series of academic studies which includes original monographs, revised dissertations, collections of essays and conference papers, and aims to cover any aspect of Baptist history and thought. While not all the authors are themselves Baptists, they nevertheless share an interest in relating Baptist history and thought to the other branches of the Christian church and to the wider life of the world.

The series includes studies in various aspects of Baptist history from the seventeenth century down to the present day, including biographical works, and Baptist thought is understood as covering the subject-matter of theology (including interdisciplinary studies embracing biblical studies, philosophy, sociology, practical theology, liturgy and women's studies). The diverse streams of Baptist life throughout the world are all within the scope of these volumes.

The series editors and consultants believe that the academic disciplines of history and theology are of vital importance to the spiritual vitality of the churches of the Baptist faith and order. The series sets out to discuss, examine and explore the many dimensions of their tradition and so to contribute to their on-going intellectual vigour.

A brief word of explanation is due for the series identifier on the front cover. The fountains, taken from heraldry, represent the Baptist distinctive of believer's baptism and, at the same time, the source of the water of life. There are three of them because they symbolize the Trinitarian basis of Baptist life and faith. Those who are redeemed by the Lamb, the book of Revelation reminds us, will be led to 'fountains of living waters' (Rev. 7.17).

Series Editors

Series Consultant Editors

To Margaret
whose love and support has been inclusive of John Rippon for more
years than either of us can easily recall

Contents

Foreword
B.R. White xiii

Preface xv

Abbreviations xvii

Chapter 1
John Rippon and the Transformation of the Baptists 1

Chapter 2
The Making of an Evangelical Baptist Leader (1751-1773) 10
Tiverton (1751-1769) 11
Bristol (1769-1773) 17
Rippon and the Theology of the Baptists 29

Chapter 3
Pattern of a Pastorate:
John Rippon and Carter Lane (1773-1836) 33
A Call and a Division 35
General Pattern 38
Pastoral Leadership 39
The Carter Lane Church Community 48
Service Outside Carter Lane 67
Men for the Ministry 73
Problems of the Closing Years (1829-1836) 78

Chapter 4
'Sing Side by Side':
John Rippon and Baptist Hymnody 82
The *Selection* 86
   Preparations, Sources and Editing 89
   Arrangement and Contents 98
   Editions of the Selection 112
      IN ENGLAND 112
      IN THE UNITED STATES 117
   Copyright Disputes 118
   Success of the Selection 121

Tune Book...123
Rippon's Watts...131
Influence of Rippon's Hymnody...134

Chapter 5
Wider Horizons:
The Baptist Annual Register (1790-1802)................................**139**
Plan of the *Register* and Response by the Churches.....................143
Rippon as Editor...147
Contents of the *Register* 153
   Lists of Churches 153
     ENGLISH LISTS 153
     WELSH LISTS..157
     GENERAL BAPTISTS' NEW ASSOCIATION LIST (1790).........158
   English and Welsh Associations..158
   American Associations, and Personal Correspondence...............164
     NEW ENGLAND 169
     MIDDLE COLONIES...170
     MARYLAND, VIRGINIA, NORTH CAROLINA AND KENTUCKY 171
     SOUTH CAROLINA AND GEORGIA 172
   Reports from the European Continent....................................173
   Missions 175
   Work among Black Christians..179
   Ireland...184
   Baptist Itinerant Society..185
   Lists of Books 185
   Miscellaneous...186
End of the *Register* 188
The Influence of the *Register*..190

Chapter 6
Rippon and Baptist Historiography..**196**
Baptist *Register* 196
Other Publications...205
Rippon's Influence on Baptist Historiography 208
'Bunhill Fields History' 211

Chapter 7
'Willing Servant of all the Churches'.....................................**215**
Rippon and the Politics of Dissent...215
Baptist Activities...221
   Baptist Board..221
   Baptist Case Committee 223

Monthly Meetings...224
The Baptist Fund..224
The Baptist Missionary Society..226
Village Preaching..226
Baptist Academies...235
Activities in Dissenting Societies 237
General Body of the Three Denominations.............................237
'Book Society' 242
'Poor Africans Society'...243
Port of London Society...245
Personal Activities...246

Chapter 8
Rippon:
The Preacher and the Man..249
Theological Position...250
Preaching Method and Style...253
Popularity as a Preacher..257
The Man..258

Chapter 9
Rippon and the Baptist Union..263

Conclusion..274

Appendix 1:
Earlier Studies on Rippon..277
Appendix 2:
Rippon's Version of 'All Hail the power of Jesu's name'..............279
Appendix 3:
Examples of Hymns by Rippon...282

Table 1:
An analysis of the number of hymns allocated to each topic in
the *Selection*, showing the numbers added in later editions.............286
Table 2:
An analysis of hymn writers in the *Selection*, showing,
where known, denominational allegiances....................................287
Table 3:
An analysis of the contents of each number of the *Register*..............290

Table 4:
Showing the increase in members of the churches, as reported to
the Particular Baptist Associations (1790-1802) and printed
in the *Register*...**292**
Table 5:
An analysis of *Register* contents...**294**

Bibliography...**295**

Index..**327**

Foreword

Dr. Manley's thesis is a very good one and John Rippon's work for the Particular Baptists is well worthy of scholarly attention.

Rippon, as the willing servant of the churches, was a fine leader for the Baptists at a critical period in their history. He had an exceptionally wide influence among British Baptist churches and beyond. In his own exceptionally long pastorate (1773-1836) at the opinion-forming Carter Lane Chapel in Southwark, he patterned a model of diligence and commitment for younger men to follow.

Beyond the local pastorate, he founded and developed the *Annual Baptist Register* as a pioneering tool in trans-atlantic intelligence. He shared in the growth of Baptist hymnology within the Baptist Union by both collecting verses and providing a tune book to exploit the collected words. He contributed widely to Baptist historiography and put himself at the disposal of the infant Baptist Union and all the churches who were happy to associate with one another in its work.

In the midst of all these many labours he was an effective preacher and pastor at Carter Lane for over sixty years.

Dr. Manley's thesis has long been one of the most useful studies in the Angus Library of Baptist writings at Regent's Park College, Oxford, and one of the most frequently consulted by visiting scholars. Dr. Manley has thoroughly revised his work for publication embracing the fruits of later scholarship.

All interested in the dissenting ministry and the history of reformed and Baptist church life will benefit enormously by having access to Dr. Manley's work, which fills an important gap in Baptist historiography.

B. R. White
Oxford, 2003

Preface

My scholarly (if intermittent) interest in John Rippon extends over more than thirty years and across that long period I have accumulated innumerable debts to many scholars, librarians and friends. I have no doubt that my greatest such debt is to Dr. Barrie White, of Regent's Park College, Oxford, my supervisor for the original thesis and long-time friend and encourager. I am delighted and grateful that despite serious health problems he has been able to complete a gracious foreword for this book. His wife Margaret has also been a good friend to both 'my Margaret' (as Barrie has it) and to me.

In a more formal sense I want to record my sincere thanks to the University of Bristol for the award of a postgraduate scholarship and the trustees of the Dr. Williams's Scholarship for an Exhibition.

From the large number of those who assisted me in various ways I want especially to thank that doyen of British Baptist historians, the late Dr. Ernest Payne, who was unfailingly helpful and generous. Dr. Geoffrey Nuttall also helped me at some crucial points. Similarly, I acknowledge the practical help of two late Principals of Bristol Baptist College, Dr. Len Champion and Dr. Morris West. An earlier Baptist historian, Dr. W.T. Whitley, in so many ways a pioneer for those of us who have tried to follow and whose work is often noted in this book, was in 1891 the founding principal of the Baptist Theological College in Melbourne, Australia, that now proudly bears his name. One of my greatest privileges has been to serve as the fifth principal of Whitley College and hopefully to strengthen the strong ties of fellowship and scholarship that unite Baptists of Britain and Australia. I like to think that Rippon would have been pleased that a 'colonial' Baptist was enlisted to tell his story. After giving much recent energy to writing about Baptists in Australia it has been refreshing to revisit the story of one whose vision was for a global denomination whose 'sentiments', as he hoped, 'will in the ages to come cover the whole earth'.

My access to Rippon family history was freely offered by Miss Evelyn Rippon, a gracious and proud custodian of those traditions. Alderman W.P. Authers of Tiverton was a fount of local knowledge. To my great enrichment, Dr. W. Morgan Patterson, then of Louisville, Kentucky, was in Oxford on sabbatical leave in 1966. He introduced me to some of the complexities of North American Baptist history and in the process became a reliable friend.

Whilst sources for this study are listed fully in the bibliography, it may be useful here to note the scattered nature of important manuscript sources. Accordingly, I recall again the kindness of librarians and curators who supplied me with copies of manuscript letters. The papers collected in the British Library are valuable, although they are nearly all letters written to Rippon. To have only one side of a correspondence is inevitably a frustration. Indeed, these letters though offering much useful information, have perhaps raised more questions than answers, whilst their scope ranges far beyond the confines of this study. The magnificent records of the Carter Lane (now Metropolitan Tabernacle) church have been of basic importance. My regular access to these was made possible by Mr. W. Berkshire whose delight in the honoured traditions of his church was transparent.

Some of this book has previously been published, though here greatly revised, and I thank the editor of the *Baptist Quarterly* for permission to utilize material which appears in chapters 2 and 6, the editor of the *Journal of Religious History* for what is here included in chapter 3 and Mercer University Press for much of what is here as chapter four.[1]

In helping me prepare this work for publication I have received great help from a fresh batch of friends: Ms. Susan Mills, Librarian and Archivist of the Angus Library, Regent's Park College, Oxford; Mr Jeremy Mudditt of Paternoster Press; Dr. John Briggs; Dr. Roger Hayden; Dr Michael Haykin; Ms. Rosemary Dillon of Whitley College; my son-in-law Rev. Paul Turton and, most especially, Dr. Anthony Cross who has given me invaluable assistance with all aspects of preparation of the text in the required format as well as helping in many other ways.

Even though so many across the years have helped me with Rippon, not least 'my Margaret', it remains necessary for me to stress that all faults and errors are completely my responsibility.

Ken Manley

---

1   K.R. Manley, 'The Making of an Evangelical Baptist Leader: John Rippon's early years, 1751-1773', *BQ* 26.6 (1976), pp. 254-74; 'John Rippon and Baptist Historiography', *BQ* 28.3 (1979), pp. 109-25; 'Pattern of a Pastorate: John Rippon at Carter Lane, Southwark (1773-1836)', *Journal of Religious History* 11.2 (1980), pp. 269-88; ' "Sing Side by Side": John Rippon and Baptist Hymnody', in W.H. Brackney, P.S. Fiddes and J.H.Y. Briggs (eds), *Pilgrim Pathways. Essays in Baptist History in Honour of B.R. White* (Macon, Georgia: Mercer University Press, 1999), pp. 127-63.

Abbreviations

BHS Trans	*Transactions of the Baptist Historical Society* (1908-1921).
B.L. Add. MSS	British Library Additional Manuscripts.
BMS	Baptist Missionary Society.
BQ	*Baptist Quarterly.*
Brief Essay	John Rippon, *A Brief Essay towards an History of the Baptist Academy at Bristol; read before the Bristol Education Society, at their Anniversary Meeting, in Broadmead, August 26th, 1795* (1796).
DAB	A. Johnson *et al* (eds.), *Dictionary of American Biography* (22 vols; New York: Scribner, 1928-58).
DEB	D.M. Lewis (ed.), *The Blackwell Dictionary of Evangelical Biography 1730-1860* (2 vols; Oxford: Blackwell, 1995).
DNB	I. Stephen and S. Lee (eds.), *Dictionary of National Biography* (67 vols; London: Smith, Elder, 1888-1903).
DWB	R.T. Jenkins and J.E. Lloyd (eds.), *Dictionary of Welsh Biography down to 1940* (London: Cymrodorion Society, 1959).
ESB	*Encyclopaedia of Southern Baptists* (4 vols; Nashville: Broadman Press, 1958, 1971, 1982).
Julian	J. Julian (ed.), *Dictionary of Hymnology* (London: John Murray, 2nd edn, 1907).
LMS	London Missionary Society
Register	*The Baptist Annual Register, Including Sketches of the State of Religion among Different Denominations of Good Men at Home and Abroad* (1790-1802).
Selection	J. Rippon (ed.), *A Selection of Hymns, from the best authors, Intended to be An Appendix to Dr. Watts's Psalms and Hymns* (1787).
Tune Book	J. Rippon (ed.), *A Selection of Psalm and Hymn Tunes from the best authors, in three and four parts; adapted principally to Dr. Watts's Hymns, & Psalms, & to Dr. Rippon's Selection of Hymns; containing in a greater variety than any other volume extant, the most approved compositions which are used in London and in the different congregations throughout England; also many original tunes never before printed. The whole forming a publication of above two hundred hymn tunes* (1791).

J. Rippon, *Watts*   J. Rippon (ed.), *An Arrangement of the Psalms, Hymns, and Spiritual Songs of the Rev. Isaac Watts, D.D. including (what no other Volume contains) all his Hymns, with which the Vacancies in the First Book were filled up in 1788; and also those in 1793: now collated, with each of the Doctor's own Editions. To which are subjoined, Indexes very much enlarged, both of Scriptures and of Subjects* (1801).

CHAPTER 1

John Rippon and the Transformation of the Baptists

English Nonconformity underwent a radical transformation during the long life of John Rippon (1751-1836). In his early years the older Dissenting churches (mainly Presbyterians, Independents and Baptists) seemed to have lost their way. Some, notably among Presbyterians and General or Arminian Baptists, had drifted into rationalism and embraced heterodox theology. Others retained their orthodoxy but lacked vitality and were in numerical decline. The reasons for this latter development are complex and must involve social, economic and political factors, but the main religious blame has usually been laid on the widely-adopted High Calvinism which was especially influential among the Calvinistic or Particular Baptists.[1]

Baptists were deeply influenced by the systematic theology of their leading pastor-theologian, John Gill (1697-1771),[2] and whilst many did

---

1   For a balanced survey of the situation among Particular Baptists, see M.A.G. Haykin, *One Heart and One Soul, John Sutcliff of Olney, his friends and his times* (Darlington: Evangelical Press, 1994), pp. 15-33.

2   For Gill, see D.M. Lewis (ed.), *The Blackwell Dictionary of Evangelical Biography 1730-1860* (2 vols; Oxford: Blackwell, 1995) (hereafter *DEB)* and the memoir by Rippon in J. Gill, *Exposition of Old Testament* (6 vols, London: 1810 ed.), 1, pp. ix-lxiv (republished: Harrisonburg, Va.: Gano Books, 1992). A vigorous debate over whether Gill is accurately described as High or Hyper-Calvinist continues. It seems simplest to use the commonly-accepted description of 'High'; but for the man and his theology, see T. George, 'John Gill' in T. George and D.S. Dockery (eds.), *Baptist Theologians* (Nashville: Broadman, 1990), pp. 77-101; G.M. Ella, 'John Gill and the Charge of Hyper-Calvinism', *Baptist Quarterly* (hereafter *BQ*) 36.4 (1995), pp. 160-77; M.A.G. Haykin (ed.), *The Life and Thought of John Gill (1697-1771): A tercentennial Appreciation* (Leiden: E.J. Brill, 1997); R.W. Oliver, 'John Gill', in M.A.G. Haykin (ed.), *The British Particular Baptists 1638-1910*, (2 vols; Springfield, Missouri: Particular Baptist Press, 1998, 2000), 1, pp. 145-65, which has a critical list of recent research on Gill and his influence.

not necessarily follow all the intricacies of his teaching what was of special significance was the view that offering a direct evangelistic appeal to all hearers was inappropriate. Scholarly debate has questioned whether even Gill strictly held that position, and certainly his writings evidence a more evangelical Calvinism than some have acknowledged. Yet, as Michael Haykin has observed, when Gill's fellow-preachers did follow his teaching on faith and evangelism many embraced a High Calvinist position and 'refrained from urging upon the lost their responsibility to embrace Christ and trust in him alone for their salvation'.[3]

However, an evangelical form of Calvinism, dating from the seventeenth century, was preserved among many Particular Baptists outside London. Concentration on Gill and his influence has often distorted the picture. Roger Hayden has demonstrated that in the west of England, where the 1689 Confession was consistently maintained within a vigorous association life and a succession of evangelistic preachers were produced at the Bristol Academy, a more positive picture emerges.[4] London, it is argued, was not typical of Baptist life: there was no real association life but rather a ministers' fraternal and administration of a denominational fund provided a form of Baptist life that lacked the cohesion and vitality found elsewhere. Tensions about hymn-singing had earlier polarized Baptist life in the metropolis and a divided community declining in vitality provided just the environment in which Gill and his followers gained status and influence.[5]

Even in London, it has been argued by R.P. Roberts, no more than a third of the churches in the period 1727-60 were consistently High Calvinist.[6] But after all this necessary balance has been drawn in an estimate of Baptist life during the eighteenth century, the common witness was undoubtedly that by about 1760 Particular Baptists in London and in many regions, for whatever reason (and Gill's theology is most commonly cited), evidenced little spiritual vigour.

Rippon would not have blamed Gill for this sad reality. He succeeded Gill as pastor of his London congregation in 1773 and was deeply sensitive of this honour. Although Rippon later wrote a laudatory memoir of Gill and showed warm admiration for his achievements, he disagreed with what he understood to be Gill's approach to evangelism and

---

3   Haykin, *One Heart and One Soul*, p. 19.

4   R. Hayden, 'Evangelical Calvinism among eighteenth-century British Baptists with particular reference to Bernard Foskett, Hugh and Caleb Evans and the Bristol Baptist Academy, 1690-1791' (PhD thesis, University of Keele, 1991).

5   M.D. MacDonald, 'London Calvinistic Baptists 1698-1727: tensions within a Dissenting Community under Toleration' (DPhil thesis, Oxford University, 1982).

6   R.P. Roberts, *Continuity and Change: London Calvinistic Baptists and the Evangelical Revival 1760-1820* (Wheaton, Ill.: R.O. Roberts, 1989), p. 42.

embodied much that was typical of the changes that came to Nonconformity.

Certainly by the end of the eighteenth century, and the beginning of the nineteenth, in a period of political and economic crisis and social discontent, Nonconformity had revived.[7] Indeed, historians customarily distinguish between Old Dissent and the New Dissent which had imbibed so much from the Evangelical religion which emerged in Britain from the 1730s.[8] Along with many other Protestants in England, Particular Baptists experienced renewal. The broad expressions of this new vitality are familiar: humanitarian and philanthropic movements, denominational organizations, missionary and Bible Societies, evangelism restored to its rightful place in the life of the church, Sunday schools, developments in theological and secular education. What had brought this change, especially to the Particular Baptists?[9]

The answer is usually linked precisely with the Evangelical Revival, that movement which established new denominations and influenced older traditions in England, that 'bracing breeze which had come sweeping down from the hills of Methodism over Baptist meadows, as well as Independent fields'.[10] To adopt a more modern metaphor: 'Dissent had drawn an enormous blood-transfusion from the veins of the Evangelical Revival'.[11] John Walsh used this image to show that Dissent received several of its leaders, even whole congregations, from the Revival; and especially converts from the preaching of the Calvinist evangelist, George Whitefield (1714-1770).[12] There was also adaptation of a 'legacy of method' which included itinerant preaching and the adoption, by some at least, of something like the Methodist connexional system. The worship of Dissent, especially in its style of preaching and the hymns sung, was also affected. Doctrinal rigidity began to relax in the enthusiasm for foreign missions.[13]

---

7   See M. Watts, *The Dissenters* (2 vols; Oxford: Clarendon Press, 1978, 1995), 1, pp. 394-490; 2, pp. 5-158; W.R. Ward, *Religion and Society in England 1790-1850* (London: Batsford, 1972).

8   D.W. Bebbington, *Evangelicalism in Modern Britain: A History from the 1730s to the 1980s* (London: Unwin Hyman, 1989), p. 1.

9   See especially W.R. Ward, 'The Baptists and the Transformation of the Church, 1780-1830', *BQ* 25.4 (1973), pp. 167-84.

10   J. Stoughton, *History of Religion in England* (8 vols; London: Hodder and Stoughton, 1901), 6, p. 364.

11   J.D. Walsh, 'Methodism at the end of the Eighteenth Century', in R. Davies and G. Rupp (eds.), *A History of the Methodist Church in Great Britain* (4 vols; London: Epworth, 1965-88), 1, p. 293.

12   Walsh, 'Methodism', pp. 293-308.

13   For a survey of the impact of the Wesleys and Whitefield on eighteenth-century Baptists, see W.M. Patterson, 'The Evangelical Revival and the Baptists', in W.H.

However, whilst much Dissent undoubtedly assumed a Methodist character, the influence of the Revival must not be over-simplified. That sturdy Congregationalist, B.L. Manning, quite strongly rejected the imagery of Dissent as being awakened from a deep spiritual slumber by a Wesleyan trumpet.[14] The rigidity of Calvinism may have restricted its appeal but it preserved the Particular Baptists and Independents from the theological rationalism of Arianism and Socinianism, the theological systems which denied the essential deity of Christ, and which so blighted the Presbyterians and General Baptists during the eighteenth century.[15] Manning claimed that it was the confluence of the central doctrines of historic Christianity with the Evangelical Revival that produced the modern missionary movements.[16]

The new approach to mission and the development of organizations to express their evangelical activism flowed largely from the renewal of a moderate Calvinism.[17] High Calvinism's influence may not have been as extensive as has sometimes been implied, for there were always some preachers who maintained an evangelistic ministry.[18] Furthermore, although there were some numerical gains from the Calvinistic wing of the Revival, the widespread adoption of a more moderate Calvinism is rightly linked with the theological writings of Andrew Fuller (1754-1815) among the Baptists, and Edward Williams (1750-1813) among the Independents.[19] Both these men rejected the view that to direct an appeal to the consciences of sinners was futile: after all did not the preachers of the New Testament, and revered figures like John Bunyan, do just that very thing? Yet the rapid spread of 'Fullerism', as the moderate position became widely known, is perhaps explained by the fact that in many churches just such a position had long been practised, if not theologically justified, by many preachers. Certainly the preaching of the moderate theology was the key factor in the remarkable expansion of the

Brackney, P.S. Fiddes, J.H.Y.Briggs (eds.), *Pilgrim Pathways* (Macon, Ga.: Mercer University Press, 1999), pp. 243-61.

14   'Congregationalism in the Eighteenth Century', in *Congregationalism through the Centuries* (London: Independent Press, 1937), p. 70; republished in B.L. Manning, *Essays in Orthodox Dissent* (London: Independent Press, 1939), p. 185.

15   See Watts, *The Dissenters*, 1, pp. 464-78.

16   Manning, 'Congregationalism', p. 80; For a similar claim regarding Gill's influence in preserving orthodoxy, see T. Nettles, *By His Grace and for His Glory. A Historical, Theological, and Practical Study of the Doctrines of Grace in Baptist Life* (Grand Rapids: Baker, 1986), pp. 73-107.

17   L.G. Champion, 'Evangelical Calvinism and the structures of Baptist church life', *BQ*. 28.5 (1980), pp. 196-208.

18   See below, chapter 2.

19   For Fuller see below, chapter 2, and for Williams, see *DEB*; W.T. Owen, *Edward Williams, D.D 1750-1813. His Life, Thought and Influence* (Cardiff: University of Wales Press, 1963).

Nonconformist churches, as contemporary historians realized: 'the grand means of augmenting the dissenting body, was the faithful and zealous preaching of the Gospel by its ministers'.[20]

David Bebbington's persuasive thesis concerning the emergence of Evangelicalism stresses that there was a measure of continuity between elements of the Reformed tradition embodied in Dissent and the Revival. Following Geoffrey Nuttall, he notes 'the eagerness for unity in Christian work, a consequent impatience with divisive doctrinal tests and a stress on personal experience in devotion to Christ'.[21] This tradition runs from Richard Baxter through Philip Doddridge to Andrew Fuller; there were 'Evangelicals before the Revival'.[22] Bristol Baptist Academy, where Rippon was a student, was a central source of this influence among Baptists, 'producing a stream of ministers with vital spirituality, evangelistic concerns and a catholic outlook'.[23]

At the same time, argues Bebbington, there were elements of discontinuity with the old Reformed tradition. For Dissenters this included religious influences from the Continent, notably that of the Moravians. Whilst their piety was pronounced in the shaping of Methodism, their example of missionary work was significant in the thinking of William Carey, pioneer of Baptist missions.[24] Certainly, Rippon admired the Moravians and was committed to promote knowledge of them among his own people.

Central to the new Evangelicalism, argues Bebbington, was the doctrine of assurance, that profound sense of acceptance by God in a true believer. 'Whereas the Puritans had held that assurance is rare, late and the fruit of struggle in the experience of believers, the Evangelicals believed it to be general, normally given at conversion and the result of simple acceptance of the gift of God'.[25] This teaching transformed Protestantism and brought changes in patterns of piety. A key figure here was the American theologian, Jonathan Edwards (1703-1758). In his writings, following the revival at Northampton, Massachusetts, in 1734-35, he provided a theological framework for interpreting Christian experience, and in particular, was the key factor in shaping moderate Calvinism among English Baptists.[26] Bebbington emphasizes that 'the

---

20 D. Bogue and J. Bennett, *History of Dissenters* (4 vols; London:1810-12), 4, p. 312.

21 Bebbington, *Evangelicalism*, p. 34.

22 G.F. Nuttall, quoted by Bebbington, *Evangelicalism*, p. 34.

23 Bebbington, *Evangelicalism*, p. 34.

24 B. Stanley, *The History of the Baptist Missionary Society* (Edinburgh: T. & T. Clark, 1992), pp. 2-3, 39-40.

25 Bebbington, *Evangelicalism*, p. 43.

26 For the influence of Edwards, see chapter 2.

fulcrum of change was the doctrine of assurance'.[27] From this confidence sprang the activism of the new Dissent.

One of the more important Particular Baptist leaders during this period of transformation, John Rippon was almost certainly the leading London Baptist for a generation or more. Rippon's story, it will be argued, serves to illuminate almost every facet of the Baptists' rapid expansion and renewed vigour during his long life.

The importance of Rippon's contribution to Nonconformity, especially to the Particular Baptists in both Britain and America, is that he represented a combination of the best elements of both the old and new traditions. He was reared in the old Nonconformity, deep in the heart of the West Country. Yet from his home church in Tiverton, and from the Academy at Bristol, which owed much of its methods and theology to the Independent divine, Philip Doddridge (1702-51), Rippon emerged with a virile evangelistic fervour.[28] He always remained a loyal Dissenter, agitated against injustices suffered by fellow-religionists, and increasingly tried to preserve the true historical and doctrinal heritages of Nonconformity. Continuity with the past was important to him. At the same time, he was linked with Fuller as a promoter of the new theology, and also introduced to the Baptist community many of the songs of the Revival, endorsing their Evangelical piety.

Rippon was in a unique position to exercise a widespread influence. He came from Bristol to the pulpit occupied for over fifty years by Gill. Here Rippon maintained a long and patently evangelistic ministry. His ministry was so successful that this in itself argued the force of 'Fullerism'. Yet Rippon preserved and enlarged the best traditions of Carter Lane. He remained concerned with the necessity for due church order, and enlarged the social responsibility of the church to its own members. But from the secure confidence of a happy ministry, Rippon was able to lead the Baptists of his day in significant ways.

When Rippon began his ministry, the Particular Baptists had no denominational structure to link congregations that were widely scattered; many gathered in small market-towns or villages. An emphasis on the autonomy of the local church could restrict cooperative ventures. Dissenting congregations were largely 'isolated and introspective'.[29] As D. W. Lovegrove summarizes: 'The very strength of independency, the internal cohesion of the gathered church, became its weakness as geographical remotenesss conspired with autonomy and lack of common

---

27   Bebbington, *Evangelicalism*, p. 74.
28   For Doddridge, see *DEB*.
29   Bebbington, *Evangelicalism*, p. 32.

purpose to foster numerical decline'.[30] Of that sad decline there seems ample evidence, from statistics and discerning commentators.[31]

Rippon's influence on the thought and denominational patterns of the Baptists was unique. He began by sensing the need for a comprehensive denominational hymn-book, one which, with the popular books of Isaac Watts (1674-1748), would provide a comprehensive resource for the homiletical bias of Baptist worship. Any good hymnbook helps to interpret and define the Christian faith for its own generation. Rippon was aware of this responsibility and the phenomenal success of his publications meant that he exerted a profound - and often overlooked - theological and unifying influence on his fellow-Baptists.

Again, it was Rippon who, by the publication of his *Baptist Annual Register* (1790-1802), not only provided a unique expression of the denomination's new maturity and confidence but also promoted a deeper mutual awareness among Baptists. Whilst this periodical was published the denomination came to life. The number of members increased from about 17, 000 in 1790 to 24, 000 in 1800, rising to 86, 000 by 1838, an increase exceeding population growth.[32] The number of churches associated with the Western and Midland Associations approximately doubled between 1780 and 1820.[33] Moreover, there were great numbers of 'hearers' who attended churches but did not become members. In 1792 the Baptist Missionary Society was established, and in 1797 a society for Village Evangelism - the forerunner of a Home Mission Society - also began. Rippon gave these societies, as well as the revival in English Association life and the expansion in both American and British churches, a wide publicity. He and his church gave personal support to these denominational movements. The leading place of Rippon and his church was formally recognized when, with Rippon as chairman and his church as host, the first real national organization of the Particular Baptists, the Baptist Union, was formed in 1812.

Considering Rippon's influence on the Baptists of both Britain and America, it is surprising that no adequate biography of him has previously been attempted. His death failed to produce a worthy memoir, probably for the simple reason that he had outlived his own contemporaries. In his last years he was eccentric and difficult, but the

---

30   D.W. Lovegrove, *Established Church, Sectarian People. Itinerancy and the Transformation of English Dissent, 1780-1830* (Cambridge: Cambridge University Press, 1988), p. 7.

31   For discussion of the statistics, based mainly on the list of Rev. John Evans (1715-18) and lists prepared in 1773 by Rev. J. Thompson, see Watts, *The Dissenters*, 1, pp. 267-71, 491-510 and 2, pp. 22-29; Haykin, *One Heart and One Soul*, pp. 24-26.

32   A.D. Gilbert, *Religion and Society in Industrial England* (London: Longman, 1976), p. 37.

33   Bebbington, *Evangelicalism*, p. 21.

younger men respected him and realized the importance of his earlier activities. Again, there were other contemporary Baptists of importance, especially William Carey (1761-1834), Andrew Fuller, and Robert Hall (1764-1831) who claimed extensive biographical attention. Only formal notices were published of Rippon's death.[34] The sermons preached at his funeral were published in the *Pulpit*, but these contained little biographical detail.[35] A review of earlier studies on Rippon is found in Appendix 1.

Much personal detail of Rippon's life is not recoverable. Yet his importance to the Baptists of both Britain and America is clearly apparent. Thus, this study has been written around the general areas of Rippon's significance to the Baptists. His own experience offered a useful introduction to the importance of Bristol Academy in the developing life of the Baptists. Then in London he ministered in what became one of the leading Baptist churches in the country, and the way in which his personality and theology were impressed upon the life of this congregation offered an intriguing study of a Baptist church during an era of denominational expansion. Rippon's importance to Baptist hymnody was seen to have basic significance by quietly moulding and unifying the spirituality and thought of the denomination. This unifying influence was even clearer in his *Register*, and in his other personal activities. He became a Baptist leader in many senses, and exerted a determinative influence on the patterns of denominational life. At the same time his work as an historian was vital for future Baptist historiography. Paradoxically, Rippon also supported the flourishing of that undenominational evangelical religion that marked the end of the eighteenth century.[36]

At least one of Rippon's contemporaries realized his importance. Joseph Ivimey (1773-1834) was the leading Baptist historian of the period, but predeceased Rippon by two years.[37] Nevertheless, after speaking about the *Register*, Ivimey wrote of Rippon in 1830, 'He certainly deserves much greater respect from his denomination than he has ever yet received'.[38] Whilst this present study is not written from the standpoint of any narrow denominational interest, it is to be hoped that Baptists - and all interested in English religious history - may be helped to place Rippon's achievements in proper historical perspective.

'Redeeming love proclaim!' This was something of a personal motto for Rippon and offers a unifying theme for our story. On the title page

---

34   *The Times*, 20 December 1836; *Annual Register for 1837* (1838), p.162; *Baptist Magazine* 29 (1837), p. 35.

35   *Pulpit* 29 (1837), pp. 289-301, 308.

36   Ward, 'The Baptists and the Transformation of the Church', p. 171.

37   For Ivimey, see *DEB*.

38   *History of the English Baptists* (4 vols; London: 1811-1830), 4, p. 62.

of each of the four volumes of his *Baptist Annual Register* (1790-1802) Rippon published verses which suggest both his evangelical vision for the world and the confidence of this period among fellow-Baptists:

> From East to West, from North to South,
>   Now be his name ador'd!
> EUROPE, with all thy millions, shout
>   Hosannahs to thy Lord!
>
> ASIA and AFRICA, resound
>   From shore to shore his fame;
> And thou, AMERICA, in songs,
>   Redeeming love proclaim![39]

---

39   These verses are taken from the long hymn by Thomas Gibbons, 'Great God, the nations of the earth', which Rippon used in his *Selection of Hymns* (1787) as hymn 420.

CHAPTER 2

The Making of an Evangelical Baptist Leader (1751-1773)

Although some Baptist leaders of the eighteenth century entered the denomination as products of the Evangelical Revival, notably Robert Robinson (1735-1790) and John Fawcett (1740-1817), who were both converts of Whitefield, it is remarkable how many emerged from within Baptist church life.[1] Several influential ministers were themselves sons of Baptist ministers. For example: Hugh (1713-1781) and Caleb (1737-1791) Evans, Andrew Gifford (1700-1784), Samuel Stennett (1727-1795), John Ryland (1753-1825), and Robert Hall.[2] Perhaps the background of these men offers some balance to the depressing picture of eighteenth-century Baptist piety that is often drawn.

John Rippon was another prominent leader reared within a devout Baptist family that was active in the life of a local congregation. This is where any analysis of the formative influences that helped shape Rippon should begin. Thus, an examination of Rippon's early life in Tiverton, and then of his time in the Bristol Academy helps to trace the formation of this evangelical Baptist leader. In particular, this study confirms that Bristol Academy played a significant role in the denomination's gradual adoption of a more moderate Calvinism.[3]

---

1   For Robinson, see G.W. Hughes, *With Freedom Fired* (London: Carey Kingsgate Press, 1955); L.G. Champion, 'Robert Robinson. A Pastor in Cambridge', BQ 31.5 (1986), pp. 241-46; and *DEB*. For Fawcett see *DEB*; I. Sellers, 'Other Times, Other Ministries: John Fawcett and Alexander McLaren', *BQ* 32.4 (1987), pp. 181-99. See W.T. Whitley, 'The Influence of Whitefield on Baptists', *BQ* 5.1 (1930), pp. 30-36; R. Brown, *The English Baptists of the Eighteenth Century* (London: Baptist Historical Society, 1986), pp. 80-82.

2   For the two Evans, see below and for the others see *DEB*.

3   See G.F. Nuttall, 'Calvinism in Free Church History', *BQ* 22.8 (1968), p. 425; N.S. Moon, *Education for Ministry: Bristol Baptist College 1679-1979* (Bristol: Bristol Baptist College, 1979), pp. 18-21; Hayden, 'Evangelical Calvinism'.

Tiverton (1751-1769)

John Rippon was born 29 April 1751 in Tiverton, Devonshire. Since the fifteenth century Tiverton's prosperity had been linked with the cloth industry. But wars, competition from Norwich and the north, together with a resulting fall in the Dutch trade, caused a steady decline through the eighteenth century in the Devon cloth industry, especially at Tiverton.[4] Baptists had been in Tiverton since at least 1626, for that year Tiverton Baptists joined with churches at London, Lincoln, Salisbury and Coventry in corresponding with Dutch Mennonite churches.[5] These first Baptists were Arminian, or General Baptists. By 1656, when William Facy represented Tiverton at the Baptist Western Association, the church had become Calvinistic, possibly due to the influence of Thomas Collier.[6] In 1769 the church had sixty-six members.[7]

Family tradition claims the Rippons were descended from Huguenots who had fled from France following the 1572 massacre,[8] and official records demonstrate Rippons were in Tiverton from at least the early seventeenth century.[9] Exact relationships have not been traced, but Grace and Mary Rippon were members of the Baptist church by 1739.[10] John Rippon 'Senior', Dr. Rippon's grandfather, joined the church on 16 March 1746.[11] He was almost certainly a weaver for he was accused by the

---

4   W.G. Hoskins, *Devon (A New Survey of England)* (London: 1954), pp. 127-30.

5   See B. Evans, *Early English Baptists* (2 vols; London: 1864), 2, pp. 21-51; C. Burrage, *Early English Dissenters* (2 vols; Cambridge: Cambridge University Press, 1912), 1, pp. 270-76; *Transactions of the Baptist Historical Society* (hereafter *BHS Trans.*) 3 (1912-13), pp. 1-7, 193-211; 4 (1914-15), pp. 124, 228-54. There is no documentary evidence for the tradition of the church as existing from 1607, as in H.B. Case, *The Baptist Church in Tiverton* (Tiverton: 1907). See also J.P. Carey, *Planting of the Baptist Church in Tiverton, being Extracts from Ancient Documents and Arguments Deduced therefrom* (Tiverton: 1876).

6   G.F. Nuttall, 'The Baptist Western Association 1653-1658', *Journal of Ecclesiastical History* 11.2 (1960), p. 215. W.T. Whitley (ed.), *Minutes of the General Assembly of the General Baptists* (2 vols; London: Baptist Historical Society, 1907, 1910), 2, pp. 53-54, note 3; *BHS Trans.* 3 (1912-13), p. 6. For Collier, see see L. Stephen and S. Lee (eds.), *Dictionary of National Biography* (67 vols; London: Smith, Elder, 1888-1903), hereafter *DNB*.

7   Tiverton Baptist Churchbook, 1769 membership list.

8   Ms. E. Rippon of London to author, 1 February 1970. (Ms. Rippon was a descendant of Dr. John Rippon's brother Theophilus.)

9   Parish Register of St. Peter's, Tiverton, records the baptism of 'Richard Rippon' in April 1608: there are several references to Rippons from this time onwards.

10   Tiverton Churchbook, membership list, May 1739.

11   Following the practice of the Tiverton Churchbook the three generations of John Rippons are designated as 'Senior', 'Junior', and 'Minor'. Note that Case, *The Baptist Church in Tiverton*, ch. 6, has confused the three Rippons.

church of participating in a town riot, known to have been common because of the introduction of Irish worsted, in December 1749.[12] In a more sedate old age Rippon 'Senior' became the 'doorkeeper' of the meeting-house, and died on 30 March 1772.[13]

John Rippon 'Junior' (1730-1800),[14] a sergemaker,[15] father of the later Dr. Rippon gave his 'experience' to the church on 4 November 1759. His written account of this survives in a small note-book inscribed with his name and significantly dated 3 November 1759.[16] Evidently he rehearsed in writing what he wanted to say to the church. Full of scriptural quotations and lamentations of an 'undone Estate', the book became a spiritual diary. From this it is learnt that the ordeal of speaking to the church so affected Rippon that 'he could not forbear to burst out into a flood of tears'. He was baptized on 18 November and admitted to church membership on 25 November 1759.[17] John Rippon 'Junior', together with Samuel Dunscombe, was called to the work of preaching on 24 August 1763 after a trial of over twelve months.[18] Dunscombe went to Bristol for formal training and later settled at Cheltenham.[19]

Rippon 'Junior' remained at Tiverton preaching wherever 'Providence' directed. When Thomas Lewis in December 1765 left the Tiverton pastorate to settle in Exeter, Rippon supplied many pulpits for neighbouring ministers who came to preach at Tiverton.[20] Accordingly, Rippon became well known in the district and received an invitation to settle as minister at Bradford, Wiltshire, in 1769. Unfortunately, that church could not support Rippon and his young family, so the advice of Hugh Evans of Bristol to refuse the invitation was followed.[21] The times in Tiverton became even harder: by 1770 the population had decreased by eighteen hundred from what it had been forty years previously, and the number of poor in the parish had risen alarmingly.[22] Tragedy came into the life of the would-be pastor, and on 1 October 1775 the church

---

12   Tiverton Churchbook, 31 December 1749. M. Dunsford, *Historical Memoirs of the town and parish of Tiverton* (Exeter: 1790), pp. 230-32.

13   Tiverton Churchbook, note in membership list compiled 2 September 1769.

14   J. Rippon (ed.), *Baptist Annual Register* (hereafter *Register*) 3 (1798-1801), p. 260, note *.

15   H. Evans to J. Rippon ('Junior'), Bristol, 4 June 1769; British Library Additional Manuscripts (hereafter B.L. Add. MSS.) 25386, f. 444.

16   In Dr. Williams's Library, London.

17   Tiverton Churchbook.

18   Tiverton Churchbook, 21 July 1762, 10 June and 24 August 1763.

19   For Samuel Dunscombe (1738-1797), see *Register* 3 (1798-1801), pp. 122-24.

20   Tiverton Churchbook, December 1765. For Rippon supplying Hampton, see *B.Q* 3.2 (1926-27), p. 95.

21   H. Evans to J. Rippon, Bristol 4 June 1769, B.L. Add. MSS; 25386, f. 444.

22   M. Dunsford, *Memoirs of Tiverton,* pp. 56-57.

sorrowfully recorded 'the great reproach brought on religion by the evil conduct of our brethren John and William Rippon in their running so much into debt and having not sufficiency to pay what they owe; on which account they had been obliged to leave their families and habitations and fly the country...'.

Both offenders were excluded from the church. Far from being in pastoral charge, Rippon 'Junior' was not even a member of a church and was in complete disgrace. Happily, however, both men were later restored to the church.[23] Eventually Rippon's great desire was realized when he became the pastor at Upottery, Devonshire, some ten miles from Tiverton, whence he was dismissed 30 October 1785. By this time he was aged fifty-five and his eldest son had been in the ministry for ten years. Unfortunately, some Upottery members adopted Antinomian views much to the distress of their pastor.[24] The church had only eighteen members at his death on 24 December 1800.[25] Two years earlier his son had written of him, in connection with his ministry at Upottery: 'A man of the sweetest of tempers presides over this little society. Good judges say, he preaches better and better. May his last days be, as we trust they eminently are, his best days'.[26]

John Rippon 'Junior' (so described in the Parish Register) married Jane Hopkins, on 8 February 1750. There were three sons, John; Thomas born 1 August 1760 and Theophilus born 29 January 1762,[27] and one daughter Mary, received into the church 2 November 1768 and whose married surname was Cozins.[28] Thomas (1760-1835), like John, lived most of his life in London.[29] Trained in the strict school of Abraham Newland,[30] Thomas succeeded him as chief cashier for the Bank of England. Possibly haunted by the memory of his father's business failure, Thomas took only three days holiday in fifty years service and by thrift and precise judgment accumulated considerable wealth.[31] He published *An elegant Engraving of a Geographical Clock...* in 1794.[32] John frequently had his mail sent care of Thomas at the Bank. Little is

---

23   John on 25 May 1777 and William on 25 January 1802.

24   W.T. Andress, *History of Newhouse Upottery* (Taunton: 1932), p. 12.

25   *Register* 3 (1798-1801), p. 260 note.

26   *Register* 3 (1798-1801), p. 10 note.

27   Tiverton Baptist Birth Register (in Public Record Office).

28   Tiverton Churchbook.

29   See *DNB,* and W. Marston Acres, 'A Former Chief Cashier', *The Old Lady of Threadneedle Street* (Staff Journal of Bank of England) 3, no. 22 (June 1926).

30   For Newland (1730-1807) see *DNB.*

31   *DNB* says £60,000; the probate was for £40,000.

32   *Register* 2 (1794-97), p. 221. A copy is in the Angus Library.

known about Theophilus but by 1809 he was still in the Exeter district.[33]
Various other Rippons were associated with both the Baptist and
Congregational churches but precise relationships cannot be
determined.[34]

John Rippon 'Minor' was thus born into a devout Baptist home where
the talk must often have been of religious experience and meetinghouse
affairs. This would have increased after the death in December 1759 of
the aged Rev. Henry Terry,[35] for his successor, a Welshman named
Thomas Lewis, boarded with the Rippon family.[36] Described by Rippon
as 'that reverend and dear man', Lewis was ordained on 24 September
1760. For the next five years Rippon was in the closest possible contact
with Lewis. Nothing is known of Rippon's schooling, but it is conceivable
that Lewis educated him, for many Dissenting pastors supplemented their
income by teaching. Lewis left Tiverton for Exeter in December 1765.

About this time young Rippon, fourteen years old, began laboriously
taking notes of sermons he heard. Whilst the extant volume does not bear
Rippon's name it is clearly his work.[37] The title page reads, 'Sermons
Preach'd At the Baptist Meeting in Tiverton Anno Dom; 1765', and the
book contains 180 pages of notes of sermons preached between 1765
and 1767. The seriousness of Rippon's young mind is evident, but the
book's main value is as an indication of the type of teaching delivered
from the pulpit. The first ten sermons were preached by Lewis and are
typically Calvinistic in their sombre emphasis. A good example is the first
entry, a 'Lecture' preached 6 January 1765. The New Year's text was the
discomforting Jeremiah 28:16, 'This year thou shalt surely die'. The
many headings and sub-headings typical of the preaching style of the
day were duly noted, whilst the value of the text was undisputed:

> It will lead to watchfulness - This is ye Case Especially with the young - you are
> ready to Say. you shall have many years, Is not this the Language of thy heart, ys is
> ye way to harden yourselves = If ys is rightly attended that is ye Subject It wod Lead
> to wait for our Coming Lord -

After Lewis had left, various local ministers visited Tiverton. Two of
these in particular influenced Rippon. The first was the Rev. Henry

---

33   From a reference in a letter, R. Hatch to J. Rippon, Exeter 11 November 1809,
B. L. Add. MSS. 25387 f. 93.

34   W.P. Authers, *The Tiverton Congregational Church 1660-1960* (Tiverton:
Tiverton Congregational Church, 1960), p. 26 refers to a Jenny Rippon.

35   Case, *History of the Baptist Church in Tiverton*, p. 41.

36   *Register* 1 (1790-93), p. 129 note. Lewis (1730-94) trained at Bristol, see list
the of ministerial students in Hayden, 'Evangelical Calvinism'.

37   The evidence is: (i) date of compilation; (ii) one sermon by 'father'; (iii)
handwriting; (iv) shorthand is similar to a method later used by Rippon. The volume is in
the Angus Library.

Philips (1719-1789) whose memoir Rippon was later to write.[38] Another Welshman, Philips was a convert of the Welsh 'enthusiast' Howel Harris.[39] With Philips the Evangelical Revival directly touched Rippon. Whilst in Tiverton, Philips also stayed with Rippon's family and clearly made a deep impression on young Rippon:

> Mr. Philips's freedom and affection procured him the love of the whole family. O how he used to pray with us! Some of the sermons that he preached in that town, on the one thing needful -- on the parable of the rich man and Lazarus -- on 42nd Psalm, 5th verse -- on Phil iii 13, 14, Isa. xxxviii. 17 and particularly on Rev. xxii 17 made a deep impression, if I mistake not, on the minds of several who heard them.[40]

The last of these sermons was one recorded by Rippon in his book of notes. It suggests that Philips was an advocate of a direct appeal to the conscience of his hearers; this was to be expected from a convert of Howel Harris. Though Calvinistic in its emphasis upon the prior call of God; 'no man will come to X till they are drawn by ye Effectual calling of God'; the evangelical appeal was pronounced as the last heading shows: 'The Universality of ye Invitation and a further Description of those yt are Invited Whosoever will Let him come and take ye water of Life freely'. Such an approach was far distant from the 'non-invitation, non-application' preaching castigated by Joseph Ivimey.[41] Philips settled at Salisbury where he remained from 1766 until his death.[42]

The other minister to influence Rippon was the Rev. Robert Day (1721-1791), minister at Wellington, Somerset, from 1745 until his death; and for whom Rippon also compiled an affectionate memoir.[43] Rippon described Day's coming to the churches of the area; 'He appeared among them, to use one of his own expressions "with a sacred shine upon his countenance", we saw his face as an angel of God'.[44] Day baptized Rippon and four others in Tiverton on Friday 25 September 1767.[45]

---

38   *Register* 1 (1790-93), pp. 128-38. For the context and details of Philips, see D.D. Morgan, 'Smoke, Fire and Light; Baptists and the Revitalisation of Welsh Dissent'; *BQ* 32.5 (1988), pp. 224-32 and *DEB*.

39   For Harris (1714-1773) see *DEB* and G.F. Nuttall, *Howel Harris 1714-1773. The Last Enthusiast* (Cardiff: University of Wales Press, 1965).

40   *Register* 1 (1790-93), p. 129 note.

41   Ivimey, *History of the English Baptists*, 3, p. 267.

42   See O.A. Moore, *Brown Street Baptist Church Salisbury 1655-1955* (Salisbury: 1955), pp. 13-20.

43   *Register* 1 (1790-93), pp. 260-67.

44   *Register* 1 (1790-93), p. 263 note.

45   Tiverton Churchbook. Cf. *Register* 1 (1790-93), p. 263 note.

Shortly after Rippon's baptism a young student from Bristol Academy, Daniel Sprague, came on a year's probation to the Tiverton church. The letter of invitation to the pastorate was signed by the three John Rippons on 26 February 1769.[46] But by the time of Sprague's ordination, 12 July 1769, John Rippon 'Minor' was himself a student in Bristol. On 4 June 1769 Hugh Evans, President of the Academy, had written to John Rippon 'Junior', 'Your son goes on very well and will I trust, be a great comfort to you and a blessing to many'.[47] Rippon had begun training for his life's work.

The most important result of Rippon's boyhood and early manhood in Tiverton was the formation of a genuine religious conviction, undoubtedly of prime importance for his life's work. To what extent his future specialised hymnodic and historical interests had developed at Tiverton is uncertain, but he may well have been encouraged by the town and chapel.

The Tiverton church had agreed, at Henry Terry's insistence and amidst considerable controversy, to permit hymn singing in 1732.[48] Since 1761 they had decided to stand whilst singing, although some retained scruples about the 'Decency of ye posture'.[49] Rippon's father was familiar enough with the hymns of Watts to quote him whilst giving his 'experience', but whether he was sufficiently an enthusiast to stimulate a love for Watts' work in his son is unknown. As to Rippon's historical interests there are two points of possible relevance. The first is the antiquity of the church: the man who was to give considerable time and energy to preserving and writing the history of other churches was himself reared in what claims to be one of the very oldest Baptist churches in England. Coupled with this is the presence in the town of a distinguished local historian, Martin Dunsford, whose family had long associations with Dissenters. His brother, Jabez (1741-1795), was a leading Baptist deacon whilst Martin was a member of the Congregational church, although one 'M. Dunsford' was later active in the inauguration of Western Unitarianism.[50] Rippon knew the family well, and wrote a detailed family history;[51] he subscribed to Dunsford's history of Tiverton[52] and advertised it in his *Register*.[53] Acquaintance with this

---

46   Tiverton Churchbook.

47   B.L. Add. MSS. 25386, f. 444.

48   Case, *History of the Baptist Church in Tiverton*, p. 31.

49   *History of the Baptist Church in Tiverton*, p. 43.

50   W.T. Whitley, *Baptist Bibliography* (2 vols; London: Kingsgate Press, 1916, 1922), 2, ref. 54-792.

51   *Register* 2 (1794-97), pp. 303-308.

52   Dunsford, *Memoirs of Tiverton*, list of subscribers.

53   *Register* 1 (1790-93), pp. 322-23.

history enthusiast can only have stimulated the historical interests of Rippon.

Throughout his life Rippon maintained a lively interest in the Tiverton Baptist church and assisted it in various ways.

Bristol (1769-1773)

Rippon was eighteen years old when in the spring of 1769 he arrived in Bristol to commence his ministerial studies. The city was a leading port for the American trade, second only to London in size and importance. The bustling activity of the docks in the heart of the city and the virile life of the historic Dissenting churches must have excited young Rippon; but the most determinative influences upon him came from the Baptist Academy.[54]

The origin of the Academy is traced to the will of Edward Terrill (1635-1686), a writing master and ruling elder of the Broadmead church in Bristol.[55] Dated 3 June 1679, this deed provided an endowment for the Broadmead pastor who should be a holy man, well skilled in Greek and Hebrew, and who was to devote three afternoons per week to the instruction of young men intended for the ministry.[56] Caleb Jope was evidently the first selected to fulfil Terrill's designs, but he was unsuccessful and not until the appointment of Bernard Foskett (1685-1758) in 1720 did the Academy function effectively.[57]

During the thirty-eight years of Foskett's tutorship approximately sixty-four students, in equal numbers from England and Wales, were prepared for the Baptist ministry.[58] These included distinguished men like Benjamin Beddome (1717-1795), Thomas Llewellyn (1720-1793), John Collett Ryland (1723-1792), John Ash (1724-1779) and Benjamin

---

54 For the Academy, see Moon, *Education for Ministry,* and Hayden, 'Evangelical Calvinism'. Rippon's essay on Bristol is a basic source for the early period: J. Rippon, *Brief Essay towards an History of the Baptist Academy at Bristol* (London: 1796) (hereafter *Brief Essay*). See also S.A. Swaine, *Faithful Men; or Memorials of Bristol Baptist College* (London: 1884).

55 For Terrill and the Broadmead church, see E.B. Underhill (ed.), *Broadmead Records* (London: 1847); R Hayden (ed.), *The Records of a Church of Christ in Bristol 1640-1687* (Bristol: Bristol Record Society, 1974); C.S. Hall and H. Mowvley, *Tradition and Challenge: The Story of Broadmead Baptist Church, Bristol from 1685 to 1991* (Bristol: Broadmead Baptist Church, 1991).

56 J. Rippon, *Brief Essay,* p. l3.

57 R. Hayden, 'The Contribution of Bernard Foskett', in *Pilgrim Pathways* (1999), pp. 189-206; and *DEB.*

58 J. Rippon, *Brief Essay,* pp. 14-23.

Francis (1734-1799).[59] Two of Foskett's students succeeded him as President: Hugh Evans in 1758, although he had been an assistant since 1739; and his son, Caleb Evans, who assisted his father from 1759 and then succeeded him after his death.[60] Both these men were tutors when Rippon entered the Academy.

The contribution of the Dissenting academies to English education has been increasingly recognized.[61] Following the Act of Uniformity of 1662 these had been commenced with the primary aim of training ministers, but soon began giving a broad and progressive education to young Dissenters whatever their future calling. Foremost among the eighteenth century academies was that established at Northampton by Philip Doddridge. Bristol Academy under both Hugh and Caleb Evans was conducted in the Doddridge tradition as evidenced in at least three aspects.[62] It was personal rather than institutional, a small group of pupils gathered around a notable tutor. The teaching was given in the President's home where the students also lived. This family atmosphere produced a body of disciples daily learning from their master's example. When Rippon entered the Academy he was one of very few students. Details before 1770 are sketchy, but few men are known to have been resident immediately before then. Secondly, the Academy was closely related by its foundation to the Broadmead church. The tutor at the Academy was also pastor at the Church. His example in the pulpit and in the life of the church provided a means of ministerial preparation of the highest order. Thirdly, the routine and curriculum adopted at Bristol closely followed the formative patterns devised by Doddridge.

Bristol was the only Baptist Academy specifically designed for ministerial education. London Baptists in 1752 had formed an Education Society but its function had been to assist individual students to be trained by various ministers such as Thomas Llewellyn, Samuel Stennett

---

59   For all these, see *DEB*.

60   For Hugh and Caleb Evans see Moon, *Education for Ministry;* Hayden, 'Evangelical Calvinism'. For Hugh Evans, see: C. Evans, *Elisha's Exclamation. A Sermon Occasioned by the death of the Rev. Hugh Evans* (Bristol: 1781); Rippon, *Brief Essay,* pp. 23-31; *Dictionary of Welsh Biography* (hereafter *DWB*) and *DEB*. For Caleb Evans, see: S. Stennett, *The Mortality of Ministers contrasted* (London: 1791); Rippon, *Brief Essay,* pp. 31-51; K. Wellum, 'Caleb Evans (1737-1791)' in *The British Particular Baptists 1638*-1910, 1, pp. 213-33; *DWB and DEB*.

61   H. McLachlan, *English Education under the Test Acts, being the history of the Nonconformist academies from 1662-1820* (Manchester: University Press, 1931); J.W. Ashley Smith, *Birth of Modern Education. The Contribution of the Dissenting Academies 1660-1800* (London: Independent Press, 1954).

62   Cf. Ashley Smith, *Birth of Modern Education*, p. 215; A.V. Murray, 'Doddridge and Education', in G.F. Nuttall (ed.), *Philip Doddridge 1702-51. His Contribution to English Religion* (London: Independent Press, 1951), p. 120.

and William Nash Clarke (1732-1795).[63] However, the year after Rippon's commencement at Bristol the nature of the Academy was revised with the formation of the Bristol Education Society. Rippon recalled that the idea and its fulfilment came from Caleb Evans: 'He devised - he planned - he executed'.[64] The scheme was to invite gifts of capital and annual subscriptions to ensure that adequate funds were available for the training of suitable applicants. On 1 January 1770 a letter was sent from Bristol advertising the scheme and underlining the dire need: insufficient ministers to supply destitute churches and suitable applicants unable to receive the necessary training. Bristol could only meet a small part of this need from the Terrill fund. Largely due to Caleb Evans' 'anxious solicitude' and 'unremitted exertions' the meeting called for 7 June 1770 was an unqualified success:[65] the Society was duly formed, an account of its formation was printed, and within the year £474. 19. 0 capital had been given together with £106. 1. 0 through annual subscriptions.[66] Students applying had to be recommended by a Baptist church but no credal tests were applied.

Rippon was fortunate to be in the Academy at this significant time. The extant records of the Academy date from 1770 and from these it does not appear that Rippon was ever given financial assistance by the Society: he was accepted before the Society's formation and presumably was supported privately. But in other ways the beginnings of the Society benefited him. There was the example of what could be achieved by a carefully planned programme: in later days Rippon was to lead in a number of new religious organizations. More immediately, the course to be followed by the students was given careful thought. Reports upon students supported by the Society were recorded in detail and these indicate the Academy's curriculum.

Undoubtedly the greatest single obstacle to the success of the new Society was the idea, still prevalent among Baptists, that an educated ministry was synonymous with an unspiritual or 'carnal' ministry. Considerable pains were taken by the leaders of the infant Society to refute this position, and their efforts provide a useful guide to their whole approach to the responsible task of ministerial education. In the introduction to the 1770 account of the Society's formation it was insisted that learning was subordinate to genuine piety, but did not even the most pious ministers (such as Dr. Gill) admit the value of learning? Answering a common objection, it was also argued that learning was not designed to replace or perfect the work of the Holy Spirit, indeed the

---

63   Ashley Smith, *Birth of Modern Education,* pp. 206-210; H. Foreman, 'Baptist Provision for Ministerial Education in the 18th Century', *BQ* 27.8 (1978), pp. 358-69.
64   Rippon, *Brief Essay,* p. 33.
65   Rippon, *Brief Essay,* p. 34.
66   *An Account of the Bristol Education Society* (Bristol: 1770).

Spirit could use the ordinary means of education to improve God-given gifts.

The intimate and domestic nature of the Academy is reflected in the many personal recollections given by Rippon in his *Essay* on the Academy. Hugh Evans was specifically remembered for his prayers, preaching, teaching, and personal interest in each student. So friendly and respected was Evans that Rippon commented that most students regarded him more as a father than a tutor.[67]

At the direct instigation of Hugh Evans, Rippon was formally called into the ministry by the Tiverton church. Although Rippon had entered the Academy in 1769 with the clear intention of training for the ministry, this 'call' had never been ratified in any way by his home-church. This does not appear to have been unique. Thomas Dunscombe, brother of Samuel, a friend of Rippon's from Tiverton and one of the first two students supported by the new Education Society, was also accepted prior to the church's call.[68] Joseph Kinghorn in 1784 wrote from Bristol that not all students were described as 'preachers', and only those with a definite call from their home church were permitted to conduct public services.[69] Rippon's case first came before the Tiverton church on 23 December 1770:

> In consequence of a letter being received from the Rev. H. Evans of Bristol by the Pastor of this Church relative to our Brother John Rippon Minor who was under his tuition, in which he desires the Church to exercise his abilities, and if they approved of him to call him to the Work of the ministry, that he might hereby be capable of supplying some destitute church occasionally around Bristol there being so many in want at this time of some to break the bread of life to them; the Church was stopd & consulted upon the affair, & it was agreed to hold the Wednesday following as a day of fasting & prayer on account of the melancholy state of the Nation at present, & our low state as a church seeing there appears little or no moving upon the sanctuary waters at which time it was appointed that br Rippon should exercise his gift.[70]

Accordingly, Rippon preached on 26 December and it was then agreed to call him to the work of the ministry:

> the Pastor of the Church did in their name & by their authority & as their mouth call him to go forth and preach the gospel of Xt wheresoever Providence may open a door unto him, hoping the Lord has given him abilities for to be useful to his fellow men.

---

67   Rippon, *Brief Essay*, pp. 27-28.
68   Tiverton Churchbook, 7, 10 July 1771.
69   M.H. Wilkin, *Joseph Kinghorn of Norwich* (Norwich: 1855), p. 77.
70   Tiverton Churchbook.

This whole procedure is of interest. The influence of the Presidents of the Academy was of great importance. Hugh Evans was active in Association affairs whilst local churches sought his advice especially about ministerial settlements. In this example, the Tiverton church readily and speedily followed his suggestion, although the fact that the Tiverton pastor was a recent Bristol graduate may have facilitated the business. On the other hand, it is equally important to note that Evans would not permit any student to preach in public unless he had been regularly called by his home church. This concern for a stated call was an important aspect of Baptist polity and Rippon himself was later to draw up detailed rules in his own church to prevent any form of irregular ministry.

Evans' personal assistance to Rippon is also evidenced by his activity in the latter's settlement at Carter Lane, as will be shown. Clearly Hugh Evans was an attractive and influential figure, greatly venerated by Rippon.

Similarly, Caleb Evans was also deeply respected: 'We all of us felt a sincere affection for him, and in some of us it seemed to be a mixture of the filial and fraternal.'[71] Evans appears to have displayed the strengths and weaknesses of the stereotypical Welsh temperament. His preaching, for example, was eloquent and passionate; but, on the other hand, his emotions could be easily roused. Rippon remembered that, 'His temper was not formed for approving virtue with coolness, nor for censuring vice with apathy';[72] whilst Samuel Stennett cautiously observed that 'on some extraordinary occasions, he might in a small degree be carried beyond that evenness of temper he aimed always to preserve'.[73] Evans was involved in a defence of the Trinitarian faith against the Rev. E. Harwood,[74] opposed John Wesley over his attitude to the American Revolution,[75] and provoked the eccentric Antinomian, William Huntington, who was to have a profound influence on the growth of the Strict Baptist denomination, to a bitter attack.[76] Like his father before him, Caleb was active in the life of the churches of the west.[77]

---

71   Rippon, *Brief Essay*, p. 42.
72   Rippon, *Brief Essay*, p. 43.
73   *The Mortality of Ministers*, p. 30.
74   See Whitley, *Baptist Bibliography*, refs. 22-766; 17-767.
75   *Baptist Bibliography*, refs. 7-775 to 9-775, 5-776 to 9-776.
76   *Baptist Bibliography*, ref. 30-789. For Huntington (1745-1813) and the Strict Baptists, see K. Dix, *Strict and Particular. English Strict and Particular Baptists in the nineteenth century* (Didcot: Baptist Historical Society, 2001), pp. 6-29.
77   Cf. S. Stennett, *The Mortality of Ministers*, p. 40. See N.S. Moon, 'Caleb Evans, Founder of the Bristol Education Society', *BQ* 24.4 (1971), pp. 175-90; R. Hayden, 'Caleb Evans and the Anti-Slavery Question', *BQ* 39.1 (2001), pp. 4-14; J.E. Bradley, *Religion, Revolution and English Radicalism: Nonconformity in Eighteenth-*

In two areas did the interests of Evans specifically stimulate Rippon. Combining with John Ash of Pershore, Caleb Evans published in 1769, the year Rippon came to Bristol, *A Collection of Hymns Adapted to Public Worship,* which soon became known popularly as the 'Bristol Collection'.[78] This book was later replaced in popularity among Baptists by Rippon's *Selection* published in 1787 and a closer comparison of the two works will be found in the later discussion of Rippon's hymnody. It is sufficient to note here that Rippon's interest in hymns can only have been stimulated, if not kindled, by the effort of his distinguished seniors. Again, Evans' public support for the Americans in their conflicts with the British can only have deepened Rippon's interest in everything American. Rippon's great debt to Caleb Evans is suggested by the print of his portrait which he published opposite the title page of the first volume of his *Register*.

The enlarged scope of the Academy in 1770 led to the appointment of James Newton (1734-1790) as classics tutor.[79] Assistant to John Tommas (1724-1800),[80] pastor of the Pithay church Bristol, Newton exerted a quiet influence upon his students. Rippon recorded, 'Some of us...who in our later years at the academy were under his care, perfectly recollect with what humility, prudence and affection, he entered on his office among us, and with what patience and assiduity he sustained it.'[81] In 1784 Joseph Kinghorn rather shrewdly observed of Newton, 'A student will soon be intimate with him who learns plenty of Latin and Greek'.[82]

The broad basis of the Academy's formal course was defined by Hugh Evans in 1773:

> To instruct them into the knowledge of the languages in which the scriptures were written, to give them a just view of language in general, and of their own in particular, to teach them to express themselves with propriety upon whatever subject they discourse of, and to lead them into an acquaintance with those several branches of literature in general, which may be serviceable to them, with the blessing of God, in the exercise of their ministry.[83]

Century Politics and Society (Cambridge: Cambridge University Press, 1990) makes extensive use of Evans' sermons (see index).

78   See E. Sharpe, 'Bristol Baptist College and the Church's Hymnody', *BQ* 28.1 (1979), pp. 7-16.

79   For Newton see *Register* 1 (1790-93), pp. 150-154. Whitley, *Baptist Bibliography,* ref. 16-782 is incorrect; this work was by John Newton. See J. Bull, *John Newton of Olney and St Mary Woolnoth* (London: 1868), p. 259.

80   Cf. *Register* 3 (1798-1801), pp. 313-19.

81   Rippon, *Brief Essay,* p. 35.

82   Wilkin, *Joseph Kinghorn,* p. 71.

83   *The Able Minister* (Bristol: 1773), p. 43.

The details of the curriculum agree with Doddridge's approach.[84] The plan was advertised to include: English Grammar, the 'learned Languages', Logic, Oratory, Geography, Astronomy, Natural Philosophy, Moral Philosophy, Evidences of Christianity, Jewish Antiquities, Chronology, Ecclesiastical History, and a System of Divinity.

A good illustration of this scheme in practice is the course followed by Thomas Dunscombe.[85] During his first year he translated the Gallic and Civil Wars in Caesar's Commentaries; the first six books of Virgil's *Aeneid*; two works by Grotius on the Truth of the Christian Religion;[86] the three first orations of Cicero; the four Gospels from the Greek; two centuries of Turretinus;[87] and thirty chapters of Ecclesiastical History had been translated from Latin. Gill's *Body of Divinity* (1770) and the first part of Watts' *Logic* (1724) had been abridged; Willymott's Particles[88] had been studied and a weekly essay on a Scripture passage had been written. Rippon presumably followed a similar course.[89] It is, however, to be noted that Dunscombe was highly regarded for his classical skill and it is possible that other students did much less classical work. John C. Ryland (1723-1792) in 1773 wrote to James Manning in America that Rippon was one of thirty-one listed Baptist ministers in England who could read Greek.[90]

Further insight is provided by the list, *A Few useful books for a young Minister*, which Caleb Evans gave to one of his students, probably Dunscombe, in 1773 and which Rippon later published.[91] After Bibles and Lexicons the list is divided into Expositions; On Revelation and the Deistical Controversy; Divinity; Practical Writers; Lives; History; Miscellaneous. The writers most cited are Watts (four works) and Doddridge (three); the latter is 'to be valued for sublimity, perspicuity, penetration, and unbounded love'. Both these writers together with others listed here were much quoted by Rippon in his later works. For example,

---

84   Murray, 'Doddridge and Education', pp. 102-21.

85   (A. Dakin), *Bristol Baptist College-250 years 1679-1929* (Bristol: 1929), p. 23.

86   H. Grotius, *De Veritate Religionis Christianae* (1622).

87   J.A. Turretinus, *Historiae Ecclesiasticae Compendium a Christo nato usque ad annum MDCC* (1734).

88   W. Willymott, *English particles exemplify'd in sentences design'd for Latin exercises: with the proper rendering of each particle inserted in the sentence* (1703).

89   For details of the studies done by John Sutcliff (1752-1814) in 1773-74, see Haykin, *One Heart and One Soul*, pp. 53-54.

90   R.A. Guild, *Early History of Brown University, including the Life, Times, and correspondence of President Manning 1756-1791* (Providence, R I.: 1897), p. 245.

91   Dunscombe was ordained in 1773, and the list refers to Turretine 'which you translated'. *Register* 1 (1790-93), pp. 253-56. Cf. Ashley Smith, *Birth of Modern Education*, pp. 282-84.

Rippon commented about Doddridge's *Rise and Progress of Religion in the Soul* (1745):

> Who can read the close of even the first chapter and not feel a present deity? I know of no other forty lines in prose which ever produced a greater effect on my own mind than the concluding part of that chapter.[92]

This section was 'The Meditation of a Sinner, who was once thoughtless, but begins to be awakened'. Again, Rippon admitted in the introduction to his *Discourses on the All-Sufficient Gracious Assistance of the Spirit of Christ* (1800) that several quotations from 'Dr. Owen, Dr. Goodwin, Mr. Charnock and other favourite authors' had been noted 'in my very earliest studies'.[93] The High Calvinists were represented by Gill ('the touchstone of orthodoxy with many') and Brine. Also to be noted as significant for Rippon's development are the books of President (Jonathan) Edwards (1703-1758), whom Evans described as 'the most rational, scriptural divine, and the liveliest Christian, the world was ever blessed with'. One of Edwards' books recommended was his *Freedom of the Will*, which greatly influenced both Ryland and Fuller in their movement towards a moderate Calvinism. The influence of Edwards on British Baptists has been analyzed as 'theological, devotional and practical',[94] and it is notable that his books were so highly commended in the Bristol Academy

Over and beyond the formal tuition, the Bristol tutors sought to fulfil their responsibility by inculcating properly devout habits. On 12 April 1770 Caleb Evans delivered an 'Address to the Students' which greatly impressed at least Dunscombe who kept the original manuscript and Rippon who published it and recommended it to later students.[95] After emphasizing that the only true motive for ministerial work was love for Christ, Evans urged the advantages of diligence, regularity, steadiness, and perseverance for successful study. Possibly Evans' suggestion of compiling a 'common place book' was the origin of Rippon's later compilation of notes entitled 'Rough Schemes of scriptural subjects'.[96]

---

92   J. Rippon, *Discourse on the Origin and Progress of the Society for Promoting Religious Knowledge among the Poor* (London: 1802), p. 37.

93   J. Rippon, *Discourses on the All-Sufficient Gracious Assistance of the Spirit of Christ* (London: 1800), p. 6.

94   E.A. Payne, 'The Evangelical Revival and the Beginnings of the Modern Missionary Movement', *Congregational Quarterly* 24 (1943), pp. 227-29. For Edwards, see *DEB*.

95   T. Dunscombe, *Tribute of Affection to the Memory of the late Dr. Evans* (Oxford: 1792), p. 33; Register 2 (1794-97), pp. 345-51.

96   In the Angus Library. Whitley, *Baptist Bibliography*, ii, dated it 1800: ref. 61-800.

Reference has been made to the weekly preaching by students. This 'conference' could be quite an ordeal: even such a talented youth as Robert Hall found the experience unnerving and gave up in despair.[97] Only after a student had been regularly called by his home church was he permitted to conduct services, as has been noted. Rippon is known to have preached at centres as far removed as Faringdon in Berkshire[98] and Falmouth in Cornwall, the latter during the summer vacation of 1771.[99]

Significant for any young student is the influence of his fellow students. Dunscombe was his closest friend, and their extant correspondence reveals a lively and affectionate relationship.[100] Many of Rippon's student-friends greatly assisted him in his later works, especially by supplying information for the *Register* and assisting in its sale. Special mention should be made of John Sutcliff (1752-1814) who entered the Academy in 1772, and who became a cautious but wise leader of the Missionary Society.

Clearly of central importance was the theological position of the tutors. W.T. Whitley suggested that under Hugh and Caleb Evans the Academy became tainted with Socinianism.[101] This conclusion may be doubted, indeed there are several indications that there was a hardening against heterodoxy. The only evidence cited by Whitley is quite misleading. He referred to the defection from the Particular Baptists to the General Baptists of William Richards (1749-1818), a Welshman of independent mind, in 1798. Richards was only in the Academy for a period of two years, more than twenty years before his defection, and was influenced by a general Welsh movement towards Socinianism.[102] Others also later became Socinians,[103] but in no case is there evidence of a link with the Academy's teaching. Certainly both Hugh and Caleb were tolerant. The inescapable conclusion has been that both men were strictly orthodox in their Christology, and believers in a moderate Calvinism.[104]

Hugh Evans published only a few sermons which argued for a duly ordered and educated ministry. Examination of notes of sermons

---

97   Swaine, *Faithful Men*, p. 102.

98   E.A. Payne, *The Baptists of Berkshire* (London: Carey Kingsgate Press, 1951), p. 86.

99   L.A. Fereday, *The Story of Falmouth Baptists. With Some account of Cornish Baptist beginnings* (London: Carey Kingsgate Press, 1950), p. 48.

100   Cf. B.L. Add. MSS. 25386, f. 421.

101   W.T. Whitley (ed.), 'Calendar of Letters 1742-1831: Collected by Isaac Mann', *BQ* 6.4 (1932-33), p. 184; *Minutes of the General Baptists,* 2, p. 244, n. 14.

102   For Richards, see *DNB* and. J. Evans, *Memoirs of the life and Writings of the Rev. William Richards, LL.D.* (London: 1819), pp. 10, 109-117.

103   These included Job David, Rippon's friend at Frome.

104   See especially, Hayden, 'Evangelical Calvinism'.

preached by him in 1766, as recorded by a member of Broadmead,[105] suggests his Trinitarian orthodoxy. For example, Christ is described as 'rich in all the Glories of the Deity', whilst the Holy Spirit is a 'distinct Person from the father & Son'.[106] Again, the Antinomian position, that believers are not required to obey all the moral laws, was rejected.[107]

More materials are available for Caleb Evans who was 'closely attached to the system of theology which we call Calvinism'.[108] His first serious publication was a defence of the Deity of the Son and Holy Spirit.[109] Most valuable as a basis of his Calvinism is his Confession of Faith that he delivered at his ordination on 18 August 1767.[110] It is to be observed that this ordination was somewhat belated and represented not so much a young man's simple repetition of expected formulas as a mature belief. Evans referred to his belief in the unity of the Godhead in three divine Persons; original sin; universal depravity; redemption of the elect; the vicarious atoning sacrifice of Christ; the necessity of regeneration; baptism and the Lord's Supper as institutions of Christ; resurrection of the dead; the last judgment. Far from being Socinian, Caleb Evans in 1788 could write of Joseph Priestley (1733-1804), then their principal advocate: 'surely he has gone to the *ne plus ultra* of heresy. Further he cannot go and retain the name of Christian, for the substance of Christianity he has long since discarded'.[111]

Of special significance, however, in Caleb Evans' theology is a number of indications that he was an advocate of that moderate, evangelistic Calvinism which Andrew Fuller was later to champion so effectively. For example, on 16 August 1775, Evans preached to the Education Society a sermon entitled *The Kingdom of God* in which he insisted that to pray for the Kingdom necessitated a corresponding personal activity to promote its advance:

> When we pray for the advancement of this kingdom, if we are not willing to do all we can to advance it, our prayers cannot be genuine, they are hypocritical;... When we pray that the kingdom of God may come we are supposed to express a willingness to do whatever God may enable us to do, as workers together with him.... Then surely we cannot but prize the gospel, a gospel ministry, gospel

---

105   MS. Book of Sermons in Angus Library.

106   See sermon on John 16:8.

107   See sermon on Proverbs 28:9.

108   Rippon, *Brief Essay*, p. 43.

109   *The Scripture doctrine of the deity of the Son of God and Holy Spirit* (Bristol: 1766).

110   *A charge and sermon, together with an introductory discourse and confession of faith, delivered at the ordination of the Rev. Caleb Evans* (Bristol: 1767).

111   C. Evans to J. Manning, Bristol, 20 September 1788, in Guild, *Early History of Brown University*, p. 460.

means of grace, and be ready cheerfully to embrace every opportunity of spreading the gospel and encouraging its ministers.[112]

Evans' own sermons evidence a direct appeal to the unconverted, as demonstrated in a series of sermons preached in 1789 entitled *Christ Crucified*:

> Are there any here who are convinced of sin, who feel the burden of it upon their consciences, and find it too heavy for them to bear, who know in themselves that a just and holy God might justly abandon and cast them off, and give them up to despair and misery for ever, and who are secretly and anxiously crying out, What shall we do to be saved? We preach to them Christ crucified...[113]

The importance of Evans' moderate Calvinism cannot be over-emphasized, for he influenced scores of Bristol students. In 1775 Evans said that, next to the education of pious candidates, the aim of the Education Society was 'the encouragement of missionaries to preach the gospel wherever providence opens a door'.[114] Earlier in 1773 the Society had financed a 'Gospel Mission' into Cornwall; the details are unknown other than that the 'Rev. Francis' was missioner.[115]

Presumably this was some form of itinerant tour on a more modest scale than that undertaken by Steadman and Saffery in 1796.[116] But the implications are clear. Years before Fuller published his *Gospel Worthy of all Acceptation* (1785) Bristol men had been influenced towards the same position. Evans may not have had the courageous vision of William Carey to take the Gospel to heathen lands, but fourteen years before the formation of the Missionary Society he had been speaking of missionaries preaching wherever God led them. It is significant that some of the most enthusiastic supporters for the new Missionary Society were Bristol men like John Sutcliff, Samuel Pearce (1766-1799), William Staughton (1770-1829), and John Rippon. The significance of Bristol Academy's influence upon the gradual decline of the High Calvinism of men like Gill and Brine, and the spread of 'Fullerism' can scarcely be overstated.

---

112   C. Evans, *The Kingdom of God* (Bristol:1775), pp. 20-21.

113   C. Evans, *Christ Crucified; or the Scripture Doctrine of the Atonement briefly illustrated and defended* (Bristol: 1789), p. 53.

114   *The Kingdom of God*, p. 24.

115   Cf. *Account of Bristol Education Society for 1773*, p. 29; *Account for 1774*, p.17. Benjamin Francis was the missioner, see J. Ryland, *The Presence of Christ the Source of Eternal Bliss. A Funeral Discourse occasioned by the death of the Rev. Benjamin Francis; to which is annexed A sketch of Mr. Francis's Life by Thomas Flint* (Bristol: 1800), p. 46. For Francis, see M.A.G. Haykin, 'Benjamin Francis (1754-1799)' in *The British Particular Baptists*, 2, pp. 17-28.

116   *Register* 2 (1794-97), pp. 459-64.

Clearly Rippon's time in Bristol exerted a profound influence upon him. The daily routine of his studies, the strong evangelical emphasis of his tutors, the companionship of his friends, the worshipping life of the Bristol churches all helped mould the direction of Rippon's life. He became a subscriber to the Education Society in 1773, the year he left the Academy, and gave an annual subscription for the rest of his life. Accorded the distinct honour of delivering the annual address to the Society in 1795 Rippon sought to repay something of his debt by carefully compiling materials towards a history of the Academy. Young men called to the ministry by his own church were, whenever possible, quite firmly directed to Bristol for their training.

A useful prelude to an examination of Rippon's ministry at Carter Lane is the charge preached by Caleb Evans to Thomas Dunscombe at Coate, Oxfordshire, on 4 August 1773.[117] Rippon was in the congregation,[118] and only the preceding Sunday had written to the Carter Lane church accepting their invitation to become pastor.[119] His beloved mentor was the preacher, his closest friend was beginning his life's work, and he himself was on the threshold of a long ministry. Evans addressed himself to the practical aspects of the work of the ministry and two of his most promising students presumably drank in every word.

Six aspects of the minister's public work were noted by Evans.

1. *Preaching the word.* Delivery should be without awkward gesture or affectation, Evans exhorted. Most pointedly he urged that Dunscombe should preach directly to the consciences of his hearers: 'Preach to them the ability of Christ to save; to save unto the uttermost, to save all that come to God by him. Preach the willingness of Christ to save'.

2. *Public Prayer.* Method, but not formality was counselled, whilst 'preaching prayers' should be avoided.

3. To preside over and regulate the *singing of psalms.* Rippon's hymnbooks were to result from his pastoral work, and he doubtless heeded Evans' advice: 'And a most enlivening, delightful part of worship it is when properly conducted. Do not think it beneath your attention, my brother, to endeavour to chuse out for your people suitable compositions.'

4. To *administer the ordinances* of baptism and the Lord's Supper, conforming to the pattern of the Word of God.

5. To preside in the *government of his (Christ's) house.* Evans suggested that ministers should *rule*, but not *lord* it over the church. Discipline should be according to the Bible and characterized by tenderness and humility.

---

117   C. Evans and H. Evans, *A Charge and Sermon; delivered at the ordination of the Rev. Thomas Dunscombe at Coate, Oxon, August 4th 1773* (Bristol: 1773).

118   J. Stanley, *The Church in the Hop Garden* (London: n.d.), p. 132.

119   Carter Lane Churchbook, 1 August 1773.

6. *Visitation.* Prudence was necessary so that a minister was not a stranger to his people and yet was not always visiting so as to neglect other duties.

The next chapter will demonstrate the extent to which Rippon's ministry followed the advice of his tutor.

Rippon and the Theology of the Baptists

At this point it will be helpful to analyze Rippon's position, as far as can be ascertained, in the Calvinistic controversy so vital to the future of the Baptists. When Rippon began his public ministry the majority of Particular Baptists still appear to have advocated what is conveniently described as the High Calvinist position. This gave false emphasis to a more 'strict' Calvinism; it constituted a lack of balance rather than an heretical deviation.[120] Its most obvious development, occasioned by an undue concern to avoid any faint suspicion of Arminianism or Pelagianism, followed a terrifyingly simple logic: (1) Christ died only for the elect; (2) Only the elect have the ability, or duty, to repent and believe; (3) Those not of the elect do not have the ability, or duty, to repent and believe; (4) To preach to all, including those not of the elect, was accordingly futile and, more seriously, impinged on God's glory and the freedom of grace.

The tragedy was that this 'non-invitation, non-application' preaching[121] obscured the very evangelical truths these Calvinists were so concerned to preserve. This doctrine was not John Calvin's, nor the Puritans'. Indeed, that it was held to be an innovation is suggested by the title of an attack by Matthias Maurice on their negative theology, *A modern question modestly answer'd* in 1737; and the controversy was frequently called 'the Modern Question'.[122]

---

120 Fuller claimed there were three forms of Calvinism: (i) High - *i.e.* Gill's. (ii) Moderate - 'Baxterian', that is, similar to the famous Puritan divine, Richard Baxter (1615-1691) or 'Arminian'. (iii) Strict - Fuller's own position which he believed was like Calvin's. See J. Ryland, *The Work of Faith, the Labour of Love, and the Patience of Hope illustrated in the Life and Death of the Reverend Andrew Fuller late Pastor of the Baptist Church at Kettering* (London: 1816).

121 Ivimey, *History of the English Baptists*, 3, p. 267.

122 For this controversy and its aftermath, see G.F.Nuttall, 'Northamptonshire and The Modern Question: A Turning-Point in Eighteenth-Century Dissent', *Journal of Theological Studies* 16.1 (1965), pp. 101-23.

Under the influence of John Skepp,[123] John Brine[124] and John Gill, High Calvinism was widely adopted by many who did not always understand the theological issues involved. It must be carefully noted that not all Baptists embraced it. In the north, Alverey Jackson (d. 1763) of Barnoldswick, Yorkshire, in 1752 published *The Question Answered* which maintained faith as the duty of all who hear the Gospel. Later John Fawcett, a convert of Whitefield, refused to be bound by Gill and promoted village evangelism.[125] More significant, perhaps, was the group of men who came from the West to exert genuinely evangelistic ministries. Notable among these was Andrew Gifford, a warm admirer of Whitefield, and known to have been an evangelist in his ministry in London.[126] Bristol Academy produced Benjamin Beddome (1717-95) of Bourton-on-the- Water, Gloucestershire, and Benjamin Francis who were also active evangelists.[127] Undoubtedly many ministers preached a better Gospel than their theology would imply. John Ryland Junior commented:

> Many of these ministers indeed endeavoured to address the consciences of men as
> far as their system would allow; and some of them could hardly refrain from
> expressing themselves inconsistently with their creed.[128]

But the decade or so after Rippon began preaching in London (1773) was the most significant. Gill and the older men had all died. The story is most clearly traced in the Midlands, within some churches of the Northamptonshire Association. By 1776 John Ryland Junior and John Sutcliff (a protege of John Fawcett) were discussing the issue and were greatly influenced by the writings of Jonathan Edwards, leader of the Great Awakening in North America.[129] Edwards provided a metaphysical

---

123 For Skepp (d. 1721), see Ivimey, *History of the English Baptists*, 3, pp. 363-66.

124 For Brine (1703-1765), see P. Toon, *The Emergence of Hyper-Calvinism in English Nonconformity 1689-1765* (London: The Olive Tree, 1967), pp. 100-139; and *DNB*.

125 Fawcett embodied his attitude in the couplet:
'To be brief, my dear friends, you may say what you will,
I'll ne'er be confined to read nothing but Gill.'
See J. Fawcett (Jr) , *Memoirs of John Fawcett* (London: 1818), pp. 108, 154.

126 L.G. Champion, *Farthing Rushlight. The Story of Andrew Gifford 1700-1784* (London: Carey Kingsgate Press, 1961), pp. 25-28.

127 *Register* 2 (1794-97), pp. 314-26; M.A.G. Haykin, 'Benjamin Beddome (1717-1795)', in *The British Particular Baptists 1638-1910*, 1, pp. 167-82; T. Flint, *A Sketch of Mr. Francis's Life,* pp. 45-46.

128 J. Ryland, *The Work of Faith*, p. 8.

129 *The Work of Faith,* p. 56. For a review of Edwards' significance for English Baptists, see Payne, 'The evangelical revival and the modern missionary movement';

clue for solving the 'Modern Question' by his distinction between *moral* and *natural* ability.[130] Use of a person's natural ability was what made a person strictly accountable to God; whilst moral ability was the disposition to use natural ability for right purposes. As D. Bebbington summarizes: 'Natural inability operated when human beings could not do what they wanted to do. Moral inability operated when they did not do something because they did not want to do it'.[131] Since a person's will is vitally concerned, each individual is blameworthy for rejection of the Gospel. Every sinner should therefore be confronted with this duty as forcefully as possible. This notion of 'faith-duty' was to be a focus of intense debate among Calvinistic Baptists in the ensuing decades. Ryland gave this insight to Robert Hall Senior (1728-1791),[132] and, in turn, Hall advised young Andrew Fuller to read Edwards.[133] This sharing through a network of friends was a turning point for the controversy.[134]

Edwards' distinction between moral and natural ability was 'one of the foundation stones of Fuller's doctrine',[135] and helped him with his own dilemma. The result was his *Gospel Worthy of all Acceptation*, written in 1781, but not published until 1785. When this book did appear, and it was as much a symptom as a cause, the foundation of the denomination's new vigour, characterized by the new Missionary Society, was well laid.

Rippon was not a theologian, but his own position was very soon apparent: he was an ardent advocate of 'Fullerism', that is, he preached the Gospel as forcefully as he could to all his hearers. This may be documented from his first published sermon in 1784,[136] but most probably was characteristic from the commencement of his public ministry. This is strongly suggested by the remarkable number of sixty people who joined the church during his first year's ministry.[137]

Watts, *The Dissenters*, 1, p. 459; Bebbington, *Evangelicalism*, pp. 47-48, 63-64; Haykin, *One Heart and One Soul*, pp. 139-46, 154-55, 158-71.

130 *Inquiry into the Modern Prevailing Notions respecting that Freedom of the Will which is supposed to be essential to Moral Agency* (1754).

131 D.W. Bebbington, *Holiness in Nineteenth-Century England* (Carlisle: Paternoster, 2000), p. 33.

132 J. Ryland, *The Work of Faith*, p. 9, note 1. For Robert Hall, Senior, see M.A.G. Haykin, 'Robert Hall, Sr. (1728-1791)', in *The British Particular Baptists 1638-1910*, 1, pp. 203-210.

133 *The Work of Faith*, p. 58.

134 For a review of Fuller's theology and the various influences shaping it, see E. F. Clipsham, 'Fuller and Fullerism', *BQ*. 20 (1963) pp. 99-114, 146-54, 214-25, 268-76; T.J. Nettles, 'Andrew Fuller (1754-1815)' in M.A.G. Haykin, *The British Particular Baptists 1638-1910*, 2, pp. 97-141.

135 Clipsham, 'Fuller and Fullerism', p. 111.

136 See below, chapter 8.

137 See below, chapter 3.

The problem is that at no one point can any decisive influence that produced this result be clearly documented. Nevertheless, at several points, his years of preparation brought him into contact with a moderate evangelical Calvinism; presumably the combination of all these influences moulded his attitude. First, at Tiverton he came into contact with Henry Philips, who it has been noted, was a convert of Howel Harris. At Bristol, several factors have been noted: his tutors were themselves moderate Calvinists; he was commended to read Jonathan Edwards' works; Doddridge's personal and vital religious writings influenced him; he probably came into contact with men like Benjamin Francis, and others, in the Associations; he formed a lasting friendship with John Sutcliff who himself had been schooled by John Fawcett.

Then he moved to London. It will be shown that a group left Carter Lane because of his preaching. Is it a mere coincidence that among the first to oppose Fuller's writings was William Button, whom that group had chosen as an alternative to Rippon? Again, in London Rippon was in contact with at least two London ministers who practised a direct appeal. One was Andrew Gifford, and Rippon, though more than fifty years younger than Gifford, became so close to him that he preached his funeral sermon. Abraham Booth (1734-1806),[138] in London since 1769, published *Glad Tidings to Perishing Sinners; or the genuine Gospel a complete Warrant for the Ungodly to believe in Jesus* in 1796, the title of which amplifies his position. Although he was in London, Rippon was in constant touch with Sutcliff,[139] and Ryland Junior, from whom he had a weekly letter for six years.[140] Accordingly, he was in touch with the movements stirring in the Northamptonshire Association. Rippon's whole-hearted adoption in his ministry of this moderate Calvinism is of basic significance for understanding the contribution he brought, not only to his own church, but also to the whole denomination.

---

138 For Booth, see *DNB*; *Memoir* by Rippon (1806); E. A. Payne, 'Abraham Booth 1734-1806', *BQ*. 26.1 (1975), pp. 28-42; R.W. Oliver, 'Abraham Booth (1734-1806)' in *The British Particular Baptists 1638-1910* , 2, pp. 31-54.

139 Cf. letters to Sutcliff, preserved in Historical Society of Pennsylvania.

140 J. Rippon to R. Furman, 18 July 1793; in S.W. Lynd, *Memoir of the Revd. William Staughton D.D.* (Boston: 1834), pp. 27-28.

CHAPTER 3

Pattern of a Pastorate:
John Rippon at Carter Lane (1773-1836)

John Rippon exerted a significant influence on his denomination but his main responsibility for the extraordinary period of sixty-three years was the pastorate of Carter Lane Baptist church. Indeed, it was the effectiveness of his pastoral ministry that commended him to the wider constituency. The unusual length of Rippon's pastorate provides a striking illustration of one paradoxical feature of congregational-type churches: the fluctuating signs of success are closely linked to the personality, theology, ability, health and age of the pastoral leader.

Historians of Dissent are increasingly concerned to trace the inner life of church communities, to understand the life and faith of ordinary people who shared in the worship and service of individual congregations.[1] Local studies, such as that attempted here, should help produce a more comprehensive picture of Baptists during a period of considerable change. Although Carter Lane was the leading London Baptist church its general pattern of life seems to be typical of other churches at the time, especially in London.

In 1773 the London churches were of central economic significance for the denomination as a whole. The majority of the provincial churches were desperately poor, and many were dependent upon the charity of London Baptists. Since 1717 the Particular Baptist Fund, largely financed by investments of capital raised by collections from the London churches, had given annual sums to poor ministers, and to help train students for the ministry. Again, whenever a country church embarked

---

1   See Watts, *The Dissenters*, 1, pp. 303-366; 2, ch. 2. Karen Smith has argued that excessive concentration on theological changes has led to an over-simplified interpretation of development among Particular Baptists and that the community experience of the church is in fact far more central. Her study on regional Baptists is especially helpful, see K.E. Smith, 'The Community and the Believer: A Study of Calvinistic Baptist Spirituality in Some Towns and Villages of Hampshire and the Borders of Wiltshire, c.1730-1830' (DPhil thesis, Oxford University, 1986).

on a building project, the pastor came to London to beg for donations from wealthy Londoners. Between 1724 and 1824, an estimated £30,000 was given by London Baptists for this purpose.[2]

Although the initiative of an independent group, largely within the Northamptonshire Association, led to the formation of the Baptist Missionary Society and a consequent renewal of much Baptist life, the economic strength of the denomination remained in London. Moreover, the main contact of Dissenters with Parliament was through the Dissenting Deputies, composed entirely of representatives from London churches.

Some ministers outside the metropolis were sharply critical of London Baptists and resented their economic power. Andrew Fuller, once described by William Wilberforce as one 'who bore about him very plainly the vestigia ruris' and 'the very picture of a blacksmith', had a countryman's inbred suspicion of London, 'that vortex of vanity'.[3] Robert Robinson of Cambridge was an outspoken critic:

> What is there in London air that thus metaphorses (sic) mankind? How is it that, as soon as a poor brother gets ordained in London, he becomes a London minister; that is, he buys us with other people's money-the funds: he ceases to advise, and commences dictator; he gravely sits in judgment on us, our wives, little ones and substance; and perhaps when we have travelled to oblige these great men, I know not how far, we come back laden with a good coat, or great wig; too little and bald for the clerical coffee-house, and hugging our chains, we admire the gifts as grapes of Eschol! Well, the carnality of the whole disgusts me...[4]

Rippon, however, never forgot his Devonshire roots and worked hard in London to promote the needs of rural churches and to plead for their generous support.[5]

Rippon's church was one of the leading London Baptist churches. With two sister churches, Carter Lane had evolved from an original church formed by Benjamin Keach circa 1672.[6] With a separate

---

2   S.J. Price, A Popular History of the Baptist Building Fund (London: Kingsgate Press, 1924), p. 55.

3   R.L. and S.W. Wilberforce, The Life of William Wilberforce (5 vols; London: 1838), 3, p. 389; A. Fuller to W. Ward, 15 July 1812 (typescript copy in Angus Library).

4   Hughes, With Freedom Fired, p. 56.

5   See chapter 7.

6   Ivimey, History of the English Baptists, 2, p. 363. For Keach (1640-1704) see DNB; J.B. Vaughn, 'Benjamin Keach' in Baptist Theologians, pp. 49-76; M.A.G. Haykin, Kiffin, Knollys and Keach-Rediscovering our English Baptist Heritage (Leeds: Reformation Today Trust, 1996), pp. 83-97; T.J. Nettles, 'Benjamin Keach (1640-1704)' in The British Particular Baptists 1638-1910, 1, pp. 95-130.

existence from 1719,[7] the church met from 1720 at Goat Yard, Horsleydown, and from 1757 at Carter Lane, off Tooley Street, Southwark. For the whole of its separate existence it had known only one pastor, John Gill, whose stature as a theologian and scholar among Baptists meant that his church acquired a certain prestige. However, when he died on 14 October 1771, after fifty-two years as pastor, the church entered upon its 'State of Widowhood' with only about 110 members, a net increase of only sixteen since 1719.[8]

That Carter Lane was so firmly within the traditions of Old Dissent, and had enjoyed the ministry of such an exponent of Calvinist orthodoxy, adds interest to our study. Rippon was an enthusiastic and convinced advocate of an evangelistic and moderate Calvinism. His pastorate at Carter Lane offers a striking example of Old Dissent becoming New Dissent. The transition was not without difficulties.

A Call and a Division

To agree on a successor for John Gill proved the first major problem. During 1772 both Benjamin Francis of Horsley, Gloucestershire, and John Fawcett then at Wainsgate, Yorkshire, declined to come.[9] According to a popular story, Fawcett had agreed to come to London but after the farewell services could not actually bear to leave his people, decided to stay and promptly wrote the hymn, 'Blest be the tie that binds', which Rippon helped popularize.[10] Significantly, both Francis and Fawcett were known to favour a direct evangelical appeal.[11] Gill had personally suggested Francis as a suitable successor.[12] The church then considered Rippon, still a young Bristol student, who seems to have visited the church at the suggestion of Hugh Evans, his Bristol tutor, and first preached at Carter Lane in October 1772.[13] After preaching for seven weeks, he was

---

7   For an account of this division resulting in the new church, see B.R. White, 'Thomas Crosby, Baptist Historian', *BQ* 21.4 (1965), pp. 154-64; B.R. White, 'John Gill in London, 1719-1729: A biographical Fragment', *BQ* 22.2 (1967), pp. 72-91.

8   In 1719, 94 had signed the Covenant: cf. White, 'Thomas Crosby', p.162, and 110 is based on a list of members compiled after Rippon's settlement. In 1753 Gill, with 153 'hearers', had one of the two biggest London Baptist congregations: *BHS Trans.* 6 (1918-19), p.155.

9   Brown, *English Baptists of the Eighteenth Century*, p. 94.

10   Brown, *English Baptists of the Eighteenth Century*, p. 94.

11   J. Ryland, *Funeral Discourse*, p. 46; Fawcett Jr., *Memoirs of John Fawcett*, p. 154.

12   B.F. and L.F. Flint, *Brief Records of the Flint Family, with its Collateral Branches* (London: 1874), p. 21.

13   Carter Lane Churchbook, 7 December 1772.

requested to return for a further period of two or three months. Evans was informed of this request, and in reply to his direct query, was informed that the church's 'approbation' of Rippon was 'very general'.[14]

Rippon had a long period of probation, for he was not ordained until 11 November 1773, more than twelve months after his first sermon in Carter Lane. The main reason for this was a measure of opposition: the vote to invite Rippon, taken on 4 March 1773, was far from unanimous: '33 sisters in favour, four contrary; 21 brethren for, 10 contrary'. Rippon, who was not officially told of this split vote, wrote from Bristol on 7 April.[15] He was clearly aware of the prestige and honour of serving in London in succession to Gill - 'that pious, learned & truly valuable Pastor' as he tactfully described him - but was equally sensitive of his own youth and inexperience: 'I may well say I am a child & cannot undertake the important Trust'. He compromised by proposing that he should return and preach for a further period before giving a definite answer.

Perhaps he sensed the division. In any case, on 7 July the group opposed to Rippon told the church they were unaltered in their opinion, so he was then given an official list of the 'neuter' voters. Eventually, after much agony of mind, Rippon accepted the call on 1 August 1773. The opposition then hardened into a threat of secession,[16] but his supporters refused to be dissuaded from calling Rippon and in fact generously voted to give the separators £300: £100 as 'equitable', since some of them had helped build the Carter Lane meeting-house, and £200 to 'shew our goodwill and affection'.[17] This remarkable decision increased the church debt to some £650.[18] Eventually thirty members, seventeen men and thirteen women, were dismissed and formed into a separate church which later built on Dean Street, Borough.[19]

This kind of division was an unfortunately common occurrence among Dissenters. Some may have objected to Rippon's youth. C.H. Spurgeon (one of Rippon's successors) recounts the story of the youthful Rippon running up the pulpit stairs two at a time.[20] But as Dean Street eventually

---

14   Carter Lane Churchbook, 26 December 1772.

15   Copy in Churchbook, 11 April 1773.

16   Carter Lane Churchbook, 25 September 1773.

17   Carter Lane Churchbook, 4 November 1773.

18   Carter Lane Churchbook, 7 February 1774.

19   Carter Lane Churchbook, 10 January 1774, cf. Ivimey, *History of the English Baptists*, 4, pp. 335-37. Rippon showed his own goodwill by sharing in the service of formation: B. Wallin, *The Church an Habitation of God, through the Spirit* (London: 1774), p. viii.

20   C.H. Spurgeon, *The Metropolitan Tabernacle: its History and Work* (London: 1876), p. 48.

called as pastor William Button (1754-1821), son of one of their deacons and younger than Rippon, age alone was not the reason.[21] The recorded explanation was simply that Rippon's ministry 'has not been bless'd to our souls'; but exactly what personal and theological prejudices this involved is uncertain.[22] Many who left were old warriors of Gill: three of the four deacons; George Keith, Gill's son-in-law, and Richard Hall who held the chapel mortgage. In their letter requesting dismissal they offered a pointedly Calvinistic statement of beliefs. William Button became one of the first to write against Andrew Fuller's influential advocacy among Baptists for a general evangelistic appeal.[23]

Of course it was just what the conservatives feared in Rippon that attracted others. Youthful and lively, he provided a dramatic contrast with Gill. Rippon's attraction for 'the rising generation' was a significant factor in his call.[24] Indeed, in accepting the call Rippon revealed a measure of moral courage and mature judgment. He confessed that he had often entered the pulpit with a 'heavy heart', 'trembling has seized all my nerves' and he had been tempted 'to abandon your Church and never more to speak a word for God in any public Assembly'. Nevertheless, he heeded advice from his Bristol tutors, 'persons of first rank in the baptist Denomination', deacons of other churches, and, of course, many Carter Lane people, to accept the call. He realized that, whatever his decision, disharmony could result. There was a sense of destiny in the way in which he called on 'Heaven & Earth, Angels and you my fellow Christians' to witness his acceptance of the charge. His dedication was expressed in characteristically emotional and dramatic terms:

> And now my beloved what more can I say; here is my body & soul at your service; here are the marks of my hand & here are the dictates, ye undisguised dictates of my heart. I have now deliver'd my self up into your hands, you may if you please soon break my heart & dispatch me to glory - But - But I count not my very life dear to me so that I may but finish my course & the work of ye ministry which I have received.[25]

The fellowship of the London Baptist community was symbolized in Rippon's ordination service, before a 'vast concourse of people' on

21   Ivimey, *History of the English Baptists*, 4, pp. 335-36.

22   Carter Lane Churchbook, 11 October 1773.

23   Carter Lane Churchbook, 10 January 1774, 8 October 1775; *Baptist Magazine* 20 (1828), pp. 148-51; W. Button, *Remarks on a Treatise, entitled, The Gospel Worthy of all Acceptation by Andrew Fuller* (London: 1785).

24   J. Rippon, *Memoir of Gill*, p. 130; Carter Lane Churchbook, 4 March, 1 August 1773.

25   Carter Lane Churchbook, 1 August 1773.

Thursday 11 November 1773.[26] The London ministers invited to share in this service had only agreed to do so after reassurances by the church and examination of the churchbook satisfied them that there had been no irregularities in Rippon's call, as his opponents had suggested.[27] Benjamin Wallin (1711-1782) of the Maze Pond church and Samuel Stennett (1727-95) of Little Wild Street church, the two leading London ministers, preached and five other ministers shared in the service.[28] Rippon gave a 'very particular declaration' of his faith, although laying-on of hands does not seem to have been practised.[29] He was subsequently received by the Baptist Board, the London ministers' fraternal, on 16 March 1774.[30] Rippon was thus fully incorporated into the close-knit life of London Baptists, and in his senior years he was to become the undoubted leader of the metropolitan Baptists.[31]

General Pattern

Statistics provide a starting-point for establishing the general pattern of Rippon's pastorate. Between 1773 and 1836, according to detailed church records, 1,162 members joined the church (exactly 1,000 by 'experience' and baptism, 156 by transfer from other Baptist churches, and six were restored after previous exclusion); whilst 300 left the church (144 dismissed to other churches, 156 excluded). Deaths were not systematically recorded so that the maximum membership of the church cannot now be accurately determined. By 1814 Walter Wilson, the Independent historian, described Carter Lane as 'the most numerous of the denomination';[32] perhaps 450 is as high as the membership can have been.[33] Many additional 'hearers' (not members) would have attended the Sunday services.

---

26   Carter Lane Churchbook, 13 December 1773.

27   Carter Lane Churchbook, 27 October, 4 November 1773.

28   Carter Lane Churchbook, 13 December 1773. For Stennett, see B.A Ramsbottom, 'The Stennetts', in *The British Particular Baptists 1638-1910*, 1, pp. 140-43. The other ministers were Robert Baskerville, William Nash Clarke, John Reynolds, Abraham Booth, Josiah Thompson (Jr.). For these men, see Ivimey, *History of the English Baptists*, 4, *passim*.

29   Details of this confession were not recorded.

30   'The Baptist Board Minutes', *BHS Trans.* 6 (1918-19), p. 83.

31   Cf. Brown's judgment that Rippon was 'London's most influential minister in the eighteenth century': *English Baptists of the Eighteenth Century*, p. 123.

32   W. Wilson, *History and Antiquities of Dissenting Churches in London* (4 vols; London: 1808-14), 4, p. 213.

33   There were 391 members in 1808 (list in Churchbook).

The increase in numbers was most dramatic in Rippon's early years. The largest increase was sixty in his first year (1774). After the Dean Street church had been formed the church had only 81 members, but this figure was doubled within three years. The general pattern is indicated by the increases in each decade: 1773-83: 246; 1784-93: 217; 1794-1803: 247; 1804-13: 169; 1814-23: 146; 1824-33: 63. (From 1834 to 1836 the church had an assistant pastor and 74 were added.) As would be expected, the second half of the pastorate compares unfavourably with the first.

There was a similar increase, in broad terms, in several London Baptist churches during this period. Some inner churches, such as Little Wild Street, suffered a rapid decline; but Prescott Street had 236 members in 1790; Eagle Street increased from 175 in 1805 to 470 in 1834 whilst, remarkably, James Upton began at Lambeth with 12 in 1785 and by 1834 had over 400 members.[34]

The increase at Carter Lane thus appears to have been above average, especially in the early years, but by no means unique. In Rippon's last years, the church greatly declined (a pathetic parallel to Gill's last days) and at his death there can only have been about 200 members.[35] Indeed, his last years imposed an almost intolerable strain on the patience and loyalty of his church. Only the momentum gathered in Rippon's vigorous years saved the church from complete disintegration.

Pastoral Leadership

In considering Rippon's pastoral leadership three aspects are of central importance: his preaching and conduct of public worship; his pastoral methods; and his role in church government.

Rippon's guiding maxim was scriptural: 'All things in the service of God are to be done decently and in order.'[36] This was applicable to preaching, public prayers, congregational hymnsinging, and the 'ordinances', which was the common Baptist term for Baptism and the Lord's Supper. Rippon's preaching is considered separately,[37] but is obviously of basic significance for his effectiveness in both his church

---

34   C. Woollacott, *Brief History of the Baptist Church in Little Wild Street, Lincoln's-Inn Fields; from 1691 to 1858* (London: n.d.), p. 66; E.F. Kevan, *London's oldest Baptist Church* (London: Kingsgate, 1933), p. 96; A.T. Ward, *Kingsgate Chapel* (London: Kingsgate, 1912), pp. 44-45; S.J. Price, *Upton* (London: Carey Press, 1935), pp. 28, 42.

35   Membership list of 1838 had 194 members received during Rippon's time.

36   J. Rippon, *Arrangement of Watts* (London: 1801), p. ix. Compare 1 Cor. 14: 40.

37   See chapter 8.

and his wider ministry. Two general observations may, however, be made
here.

First, Rippon's preaching was directly evangelistic. There are
numerous testimonies to people being first 'awakened', or 'led to
seriousness' by Rippon's sermons. Many agreed with H. Calldee, when
she wrote, 'Dear Sir I shall have reason to Bless God to all Eternity for
Ever hearing the sound of your voice as the Lord very much Blesses your
ministry to me.'[38]

Secondly, Rippon's sermons were doctrinal in content and especially
designed to impress the necessity of holy living. He detested any
suspicion of Antinomianism, that 'bastard zeal for the doctrine of
salvation by grace',[39] which teaches that Christians are by grace set free
from the need of observing any moral law. Some exponents of High
Calvinism were accused of holding this view, and as late as 1804, Andrew
Fuller believed: 'Nowhere does antinomianism grow more strongly than
in London'.[40] But as one periodical soberly reported of Rippon's
preaching: 'He never omits to remind them (his hearers) occasionally,
that the faith he recommends to them must, and ever will be,
accompanied with holy obedience and good works as the necessary effect
of it'.[41]

Dissenters at the end of the eighteenth century strongly reacted against
any 'formality' in services, and Rippon, as with other of his
contemporaries, even omitted regular Bible-reading from the public
services.[42] In 1811, one hearer lamented, 'how much I wished you would
read a Psalm or chapter or some portion of Scripture in the morning &
afternoon Worship.'[43] Rippon's public prayers were inevitably
extempore, long, with pointed and detailed intercessions and always
concluded with a doxology. Like many another non-liturgical pastor,
Rippon's words were so frequently repeated that William Aikin could
quote his exact words: 'We have all of us, O Lord! totally ruined and
destroyed ourselves, and it would be righteous in thee to banish us for
ever from thy blissful presence.'[44]

---

38   B.L. Add. MSS. 25386, f. 176.

39   D. Bogue and J. Bennett, *History of Dissenters from 1608 to 1808* (4 vols.;
London: 1808-1812), 4, p. 392.

40   A. Fuller to W. Ward, 27 October 1804, as cited by Haykin, *One Heart and One
Soul*, p. 319.

41   *New Spiritual Magazine* 6 (1785), p. 1708.

42   See R.T. Jones, *Congregationalism in England 1662-1962* (London:
Independent Press, 1962), p. 223.

43   'Your sincere well-wisher', to Rippon, 10 May 1811, B.L. Add. MSS. 25389, f.
576.

44   *Baptist Magazine* 24 (1832), p. 465.

Rippon gave special care to the improvement of congregational singing. His appreciation of the various elements of public worship was offered in the preface to his *Tune Book* (*circa* 1791):

> In *hearing the word of God*, we place ourselves at his feet as the children of ignorance, hoping to be made wise unto salvation: Performing the *work of prayer* we are only Beggars of a superior class; but when the *high praises* of God, in our mouths, are inspirited with gratitude to him who sitteth upon the throne of the Lamb, then we rise above the lower forms of Christianity.[45]

A concern for good hymnody in his own church was a catalyst for Rippon's extensive hymnodic work.[46]

Carter Lane employed, in the custom of the day, a precentor, or clerk, who led the singing from the 'neat mahogany Clerks desk' donated to the church in 1780.[47] The church had agreed in 1767 that 'the whole Psalms or Hymn or such verses as are app'd to be sung be first read & afterward every line separately'.[48] Rippon deplored the stultifying effect of this lining-out,[49] but the custom seems to have persisted in his church. To find a good clerk, especially with Rippon's specialised interest, was not always an easy task. Robert Keene[50] served in this way, but in 1824 S. Denham, a 'man of very *nervous* constitution', insisted that he could only do the task if he was allowed to choose the hymns. He liked to have the hymn and tune fixed in his mind before leaving his house.[51] Rippon normally read out the hymns himself.

The two 'ordinances' were central in the worship of the church. From 1716 Baptists in London had shared a communal baptistery erected at Horsleydown.[52] But in 1779 Carter Lane had added its own 'large baptistery, with every conveniency for baptizing'.[53] Appropriate garments for baptismal candidates were provided, and each candidate paid 2s. 6d. for the preparation of the baptistery, and not less than 1s. each to attendants (this charge was removed in 1800).[54] Baptisms were

---

45   Rippon, *Tune Book,* p. iii.

46   See chapter 4.

47   Carter Lane Churchbook, 28 February 1780.

48   Carter Lane Churchbook, 6 July 1767.

49   J. Rippon, *A Selection of Hymns* (London:1787), pp. vii-viii.

50   For Keene, see below, chapter 4.

51   S. Denham to Rippon, 13 October 1824, B.L. Add. MSS. 25386 f. 370.

52   Ivimey, *History of the English Baptists*, 3, pp. 136-38.

53   Wilson, *History and Antiquities of Dissenting Churches,* p. 213; Carter Lane Churchbook, 27 September 1779.

54   Carter Lane Churchbook, 20 March 1780; 22 September 1800. No further charges were then listed.

usually, but not invariably, on a Sunday.[55] Rippon collected several baptismal hymns for his *Selection*, and added thirteen 'single verses' which ministers could repeat during the baptismal service.[56]

Rippon baptized more than 900 people, not all of them from his own congregation.[57] William Newman (1773-1835), later to become president of Stepney Academy, was baptized by Rippon, with twenty-one others, in 1791.[58] Rippon's pastoral concern for those being baptized is illustrated in a letter he wrote to Newman during the week preceding his baptism: he hoped Newman would be 'composed' all the week, and would 'be enabled to perform an act of worship to the adorable Trinity' in the 'ordinance'.[59] Two Independent pastors were baptized by Rippon in 1798;[60] an event which provoked considerable interest and satisfaction among some of Rippon's friends.[61]

Rippon left any baptismal controversy to colleagues like Abraham Booth,[62] but did re-publish a small tract on baptism by Samuel Wilson.[63] Two comments from interested observers at services conducted by Rippon suggest the level of his baptismal apologetic was not very profound: one corrects Rippon's notion that Roman Catholics baptized with oil,[64] and the other was unconvinced by Rippon's argument that Christ himself had not been baptized as a baby.[65]

The Lord's Supper was held monthly, for most of the period on the first Sunday afternoon of the month. The value of this sacrament is

---

55   E.g. B. Coxhead was baptized on a Tuesday, and Thomas Mortimer on a Thursday. See *Baptist Magazine* 44 (1852), p. 326; Carter Lane Churchbook, 15 January 1775.

56   See below, chapter 4.

57   939 had been received 'by experience' by 1829, but 57 were 'already baptized' (some possibly by Rippon). Others who did not become members were also baptized by him.

58   G. Pritchard, *Memoir of the Rev. William Newman, D.D.* (London: 1837), p. 42; R.E. Cooper, *From Stepney to St. Giles'. The Story of Regent's Park College 1810-1960* (London: Carey Kingsgate Press, 1960), p. 29.

59   Pritchard, *Memoir of Newman*, p. 41.

60   *Register*, 3 (1798-1801), p.39, note 348: Mordaunt Cracherode became Baptist minister at Hull; and William Waterman was an Independent minister in London.

61   Cf. B.L. Add. MSS. 25388, f. 476; 25389, f. 82, 145.

62   Cf. A. Booth, *Paedobaptism Examined* (2 vols., London: 1784). For his controversy with Edward Williams, see Owen, *Edward Williams*, pp. 35-47.

63   *A scripture manual: or, a plain representation of the ordinance of baptism* (1750, and frequently reprinted). For Wilson (1702-1750), see Ivimey, *History of English Baptists*, 3, pp. 542-53. Rippon advertised his edition of Wilson in his publications for 1793, *Register*, 2 (1794-97) p. 85. Booth published a revised version in 1797.

64   E. Young to Rippon, 4 December 1807, B.L. Add. MSS. 25389, f. 561.

65   'An impartial observer' to Rippon, (n.d.). B.L. Add. MSS. 25389, f. 585.

suggested by Benjamin Coxhead's recollection of his first sharing in the service: 'This was peculiarly delightful to my heart, and it is still a very sweet and significant ordinance to me'.[66] Occasionally the service was postponed, usually because Rippon was 'in the country' or 'ill'.[67] There does not appear to have been any service of preparation the evening before the ordinance, otherwise the broad pattern of the service presumably corresponded to the order carefully described by Isaac Watts, an account of such interest that it was published by Rippon.[68]

Pastoral visitation was thought to have declined at this time because of the increasing multiplicity of pastoral duties.[69] This strangely modern complaint may well have been true of Rippon who had many commitments. Certainly, his predecessor Gill had not been a regular visitor.[70] Still Rippon obviously did visit whenever there was illness or some special need, as several appreciative letters suggest. One important and frequent duty in the eighteenth century was to visit the dying. Whenever possible a 'dying testimony' was elicited.[71] H.D. Rack has claimed that a distinction has to be made between the Calvinist Evangelicals and the Arminian Methodists on this point. Whilst both were concerned about 'holy dying', Calvinists 'tended to trust less to feelings and were inclined rather to fall back on God's grace and mercy and the hope of election' and 'were more prone to a heightened stress on human helplessness and total dependence on grace'. Methodists 'often laid more stress on the evidence of feelings and looked for a specific 'assurance' of salvation'. This meant that Methodist death-beds could be the 'scenes of special probings and questionings' and even badgering the dying.[72]

The way in which Rippon sought both to comfort the dying and obtain this testimony is illustrated from two different sources. The first suggests Rippon conformed to the Calvinist concern to evoke a sense of sinfulness, but his evangelical concern for the offer of salvation to be personally received is also evident. Harriet Bowyer was the delicate nineteen-year old

---

66   *Baptist Magazine* 44 (1852), p. 326.

67   Six occasions were recorded: Carter Lane Churchbook, 21 July 1777, 16 September 1803, 17 January 1819, 3 July 1825, 14 December 1828, 3 January 1830.

68   *Register*, 4 (1801-02), pp. 593-603. Days of preparation were held in some Baptist churches, see Hayden, 'Evangelical Calvinism', p. 206.

69   Bogue and Bennett, *History of Dissenters*, 4, p. 351.

70   Rippon, *Memoir of Gill*, p. 117.

71   Compare the studies on the Victorian era by P. Jalland, *Death in the Victorian Family* (Oxford: Oxford University Press, 1996); H.D. Rack, 'Evangelical Endings: Death-beds in Evangelical Biography', *Bulletin of the John Rylands Library University of Manchester*, 74 (1992), pp. 39-56; L. Wilson, *Constrained by Zeal; Female Spirituality amongst Nonconformists 1825-1875* (Carlisle: Paternoster, 2000), pp. 154-67.

72   H.D. Rack, 'Evangelical Endings', pp. 46-48.

only daughter of one of Rippon's most distinguished members, the artist, Robert Bowyer.[73] As she was dying, Harriet was moved to Portsmouth for the sea air. Rippon, 'her dear Uncle and friend', wrote her a long letter which was evidently his substitute for a pastoral visit.[74] He first quoted various scriptures urging the necessity of the new birth, and some hymns, including 'Come, ye sinners, poor and wretched'. Then he proposed a series of six questions, which provide the clearest evidence of Rippon's evangelistic purpose:

> Do you feel that you are a sinner, a great sinner, in the sight of God? Is sin a trouble, a burden to your soul? And do you hate it, really hate it, on account of its exceeding sinfulness? if so, write only the word 'Yes', on this line for which I leave room.... Do you believe that Christ is able, and that he is as willing as he is able, to save all them to the uttermost who come unto God by him? And have you, at any time, attempted to go to him? Would you now apply to him, if you could? I'll leave room for your answer. . .

All these questions were answered in the affirmative, and as well as hopefully bringing Harriet peace of mind, this provided an excellent testimony for her funeral sermon.

The second example comes from the last days of William Lepard (1700-1799), a church member for 82 years, and a deacon for 56 years, something of an institution in the church.[75] Rippon visited the old man frequently in his last illness, and had a *verbatim* account of his last conversation recorded.[76] After hearing the old saint reminiscing about his family and his religious experiences, Rippon asked him several questions which included: 'Are you in any pain, Sir?'; 'Do you know, Sir, what day it will be to-morrow?' (Sunday); 'Do any of the truths and promises which comforted you formerly, support you now, Sir?' After gaining various messages for the congregation, Rippon concluded the visit:

> My heart and voice said, let me die the death of the righteous, and let my latter end be like his. With this desire, assured that God would safely convey him over the rivers I pressed his dying hand to my lips, and he as affectionately kissed mine in return. 'The Lord be with you' said he; I replied, 'and with your spirit!' and so we parted on Saturday evening about nine of the clock.

Even in his own advanced age, Rippon still visited the dying:

---

73   *Register*, 3 (1798-1801), pp. 96-101. For Bowyer, see later in this chapter.

74   *Register*, 3 (1798-1801), pp. 98-99.

75   J. Rippon, *Discourses on the All-Sufficient Gracious Assistance of the Spirit of Christ, To which are added Memoirs of William Lepard* (London: 1800).

76   Rippon, *William Lepard*, p. 111.

His pastor being informed that Mr. A(ikin) was dying (though himself very feeble) resolved to go and see him immediately, saying, it would be a holy gratification to him if he could but place his hand on our friend's forehead before he died. On it being intimated that he was unable to walk so far, and had better have his coach ordered, he replied, 'Coach child, no, for before the horses are put to, brother Aikin may be in heaven.' Leaning on the arms of two of his members Dr. R. walked about half a mile and accomplished his wish, laid his hand on the cold and dying forehead of his friend, affectionately pronouncing his farewell benediction.[77]

Children were present in the Carter Lane services although the introduction of special children's talks was a later nineteenth century innovation.[78] Benjamin Coxhead wrote, 'I had from my childhood sat under the ministry of Dr. Rippon';[79] and Thomas Olney had a special 'little chair' fixed to his pew for the youngest of his children.[80] But the extent to which a service of 'dedication' for infants was adopted is uncertain. There are references to this in some church covenants,[81] whilst Abraham Booth offered this comment on his own practice:

Being sometimes requested by the parents of a new born child, to unite with them in addressing the Father of all mercies, we comply. On which occasion, we frequently read some portion of Scripture; give a word of exhortation to the parents, respecting the education of their child; return thanks to the Giver of all good, for the recent blessings bestowed on the family; and recommend the infant to God by earnest prayer. This is all, to the best of my knowledge, which the generality of us either practise or approve on such an occasion.[82]

Whether this was in the home or a public service is not clear. Booth was refuting the suggestion of Dr. S. Addington that Baptists had invented 'their own' ceremony for children.[83] That some went further than Booth is implied by Booth's conclusion:

If however, there be any Baptist ministers who take infants in their arms, give them names, pronounce a blessing upon them, and call this *dedicating* children to

---

77   *Baptist Magazine* 24 (1832), p. 468.

78   E.A. Payne, *The Fellowship of Believers* (London: Carey Kingsgate Press, 2nd edn, 1952), p. 96.

79   *Baptist Magazine* 44 (1852), p. 326.

80   Spurgeon, *The Metropolitan Tabernacle*, p. 83.

81   See P. Stock, *Foundations* (Halifax: 1933), p. 70 for the 1743 Salendine Nook Covenant; A. Taylor, *History of the General Baptists*, (2 vols.; London: 1818) 2, p. 30; *B.Q.* 19.7 (1962), p. 290.

82   Booth, *Paedobaptism Examined*, 2, p. 343.

83   For Addington (1729-1796) of Miles's Lane Independent church, see *DNB*.

God; we despise their conduct as a paltry substitute for infant sprinkling, and leave them to the severest censure of our opposers.[84]

Rippon did include in his *Selection* hymns suitable for such a service, especially in the 27th edition (1828). (After his death, the *Comprehensive Rippon*, 1844, included a section for 'Infant Dedication', suggesting the widespread adoption of the practice.)

Rippon was also an enthusiastic advocate of catechizing. This method of teaching the faith had partially declined in popularity earlier in the century, but the Evangelicals revived it,[85] and many Dissenters practised it.[86] Rippon gave a lecture at Fetter Lane on the subject,[87] and offered 'pointed advice' to Benjamin Coxhead at his ordination about catechizing, which Rippon felt was 'a work *now* much neglected, but from which the genuine Protestant Dissenters have derived *peculiar advantages* in better times'.[88] Although both Benjamin Beddome and John Sutcliff produced Baptist catechisms,[89] Rippon preferred a 1693 *Baptist Catechism*, prepared by William Collins and Benjamin Keach, commonly known as 'Keach's Catechism'.[90] This catechism, which was based on the shorter Catechism of the Westminster Assembly, also taught the Baptist content of their 1689 Confession. Rippon published in 1794 two revised versions of 'Keach's Catechism', one with the 'Scripture proofs' printed, and one without.[91] Rippon's catechizing was not only for children but also for prospective church members.[92]

One cause and consequence of a long ministry is the affection that exists between pastor and people. Several referred to Rippon as their 'Father in Christ', or some variant of this. A strong bond of respectful affection is suggested by the following letter:

---

84   Booth, *Paedobaptism Examined,* p. 344.

85   P. Sangster, *Pity My Simplicity, The Evangelical Revival and the Religious Education of Children 1738-1800* (London: Epworth Press, 1963), pp. 40-42.

86   For details of the revival of catechizing in the Northamptonshire Baptist Association, see Haykin, *One Heart and One Soul,* pp. 153-54.

87   I. Prachey to Rippon, 3 October 1807, B.L. Add. MSS. 25388, f .238. Cf. *Evangelical Magazine* 15 (1807), p. 431.

88   *Register* 3 (1798-1801), p. 245.

89   B. Beddome, *A scriptural exposition of the Baptist Catechism,* (Bristol: 1752, revised 1776); J. Sutcliff, *The first principles of the oracles of God.* (Northampton:1784). Sutcliff's catechism was notable for the explicit emphasis on 'Fullerism', in which the distinction between moral and physical inability was explained: see Haykin, *One Heart and One Soul,* p. 153.

90   B. Keach, *Instructions for Youth ... with a scripture catechism* (London: 1693).

91   *Register* 2 (1794-97) p. 85. (Copy in British Library.)

92   E. Whebell to Rippon, 12 October 1797, B.L. Add. MSS. 25389, f. 448.

I have frequently thought of your seasonable admonition & prayer on my behalf, which perhaps you may not recollect, 'My dear child, the Lord go with you wherever you go; walk closely & humbly with thy God.' 0 that those sweet ejaculations may be fulfilled in my experience![93]

Rippon's role as 'Father' and 'Friend' brought him all manner of unusual requests from his people. These ranged from finding a wife, - 'she must be a woman of property' was the directive[94] - to finding lodgings or domestic posts,[95] and speaking in bankruptcy courts.[96] What is clear is that for many households, as with the Lepards for example, Rippon was virtually regarded as one of the family.[97]

The ultimate authority (under Christ) in a Congregational or Baptist church resides in the church meeting, although the deacons have considerable responsibility for many practical affairs. At Carter Lane, however, Rippon was undisputed leader and did not suffer petty arguments:

'How is it, Doctor, that your church is always so peaceful?' said a much-tried brother minister. 'Well, friend,' said Rippon, 'you see, we don't call a church meeting to consult about buying a new broom every time we want one, and we don't entreat every noisy member to make a speech about the price of the soap the floors are scrubbed with.'[98]

Spurgeon, who told this anecdote, concluded that Rippon ruled 'with dignity and discretion', but 'perhaps ruled too much'.

Indeed, the long ministry he exercised and his firm, wilful mind meant that he came to occupy an almost dictatorial position. He was an emotional man, and overwork and sensitivity often meant he was easily offended. Confused church members and deacons wrote on various occasions apologizing for 'slights' they had unwittingly committed.[99]

Moreover, Rippon could act in complete independence of his deacons, as will be shown. This was, after all, exactly how he began his ministry, for three out of the four deacons left to form the Dean Street Church. Again, Rippon had the church agree to grant transient communion to members of 'mixed communion' churches, despite the unanimous objection of his deacons. Again, he began the almshouses on his own initiative and had a clause inserted stipulating that no deacon could interfere in the appointment of almswomen.

---

93   M. Colebrook to Rippon, 15 February 1800, B.L. Add. MSS. 25386, f. 258.
94   W. Garnsey to Rippon, 2 April 1804, B.L. Add. MSS. 25387, f. 62.
95   M. Anderson to Rippon, 21 April 1795, B.L. Add. MSS. 25386, f. 13.
96   W. Garnsey to Rippon, 2 October 1796, B.L. Add. MSS. 25387, f. 53.
97   Rippon, *Memoir of Lepard*, p. 111.
98   Spurgeon, *The Metropolitan Tabernacle*, p. 52.
99   Cf. B.L. Add. MSS. 25387, f. 298; 25388, f. 159.

The inevitable result was that in Rippon's old age, when he retained the will to govern long after the capacity had gone, the church was placed in an intolerable position. Two deacons eventually threatened to resign, and only this drastic proposal brought some sense to the old pastor. The origins of this unfortunate situation may undoubtedly be found in the earlier years of Rippon's ministry.

The Carter Lane Church Community

The Carter Lane congregation, repeatedly described as 'one of the wealthiest within the pale of Nonconformity', was in fact composed of many different types of people.[100]

Occupations of the church trustees appointed in June 1793 reveal the following: two 'gentlemen', two stationers, tailor, jeweller, cheesemonger, tallow chandler, brewer, haberdasher, oilman, coal merchant, sail maker, butcher.[101] These conform to the general group of merchants, artisans, and tradesmen thought to have been the dominant social class of the Dissenters from 1740 to 1800.[102]

Some of them also conform to another type: successful men who had begun in lowly circumstances. M.D. George suggested that in eighteenth-century London 'sobriety and steadiness must have had a scarcity value, and could hardly fail to raise a journeyman to the position at least of a foreman or manager, probably of an employer'.[103] William Lepard Senior, for example, as a bricklayer's apprentice had so won the confidence and respect of his master that the business 'worth hundreds a year' was given to him. Accordingly, he and his family enjoyed 'comfort and credit'.[104] His son, William Lepard Junior (d. 1805), described as a 'stationer', owned the Hamper Mills at Watford, where he conducted religious services for his workmen.[105] Benjamin Lepard (d. 1844) was also active in both church and denominational affairs.[106]

---

100 Spurgeon, *The Metropolitan Tabernacle,* p. 52; cf. A.C. Underwood, *History of the English Baptists* (London: Carey Kingsgate Press, 1947), p. 178; E.W. Hayden, *A Centennial History of Spurgeon's Tabernacle* (London: Clifford Frost, 1962), p. 5.

101 Carter Lane Churchbook, 17 June 1793.

102 E.D. Bebb, *Nonconformity and Social and Economic Life 1660-1800* (London: Epworth Press, 1935), pp. 53-57. For the period 1791-1851, see Watts, *The Dissenters,* 2, pp. 303-27.

103 M.D. George, *London Life in the Eighteenth Century* (Harmondsworth: Penguin, 2nd edn, 1966), p. 304.

104 Rippon, *Memoir of Lepard,* pp.108-109.

105 Carter Lane Churchbook, 29 April 1805; *Memoirs of Mr. John James Smith, late of Watford, Herts.* (1821), pp. 46-47. (Smith was son-in-law of Lepard.)

106 *Baptist Magazine* 36 (1844), pp. 196-97.

Clearly several members were comfortable, if not exactly affluent. Peter Sharp (d. 1800), as church treasurer from 1774 until near his death, lent the church £400 in 1793.[107] Indeed, the church treasurer was usually required to bear the burden of the church's debt, often several hundreds of pounds, until a special collection could be taken. James Norton (d. 1822), a jeweller, one of Sharp's successors, was able to allow the church debt to reach £300.[108] Robert Westley (1742-1830), a tailor, was 'not opulent' at his death, but left £170 in legacies to the church and the denomination.[109] Robert Davies (d. 1830), a cheesemonger, could lend the church £180 in 1796.[110]

During the second half of Rippon's ministry several successful citizens were active in the church. William Burls (1763-1837) was a merchant who also had been given his employer's business as a direct reward for his ability, industry, and integrity.[111] Burls was not only treasurer in the church but was prominent in denominational affairs, especially with the Baptist Missionary Society. Samuel Gale was a solicitor married to Rippon's daughter, Martha.[112] Gilbert Blight (1767-1847), a 'stationer' with prosperous business premises at the Royal Exchange, was honoured as a Freeman of the City of London in 1809.[113] James Low (d. 1863), a 'papermaker', was prominent in the Baptist Union, of which he was both Treasurer (1834-47) and President (1847). In 1832, John Bousfield could lend the church £1,000.

In addition to Rippon, four members have found a place in the *Dictionary of National Biography*. Joseph Swain and William Henry Angas achieved distinction as Baptist ministers. Both the others were artists. Robert Bowyer (1758-1834) was probably the only member of the church who moved in the fashionable world of the Court. He was appointed miniature painter to George III in 1789 and exhibited regularly at the Royal Academy between 1787 and 1828. He was also a publisher and collector of lavishly illustrated books, especially on historical subjects, and exhibited many of these at his 'Historic Gallery' in Schomberg House, Pall Mall.[114] Samuel Medley Junior (1769-1857), son of the Baptist pastor at Liverpool, also exhibited at the Royal

---

107 Carter Lane Churchbook, 18 May 1800; 17 June 1793.

108 Carter Lane Churchbook, 2 December 1822; 31 October 1814.

109 *Baptist Magazine* 22 (1830), pp. 265-68.

110 *Baptist Magazine* 22 (1830), p. 563; Carter Lane Churchbook, 26 February 1776.

111 See E.A. Payne, *The Excellent Mr. Burls* (London: Carey Press, 1943); *DEB*.

112 Reference in Rippon's will (in Somerset House).

113 See G. Hawker, *A Biographical Sketch of Francis James Blight, F.R.S.E., Publisher* (London: Elliott Stock, 1931), pp. 23-35.

114 K.R. Manley, 'Robert Bowyer: Artist, Publisher and Preacher', *BQ* 23.1 (1969), pp. 32-46, and *DEB*.

Academy in 1792. He became a successful portrait artist, but finding the oils affected his health, turned to an equally successful living from the Stock Exchange. Medley left the Carter Lane church for Hackney in 1812, and later became one of the founders of University College, London.[115]

Joseph Fox (d. 1816), a surgeon and dentist, for several years lectured at Guy's Hospital.[116] Fox was an active supporter of the efforts of Joseph Lancaster (1778-1838) to teach poor children by the 'monitorial' method, and became one of the secretaries of the British and Foreign School Society founded by Lancaster.[117] Another medical member, William Johns, was a young druggist, whom the BMS trained as a surgeon prior to sending him out to India, where he was, briefly, acting-surgeon at Serampore.[118]

Several teachers were in the congregation, including Thomas Mabbott, 'master of Bartholomew Close Dissenters' School',[119] Josiah Wilkinson, 'classical tutor at the Academy at Hull' before he entered the Baptist ministry;[120] Rev. J. J. Douglas who conducted a school after returning to London after a period as Baptist minister,[121] and one Mrs. Colebrooke who conducted a boarding school at Islington where 'she used frequently to address the young ladies committed to her care in a very striking and affectionate manner' respecting eternal things, and especially when the death of any young person gave her an opportunity.[122] James Biggs opened a 'Protestant Establishment at Brussels, for the Education of Young Gentlemen' in 1816 - the year after Waterloo.[123] Not all teachers were in a secure position, as Ann Godwin had 'two or three shillings a week from her keeping a school was all she and three young Children had to subsist on so that she often had not a Loafe of bread for herself and family'.[124]

Carter Lane, near London Bridge, was not far from the docks and seamen were frequently in the congregation. Captain Angas joined the church prior to becoming a Baptist pastor and missioner to seamen.[125] John Peck's reception into church membership was postponed a few

---

115   Carter Lane Churchbook, 9 March 1812; *DEB*.
116   For Fox, see Ivimey, *History of the English Baptists,* 4, pp. 382-84; *DEB*; Briggs, *English Baptists of the Nineteenth Century*, p. 341.
117   For Lancaster, see *DNB*.
118   See below in this chapter.
119   *Register* 3 (1798-1801), p. 310.
120   Carter Lane Churchbook, 17 July 1803.
121   *Baptist Magazine* 35 (1843), p. 480.
122   *Register* 3 (1798-1801), p. 96.
123   J. Biggs to Rippon, Brussells, 16 August 1816, B.L. Add. MSS. 25386, f. 90.
124   Carter Lane Churchbook, 29 December 1788.
125   See below in this chapter.

months because he had 'gone to sea'.[126] Several captains took messages and parcels for Rippon to America. One Captain Applegath, who visited the Serampore missionaries, was well known to Rippon and was probably the uncle of one of Rippon's members, Augustus Applegath.[127] Conditions for the seamen of the Fleet were intolerable, but the help given by Rippon's ministry is reflected in a long letter written by one Henry Roberts, of HMS Minerva in February 1796, the year before the famous mutiny at Spithead.[128] Roberts wrote that even though 'providence' had placed him 'to use your own words - in a floating Hell - yet in that machine in which so much misery floats I sometimes feel my heart expand & bless the providence which conducted me to Carter Lane'. Roberts asked Rippon's advice about the ethics of 'clandestinely' leaving the Service.

Then, of course, there were young apprentices and domestics in the congregation. John Giles was apprenticed to a 'silk ribbon and gauze manufacturer',[129] Joseph Swain to an engraver,[130] and William Aikin to a glass engraver.[131] Some 109 members, to judge from their addresses, appear to have been in domestic service.

Broad aspects of the congregation's social composition have emerged: merchants, craftsmen, seamen, teachers, professional men, domestic servants. The majority were women, comprising 64% of those added to the church in Rippon's time. If some were very rich, others were very poor, as allocation of church funds to seventy members indicates. If many were successful in business, at least 29 became bankrupt. Carter Lane represented a cross-section of middle and lower class London society. There is every impression of a close-knit community, even if there could be a degree of patronizing in the relationships. William Bousfield, a successful 'man of business', was noted for his 'kind and condescending familiarity' with the poor members.[132]

There were numerous family groups, notably the Lepards, but also others like the Davies family, as when Robert Davies delightedly gave the moral character for his three daughters when they were received at one service.[133] Many young men chose their future wives from the ladies of

---

126 Carter Lane Churchbook, 2 June 1793.

127 Cf. *Register* 3 (1798-1801), p. 169. A. Applegath to Rippon, Bristol, 4 April 1810, B.L. Add. MSS. 25386, f. 19.

128 B.L. Add. MSS. 25388, f. 440. For the Spithead mutiny, see J.S. Watson, *The Reign of George III 1760-1815* (Oxford: Oxford University Press, 1960), pp. 172-73.

129 *A Brief Sketch of the Life and Character of the Rev. John Giles*, (London: n.d.), p. 4.

130 For Swain, see *DNB* and *DEB*.

131 *Baptist Magazine* 24 (1832), p. 465.

132 *Baptist Magazine* 27 (1835), pp. 468-69.

133 Carter Lane Churchbook, 21 May 1798.

the church: by 1806, some forty ladies' maiden names had been altered to surnames of male members. Another 39 members were in the employ of 32 Carter Lane families.

Carter Lane was joined by one of three methods: by a verbal 'experience' and baptism, by dismissal from another Baptist church, by restoration after exclusion. To give an 'experience' before the church could be an ordeal for sensitive souls: Mildred Alston was so 'intimated [sic] by the number of members' that her statement was unsatisfactory and her reception was delayed a year.[134] In the unusual case of a mute, a written statement was accepted: Elizabeth Webbell gave so 'pleasing' an account that it was copied into the church minute book providing an excellent example of what constituted an acceptable 'experience'.[135] Essential elements included: a confession of sinfulness, and subsequent peace through faith in Christ, conviction about believer's baptism, appreciation of the church and its ministry together with an ardent desire to be accepted as a church member. Supreme importance was given to an experience of conversion.[136] The moral character of all candidates also needed attestation, and, if necessary, messengers were appointed to seek this. In six cases membership was not granted because the moral character was judged to be unsatisfactory.[137] Generally, baptism followed the 'experience', although even the fifty-seven 'already baptized' had to give a verbal 'experience'. Members were also required to give assent to *A Doctrine of the Faith and Practice of the church of Christ in Carter Lane, Southwark*, a statement drawn up by Gill, but still used in Rippon's time.[138] Formal reception was expressed by giving the 'right hand of fellowship' at a communion service.

Of the 156 members received by transfer from other churches, 47 came from the London area and the remainder from country or overseas churches. During the same period, 131 were dismissed, 96 to London churches but mainly to the outer areas. If the dismissing church was without a pastor, Carter Lane refused to accept the letter of dismissal since they felt a pastor was necessary for such a duty.[139]

'Transient communion', which enabled visitors to share in the Lord's Supper, was normally granted only to men like William Hunter, whose

---

134   Carter Lane Churchbook, 28 November 1785, 24 November 1786.

135   Carter Lane Churchbook, 24 September 1781. For a review of earlier Congregational experiences, see J.H. Taylor, 'Some Seventeenth-Century Testimonies', *Transactions* of Congregational Historical Society, 16 (1949), p. 66.

136   For an important review of conversion among Dissenters, see Watts, *The Dissenters*, 2, pp. 49-80.

137   Carter Lane Churchbook, 7 March, 4 April, 27 June, 16 December 1774, 29 May 1781, 26 April 1786.

138   For the text, see Rippon, *Memoir of Gill*, pp. 14-19.

139   Carter Lane Churchbook, 26 January 1784.

business involved spending half his time in Liverpool and half in London.[140] On 4 July 1824 Rippon noted thirteen present under this rule, and they came from places as far apart as Reading, Bramley (Yorkshire), Calcutta and New York.[141] Rippon himself was a transient communicant at the Pithay church in Bristol.[142]

The 'terms of communion' issue greatly divided Baptists at this time.[143] The strict-communionists, who included influential men like Booth, Fuller, Ivimey, and Joseph Kinghorn of Norwich, claimed that communion should be open only to those baptized as believers. The mixed-communionists, with John Ryland and Robert Hall (Jr.) as main advocates, insisted that the Lord's Table should be open to all true believers, irrespective of their views on baptism. Rippon favoured mixed-communion, even though his church practised closed communion. The issue was raised when three members from College Street Church, Northampton, applied for transient communion in 1783.[144] The problem was that this church practised mixed-communion, and moreover, although this was not stated in the Carter Lane records, also practised 'open' membership, that is, both baptized and unbaptized believers were admitted to membership.[145] The deacons unanimously opposed the granting of transient communion in these circumstances. Rippon, 'being of a different opinion', brought it to the church together with several statements in writing from various ministers on the subject. He insisted that it was 'not improper or unscriptural, and that his own conscience would be much hurt if they were not admitted to transient communion'. After 'much debate', it was agreed, by the margin of seventeen votes to thirteen, that such applications could be admitted. Rippon preferred mixed-communion, but such a narrow vote obviously prevented his introduction of it.

Despite this refusal to follow the deacons' judgment, the position of deacon was highly regarded in Baptist churches. Their duty, according to Gill, was 'to serve tables': the Lord's Table, the minister's table, and the poor's table.[146] Thus, deacons served at communion but, at least at Carter Lane, never presided. They collected the pew subscriptions which constituted Rippon's salary. Each deacon had a 'division', or group of members who were his responsibility, especially any experiencing

---

140 Carter Lane Churchbook, 13 November 1774.

141 B.L. Add. MSS. 25388, f. 398.

142 *Register* 3 (1798-1801) p. 319.

143 For this controversy, see M. Walker, *Baptists at the Table* (Didcot: Baptist Historical Society, 1992), pp. 32-83.

144 Carter Lane Churchbook, 18 August 1783.

145 Cf. E.A. Payne, *College Street Northampton 1697-1947* (London: Kingsgate, 1947), pp. 10-11.

146 J. Gill, *Body of Divinity*, 3 (1770), p. 291.

hardship. Towards the end of Rippon's life the deacons had to assume a larger control of affairs, and only their devoted service preserved the church from complete collapse.

Carter Lane deacons were drawn almost exclusively from those known to be 'successful' men. Deacons were normally appointed for life so there were only fifteen during Rippon's pastorate. (One of these resigned and left the church because 'the ministry of the word under our Pastor had not been blest to his soul', and one moved to Birmingham.)[147] No set number of deacons was thought to be necessary, but whenever the need became apparent new deacons were appointed. The full list reveals many who were active in the denomination: William Lepard Senior (appointed 1743), Peter Sharp (1774), Joseph Carroll (1774), William Lepard Junior (1777), Stephen Misnard (1777, but was excluded 1790), James Norton (1791), Robert Westley (1791), William Burls (1802), Benjamin Lepard (1802, to Birmingham 1825), David Hudson (1802), Gilbert Blight (1823), Chapman Barber (1823), Thomas Evans (1823), Samuel Gale (1827), and James Low (1835).

The election and 'ordination' of deacons was a serious matter. As three of the four deacons had left the church to form the breakaway Dean Street church, two men were appointed to assist the aged William Lepard in 1774. Their appointment was preceded by a special prayer meeting.[148] Actually, three men were elected by ballot, and given a fortnight to consider the invitation, but one man declined on the grounds of 'so much business of his own to attend to'.[149] Hence, only two men were 'invested' - by 'the right hand of fellowship', since Gill had disagreed with the laying-on of hands for deacons,[150] although this had been done in Gill's earlier years at the church.[151]

However, when the 1791 appointments were made, John Giles, a young man whom the church had recently called to be a preacher and on whom Rippon had laid hands, suggested that the deacons should be similarly ordained.[152] But the serving deacons, and others, objected and 'a warm dispute being likely' Giles agreed to withdraw his motion. It is tempting to see the influence of Rippon in young Giles' suggestion, especially as a month later Rippon raised the matter so that procedure for future preachers and deacons could be determined.[153] This time it was decided

---

147 Carter Lane Churchbook, 25 October 1790; *Baptist Magazine* 36 (1844), p. 196.

148 Carter Lane Churchbook, 16 December 1773. For extracts from the Churchbook relating to the appointment of deacons, see *BQ* 17.2 (1957), pp. 87-91.

149 Carter Lane Churchbook, 10 January 1774.

150 Gill, *Body of Divinity*, 3, pp. 269-70.

151 Ivimey, *History of English Baptists*, 3, p. 434.

152 Carter Lane Churchbook, 21 March 1791.

153 Carter Lane Churchbook, 4 April 1791.

to practise laying-on of hands, by the narrow majority of two votes (30 to 28). Accordingly in 1802, and 1823, deacons 'were set apart by Prayer and laying-on of hands by our Pastor'.[154] Special meetings for prayer always preceded the elections and the ordination was held at a service at a later date.

By 1827, when Rippon was old and church meetings were irregular, the whole election and appointment was speedily concluded.[155] Rippon gave a short address on the subject, two deacons already in office nominated two men, the church agreed, and the two new deacons assumed office. There is no indication that laying-on of hands was practised. Finally, in December 1835 when James Low was appointed, the deacons again made the nomination, and there was 'some discussion as to the mode of nominating and choosing deacons'.[156] By this time Rev. Charles Room, Rippon's assistant, was in the chair in Rippon's absence, and clearly there was some confusion over procedure. Laying-on of hands was not practised, Low simply acknowledged his acceptance of the office. There was, then, considerable variation in the manner of election and appointment of deacons.

Whilst the focal point of the church's life was naturally the Sunday services the members could share regularly in other activities. Various 'lectures' were associated with the church, although their origins and arrangements are not always clear. Robert Robinson of Cambridge was intended to deliver monthly lectures on Baptist history at Carter Lane, but few of these were evidently given. One member referred to Rippon's studies in Bunyan's *Pilgrim's Progress* on Thursday evenings, but this may well have been in conjunction with a prayer-meeting. A 'Lord's day morning Lecture' was 'renewed' in 1818, but when it was first begun is unknown. Certainly it was Thomas Olney's great delight 'to be at the service by half-past six o'clock to collect the necessary funds, and to welcome the various ministers'.[157]

In Baptist churches the church meeting is the final authority for governing the church, and at Carter Lane these were held monthly, from 1776, on the third Monday after the 'ordinance day'.[158] However, from 1820 church meetings were held irregularly,[159] as much a symptom as a cause of the gradual decline of the church. Michael Watts has suggested

---

154 Carter Lane Churchbook, 6 December 1802, 28 March 1823.

155 Carter Lane Churchbook, 27 May 1827.

156 Carter Lane Churchbook, 17 December 1835.

157 Ivimey, *History of English Baptists*, 4, pp. 48–49; D. Chambers to Rippon, 2 November 1796, B.L. Add. MSS. 25386 f. 227; Carter Lane Churchbook, 15 March 1818; Spurgeon, *The Metropolitan Tabernacle*, p. 84.

158 Carter Lane Churchbook, 20 May 1776.

159 3 meetings in 1820, 5 in 1821, 6 in 1822, 5 in 1823, 7 in 1824, 4 in 1825, 3 in 1826, 6 in 1827, 2 in 1828, 5 in 1829.

that Rippon's real motive for calling church meetings infrequently may have been fear that such meetings would discuss replacing him with a younger minister, but there is no hint of this in his extant correspondence and, in the light of the deep respect and affection consistently accorded to him, does not seem likely.[160]

No record of attendances was kept, but from the votes taken at certain elections, the following figures are suggested: 148 on 21 March 1791, and 130 on 22 November 1802. Every member - including women - had a vote.

Rippon clearly placed a strong emphasis on the value of gathering for 'social' prayer. An interesting decision was taken in 1779 to hold a prayer meeting on the first Monday in each quarter, 'to begin at 5 in the evening precisely, hoping the Lord will be pleased to revive his Work in the midst of the Churches & in this'.[161] This seems strikingly similar to the scheme of regular prayer for revival urged by Jonathan Edwards, a plan adopted by the Northampton churches in 1784, and widely promoted among the Baptists from about 1789, when Rippon's friend Sutcliff published an edition of Edwards' *Humble Attempt*. This prayer call has been directly linked with the renewal of life among Particular Baptists.[162] Rippon certainly supported this programme from this time, for in May 1790 a South Carolina pastor wrote to thank him for the suggestion.[163] If the 1779 decision was along the lines of the later Prayer Call, Rippon was perhaps the first English Particular Baptist to introduce special regular prayer for revival. Certainly, in 1791 and 1793, special additional prayer meetings for revival were held; at least one member traced her conversion to those gatherings, and in both years more than thirty were added to the church.[164] Rippon also introduced a Sunday morning prayer service at 9.30 a.m. At some time, a weekly night gathering was also begun, but the details of its commencement are not recorded. Days of national significance were marked with special prayer meetings, such as thanksgiving for the 'very plentiful harvest' of 1801.[165] The Treaty of Amiens (1802) was acknowledged by a special

---

160 Watts, *The Dissenters*, 2, p. 193.

161 Carter Lane Churchbook, 17 May 1779.

162 J. Edwards, *Humble Attempt to Promote Explicit Agreement and Visible Union of God's People in Extraordinary Prayer* (1749); E.A. Payne, *Prayer Call of 1784* (London: Baptist Layman's Missionary Movement, 1941); Haykin, *One Heart and One Soul*, pp. 158-71.

163 *Register* 1 (1790-93), pp. 107-108.

164 Carter Lane Churchbook, 18 April 1791, 30 April 1793. E. Crudge to Rippon, (n. d.), B.L. Add. MSS. 25386, f. 325.

165 Carter Lane Churchbook, 21 September 1801. This year's harvest, however, was 'poor'; see T.S. Ashton, *Industrial Revolution 1760-1830* (London: Oxford University Press, 1948), p. 145.

meeting of thanksgiving, but this 'truce of exhaustion' soon expired, and as Napoleon gathered his troops on the other side of the Channel, the Carter Lane Baptists joined with other Dissenters and prayed 'on account of the State of the Nation'.[166] These references provide some indication of the community's devotional life.

The Sunday School does not appear officially in the church-book, suggesting that, as was not uncommon, its beginnings were independent of the church meeting. Possibly, as has been claimed, this school began in emulation of one established by the Maze Pond Church in 1801.[167] Certainly in 1802 a dismissal for a member was signed by 'our Pastor, the Teachers, Deacons & several Brethren', a formula used only in 1802 and 1803.[168] In 1807 six teachers wrote to Rippon complaining that, despite repeated requests, they still had not been formed into a proper society.[169] The 'Teachers of the Sunday School, Dr. Rippon's' contributed to the BMS in 1811-12.[170] When the new buildings were erected in New Park Street in 1833 schoolrooms and seating accommodation for 200 children were provided.[171] But no further details of the Sunday School survive.

Friendly societies were found to be necessary in the eighteenth century: some 1,600 existed in London in 1797.[172] Many of these were closely associated with public houses so it was only natural that Dissenters should begin their own. On 20 October 1783 a society known as the 'Union Society for relief of one another in Sickness' was formed, commonly referred to as the 'Brotherly Society'.[173] A similar group, the 'Sisterly Society', was commenced in 1794, and by 1836 was known as the 'Female Benevolent Society'.[174] Several Baptist churches began benefit societies, although Carter Lane's 'Brotherly Society' suffered a severe setback when one member had to be excluded from the church because he had embezzled the society's funds.[175]

---

166 Carter Lane Churchbook, 24 May 1802, 18 July 1803. Cf. *Evangelical Magazine* 11 (1803), p. 411.

167 B. Reeve, *History of Maze Pond Sunday School: 1801-1901* (London:1901), p. 12.

168 Carter Lane Churchbook, 24 May, 20 December 1802, 14 March 1803.

169 B.L. Add. MSS. 25386, f. 10.

170 BMS *Periodical Accounts* 4 (1810), p. 486.

171 *Baptist Magazine* 25 (1833), pp. 474-75.

172 M.D. George, *London Life in the Eighteenth Century*, p. 395, note 141.

173 Carter Lane Churchbook.

174 Carter Lane Churchbook, 19 May 1794, 14 January 1836.

175 J.C. Carlile, *Story of the English Baptists* (London: J. Clarke, 1905), p. 172; Unicorn Yard church had a 'Benevolent Institution': see Unicorn Yard Churchbook 24 November 1813 (Angus Library); Woolwich had a 'Poor Man's Friend' in 1799: see W. Ranwell, *Memory of the Blessed; or Biographical Sketches of some Persons connected*

Some London Baptist churches during this period gave help to the needy poor who lived near their churches: Prescott Street, for example, formed a 'Prayer and Alms Society' in 1775, Eagle Street had a 'Dorcas Society' whilst Hammersmith had a 'Society of the Distribution of Bread', which between 1813 and 1832 distributed some 7,000 quartern loaves.[176] Carter Lane does not seem to have adopted any such scheme, but did seek to care for its own poor, a tradition among Baptists from their earliest times.[177]

There were four ways in which Carter Lane cared for their own poor: by regular weekly payments; by an annual 'Christmas collection'; by members leaving legacies to be distributed among the poor; and the building of almshouses.

Seventy-one members were granted regular weekly financial assistance by the church. The way in which regular payments were allocated is illustrated by the following example:

Brother Lepard reported that our Sister Helena Southerland an Ancient Woman and an old member of this Church stood in need of assistance that about a twelve month ago what money she had in the funds, was sold out for about Thirty pounds which had been applyed for her maintenance but was now ne'er expended that being confin'd to her room she required some person to look after her, that being a Scotch Woman she had no Parish to apply to for releif. Bror. Sharp mention'd that he had made inquiry, and that our Brother Mortimer with his Wife would take care of her at Nine Shillings a Week which is considerably less than what she at present stands at. It was taken into consideration and agreed that she be allow'd Nine Shillings a week out of the Churches stock for her support under the direction of the Deacons.[178]

Several points of procedure emerge. First, the case was, as usual, reported by a deacon. Secondly, it was noted that she was a member of the church, in fact had been received on 12 May 1735. Thirdly, this case is unique in its reference to the 'funds' in which she had her own money. Members were expected to make full use of their own resources. Fourthly, a detailed statement of the member's condition was given. Often this was, as here, because of old age. Another frequent case was a deserted mother with children. But the genuine need of the person was always stressed. If practicable, members were encouraged to go into a workhouse, as Sister Brooksbank, 'a hearty young woman' was

---

with the First Baptist church at Woolwich (London: 1837), p. 53; Carter Lane Churchbook, 21 November 1796.

176 Kevan, *London's Oldest Baptist Church*, p. 95; Ward, *Kingsgate Chapel*, pp. 37-38; G.W. Byrt, *Stream of the River* (London: 1944), p. 49.

177 J.J. Goadby, *Bye-Paths in Baptist History* (London: 1871), pp. 302-309.

178 Carter Lane Churchbook, 16 September 1782.

advised.[179] Occasionally, additional assistance was given to inmates of a workhouse, as with Ann Watford who was given eighteen pence a week because 'by reason of Bodyly Illness she could not allways Eat the provision of the house'.[180] Fifthly, members were expected to apply for Parish Relief, wherever relevant. To receive this it was necessary for an individual to be resident in the parish where he or she had been given a settlement. As Helena Southerland was a 'Scotch woman' peculiar hardship existed. The church often gave a small grant in addition to the Parish Relief.

Three kinds of allowance were paid. The most common was to give a small weekly amount (commonly between 1s. and 4s.) to an individual. The second grant was specifically towards the payment of an individual's rent, often given in addition to a weekly allowance. After 1778 the maximum allowance for rent was fixed at £2 per annum.[181] The cheapest London rents at this time averaged about 2s.6d. per week.[182] The third type of assistance voted was that given to Helena Southerland, that is, a larger sum voted to provide full care for the member. This was, of course, only voted to those in advanced age or serious illness.

Only six of the members helped were men. The total outlay in any year is not easily calculated but £120. 5s. 6d. was paid in 1810. This had dropped to £50 7s. by 1832 when the church was smaller and had built almshouses. A special annual collection, originally described as a 'Christmas gift' for the poor 'to buy coals', was from 1779 referred to as the poor's 'Annual Gift'. Not only those already receiving allowances shared in this. For example, in 1798 twenty-two received gifts, although only eleven were on the 'poor list'.[183] The amount distributed was £26. 4s with individual gifts varying between two guineas and half a guinea.

Some members made bequests for the poor. Two church treasurers, Peter Sharp and William Lepard Junior, who knew at first hand the desperate need of some members, both gave such gifts: Sharp one guinea to all on the poor list, and Lepard two pounds to thirty poor members.[184] Robert Westley[185] and Benjamin Coxhead[186] both left £20 for the poor, and John Page, an ironmonger, directed that £100 should be invested and

---

179 Carter Lane Churchbook, 20 February 1792.
180 Carter Lane Churchbook, 18 June 1787.
181 Carter Lane Churchbook, 16 November 1778.
182 George, *London Life in the Eighteenth Century*, p. 100.
183 Peter Sharp's Cash Book (Metropolitan Tabernacle).
184 Carter Lane Churchbook, 16 June 1800, 29 April 1805.
185 *Baptist Magazine* 22 (1830), p. 268.
186 B. Coxhead (Jr.) to Rippon, 10 Aug. 1824, B.L. Add. MSS. 25386, f. 300.

the dividends used to help the poor.[187] Ann Aikin left £100 to be given directly to the needy.[188]

But the most remarkable legacy was for the almshouses. On 19 December 1803 Rippon advised his church that he had bought, in his own name, '£100 3 per cent Redeemed' with a view to procure almshouses 'which he considered the property of the Church'. No further mention was made of these in the churchbook until the discussions of the enforced removal from Carter Lane. Spurgeon, however, preserved a story that perhaps fills in the details.[189] Rippon proposed building the almshouses, but his deacons - not unreasonably during the war years, and in view of the church's financial commitments - were fearful of such an ambitious project. Rippon persuaded them to agree that if he could raise £500 by the following Monday the almshouses would be built. On the Monday Rippon announced that he had raised £300, whereupon the deacons wanted him to drop the whole idea. But Rippon then announced that he meant he had raised £300 more than he had said, that is, £800. As the deacons had been so fearful, Rippon refused to let them have anything to do with it. Indeed, Spurgeon observed that in his own time he had expunged a clause which specifically stated that only the pastor could elect the pensioners, 'no deacon interfering'.

That the almshouses were Rippon's idea is confirmed by his description in a will as 'the original projector, treasurer, and principal manager of certain rooms, apartments, or almshouses commonly called by the name of Dr. Rippon's almshouses'.[190] All the accommodation was for women. Not surprisingly it was reported to the church in 1830, when all the finances of the church were carefully reviewed, that the 'responses of the Alms Houses have become amply sufficient to satisfy their own demands without other aid'.[191]

As far as is known, 'Rippon's Almshouses' were the first built by Baptists in London, though Methodists and Independents had some.[192] Other Baptists soon followed, for in 1824 Lambeth built ten almshouses,

187 Carter Lane Churchbook, 3 August 1829.
188 Carter Lane Churchbook, 16 October 1833.
189 *Metropolitan Tabernacle*, p. 52.
190 Will of Sarah Lynall, printed in *New Baptist Miscellany* 3 (1829), pp. 471-73. The legacy referred to was quite remarkable. Mrs. Lynall had attended Carter Lane, although not a member, for many years. Late in life she was married to Mr. Lynall, with whom she had previously lived as a domestic, and after his death inherited considerable property. She died in 1829, and left £2,000 in Bank annuities for the almshouses to be used under Rippon's sole direction, and a further £2,000 which would revert to the almshouses after the decease of certain relatives and friends.
191 Carter Lane Churchbook, 3 September 1830.
192 Watts, *The Dissenters*, 2, p. 639.

and Eagle Street also had some.[193] But the inspiration for these was most probably Rippon's. Indeed, the charitable traditions begun earlier in the church's history were expanded and enlarged under C.H. Spurgeon with enlarged almshouses, a day school, and an orphanage.[194]

Those who covenanted together in a gathered community of believers, such as Carter Lane believed itself to be, took seriously their mutual responsibilities-not only for the body but also for the soul.[195] Every aspect of a member's life could be - and often was - exposed to the frank scrutiny of a 'brother' or 'sister'. This could become petty, legalistic and irksome but was intended to be an expression of mutual care. Most matters investigated by Carter Lane were either a serious breach of fellowship, or involved some social or moral disgrace. No exclusion was undertaken lightly, and investigations often extended over several months before any final decision was taken. Allegations of misconduct reported to the church meeting were investigated by 'messengers' who would visit the alleged offender and make all general inquiries.

The report of the messengers (who never included Rippon) was invariably accepted. One of three actions could then be taken: the matter was dropped; the member was 'suspended' from attending communion; most seriously, the member was 'excluded' from the church. Although it had been normal during Gill's time for members to appear before the church to answer any accusation, this happened only once or twice in Rippon's early years.[196] Occasionally the messengers delayed a final report, in the hope of a genuine repentance. William Knolding, for example, admitted the immorality with which he was first accused on 20 October 1783 and professed his regret. However, he was later excluded, since a 'bastard child' had been sworn to as his.[197]

In only seventeen instances was the charge dropped without any disciplinary action. These charges were of two kinds: bankrupts who demonstrated no dishonesty (twelve), and those absent from church services with a reasonable cause (five).

'Suspension' from communion took place in only fourteen instances. Gill had insisted that one was either in communion with the church, or one was not.[198] However, 'suspension' was held to have a twofold purpose. If the charge was serious, but not proven nor admitted, suspension allowed time for further inquiries without impinging on the

193 Price, *Upton*, pp. 59-68; W.T. Whitley, *Baptists of London* (London: Kingsgate Press, 1928), p. 130.

194 Hayden, *A Centennial History of Spurgeon's Tabernacle*, pp. 20-24.

195 For a review of discipline among Dissenters, see Watts, *The Dissenters*, 2, pp. 199-222.

196 Cf. Carter Lane Churchbook, 18 August 1783.

197 Carter Lane Churchbook, 17 May and 18 October 1784.

198 Gill, *A Body of Divinity*, 3, p. 308.

moral character of the church during the interim.[199] The majority of suspensions (ten) at Carter Lane resulted in eventual full exclusion, whilst the periods of these suspensions varied from one month to eleven months. On the other hand, suspension allowed an interval for testing the genuineness of any professed repentance. On 21 March 1796 the church decided that the pastor or deacons could request any member 'supposed to have acted indiscreetly in any matter' not to sit at the Lord's Table till the matter had been investigated. This, of course, was really arbitrary suspension, and explains the low number of suspensions recorded by the church meeting. No great stigma necessarily resulted. Mark Moore, suspended in 1816 for bankruptcy occasioned 'by great imprudence but not designed dishonesty', was restored in 1818, and later became a deacon of the church.[200]

Exclusion constituted the most severe form of discipline and was undertaken for three reasons (reminiscent of Calvin's teaching on church discipline): for the 'Glory of God', the 'honour of the church' and to provoke repentance in the offender.[201] The rubric for exclusion usually concluded, 'till God shall give him/her repentance for it'. Theoretically, if God did give repentance, any member could be restored after exclusion. But, in practice, only six members were restored. Three assurances were required in all such cases: the justice of the church's censure had to be conceded, repentance had to be professed, and a corresponding moral change had to be attested. The periods of exclusion prior to restoration ranged from three to twenty-two years.

Some indication of the personal tragedy that exclusion from the church could mean for an individual and his family is provided by a series of letters written to Rippon by Alexander Prior and his daughter, Elizabeth.[202] Prior had been excluded on 26 June 1797 because of 'attempts on the charity (sic) of one of our sisters who liv'd servant with him'. His daughter told Rippon of the great distress this had brought to him, seriously affecting his sleep. At the same time, she and her mother had been offended by members of the congregation who 'won't look at me their conduct is like this stand off I am holyer than thou'. Rippon's 'kindness' was appreciated although only two church members had visited them since the exclusion. Prior tried to be restored in 1801, but after due investigation the messengers could not see fit to recommend this.[203] Accordingly, Prior remained in spiritual isolation, an unhappy man, the only member during Rippon's time whose request for

---

199   For a discussion of links between the Lord's Supper and church discipline, see Walker, *Baptists at the Table*, pp. 157-61.

200   Carter Lane Churchbook, 12 August 1816, 28 December 1818, 31 May 1838.

201   J. Calvin, *Institutes of the Christian Religion*, IV.xii. 5.

202   B.L. Add. MSS. 25388, ff. 338-45.

203   Carter Lane Churchbook, 22 June 1801, 18 January 1802.

restoration was refused. It does not appear from this example that the church gave much attention to attempting to rescue those who had fallen.

During the second half of Rippon's ministry there was a decline in church discipline; between 1811 and 1836 there were only 22 exclusions. The reasons for this are complex. Rippon's advancing years and the measure of disintegration in the church fellowship would inevitably bring less awareness of members' failures. There is an impression of diminished interest in church discipline. It is interesting that there were no instances of exclusion for doctrinal errors after 1809, suggesting perhaps a generation less occupied with the *minutiae* of theological disputes. The extent to which the general social and economic conditions had improved is uncertain, but this obviously is relevant.

The total of 156 exclusions divide, almost equally, into what might be termed 'sins against the fellowship' and sins that involved a more public offence. Clearly any expressed dissatisfaction with Rippon's ministry was a disturbance to the harmony of the church. One left because he couldn't hear Rippon,[204] but more serious was the rudeness of one John Ravish. After having noted 81 sermons by Rippon in shorthand he described him as a 'legalist', and the church as a 'herd of Hypocrites'. He did not want Rippon to call to see him, 'as I do not wish to have any conversation with you knowing what it cost Eve for parleying with the Devil'.[205] Another man was excluded because, although under suspension for causing a disturbance after a church meeting, he arrived at a subsequent church meeting, 'used unbecoming behaviour to the Church and with much difficulty was persuaded to withdraw into the vestry where he remained'.[206]

Rippon in his earlier years took seriously any doctrinal errors. The main offence was Antinomianism, and Rippon's concern to eradicate this extravagance probably was why Ravish called him a 'legalist'. Four members were excluded for Antinomianism, and Rippon became so concerned that he had the church agree to the following statement:

We as a Church of Christ do agree that the Moral Law as summarily comprehended in the Ten Commandments is a rule for the conduct of men in general and for God's people in particular.

Resolv'd. That no one after a first and second admonition by Messengers from this church denying the Moral Law to be a rule for the conduct of Men in general and for

---

204 Carter Lane Churchbook, 21 December 1789.
205 Carter Lane Churchbook, 1 September 1806. Cf. B.L. Add. MSS. 25389, f. 376.
206 Carter Lane Churchbook, 29 August 1791.

God's people in particular shall be continued a member of this Church which was unamimously (*sic*) agreed to.[207]

Other doctrinal errors included denial of the Trinity and the divinity of Christ (4 cases), suggestive that Socinianism had some impact on Calvinist congregations, and 'Deistical errors' (1 case). Another left because the church held to the 'general salvation of Infants which he said we were not warranted to do from scripture'.[208]

The 'social sins' covered a wide variety. Sexual immorality was the main offence in this second group. Three were excluded for illegal marriage. One 'brother', who proposed to marry again, although his wife who had deserted him was still alive, called on Rippon for 'his advice therein'. Rippon promptly advised him 'not to do any such thing', but the lure of a woman 'whom he thought would make him comfortable' proved too much.[209] Others were excluded for adultery (two), fornication (eight), 'immorality' (fourteen), desertion of wife (one).

The uncertainties of trade, and the general economic instability of London at the end of the eighteenth century, are reflected in the fourteen excluded for bankruptcy or 'business failure'. Baptists took seriously any hint of dishonesty in business or the compromise of Christian witness: it will be recalled that Rippon's own father and uncle had been excluded from the Tiverton church for just this offence. At Carter Lane a further four were suspended, and another thirteen who failed were absolved from any charge of dishonesty. Bankruptcy became so common that in 1789 the church agreed that messengers should automatically be appointed to investigate all who became insolvent under the Statute of Bankruptcy.[210] This was softened in 1804, when it was agreed that the pastor or deacons could use their discretion as to whether a case of insolvency should come before the church. This implies that the number of bankruptcies may have been more than those already noted. Other churches faced the same problem with similar care.[211]

Again, it should be noted with reference to the number of exclusions for drunkenness (nine), that not only were these pre-temperance days but that drinking was inextricably woven into the social patterns of every-day London life.[212] Employment was found and wages paid in the alehouse for thousands of Londoners. The normal amusements of the City could bring rebuke from the church: such as being seen at a 'public skittle

---

207 Carter Lane Churchbook, 31 October 1791.

208 Carter Lane Churchbook, 22 August 1791.

209 Carter Lane Churchbook, 17 December 1787.

210 Carter Lane Churchbook, 21 September 1789.

211 Cf. Kevan, *London's Oldest Baptist Church*, p. 96; Watts, *The Dissenters*, 2, p. 205.

212 George, *London Life in the Eighteenth Century*, pp. 266-92.

ground and having there lost three of four pounds'; 'gameing frequently at public houses'; and 'indulging in Card playing, Dancing and frequenting Play-houses'.[213] Discipline for breaches of Sunday observance, especially trading on Sunday (two), occurred only in the nineteenth century. Stealing (eight) and idleness (three) were other offences.

Rippon's own summary of his congregation was reported to be that he had some of the best people in His Majesty's dominions in his church, but he used to add with a nod, 'and some of the worst!'[214]

One further aspect of the church's life requiring comment is its financial structure. Caring for the poor was only one aspect; maintenance of property and pastor was another major concern. The Carter Lane meeting-house was built in 1757 at a cost of £1, 541.[215] Under Rippon's leadership the property was constantly kept in good repair, some major expense occurring about every ten years. Alterations and cleaning in 1769 had cost £70, but in 1779 the surface of Carter Lane was repaired, and a ventilator was added to the roof, since 'in the Summer Time the heat in the Meeting was so great, as to be very inconvenient'.[216] Later that year, after a legacy of £200 from Martha Tipping for the purpose, additional land adjacent to the north side of the meeting-house was leased, and the baptistery built. The meeting-house itself was at the same time 'whitewashed and beautified'.[217]

However, in 1792, it was decided to undertake a major enlargement at a cost of £677. Whilst this was being completed, the church worshipped in the Miles's Lane Independent meeting-house, at the invitation of their minister, Dr. Addington. Payment for this enlargement dragged on, and in 1793 Peter Sharp lent the church £400. However, additional repairs costing £124 in 1802 and an unspecified sum in 1810 were completed, before the 1792 debt was paid in 1816. But in 1824 further repairs costing £228 were necessary, and between 1824 and February 1826 the church raised £411 to remove this debt.[218] Thus, during Rippon's ministry well over £1,000 was spent to maintain the chapel, described in 1814 as 'an oblong building, with galleries entirely round'.[219]

As well as the care of the property, by February 1774, just after Rippon began his ministry the church had a debt of £650.[220] This consisted of

---

213 Carter Lane Churchbook, 24 October 1785; 26 August 1793; 20 June 1796.

214 Spurgeon, *The Metropolitan Tabernacle*, p. 52.

215 Carter Lane Churchbook, 27 November 1758.

216 Carter Lane Churchbook, 14 May 1770; 19 April 1779.

217 Carter Lane Churchbook, 24 October 1779.

218 Carter Lane Churchbook, 18 June 1792, 17 June 1793, 21 June, 25 October 1802, 25 June 1810, 17 June 1816, September 1824 (no day given), February 1826.

219 Wilson, *History and Antiquities*, 4, p. 213.

220 Carter Lane Churchbook, 7 February 1774.

the £300 promised to Dean Street, paid on 9 August 1774, and mortgages raised to repay the original cost of the meeting-house. By 21 April 1777 the whole debt had been cleared.[221]

The income of the church was received in four ways: by collections, subscription, legacy or gift, rental of church property. Two collections each month were the main sources of income. The 'ordinance collection' was given at the communion service for the poor of the church. The amounts received for 1800-1 were £101 and £113; from 1815 to 1832 they declined from £104 to £41. The 'public collection' was taken at the doors of the meeting-house. Prior to 1777 there were twelve monthly collections 'for the Use of the Church', and four quarterly collections 'for Ground Rent & other Expenses'.[222] These were then combined, so that each month there were simply two collections: the 'ordinance' and the 'public'. There were, of course, additional special collections: for reduction of church debts, for the Christmas gift to the poor, for outside needs.

The general method was somewhat haphazard. The church does not seem to have been unduly concerned about whether the money was available before making any decision. The church treasurer was expected to submit regular statements of how much the church owed him. When these sums grew too large, a special collection was arranged.

The other regular source of income was the pew-subscription, the whole of which was given to Rippon as a stipend.[223] The church never gave any undertaking as to his salary, but to judge from those years for which there is evidence, his income from the church was normally in excess of £300 *per annum*. Individual subscriptions, which ranged from six guineas to two shillings, were received twice yearly by the deacons. Evidently Rippon's salary compared very favourably with his Baptist colleagues.[224] Many country ministers were almost destitute, and had to seek secular employment. The Baptist Fund normally made grants of only five guineas. However, various Independent pastors in London received salaries ranging between £400 and £600 at this time.[225]

Most of the legacies received were for the poor of the church. Especially valuable was Martha Tipping's legacy which provided for the baptistery. A small amount, about £6 per annum was received from 1826 as rent of the cellar under the vestry.[226]

---

221 Carter Lane Churchbook, 8 October 1775, 26 February 1776.

222 Carter Lane Churchbook, 18 August 1777.

223 Pew-subscription book shows Rippon's signature for receipt of the entire sums collected.

224 See K.D. Brown, *A Social History of the Nonconformist Ministry in England and Wales 1800-1930* (Oxford: Oxford University Press, 1988), pp. 154-61.

225 Jones, *Congregationalism in England*, p. 229, note 7.

226 Entries in Carter Lane Cash-Book.

There were certain regular expenses. Lease of the property was normally £14 per annum, Insurance and Taxes were between £5 and £6, three pew-openers received two guineas each per quarter, and the clerk's salary was fifteen guineas per year. Coals, presumably for a stove which heated the church, cost about £7 a year, candles between £2 and £3, and about £20 a year for wine. In addition to purchasing communion wine the church gave Rippon a dozen bottles of wine each January. Sherry and brandy were bought respectively in 1825 and 1826, perhaps the deacons feared for the welfare of their aged pastor. Visiting preachers were paid 10s.6d. per church service. Then there were cleaning and maintenance repairs, one man received £2.12s. from 1826 for sweeping Carter Lane each week.[227]

The church must have been stunned to learn on 9 August 1829 that because of an approach road being built for the New London Bridge their chapel would have to be demolished. Rippon was now almost senile, as will be shown below, and the church faced a major crisis.

Service Outside Carter Lane

Rippon and his people were thoroughly involved in the vast range of denominational, religious and philanthropic societies which flourished at this time. Rippon's personal activities require more detailed examination,[228] but a brief sketch of the church's involvement is necessary to complete the picture of its life.

Public collections to help country churches were frequently undertaken. At first such requests were considered and authorized by the Baptist Board, the ministers' body.[229] At Carter Lane, collections were held for Northampton in 1776, Scarborough, Yorkshire, in 1780, and Bricknell, Somerset, in 1784.[230] The rather chaotic method of appeals was then regularized by the Baptist Board which in 1784 established the Baptist Case Committee.[231] This committee, consisting of both ministers and laymen from the London churches, investigated all cases and authorized appeals 'in a regulated succession and an orderly manner'. Rippon assisted the work by publishing details in his *Register*.[232] Samuel Gale was 'the gratuitous Secretary and Solicitor' for the committee. In 1824, the committee was replaced by the London Baptist Building Fund,

---

227 Carter Lane Cash-Book.
228 See chapters 7 and 9.
229 Price, *Baptist Building Fund*, pp. 27-39.
230 Carter Lane Churchbook, 4 August 1776, 21 August 1780, 17 May 1784.
231 Price, *Baptist Building Fund,* pp. 40-63.
232 *Register* 1 (1790-93), pp. 289, 467; 2 (1794-97), pp. 92, 176, 533; 3 (1798-1801), pp. 60, 266.

which improved the organization of grants, with special concern for the legality of Trust Deeds. Samuel Gale was solicitor (1824-26) of the Fund, whilst C. Barber, J. Warmington and Gilbert Blight served on the committee. An earlier scheme for providing loans to churches was begun by the Baptist Union in 1817, and Chapman Barber was one of four on the committee: but this idea failed because of inadequate capital support.[233]

The principal aid for rural churches, however, came from the Particular Baptist Fund, as noted above. All the contributing London churches sent representatives who acted as 'managers' of the Fund, Carter Lane providing Benjamin Lepard, who was the 'kind and sympathizing secretary' of the Fund from 1811 to 1826,[234] Peter Sharp, Joseph Carroll, William Lepard (Jr.), John Cooper, Stephen Misnard, James Norton and Robert Westley. The church referred to this fund as 'for the poor country ministers'. The amounts collected ranged from £54 in 1773 to be regularly in excess of £100 *per annum* until after 1823; by 1836 it had fallen to £31. Carter Lane was among the biggest contributors to the Fund. The amount collected for 1798 consisted of collections received on 23 and 30 December, £6.16s.8d from 'Mr. Rippon and children' together with 13s.7d. from the following intriguing source: 'saved by farthings out of our friends pints of beer who dine at the meeting in order to give to this collection'; clearly every farthing helped![235] In 1820, Rippon persuaded the church to give £16 direct to the Uffculm, Devonshire, church out of their collection.[236] This was because the Fund managers had decided that only churches with pastors could receive grants. As Uffculm did not have a pastor, but was in desperate need, Rippon who knew the local situation intimately, asked for the £16, which was the equivalent of the two years' grant of £8 they had been denied from the Fund.

Carter Lane, together with the Prescott Street church, provided the best of the denomination's lay leadership. Abraham Booth at Prescott Street numbered three influential men among his members: William Taylor (1728-1811), a generous supporter of the Baptist Fund, and the man who gave £3,600 for the buildings of Stepney Academy; Joseph Gutteridge (1752-1844), treasurer of the Baptist Fund for forty-six years, and first treasurer of Stepney Academy; and William Fox, founder of the Sunday School Society.[237] But the influence of Rippon and his Carter Lane men was also widespread especially through the work of gifted men like

---

233 Price, *Baptist Building Fund*, pp. 41, 64-82, 88-90.
234 *Baptist Magazine* 37 (1844), p. 196.
235 Peter Sharp's Cash Book.
236 Carter Lane Churchbook, 17 January 1820.
237 Kevan, *London's Oldest Baptist Church*, pp. 135-42.

Samuel Gale, William Burls, Gilbert Blight and others whose names appeared on most of the denomination's committees.

Under Rippon's leadership Carter Lane strongly supported the Baptist Missionary Society from its small beginnings.[238] Fuller and Carey preached from the pulpit, indeed when Carey preached just before his departure for India he inspired young William Ward to promise that he would join Carey in India.[239] William Burls was the first Londoner on the BMS committee, and acted as a kind of London agent for the Mission. As the BMS grew, an increasing amount of business had to be transacted in London, and Burls allowed the missionaries to draw their bills upon him and so became personally responsible for them. He shared in the BMS agitation in 1813 over the renewal of the East India Charter, when freedom for missionary activity was obtained.[240] From 1819-21 Burls was co-treasurer of the BMS. Others to serve on the BMS committee were Chapman Barber (1822-23), Gilbert Blight (1824-28), and James Low (1836-37).[241] The Carter Lane church was host to valedictory services for John Chamberlain (1802),[242] and for their own medical missionary, William Johns (1810).[243]

The financial support for the Mission was consistent and considerable. The first list of subscribers included eight Carter Lane members: Robert Bowyer, William Burls, J. Cowell, Robert Davies, Benjamin Lepard, Samuel Medley, Robert Westley, and James Norton. Subscriptions were normally of one guinea *per annum*. Additional special gifts from individuals included £470 from Robert Davies, £70.10.0 from Rippon, and £64 from Burls. The church had special collections, notably £253 in 1806. Mrs. Arnold sent regular amounts, collected from her friends, to be used specifically for female education in Calcutta. A Carter Lane BMS Female Auxiliary contributed from 1822.[244] More than £2,600 was given to the BMS by Carter Lane members during Rippon's pastorate.[245]

---

238 For Rippon's strong support, see chapter 5.

239 S.P. Carey, *William Carey* (London: Hodder and Stoughton, 1923), p. 119. For Ward (1769-1823) see especially A.C. Smith, 'William Ward, Radical Reform, and Missions in the 1790s', *American Baptist Quarterly* 10.3 (1991), pp. 218-44 and A.C. Smith, 'William Ward (1769-1823)' in *The British Particular Baptists 1638-1910*', 2, pp. 255-71.

240 See Payne, *The Excellent Mr. Burls*. Burls' name first appears in 1811 Committee: BMS *Periodical Accounts* 4 (1810), p. 292. For the East India Company charter, see B. Stanley, *The History of the Baptist Missionary Society 1792-1992* (Edinburgh: T. & T. Clark, 1992), p. 26.

241 Annual Reports in BMS, *Periodical Accounts*, vols. 7-9.

242 BMS *Periodical Accounts* 2 (1802), p. 259.

243 Carter Lane Churchbook, 4 October 1810.

244 BMS *Periodical Accounts*, 7 (1824), p. 68.

245 Calculated from BMS *Periodical Accounts*.

The Baptist Itinerant Society was established in 1797 to promote village evangelism. Rippon was the first chairman. His son-in-law Samuel Gale was first secretary of the society and William Lepard (Jr.) was treasurer (1799-1805).[246] This Society became the Home Missionary Society in 1821, and both James Norton and James Low were collectors for it.[247] Carter Lane was host to the initial meeting of the Baptist Union in 1812 and frequently in subsequent years. William Burls was the first treasurer of the Union whilst James Low was treasurer (1834-1847) and President (1847).[248] The Baptist Irish Society was formed in 1814 in order to promote evangelistic and educational work in Ireland.[249] Burls was the first treasurer (1814-1830) of this Society, whilst Barber and Low also served on the committee.[250] Blight and John Bousfield served on the Baptist Continental Society formed in 1831 for evangelistic mission in Europe.[251] Robert Westley was active on a committee, established in 1781, to support Robert Robinson's research into Baptist history.[252] Benjamin Lepard was one of the collectors for the Stepney Academy begun in 1810.[253] Burls and Barber were also later on the Academy committee.[254] On one occasion, Carter Lane contributed five guineas to the Maze Pond Church which had been at Law with the Commissioners of the Pavements over an unjust demand in rates.[255] The reduction they acquired also benefited Carter Lane.

Carter Lane people were not only involved in every aspect of the emerging denominational structures but in numerous other Dissenting and evangelical causes: this was uniquely the age of the society. Particular Baptists generally engaged in several interdenominational enterprises in the closing decades of the eighteenth century.[256] One member, Chapman Barber, helped Rev. J. Martin (1741-1820) distribute the *Regium Donum*, the royal gift to needy Dissenting ministers, which one Dissenter

---

246   For the society see below, chapter 7. Details from Minutes of Itinerant Society (Angus library).

247   *Baptist Magazine* 13 (1821), p. 309; 14 (1822), p. 315.

248   Payne, *The Baptist Union*, pp. 26, 257, 262.

249   For this society, see *The Baptist Union*, index.

250   *The Baptist Union*, p. 47, note 8; *Baptist Magazine* 8 (1816), p. 302; 14 (1822), p. 296.

251   *Baptist Magazine* 23 (1831), p. 251, 25 (1833), p. 200.

252   Ivimey, *History of the English Baptists*, 4, p. 48. Robinson published *History of Baptism* (London:1790) and *Ecclesiastical Researches*(Cambridge: 1792). See Hughes, *With Freedom Fired*, pp. 57-60.

253   *Baptist Magazine* 8 (1816), p. 131.

254   Cf. Payne, *Excellent Mr. Burls*, p. 10; *Baptist Magazine* 9 (1817), p. 120.

255   Carter Lane Churchbook, 27 February 1775.

256   R.H. Martin, 'English Particular Baptists and Interdenominational Cooperation', *Foundations* 22.3 (1979), pp. 233-45.

castigated as 'hush-money'.[257] Carter Lane had two representatives on the Dissenting Deputies, the body dedicated to protecting the civic and religious rights of Dissenters, and in 1790 collected to help defray the expenses of the (unsuccessful) agitations to have the Test and Corporation Acts repealed.[258] Associated with the Deputies, however, was a meeting of ministers, 'the General Body of the Three Denominations', of which Rippon became a leading figure. He led the church to collect £128.14s. for the 'poor Protestants in Germany'.[259] Rippon was on the committee which arranged an appeal to relieve the plight of some Protestants in the south of France who were cruelly persecuted in 1815.[260] Reports of these events, more the 'last gust of the revolutionary storm' than any religious or systematic persecution, were difficult to authenticate, and whilst some churches hesitated to contribute, Carter Lane gave £183.5s.[261]

There were numerous other societies in which the church and its members are known to have been actively involved both financially and personally. A sense of both human need and the evangelical activism generated to meet them is provided by a list of such societies. The Protestant Dissenting School, one of whose founders in 1714 was Benjamin Stinton (1676-1719), Gill's immediate predecessor (1704-1719), provided free education and clothing for forty boys.[262] Boys would attend various chapels for a quarter at a time, after which a collection would be received. These collections were certainly taken at Carter Lane in 1775, 1777, 1779, 1781, 1785, 1794, 1797, 1801, 1803, 1809, 1812 and 1834. Joseph Fox was a secretary and generous benefactor of the British and Foreign School Society, and secretary

---

257 Ivimey, *History of the English Baptists,* 4, p. 347; Hughes, *With Freedom Fired,* p. 57.

258 Carter Lane Churchbook, 16 February 1790. The church's representatives were Joseph Flight (first appointed 1774), William Lepard Junior (1774), Peter Sharp (1788), William Burls (1800), Samuel Gale (1805), William Bousfield (1821), James Low (1836).

259 Carter Lane Churchbook, 16 December 1805.

260 For the flurry of activity generated by this incident, see C. Perrot, *Report on the Persecution of the French Protestants presented to the Committee of Dissenting Ministers of the three Denominations* (London: 1816); H.M. Williams, *On the Late Persecution of the Protestants in the South of France* (London: 1816); M. Wilks, *History of the Persecution endured by the Protestants in the South of France* (2 vols; London: 1821); *Notes, Intended as Materials for a Memoir on the Affairs of the Protestants of the Department du Gard* (London:1816), p. 51.

261 A.J. Grant, *The Huguenots* (London: 1934), p. 240; Unicorn Yard Churchbook, 18 January 1816; Carter Lane Churchbook, 17 June 1816.

262 Cf. T. Crosby, *History of the English Baptists* (4 vols., London: 1740), 4, pp. 114-23; M.G. Jones, *The Charity School Movement* (Cambridge: 1938), pp. 132-34; H. Foreman, 'Baptists and the Charity School Movement', *BQ* 27.4 (1977), pp. 150-56.

(1809-1811) of the London Society for promoting Christianity among the Jews.[263] The Widows' Fund (to assist Dissenting ministers' widows) was managed by William Lepard (1802).[264] The Society for Promoting Religious Knowledge among the Poor (commonly known as 'the 'Book Society' and for which Rippon prepared a history) had W. Lepard (1788) and B. Lepard (1803) as managers, and Norton as secretary (1821).[265] Burls was from 1809 on the committee of the British and Foreign Bible Society.[266] Norton, Blight and Barber assisted the Society for the Relief of Aged and Infirm Protestant Dissenting Ministers formed in 1818.[267] William Lepard, with Rippon, was on the committee for the Relief of Poor Africans in London.[268]

When the Edinburgh Missionary Society (founded in 1796) asked to hold a service in the Carter Lane church in 1819, Rippon reminded his church that that Society had generously helped the BMS in its early days. Dr. Alexander Waugh preached for the Scottish Society, and £60 was collected.[269]

Rippon had a generous church, which normally responded to any appeal that he brought to them. A final example of this was the urgent request for clothing in 1794 from a church of 'coloured' people in Sierra Leone, with whom Rippon had been in contact, after a French squadron had attacked the colony. Rippon's church spontaneously provided five chests of 'wearing apparel, mostly in good condition, and some of it quite new'.[270]

Michael Watts has noted that 'the elderly, the sick, the orphaned, the imprisoned, were all beneficiaries of Dissenting philanthropy'.[271] Carter Lane offers ample proof of this claim. The influence of Rippon and his church spread far beyond Southwark.

---

263   W.T. Gidney, *The History of the London Society for Promoting Christianity Amongst the Jews* (London: 1908), p. 38. Rippon subscribed a guinea to this Society in 1813:*The Jewish Repository* 1 (1813), p. 576.

264   *Register* 3 (1798-1801), p. 428. For an account of this Fund, which assisted Dissenting ministers' widows, see pp. 426-28.

265   Rippon, *Discourse on the Origin and Progress of the Society for Promoting Religious Knowledge Among the Poor* (London: 1802), pp. 76, 78; *Baptist Magazine* 13 (1821), p. 171.

266   Payne, *The Excellent Mr. Burls*, p. 9.

267   *Baptist Magazine* 12 (1820), p. 842; 20 (1823), p. 388; Ivimey, *History of the English Baptists*, 4, p. 191.

268   *Evangelical Magazine* 15 (1807), p. 244.

269   *Register* 3 (1798-1801) p. 77; for Alexander Waugh (1754-1827) see *DNB;* Carter Lane Churchbook, 1 March 1819.

270   *Register* 2 (1794-97), p. 255.

271   Watts, *The Dissenters*, 2, p. 638.

Men for the Ministry

The influence of Rippon and his church was radiated in a more personal way through the nineteen men recognized as preachers by the church, although only eleven of these assumed pastoral charge.

After the exclusion of two members for preaching without a proper 'call' from Carter Lane, Rippon proposed that the church should define its attitude to the whole issue.[272] Accordingly, Rippon drafted a statement, accepted by the church on 18 August 1788, which made the following points:

(i) that just as nobody has the right to make himself a pastor, or a deacon, so no man can 'put himself into the office of a publick Teacher', an office only 'communicated by the Church';

(ii) anyone who does preach without proper authority, throws contempt upon the church, and if he persists in this should be excluded;

(iii) if a member desires to have his gift tried, he should speak either to the pastor or a deacon who will appoint a time and place when both deacons and the same number of male members as deacons shall be present.

Rippon proposed a detailed rubric for this service that included these questions:

'To the brethren who come to hear

Brethren! - - Is it your Desire to hear our Brother at this time in the fear of God, and will you give him the best Advice in your Power?

To which they shall audibly answer.

Question - - To the Brother -who is to speak

Brother! - - Will you take the Advice that the Brethren present, or the Majority of them may give you, and abide by it in the Fear of the Lord?

He shall audibly answer, 'Yes, in the Fear of the Lord'.

This view of the necessity of a trial for discerning a preaching gift was a Baptist conviction as early as 1644.[273] Rippon's rules seemed to have had the desired effect, for only two members were subsequently excluded

---

272 Carter Lane Churchbook, 19 November 1787, 17 November 1788.

273 Lumpkin, *Baptist Confessions of Faith*, p. 166.

for irregular preaching.[274] The gifts of twenty 'brothers' were tried, and only one was given a negative answer.[275]

John Giles (1758-1827) was given a long preaching 'trial' covering five sermons.[276] Rippon ordained Giles, and gave him a special certificate on 11 January 1789. After nine months as assistant to Robert McGregor at Woolwich, to where Rippon had commended him, Giles ministered most effectively, at Eythorn, Kent. Joseph Swain (1761-1796), called in 1791, exercised a short but effective ministry at East Lane, Walworth.[277] He was a poet of some merit. Thomas Illidge, ordained in 1797, appears to have been a local preacher.[278]

George Keeley, Benjamin Coxhead (1772-1851), and James Douglas (1772-1843) were all sent by Rippon to Bristol Academy for training, where his friend John Ryland was by then President.[279] Keeley eventually settled at Ryland's former pastorate at Northampton in 1799, but later moved to America.[280] Coxhead served at Little Wild Street, London (1800-1807), and later at Truro and Winchester.[281] Douglas had only a short probation at Tiverton and Yarmouth before settling at White's Row, Portsea, (1802-1804), then at Oakham, before returning to teach in London in 1807.[282]

George Atkinson (d. 1825) and William Aikin (1770-1832) were both sent to Bristol in 1799.[283] Atkinson became pastor at Margate (1801-1825), but Aikin found study too difficult and returned to business in London. James Stuart was encouraged to undertake 'Village Worship', under Rippon's direction in 1803.[284] Josiah Wilkinson (1784-1849) was first called to preach in 1803, became minister at Saffron Walden in 1809, and became widely known for his work with the BMS, LMS and

---

274 Carter Lane Churchbook, 17 November 1800, 20 April 1801.

275 Carter Lane Churchbook, 21 May 1798.

276 *A Brief Sketch of the Life and Character of the Rev. John Giles* (London: n.d.); S. J. Price, 'Brother Giles becomes a Recognized Minister', *BQ* 5.1 (1930-31), pp. 37-41; H. Davies, *Worship and Theology in England,* (5 vols; Princeton: Princeton University Press, 1961-75), 3, pp. 137-39.

277 See *DNB* and *DEB*; Carter Lane Churchbook, 6 June 1791.

278 Carter Lane Churchbook, 28 May 1798.

279 Carter Lane Churchbook, 19 June 1797, and Records of Bristol Education Society (Bristol Baptist College).

280 Keeley was supported at Bristol by the London Education Society: see MS records of Society, (last unnumbered page); *Register* 3 (1797-1801), pp. 244-49; Payne, *College Street Chapel Northampton 1697-1947*, p. 27.

281 *Baptist Magazine* 44 (1852), pp. 328-29.

282 *Baptist Magazine* 35 (1843), p. 480.

283 *Baptist Magazine* 18 (1826), p.28; 24 (1832), pp. 465-69; Carter Lane Churchbook, 17 June 1799.

284 Carter Lane Churchbook, 17 January 1803.

the Bible Society.[285] Augustus Applegath had 'an ardent desire to become a Missionary', so was 'encouraged' by the church to study at Bristol.[286] However, his doubts and fears, movingly detailed in a letter to Rippon were such as to cause his return to London and business.[287]

William Johns, a young druggist with a 'fine mind' and 'a singular gift in prayer' according to Fuller,[288] was given training as a surgeon by the BMS. He left for India via America in 1810, but did not arrive until August 1812.[289] Although appointed acting surgeon at Serampore, Johns was forced to return to England in 1813 as the East India Company had not given permission for his entry.[290] Johns moved to Birmingham,[291] and is not to be confused with a Unitarian minister of the same name.[292]

Robert Bowyer, the artist, had been preaching to his neighbours at Byfleet, Surrey, for four or five years before he realized in 1810 that he had broken the church's rule.[293] He told Rippon that the proper thing was for the church to exclude him, but Rippon persuaded the church to grant him a formal call, without even hearing Bowyer preach.[294] This 'extraordinary case' was unique in this sense, and suggests the high esteem in which Bowyer was held by Rippon and the church.

Mark Moore was 'encouraged' as a local preacher on 1 March 1813. Jeremiah Cowell had begun preaching to his fellow-prisoners, whilst a prisoner in France during the long war.[295] Clearly this was another exception to the church's rule, although Cowell did preach before the church once before being granted a call in 1814. Cowell appears to have become a local preacher.

Thomas Rippon (1791-1825), a nephew of Rippon, was commended by the church the day after he had been received into the church from the St. Albans church.[296] Thomas Rippon had already begun studies at

---

285 Carter Lane Churchbook, 17 July 1803; *Baptist Magazine* 41 (1849), pp. 265-69.

286 Carter Lane Churchbook, 26 September 1808.

287 4 April 1810, B.L. Add. MSS. 25386, f. 19.

288 A. Fuller to W. Ward, 25 Aug. 1807: typescript copy in Angus Library (original in BMS archives).

289 BMS *Periodical Accounts* 5 (1813), p. 45.

290 BMS *Periodical Accounts* 5 (1813), pp. 198-200.

291 Carter Lane Churchbook, 12 August 1816.

292 BHS *Trans.* 7 (1920-21), p. 211, and Whitley, *Baptist Bibliography*, 2, p. 236 appears to have confused Johns with another William Johns (1771-1845), for whom see *DNB*.

293 R. Bowyer to Rippon, 6 July 1810, B.L. Add. MSS. 25386, f .116.

294 Carter Lane Churchbook, 27 July 1811.

295 Carter Lane Churchbook, 26 September 1814.

296 Carter Lane Churchbook, 5 June 1815; Thomas had been granted a dismissal by St. Albans on 7 August 1814: St. Albans Churchbook (as kindly noted by Dr. W.M.S. West).

Bristol.[297] He also studied at Edinburgh but died at an early age, whilst supplying at Two-Waters, near Hemel-Hempstead.[298] Rippon included a hymn by his nephew in his *Selection*.[299]

William Henry Angas (1781-1832) was perhaps the outstanding man of the group.[300] After colourful adventures as captain of a vessel trading with the West Indies, Angas joined the church in 1807. Ten years later he was called to preach, but went to Edinburgh, not Bristol, for his studies. Angas specialized in work with seamen, and travelled to Rotterdam in 1818 to learn Dutch and perfect his French, so as to be able better to converse with foreign seamen. In 1820 Angas visited Holland with William Ward, back from India, to interest the Mennonites in the BMS. The Mennonite church acknowledges Angas to be the awakener of a missionary interest among them.[301] Angas visited the West Indies for the BMS in 1831, but his main work was on the Continent and in English ports.

Thomas Waldron was called to village preaching on 14 June 1824. Thomas Gough was sent to Bristol, with the church's approval on 17 March 1830 but his later work has not been traced.

Rippon's concern with due church order is remarkable. His development of a formal rubric for this procedure appears to be unique among Baptists. He instituted laying-on of hands, usually only for those men entering a pastoral charge, before the church agreed to sanction this method. He insisted that all should preach only after a trial, although there were one or two exceptions to this. It may well be true, as Horton Davies has suggested, that there was an undue emphasis, in Carter Lane's rules on preaching ability, 'without a due regard for any capacity for leading worship and with little consideration of the future minister's ability as a visitor and adviser'.[302] But then this emphasis on preaching was an undoubted characteristic of the Baptist churches of the day. The only other way members could detect a possible preaching gift was by the discernment of a 'gift in prayer', mentioned in some cases.[303] But this infers a scarcely adequate motive to the public prayers of some young men, and an equally inadequate view of prayer!

---

297 Carter Lane Churchbook, 5 June 1815. However, Bristol College records indicate an application by Rippon (2 August 1814) was delayed until 14 July 1815.

298 *Baptist Magazine* 17 (1825), p. 300.

299 *Selection* (1828 ed.), hymn no. 135, part 3.

300 See *DNB* and F.A. Cox, *Memoirs of the Rev. William Henry Angas* (London: 1834).

301 H.S. Bender, C.H. Smith, C.J. Dyck, D.D. Martin (eds) *The Mennonite Encyclopedia* (5 vols; Scottdale, Pa.: Mennonite Publishing House, 1956, 1990), 1, pp. 122-23.

302 Davies, *Worship and Theology in England* , 3, p. 139.

303 For example, Carter Lane Churchbook, 21 February 1830.

Rippon's emphasis upon ministerial education wherever possible was a symptom of the times. Rippon sent eight men to Bristol, whilst two went to Edinburgh. It is surprising that none were encouraged to go to Stepney Academy, opened in 1810. Perhaps the simple explanation is Rippon's intense support for Bristol: it is revealing that Rippon refused to recommend Jeremiah Cowell when he was younger, because he was not prepared to go to Bristol for training.[304]

These men constituted a powerful medium for the strong evangelical and personal influence of Rippon. They were nearly all converted through his ministry. It was he who first encouraged them to the ministry. Benjamin Coxhead, for example, was surprised to learn from Rippon 'that he had his eye upon me in reference to the work of the ministry'.[305] All of them had to give proof of their acceptable doctrines and gifts. Thomas Illidge was delayed for a year, because at his first trial he had his ideas 'encumber'd respecting the work of the Holy Spirit'.[306] Certainly most of those who entered pastorates fulfilled notably evangelical ministries. John Giles, for example, left Woolwich because his preaching 'was not so doctrinal, or hyper-calvinistic as they wished'.[307] During his pastorate of thirty-five years at Eythorn 340 were added to the church.[308] Swain achieved a reputation for his evangelical preaching, and Angas made a unique contribution both to evangelism among seamen and to the missionary cause. Rippon's personal influence continued with these men. They consulted him about their settlements in churches, and he greatly helped them. Typical of their attitude was George Atkinson's statement, 'I shall not take any step without consulting you'.[309] Strong ties of affection bound his men to Rippon. John Giles, whom Rippon dubbed 'John the Evangelist', thanked Rippon for a special collection he had organized for him and confessed that both he and his wife often looked at the engraving of Rippon which was in their living-room.[310] Rippon preached funeral sermons for three of them,[311] and John Giles wrote in his diary when he knew he was dying, 'I am likely to go home before Dr. Rippon'.[312]

Furthermore, Rippon's men provided materials for his *Register*, and promoted the sale of his hymnbooks and sermons. More significantly,

---

304 J. Cowell to Rippon, 22 January 1801, B.L. Add. MSS. 25386, f. 286.
305 *Baptist Magazine* 44 (1852), p. 326.
306 Carter Lane Churchbook, 16 January 1797.
307 *Brief Sketch of John Giles*, p. 8.
308 *Brief Sketch of John Giles*, pp. 14, 31. See also A.C. Miller, *Eythorne: A Village Baptist Church* (London: 1924), pp. 40-41.
309 G. Atkinson to Rippon, Margate 7 October 1811, B.L. Add. MSS. 25386, f. 25.
310 J. Giles to Rippon, Eythorne, 9 October 1792, B.L. Add. MSS. 25387, f. 86.
311 Giles, Swain, and Aikin.
312 *Brief Sketch of John Giles*, p. 42.

they promoted his approach to evangelism. When Douglas was at
Yarmouth, and encountering opposition from High Calvinists, he wrote to
tell Rippon about the situation.[313] The people were opposed to
'Fullerism', but Douglas fervently wished that either Fuller or Rippon
could preach there without the people knowing who he was. This
juxtaposition of Fuller and Rippon in the minds of the Yarmouth people
and Douglas reveals that they shared the same position. But Douglas and
his colleagues from Carter Lane greatly strengthened the Baptist ministry
as they preached with a similar evangelical fervour as their old pastor to
whom they confessed they owed so much.

Problems of the Closing Years (1829-1836)

The final years of Rippon's pastorate are a sad postlude to the vigour and
effectiveness of his active years. It was not unique for a dissenter to
remain in one church for a lifelong ministry, but many did retire before
they reached Rippon's age.[314] For his church there were two inter-related
problems: Rippon's advancing senility and refusal to give up his charge,
and the compulsory removal from the Carter Lane site.

That Rippon retained the affection of his people is a tribute both to
their patience and the enduring quality of his earlier ministry. In 1822,
the fiftieth anniversary of Rippon's first preaching to the church, a
special gathering was held on Christmas Day from 10.30 a.m. until 1.00
p.m. to express their gratitude to God for their pastor.[315]

However, by 1829 Rippon's deacons had to write to him, in respectful
terms, suggesting the need for an assistant minister.[316] This was obviously
needed: Rippon could only 'minister the word occasionally', the
attendances had declined 'both of general hearers & of our fellow
Members'. Rippon made no reply, but perhaps the irony of Gill having
refused just such a request in his old age was not lost on his biographer
and successor. Then on 21 July 1829 the church was stunned to learn
that in order to make way for an approach road for a new London
Bridge, their meeting-house would have to be demolished. Fresh trustees
had to be appointed - only two of those appointed in 1793 were 'capable
of acting' - and the search for a new site was begun.[317] At the same time

---

313 J. Douglas to Rippon, Yarmouth, 5 June 1801, B.L. Add. MSS. 25386, f. 391.

314 Watts, *The Dissenters*, 2, p. 255.

315 Carter Lane Churchbook, 21 October 1822.

316 Letter in Carter Lane Churchbook, 10 April 1829.

317 Carter Lane Churchbook, 26 August 1829.

the deacons began keeping a rough minute book of church meetings, because Rippon kept the churchbook in his own possession.[318]

Location of a new site proved difficult. In the interim the church agreed, against its own wishes, to submit to Rippon's request that there should be two services, one in the morning at Unicorn Yard chapel, and in the afternoon at Miles's Lane.[319] When Miles's Lane was itself demolished in 1831, the afternoon services were held at Dean Street.[320] The move from Carter Lane must have been a sad blow to the old pastor.

Finally, Rippon's aged eccentricity became too much, and two deacons resigned. They stated their reasons for resignation as follows:

> ...because for a considerable time past, they had not experienced the cordial confidence and co-operation of our Pastor, nor received that countenance, encouragement, free communication, or reciprocal intercourse which is necessary for promoting the welfare of the Church - that our Pastor has ever chosen to act independently, and claims the entire management of all our Church affairs - that he has long since desisted from having any regular, or stated Church meetings, in consequence of which our discipline and order as a Christian Church have long been, and now are woefully neglected, whereby the design of Christian fellowship is defeated - that from these and other circumstances the office of Deacon in this Church has been rendered nugatory...[321]

These accusations, although not 'conceded' by Rippon, appear to have been perfectly justified. The church persuaded the deacons to resume their office, Rippon was persuaded to keep out of all 'temporal affairs', a monthly church meeting was resumed, and the churchbook was to be produced at every meeting.[322] This stand of Blight and Evans, the two deacons, brought a measure of stability back to the church.

The church received compensation from the City: £3,028 for the chapel, and £2,047 for the Almshouses, vestry, and schoolrooms.[323] Together with legacies of £1,253 the church had considerable money in hand.[324] Eventually a freehold site on New Park Street was bought at auction in June 1831 for £1,220. The church was not particularly impressed with the lot, but their difficulty in finding anywhere for a

---

318 Note in the 'Rough Minutes', which are exactly the same as the records in the churchbook.

319 Carter Lane Churchbook, 3, 6, 13 January 1830. The church wanted to have only one service and preferred to meet at 'Salters' Hall', where a Baptist group began about this time. See Whitley, *Baptists of London*, p. 158.

320 Carter Lane Churchbook, 16 December 1831.

321 Carter Lane Churchbook, 3 September 1830.

322 Carter Lane Churchbook, 15 July 1831.

323 Carter Lane churchbook, 15 May 1834 gives a complete statement of all the finances of the removal.

324 Carter Lane Churchbook, 3 September 1830.

reasonable price made them accept this site. Spurgeon, who came to the New Park Street site in 1854 was especially severe in his strictures on the site: low-lying, near vinegar-factories and boiler works, a 'dim, dirty, destitute' site. Whether it was as bad when first developed is uncertain, but at least Spurgeon admitted that the chapel erected was 'a neat, handsome, commodious, well-built edifice, and was regarded as one of the best Baptist chapels in London'.[325] This chapel was opened with three services on Monday, 6 May 1833. The chapel could seat some two hundred people and featured 'a bold handsome frontage of the Ionic order, built with stone- coloured bricks', with eight stone columns.[326] Its total cost including six almshouses and schoolrooms, was £6,970. Most of this was raised from funds already held, only £402, or about 5% of the cost, came from special gifts and collections.[327]

Rippon grew increasingly unable to fulfil his commitments. He refused to co-operate in the reception of new members-when asked if he would receive new members he 'would neither say yes, or no'.[328] Eventually, Rev. Charles Room (1804-1844) began preaching on 15 May 1834, and was called as assistant to Rippon on 23 August.[329] Rippon and Room seem to have been happy together, a tribute to Room's graciousness.[330] To supply for the aged pastor was something of an ordeal: the visiting preachers were not always permitted to officiate and had to endure remarks from Rippon's pew during the course of their sermons.[331]

The death of Rippon, on 17 December 1836, must have been a relief to the church. He had 'outlived his usefulness', as Spurgeon aptly remarked.[332] The church recorded a fulsome tribute to Rippon, in which they noted that 'they cannot forget in the infirmities of age, the vigour and ability of his better days.'[333]

The strengths and weaknesses of Baptist church life are revealed by Rippon's long pastorate at Carter Lane. At first the dominance of the pastor's personality helped the church grow and adapt to the challenges of a new age. But the neglect of active church government by the congregation is suggestive of the decline in true community life, and the

---

325 *Metropolitan Tabernacle*, pp. 53-54.

326 *Baptist Magazine* 25 (1833), pp. 474-75.

327 Carter Lane Churchbook, 15 May 1834.

328 Carter Lane Churchbook, 30 January 1834.

329 For Room, see BHS *Trans.* 7 (1920-21), p. 227.

330 Letter from Room to the church in Churchbook, 29 December 1836.

331 Spurgeon, *Metropolitan Tabernacle*, p. 53.

332 *Metropolitan Tabernacle,* p. 53.

333 Carter Lane Churchbook, 22 December 1836. The substance of this is in J.A. Jones, *Bunhill Memorials. Sacred Reminiscences of Three Hundred Ministers and other Persons of note who are buried in Bunhill Fields* (London: 1849) pp. 233 -34.

dominance of a stubborn old man brought the church to the brink of disaster.

Room, whose assistant-ministry had brought a recovery to the church, left immediately after Rippon's death. Joseph Angus (1816-1902) destined to become secretary of the BMS and Principal of Stepney Academy (1849-1893) brought fresh heart to the church in his ministry of two years.[334] But the most illustrious of Rippon's successors was a young minister from Cambridgeshire named Charles Haddon Spurgeon. The dramatic impact of his extraordinary ministry is such that the church is still popularly known as 'Spurgeon's Tabernacle'. But the traditions of evangelical Calvinism root back earlier than Spurgeon, and the ministry of John Rippon is worthy of its own place in the history of a remarkable church.

---

334 For Angus, see *DNB* (supplement) and Briggs, *English Baptists of the Nineteenth Century*, see index.

CHAPTER 4

'Sing Side by Side':
John Rippon and Baptist Hymnody

It has afforded me no small Pleasure to unite, as far as I could, here below different Denominations of ministers and Christians, in the same noble Work which shall for ever employ them above. My enquiry has not been, *whose* Hymns shall I choose, but *what* Hymns; and hence it will be seen, that Churchmen and Dissenters, Watts and Tate, Wesley and Toplady, England and America, sing side by side.[1]

Few issues have been as continually contentious among Baptists as changes in worship, especially the introduction of new kinds of songs. Baptists have a long history of controversy over hymn singing: whether to sing at all, what to sing and how to sing. This is in part because worship is at the heart of religious experience and deep feelings are inevitably aroused when changes are proposed or imposed. Hymns cannot be simply considered as literary texts, as J.R. Watson has argued:

(Hymns) appear limited in expression and over-determined, doctrinally orthodox, and essentially predictable in content; yet at the same time many of them seem to have the power to touch the hearts of ordinary men and women in remarkable and intense ways...hymns originate in church worship, and are primarily intended for the praise of God and for the encouragement of the faithful.[2]

It is no surprise, therefore, that eras of spiritual revival, especially among evangelicals, are usually marked by new outbursts of song. The vision and labour of Rippon at a time of great renewal among English Baptists casts an important light on the place of hymnody in such renewal. Rippon understood that hymns are a force for unity as well as for shaping and strengthening faith. His vision of various Christians-

---

1   J. Rippon (ed.), *A Selection of Hymns* (London: 1787), p. viii.
2   J.R. Watson, *The English Hymn. A Critical and Historical Study* (Oxford: Oxford University Press, 1999), pp. 7-8.

Anglican and Dissenter, Arminian and Calvinist, English and American-praising God 'side by side' sustained his wider ministry among Baptists and the larger evangelical community. This desire of Rippon is first demonstrated in the publication of *A Selection of Hymns from the best Authors* (1787), which, with his subsequent books, constituted a highly significant contribution to Baptist hymnody.[3]

Rippon lived in a time of remarkable development in English hymnody. During the seventeenth century the English hymn developed alongside the metrical psalm. Religious poems by Anglican divines, such as George Herbert and Thomas Ken, were influential as were works by Puritan leaders like Richard Baxter and John Bunyan. But Isaac Watts and those of his 'school', notably Philip Doddridge, dominated all Dissenting hymnody in the eighteenth century: 'Doddridge encourages, exhorts, expounds; he stands in the Dissenting tradition which valued the sermon as a means of grace'.[4] Gradually the songs of the Wesleyan Revival also began to be sung by Dissenters whilst the Calvinistic wing of the Revival produced hymns by Augustus Toplady (1740-1778) and the *Olney Hymns* (1779) of John Newton (1725-1807) and William Cowper (1731-1800).

Baptists, too, were in what has been called 'the golden age' of their hymnody (1760-1800).[5] The controversies over the legitimacy of congregational singing had virtually ceased,[6] and many of the most prolific hymn-writers Baptists ever produced were active: Daniel Turner (1710-1798), Robert Robinson, Samuel Medley, John Fawcett, and Benjamin Francis.[7] Of special significance were the three Baptist writers whom Rippon used most in his *Selection*. Anne Steele (1717-1778), who called herself 'Theodosia', was a poet of considerable accomplishment. Feminine sensibility and awareness of human suffering were fused with orthodox theology in her hymns.[8] Benjamin Beddome's hymns were marked by clarity and balance with a strong imagination. His hymns provide a 'link between two traditions, the Old Dissent of Watts and the

---

3   A useful review of Baptist hymnody is R.H. Young, 'The History of Baptist Hymnody in England from 1612 to 1800'. There is valuable material on Baptist hymnody in Brown, *The English Baptists of the Eighteenth Century*, and Briggs, *The English Baptists of the Nineteenth Century*.

4   Watson, *The English Hymn*, p. 183.

5   L.F. Benson, *The English Hymn, Its Development and Use in Worship* (New York: 1915), p. 215. (New edition by John Knox Press, Richmond, Va., 1962.)

6   See Brown, *English Baptists of the Eighteenth Century*, pp. 46-48.

7   For these writers, see J. Julian (ed.), *Dictionary of Hymnology* (London: John Murray, 2nd edn, 1907) (hereafter *Julian*), and *DEB*. Francis is an important example of how the Evangelical Revival shaped Baptist hymnody, see Hayden, 'Evangelical Calvinism', pp. 293-95.

8   Watson, *The English Hymn*, pp. 190-98.

pre-Romantic intensity of the Evangelicals',[9] although Horton Davies regards him as an 'indefatigable sermon summarizer in verse'.[10] Although Samuel Stennett (1727-95) is described by Watson as 'unoriginal' and his hymns 'represent the decline of the Baptist tradition into the unexciting', his work was highly regarded by contemporary Baptists.[11]

Careful study of a hymnodist like John Rippon has several values. First, when hymns are recognized as 'the folk-song of the church militant',[12] they help recover a sense of the worshipping-life of an earlier generation. The distinguished hymnologist, L. F. Benson has suggested:

> A hymn may or may not happen to be literature; in any case it is something more. Its sphere, its motive, its canons and its uses are different. It belongs with the things of the Spirit, in the sphere of religious experience and communion with God. Its special sphere is worship, and its fundamental relations are not literary but liturgical.[13]

Similarly, Ernest A. Payne commented that the hymnbook took the place for Dissenters that the Prayer Book enjoyed in the devotional life, public and private, of the Anglican.[14] The hymn was 'both an expression of an individual's religious faith and experience and an act of communal commitment and devotion'.[15] J.R. Watson expresses a similar understanding: 'Hymns are a part of the religious experience which they express; they help to create that experience'.[16] Rippon's books suggest the devotional content of Baptist worship during his lifetime and are a valuable pointer to Baptist spirituality for the period.

Secondly, hymns (as with the Prayer Book again) are invaluable for the preservation and communication of theology. John Wesley (1703-1791) described his 1780 hymnbook as 'a body of practical and experimental divinity', and used it as such.[17] 'We recite no Creed, because our hymns are full of the form of sound words', B.L. Manning declared for

---

9   Watson, *The English Hymn*, p. 202.

10   Davies, *Worship and Theology in England*, 3, p. 136.

11   Watson, *The English Hymn*, pp. 202-204.

12   E. Routley, *Hymns and Human Life* (London: John Murray, 2nd edn, 1969), p. 3.

13   Benson, *The English Hymn*, p. viii.

14   E.A. Payne, *The Free Church Tradition in the Life of England* (London: SCM Press, 3rd edn, 1951), p. 95.

15   Watts, *The Dissenters*, 2, p. 180.

16   Watson, *The English Hymn*, p. 16.

17   *A Collection of Hymns, for the use of the people called Methodists* (London: 1780).

Nonconformists.[18] Ian Bradley claims that hymns in the Victorian era were 'the most powerful single medium for the transmission of Christian doctrine and the expression of religious feeling, speaking both to committed believers and to the much larger ranks of half-believers'.[19] This process began with hymnbooks like Rippon's and the widespread use of his book among Baptists was a theologically unifying force of almost incalculable significance. Hymns belong to those who sing them. A congregation becomes 'an interpretive community':

> They interpret the hymns...in the way they have come to understand them, almost unconsciously, in the light of doctrine, belief and history. Hymns are sung by those people who share certain things: Bible-reading, doctrine, common prayer, and moral precept...congregations sing because of what they believe, and believe because of what they sing.[20]

Good hymns are related, then, to both experience and doctrine. Donald Davie has argued that this was especially true of Rippon's era:

> ...the great congregational hymns of the eighteenth century are certainly devotional writings; they appeal to experience, an experience which they sometimes try to provoke or to ease an entrance for. And yet their peculiar glory is that at their best they are doctrinally exact, scrupulous and specific. Theological niceties are *not* sterile- not so long as they can be translated into worshipping experience.[21]

Few ordinary Baptists had read John Gill's tedious tomes, but most of them sang from Rippon's book. This was a responsibility Rippon fully recognized and his book promoted the orthodox but moderate Calvinism he espoused.

Finally, Rippon's careful collection, frequent improvement, and wide distribution of many hymns by Baptists was of cardinal significance in the promotion and preservation of the best of Baptist hymnody, as well as influencing the continued use of the best hymns from other sources. The role that hymnody played in the life of the churches during this period became increasingly significant.

Rippon's three hymn-books were: *The Selection*, greatly enlarged in the tenth (1800) and twenty-seventh (1828) editions; *A Selection of*

---

18   B.L. Manning, *The Hymns of Wesley and Watts* (London: Epworth, 1942), p. 136.

19   I. Bradley, *Abide with Me, The World of Victorian Hymns* (London: SCM Press, 1997), p. xvi.

20   Watson, *The English Hymn*, p. 18.

21   D. Davie, *The Eighteenth-Century Hymn in England* (Cambridge: Cambridge University Press, 1993), p. 14.

Psalm and Hymn Tunes (c. 1791); An Arrangement of the *Psalms, Hymns, and Spiritual Songs of the Rev. Isaac Watts*, (1801).

The *Selection*

Rippon's *Selection* enjoyed a phenomenal success simply because he satisfied a deep need for a good hymn collection. When Rippon began at Carter Lane the hymns most commonly in use among Baptists were those by Isaac Watts (1674-1748), mainly from his *Hymns and Spiritual Songs* (1707) and *Psalms of David* (1719), frequently republished together and known as *Watts' Hymns and Psalms*.[22] Watts' hymns were based on Scripture but also 'represented the thoughts and feelings of a man who was engaged with the philosophical and religious ideas of his age'.[23] His joy in the created world, reflected in his hymns, resulted from his awareness of scientific discoveries. He used words with 'clarity and confidence' whilst his hymns were always designed to aid the worship of the people. Watts was a genius who combined 'the clarity of a rhetorician' with the force and energy of religious emotion.[24] Indeed, Donald Davie has suggested: 'There is quite clearly *prima facie* quantitative evidence for supposing that Watts's *Hymns and Psalms* ('Watts Entire', as it came to be called) has been more influential than any of the works of its century that we think of as most popular...'[25]

Baptists found the hymns of Watts eminently suitable: they were doctrinally orthodox, objective in tone, rich in emotion but free from frivolities. The grace of God, the person of Christ and his redemptive action were central themes of his hymns. One result of Watts' ascendancy was a bias towards 'homiletical hymnody' among the Baptists: many of his hymns were either Scripture paraphrases, or freely employed scriptural imagery. Hence they were helpful as hymns to follow the sermon. But not even Watts could be expected to find a hymn suitable for any text the pastor might choose, as Rippon observed.[26] One of two things could be done. If the pastor fancied himself a poet (and many did) he wrote his own hymn: Benjamin Beddome at Bourton-on-the-Water

---

22   See H. Escott, *Isaac Watts Hymnographer. A Study of the Beginnings, Development, and Philosophy of the English Hymn* (London: Independent Press, 1962). Still valuable is A.P. Davis, *Isaac Watts His Life and Works* (London: Independent Press, 1948).

23   Watson, *The English Hymn*, p. 133.

24   Watson, *The English Hymn*, pp. 141, 149.

25   D. Davie, *A Gathered Church. The Literature of the English Dissenting Interest, 1700-1930* (London: Routledge & Kegan Paul, 1978), pp. 33-34.

26   *Selection*, preface.

wrote a weekly hymn for his Sunday sermon.[27] Or, the clerk could give out a hymn from some other source.

The only specifically Baptist general collection available before 1787 was the 'Bristol Collection' (1769), edited by Caleb Evans and John Ash, which contained 412 hymns.[28] This was evidently designed to replace Watts' own books in popular Baptist usage since 137 of his hymns were included. Several Baptist writers, notably Anne Steele, but also Beddome, Turner, and Robinson were represented. Important though this book was, it proved to be inadequate for several reasons. Baptists were not prepared to relinquish their easy access to all of Watts' hymns - what was needed was a supplement to Watts (such as Rippon produced), not an alternative to Watts. The general usefulness of the Bristol book for public services, especially for hymns related to the sermons, was restricted. (No scriptural index was provided.) Certain doctrinal or occasional needs were neglected: no hymns specially designated for the doctrines of election or perseverance (vital Calvinistic themes), and none specifically on the Holy Spirit; only three on baptism, no general hymns for singing 'after the sermon', and very few suited to the meetings for prayer, or association gatherings. During the succeeding years many good hymns had gradually found their way into the worship of the Baptists, and many original hymns of quality had been restricted to only one or two congregations. The only other Baptist books available were collections of the poems and hymns of individual authors, such as those by Daniel Turner,[29] Benjamin Wallin,[30] Anne Steele,[31] John Needham (d. c.1786),[32] John Fellows (d. 1785),[33] and John Fawcett.[34] But these were comparatively restricted in scope, and no congregation could be expected to possess all of them. Rippon clearly understood the need for one good collection. Worshippers had no idea who had written many hymns sung in their services, nor where they could read them again for their private devotions. Rippon found that his people continually asked him, 'Why could we not have some of the best Hymns in all these Authors put together, and used with Dr. Watts?'[35] Thus the impetus for the *Selection* arose directly out of Rippon's own pastoral experience.

---

27   *Register* 2 (1794-97), p. 322.

28   *A Collection of Hymn Adapted to Public Worship* (Bristol: 1769); see E. Sharpe, 'Bristol Baptist College and the Church's Hymnody', *BQ* 28.1 (1979), pp. 7-16.

29   *Divine Songs, Hymns and other Poems* (Reading: 1747).

30   *Evangelical Hymns and Songs* (London: 1750).

31   *Poems on Subjects chiefly Devotional, by Theodosia* (2 vols; London, 1760).

32   *Hymns Devotional and Moral* (Bristol: 1768).

33   *Hymns on Believers' Baptism* (Birmingham: 1773).

34   *Hymns adapted to the circumstances of Public Worship and Private Devotion* (Leeds: 1782).

35   *Selection*, p. ii.

Rippon quickly discovered that a similar need existed in America, where Watts also reigned supreme. The first Baptist hymnbook was produced in Newport, Rhode Island, in 1766, *Hymns and Spiritual Songs, collected from several authors*. But there was a need for good, specifically Baptist, hymns, especially for baptismal services. During 1786 Rippon wrote to two Baptist leaders, Thomas Ustick in Philadelphia,[36] and James Manning, of Providence, R. I. [37] He gave them full plans of his *Selection*, asked for any American hymns of merit, and generally made plans for the sale of his books in America. The success of the *Selection* on both sides of the Atlantic demonstrated the urgent need for just such a book. Some leading Americans regretted any lingering dependence on the English, even for their hymnbooks. Samuel Jones (1735-1814) of Philadelphia wrote to James Manning about this in 1788 but Manning replied: 'I agree with you that we ought not to send to England for all our books, but our people are so backward that little is to be expected from them in the way of printing an Edition of Hymns...I hope the period is not very far distant when Books printed in England will be interdicted by us...'[38]

Rival productions in America, however, could not supplant Rippon's book.[39] For example, Samuel Jones and Burgiss Allison (1753-1827) were asked to prepare a hymnal 'for the use of the associated churches' by the influential Philadelphia Association in 1788. This collection appeared in 1790.[40] Jones tried to persuade Richard Furman (1755-1825) of Charleston to promote his book. Furman replied, 'Most of our friends in Charleston have been obtaining Rippon's Selection lately, which may be some obstacle to their purchasing this directly'.[41] Rippon was critical of Jones' book. He was surprised by the typographical errors and annoyed at the ease with which Jones simply took hymns from Watts and his own book. He was not impressed with the 'poetical talents of the Compilers'. Even though Rippon tried to soften his criticisms to Jones

---

36   Letter dated 18 August 1786 (original at American Baptist Historical Society).

37   Undated letter (1786), (original at Brown University, Providence, R.I.) For Manning (1739-1791), see R.A. Guild, *Early History of Brown University, including the Life, Times, and Correspondence of President Manning* (Providence, R.I.: 1897) and *DEB*.

38   Manning to Jones, 18 July 1788; cited by H. Davies, 'The American Revolution and the Baptist Atlantic', *BQ* 36.3 (1995), pp. 142-43. For Jones, see *DEB*.

39   W.J. Reynolds, *Companion to Baptist Hymnal* (Nashville: Broadman, 1976), pp. 11-12; and see below for editions of Rippon in USA.

40   H.S. Burrage, *Baptist Hymn Writers and their Hymns* (Portland; 1888), p. 641. For Allison, see *DEB*.

41   Furman to Jones, 19 February 1791, cited by Davies, 'The American Revolution and the Baptist Atlantic', p. 142. For Furman, see *DEB*.

the latter was offended. Rippon quickly apologised; 'I ASK YOUR PARDON A THOUSAND TIMES', he wrote to Jones.[42]

Preparations, Sources and Editing

Rippon listed four specific aims for his *Selection*. First, he emphasized that his book was intended not to supplant, but to extend the use of Watts. Rippon felt he had used more of Watts' hymns (39) from his other books than had previously appeared in any other collection. The full title of his book included, 'Intended to be an Appendix to Dr. Watts's Psalms and Hymns' and he added in the Preface: 'it would pain me very much to find any one suspecting my most cordial attachment to them'.[43] Undoubtedly, one of the principal reasons for the success of his *Selection* was that Rippon supported this loyalty to the traditions and theology of Watts.

Secondly, it was a *Supplement* to Watts. During the last quarter of the eighteenth century, several such supplements appeared. (Perhaps the most successful, prior to Rippon's, was G. Burder, *Collection of Hymns from various Authors, intended as a Supplement to Dr. Watts* [1784, 25 editions by 1827]. This contained only 211 hymns.) Rippon suggested Watts did not have many 'whole' hymns on:

> ...the Characters of Christ - the Work of the Spirit - the Christian Graces and Tempers - the Parables of the New Testament - the Ordinance of Baptism - and but few suited to Associations and General Meetings of Churches and Ministers - Ordinations - Church meetings - Meetings of Prayer - Annual Sermons to Young People, &c.[44]

These aspects Rippon supplied in his book.

Thirdly, the *Selection* was an *Appendix* to Watts, that is, it contained many hymns on the same themes: 'that we may not always sing of the same Thing in the Same Words but enjoy Variety in the Work of Praise'. Rippon realized that 'Too great a variety is scarcely to be conceived of', so added a section of general hymns suitable for singing after sermons.[45] This is a clear confirmation of Rippon's homiletical concern.

Fourthly, Rippon tried to introduce a 'Variety of Measures'. He utilized, in fact, some twenty-three metres, and for the fourth edition

---

42   Rippon to Jones, 24 August 1793, cited by Davies, 'The American Revolution and the Baptist Atlantic', p. 142.

43   *Selection,* p. iii. (All references, unless otherwise indicated; are from the fifth edition of the *Selection.*)

44   *Selection*, p. iv.

45   *Selection*, p. iv.

added a page explaining these different metres. The most frequently employed metres were Long Metre (230 hymns), Common Metre (199), and Short Metre (34).

Rippon confessed that the materials might well have 'appeared to greater advantage' had others handled them. He hoped that it would not be deemed presumptuous, for 'a Junior Brother', to 'walk abroad and gather up the Golden Ears which have long lain scattered in the Fields of Piety and Genius, that so a Sheaf of Gratitude might be presented by an affectionate Pastor to his affectionate People'.[46] Rippon had been actively interested in hymnody since 1778 when he began carefully examining all the editions of Watts.[47] He had assisted, in 1786, to produce an enlarged version, (using more of Watts' hymns) of Watts' *Hymns and Psalms*.[48] Certainly Rippon brought to the task a capacity for hard work, attention to detail, a discriminating poetic taste, and a sensitive awareness of Baptist needs.

In selecting suitable hymns Rippon examined 'more than *Ninety* printed Volumes of Hymn-Books, Hymns, Psalms, &c attentively perusing all the Collections I could obtain in this Country and from America'.[49] Thus, he had to select from literally thousands of available hymns. In fact, the only American hymns used were those by Samuel Davies (1723-1761), published by Thomas Gibbons (1720-1785) in 1769.[50] Rippon confidently claimed that his book 'ought to contain a greater variety of Subjects and Metres, than either of the Collections extant'.[51]

Some hymns, of course, had to be included because of their popularity. Hence, some 110 hymns from the 'Bristol Collection' were also in Rippon's book. Whilst several hymns were common to all books, the popular core of hymns is illustrated by the numbers which had earlier appeared in these popular collections: Burder's: 70; Conyer's 1774 *Collection*: 66; Toplady's: 55; Hill's: 45; Lady Huntingdon's: 39.[52]

---

46   *Selection*, p. viii.

47   Rippon, *Watts*, p. iv.

48   Rippon, *Watts*, p. viii.

49   *Selection*, p. v. More than sixty books probably used by Rippon have been examined in the preparation of this analysis.

50   For Davies (1723-1761), see *Julian*, pp. 280-81 and *DEB*; T. Gibbons, *Hymns adapted to Divine Worship* (1769). For Gibbons, see *Julian*, p. 420.

51   *Selection*, p. vi.

52   (R. Conyers), *A Collection of Psalms and Hymns from various authors for the use of serious and devout Christians of every Denomination. A new edition, with additions* (London: 1774); A.M. Toplady, *Psalms and Hymns for Public and Private Worship* (London: 1776); R. Hill, *Collection of Psalms and Hymns, chiefly intended for Public Worship* (London: 1783); *A Select Collection of Hymns to be universally sung in all the Countess of Huntingdon's Chapels. Collected by Her Ladyship* (London: 1780).

Then there were 'more than Three Hundred others', which had been previously printed, but had not appeared in a general collection. For example, Rippon used 101 hymns by Doddridge,[53] about twice as many as other hymnals (for example, 'Bristol' had 41); 53 by Anne Steele; 39 by Watts from other than his *Hymns and Psalms*;[54] 34 from the *Gospel Magazine* (1774-1784), although of these only ten had not appeared in other collections; 32 from the *Olney Collection*; 25 by Thomas Gibbons.[55]

About 'one-fourth part of the Whole', or as Rippon claimed in the Preface to the tenth edition, about 'one hundred and fifty' hymns, had not been previously published. About two-thirds of these original hymns may be readily identified: 38 by Samuel Stennett, who had given Rippon 'more than 70 hymns';[56] 42 by Beddome, who had given Rippon 'above 500' hymns[57] (although 13 had been in the 'Bristol Collection'); 8 by Turner, 5 by Francis, 4 by Ryland (Junior), 2 by 'K',[58] Robinson's 'Mighty God, while angels bless thee', and several anonymous hymns, some of which were by Rippon himself.

Rippon indicated the authorship for 395 hymns. Rippon did not subscribe to the theory later known as the 'death of an author', when authors' names were deliberately omitted in order to stress the content of the hymn rather than draw attention to the writer.[59] At times Rippon gave only 'a single letter', rather than the full names, indicating he was unsure of the authorship, or the hymn had been considerably altered. Authors of a further 123 hymns have been traced, so that about 70 remain as anonymous.[60] Whilst 187, or 32%, of the hymns (in the first edition) are

---

53   P. Doddridge *Hymns founded on Various Texts in the Holy Scriptures* (ed. J. Orton; London: 1755).

54   For a list of Watts' other works, see *Julian*, p. 1237.

55   A second volume of *Hymns adapted to Divine Worship* was issued by Gibbons in 1784.

56   J. Rippon to T. Ustick, 18 August 1786.

57   J. Rippon to T. Ustick, 18 August 1786.

58   'K' has been identified as: (i) George Keith, who was John Gill's son-in-law (see chapter 3); and (ii) Robert Keene. See *Julian*, p. 537. For Keene's help to Rippon with the *Tune Book*, see below in this chapter. Keene was first suggested in 1822 by Dr. Fletcher, a friend of Thomas Walker's. In the 1844 *Comprehensive Rippon* the hymn is attributed to 'Kirkham' (otherwise unknown) and in Spurgeon's *Our Own Hymnbook* (London: 1866) to George Keith. See W.J. Reynolds, *Hymns of our Faith. A Handbook for the Baptist Hymnal* (Nashville: Broadman, 1964), p. 70.

59   Watson, *The English Hymn*, p. 267 who cites the preface to R.W. Almond, *Hymns for Occasional Use in the Parish Church of St Peter, in Nottingham* (Nottingham: 1819), p. xi.

60   A full list of the authors represented in the *Selection* is given in Table 2, and where known, the denominational affiliation is added.

known to be by Baptists, Rippon was not unduly influenced by the denominational allegiances of the authors.

For a further 21 hymns, the name of the collection from which the hymn had been taken was acknowledged, although the fact that Hymn 157 was taken from the 'General Baptist Collection' was omitted after the first edition.[61] Similarly, the name of John Adams (1751-1835) as author of Hymn 108 was not given after the first edition: Adams was excluded from the Northampton church for doctrinal errors.[62] No attempt was made to conceal the use made of the Wesleys' hymns, although 'JCW' was sometimes used rather than the full name.

The most popular hymn-writer in the *Selection* was Doddridge, with 105 hymns by the 27th edition (101 in the first edition). Baptist writers most frequently utilized were Anne Steele, Benjamin Beddome, and Samuel Stennett. Eighteen Baptist poets had hymns in the first edition. Non-Baptists most often selected were Watts, Gibbons, John and Charles Wesley, John Newton, William Cowper, Augustus Toplady, John Cennick (1718-1755) and Samuel Davies. Clearly the Dissenting hymn-writers dominated. But the inclusion of some 24 Wesleyan hymns in 1787 is significant. Alexander Knox later suggested that one of the signs of the decline of Calvinism among Dissenters was the increasing use made of the Wesleys' hymns.[63]

In the preface to the tenth edition, Rippon commented about the original hymns in the first edition, 'Some of these, on different subjects, I had the pleasure of composing.'[64] Again, some in the enlarged edition were by him: 'To distinguish those in the enlargement, which are my own compositions, would neither add the embellishments of piety or poetry to them, nor, perhaps answer any other valuable end.'[65] This modesty of Rippon is a frustration for students of hymnody, but some discussion of possible original hymns by him is offered in Appendix 3.

To alter hymns was an almost necessary procedure for any self-respecting hymn-editor. In part this reflects the uniqueness of the hymn as a literary form. The Church, claims J.R. Watson, regards a hymn as

---

61   Evidently this was *Hymns and Spiritual songs, mostly collected from various authors* (1772); see Whitley, *Baptist Bibliography*, 1, p. 195, ref. 50-772, but I have not seen a copy of this work.

62   Burrage, *Baptist Hymn Writers and their Hymns*, pp. 100-102.

63   *Remains of Alexander Knox, Esq.* (4 vols; London: 1837), 3, p. 181, quoted in Walsh, 'Methodism at the end of the eighteenth century', p. 299. Although Knox had in mind the 1801 collection of James Boden and Edward Williams, the trend may be traced earlier in Rippon's book. By contrast, the 'Bristol Collection' had only three hymns by the Wesleys, so Rippon was the one who introduced many of their hymns to the general body of Baptists.

64   *Selection* (10th edn), p. iii.

65   *Selection* (10th edn), p. iv.

'primarily liturgical, textually alterable, and valuable mainly for its doctrinal content'.[66] John Wesley's famous complaint about the treatment that Charles' and his own hymns received was largely ignored.[67] Rippon freely altered several hymns, and was helped in his 'corrections' by Stennett, Turner, Francis, Beddome, and Dunscombe.[68] After the careful examination of as many alterations as have been identified, the general impression of R.H. Young may be confirmed, that Rippon's tampering 'seems to some extent defensible in that his alterations, for the most part, tend to improve the flow of verse rather than alter theological meaning.'[69] Recalling that some 150 hymns were first published by Rippon, it may also be noted that a further 229 hymns were unchanged from some earlier version (not always the original form). Certain authors, notably Doddridge, Watts, Steele, Newton, and Gibbons were rarely altered.

Rippon's alterations fall into two broad types. Some are altered for poetic style or literary improvement and others (relatively few) for doctrinal reasons. Most frequently, verses were simply omitted since hymns of ten or more verses were not generally suitable for congregational purposes. In several cases there is a suspicion that the omission was because of poor poetry or theology. One good illustration, however, is the third verse of Hymn 200 which Rippon omitted after his first edition. Based on the imagery of the Vine and the Branches (John 15) Toplady's hymn becomes ludicrous:

Grafted in thee, by Grace alone,
In Growth I daily rise,
And rais'd on this Foundation-stone
My Top shall reach the Skies.

Perhaps Rippon's chief merit as an editor was the skill shown in more extensive revisions. In at least twenty hymns one or more verses, presumably by Rippon, were added to the original version. Most of these centos passed into common use: to take only the examples listed in Julian, some twenty-four centos by Rippon were widely adopted.[70] The most popular is Rippon's extensive alteration of Edward Perronet's 'All hail the power of Jesus' name!'. This hymn, found in most modern hymnals, is usually correctly designated, 'Edward Perronet, altered John Rippon' and is the outstanding illustration of Rippon's facility for

---

66   Watson, *The English Hymn*, p. 16.
67   Wesley, *A Collection of Hymns*, preface, p. vi. See Manning, *The Hymns of Wesley and Watts*, p. 118.
68   J. Rippon to T. Ustick, 18 August 1786.
69   'The History of Baptist Hymnody', p. 131.
70   References under various hymns in *Julian*.

improving a hymn.[71] This is not the only such instance of a radical alteration. For example, Rippon's version of Toplady's hymn, 'Awake, sweet gratitude, and sing' (number 153), is the text to which later collections are indebted.[72]

Rippon also in ten instances altered a hymn from singular to plural although other changes were often added at the same time. For example, Hymn 100, verse 1, line 1, was changed from 'Where shall I hide this noxious head?' to 'Where shall we sinners hide our heads?'.[73] In only four known instances was the metre of a hymn changed. In each example the hymn is improved. For example, Hymn 264, verse 1, was altered from:

> Lord, though bitter is the cup
> Thy kind hand deals out to me,
> Cheerful I would drink it up,
> Nought can hurt which comes from thee.[74]

to:

> Dear Lord, tho' bitter is the cup
> Thy gracious hand deals out to me,
> I cheerfully would drink it up;
> That cannot hurt which comes from thee.

There are several examples of an inappropriate expression, or bad rhyme being altered. Although not averse to the description of sinners as 'worms' ('vermicular hymns' as Percy Dearmer called them),[75] Rippon did alter one hymn on the Lord's Supper, substituting 'unworthy guests' for 'unworthy worms'.[76] Again, Wesley's 'Ye that pass by, behold the man!' (Hymn 136) was altered probably for aesthetic motives. In Rippon's first edition it read as the original:

---

71   For Perronet (1726-1792), see *Julian.* See Appendix 2 for the texts.

72   *Julian,* p. 103.

73   Watts, *Horae Lyricae* (1834 edn.), p. 72.

74   B. Beddome, *Hymns adapted to Public Worship or Family Devotion, now first published from the manuscripts of the late Rev. B. Beddome* (London: 1817), hymn 206.

75   Quoted by H.W. Foote, *Three Centuries of American Hymnody* (Hamden, Conn.: Shoe String Press, 1961), p. 359.

76   Hymn 472, vs.5, line.4; cf. Watts, *Horae Lyricae,* p. 104.

> 0 thou dear suffering Son of God;
> How doth thy Heart to Sinners move!
> Help us to catch thy precious Blood,
> Help us to taste thy dying Love![77]

The image of the third line was altered in the second edition:

> Sprinkle on us thy precious blood,
> And melt us with thy dying Love!

Possibly, the change of emphasis from the activity of the sinner ('Help us to catch') to that of God ('Sprinkle on us') reflects a theological distinction.

Other infelicitous phrases altered include: the tear 'that secret wets the widow's bed';[78] Wesley's 'slaughtered Hecatombs';[79] Toplady's 'pouring eye-sight on our eyes'.[80]

Rippon was certainly concerned with sound theology in his hymnal:

> I trust it will be found, that the Hymns in this Selection are truly evangelical; but if any Sentiment or Expression has escaped me that is contrary to the sacred Oracles I hope I shall be willing to correct it whenever an opportunity may offer. It would pain me beyond Expression if there were any Hymn in the Book that might give just Reason for offence, to any serious Mind. I hope no Line, nor even Syllable, will be found tending to make the Breaches between good Men wider than they are already.[81]

Rippon accordingly avoided all polemical hymns, such as the one Toplady had included in his *Psalms and Hymns* (1776):

> In vain do blind Arminians try
> By works themselves to justify:
> Thy righteousness, O God, exceeds
> Men's dutys and their brightest deeds.[82]

But concern with theological accuracy is known to have produced alterations in about twenty hymns, although some of these are on minor or uncertain points. Rippon also utilized already 'corrected' versions of hymns, as when he used Toplady's version of Wesley's 'Blow ye the

---

77 Wesley, *A Collection of Hymns*, hymn 24.
78 Hymn 33, vs. 5, line 4; changed in second edition. This hymn was probably by S. Collett, see *Julian*, p. 1593.
79 Hymn 83, vs. 2, line 4; cf. Wesley, *A Collection of Hymns*, hymn 123.
80 Hymn 182, vs. 1, line 8; cf. Toplady, *Psalms and Hymns*, p. 21.
81 *Selection* , pp. vi-vii.
82 Hymn 79.

trumpet, blow'; and designated it as 'altered by Toplady' (hymn 57).[83]
But one hymn by Charles Wesley was certainly altered because of its
Arminian tendency, 'Father of faithful Abra'm hear', a prayer for the
conversion of the Jews. Originally the fourth verse read:

> Come, then, thou great Deliverer, come,
> The veil from Jacob's heart remove;
> Receive thy ancient people home,
> That quicken'd by thy dying love,
> The world may their reception find,
> Life from the dead for all mankind.[84]

The last two lines were altered to remove the suggestion that Christ's
atonement was for all mankind, rather than the elect (Hymn 422):

> The world may their reception view
> And shout to God, the glory due.

Again, another Wesleyan hymn, 'Thou God of glorious majesty'
(Hymn 549), verse 5 originally commenced:

> Be this my one great business here,
> With serious industry and fear,
> Eternal bliss to insure.[85]

This emphasis on man's activity was altered:

> Be this my one great business here,
> With holy trembling, holy fear,
> To make my calling sure!

Indeed, Rippon's concern with theological accuracy prompted him, in
one instance, to add an explanatory note. In the first edition, Hymn 109
(of two verses), began:

> Salvation thro' our dying God
> Is finish'd and complete:

---

83   *Julian*, p. 151. Toplady had altered 'all-atoning Lamb' to 'sin-atoning Lamb'.
84   Wesley, *A Collection of Hymns*, hymn 439.
85   *A Collection of Hymns*, hymn 58.

But in the tenth edition, Rippon added two new verses (probably of his own composition) which emphasized the regenerating influence of the Holy Spirit and added this comment:

> Christ has made a *complete* atonement for the sins of his people, in *that* sense *his* work is finished: The work of the Spirit, which at present, in some of the saints, is only *begun*, in due time shall be completed also; (and then *salvation* will be finished, but not before).

(The words in brackets were added in the twenty-seventh edition). This note is eloquent comment on Rippon's concern with theological orthodoxy.

Another anxiety of Rippon, and of orthodox Calvinists, was that distortion of their faith that issued in Antinomian practices, an issue that, as we have noted, was addressed by Rippon in the Carter Lane church. One example of an alteration because of this concern was given in Hymn 350, which Rippon took from the 'Bristol Collection'.[86] The second verse originally read:

> Accept our faint attempts to love,
> Our frailties, Lord, forgive;
> We would be like thy saints above,
> Unlike them as we live.

The last line was changed by Rippon: 'And praise thee while we live'.

There are very few changes in the sacramental hymns. One hymn (230) that Rippon adapted was by Thomas Gibbons. The fifth verse originally read:

> Now spread the banner of thy love,
> And let us know that we are thine;
> Cheer us with blessings from above,
> With heav'nly Bread, and heav'nly Wine.[87]

Rippon elected to place this hymn under 'Christian Graces - Hope', and avoided any misunderstanding of the significance of the communion elements by deleting the sacramental reference in the fourth line to read: 'With all the joys of hope divine'.

One baptismal hymn (450), by Joseph Stennett, originally read in verse three:

---

86   Hymn 312.
87   T. Gibbons, *Hymns adapted to Divine Worship*, Book 2, hymn 50.

> O sacred rite! by this the name
> Of Jesus we to own begin;
> This is our resurrection pledge,
> And seals the pardon of our sin.[88]

Rippon avoided any reference to baptism as a 'seal', by making the last line read: 'Pledge of the pardon of our sin'. The other theological changes are minor, such as Providence providing not 'all they want',[89] but 'all they need'. (Hymn 288, verse 3, line 4).

Rippon's guiding maxim was constant: he wanted to include hymns that congregations would actually want to sing. Not all hymns work as *congregational* hymns and Rippon's editorial vision was to provide just such hymns. In the process he was concerned to be non-sectarian, to invite all believers to 'sing side by side'.

Arrangement and Contents

Rippon's *Selection* not only contained more hymns than other contemporary collections ('Bristol' with 412 and Toplady's with 419 were the nearest to Rippon's 588 hymns) but was better organized. He arranged the book into seventeen distinct subjects, and gave sub-headings to each page. The pages were numbered so as to agree with the numbers of the hymns on each page, a simple device that greatly speeded up the location of hymns. (In later editions Rippon also suggested a suitable tune from his *Tune Book* for each hymn.) Four general indices were added.[90]

J.R. Watson has castigated the arrangement of Dissenters' hymnbooks during this period:

> These collections were often curiously haphazard in their arrangement: there seems to be no discernible structure in any of them, and no reference to the great festivals of the Christian year. The hymns have a kind of accidental, serendipitous occurrence...[91]

---

88   J. Stennett, *Hymns composed for the Celebration of the Holy ordinance of Baptism* (London: 1712), hymn 12.

89   Beddome, *Hymns adapted to Public Worship*, hymn 549.

90   (1) A Table to find any Hymn by the first Line, which unlike many contemporaries, was highly accurate; (2) 'General Contents', which gave the subject-headings; (3) A Table of Scriptures, an index to suitable hymns for various texts; (4) Contents, a subject-index, with approximately 760 entries.

91   Watson, *The English Hymn*, pp. 266-67.

Watson acknowledges Rippon's as 'the most successful' of these compilations and that his was the 'principal example' of collections intended to supplement Watts.[92] His strictures about arrangement do not really apply to Rippon. Of course hymnbooks by Dissenters of the time did not refer to the 'great festivals of the Christian year': they did not observe them! Rippon pioneered a pattern of arrangement that is clear and logical.

Indeed, R.H. Young has claimed to trace a connection between the arrangement of the *Selection* and the 1677 Particular Baptist Confession of Faith (reaffirmed in 1689).[93] Rippon was familiar with this Confession, and republished it in 1791, but whether he consciously followed it is uncertain. The parallels are only to be expected. Most of the thirty-two 'chapters' or sections of the Confession may be illustrated from the *Selection*, all save a few on oaths, civil magistrates, etc. Rippon, however, began with 'God', not with 'the Holy Scriptures' as did the Confession. The *Selection* evidences both a distinctly Calvinist orthodox theology and a strong evangelistic spirit.

Analysis of the *Selection* reveals much of the theology and piety of Baptists, as understood and promulgated by Rippon. The seventeen main headings begin with fundamental doctrinal themes: God, Creation and Providence, Fall of Man, Scripture, Christ, the Spirit. From the foundation of this theological base the book moves to Christian experience: Christian Life, Worship, the World (its vanity), the Church, Baptism, the Lord's Supper. The last group provides hymns for 'Times and Seasons', Time and Eternity, Death and Resurrection, Judgment and, in last place, a sober but small collection of hymns on Heaven and Hell. The number of hymns Rippon allocated to each section may be seen in Table 1. A large number of hymns, 86 or 15%, are devoted to the Scriptures; 87 or 15% to the Holy Spirit; and 77 or 14% to Christ (although obviously many hymns in other sections have a strong Christological significance). The sections enlarged during succeeding editions are also shown in Table 1.

Lionel Adey has argued that much English hymnody became, in effect, an instrument of class domination, of coercion.[94] He detects two broad traditions from the time of the Wesleys until the First World War: the Learned and the Popular. Despite the fact that Watts and Doddridge, both described as belonging to the Learned tradition, were so popular for so long among Baptists, Adey insists that Baptists generally belonged to the Popular tradition. Rippon's *Selection* is rightly recognized as a major influence on Baptists and, it is suggested, was a factor in moving Baptists

92   Watson, *The English Hymn*, pp. 266, 335.

93   'The History of Baptist Hymnody', p. 162. Cf. Lumpkin, *Baptist Confessions of Faith*, pp. 241-95.

94   L. Adey, *Class and Idol in the English Hymn* (Vancouver: University of British Columbia Press, 1988).

even more firmly into the Popular tradition. This thesis seems to be based more on class analyses of Baptist congregations than any actual study of the hymns themselves.

Adey is also critical of the Calvinism and 'unworldly substance' of Baptist hymnody:

> Predisposed to elephantiasis by the requirement to provide for every conceivable sermon topic, these Baptist hymnals make tedious reading. Their metaphors require the singer constantly to prostrate himself before the divine majesty and give thanks for his deliverance by the blood of Christ from turmoil within and hell-fire hereafter. This life he must envisage as his pilgrimage across a desert or tempestuous sea.[95]

But the crucial question is: did the Baptists of the time find this 'suffocating repetitiousness' as tiresome as a modern critic? All the contemporary evidence suggests that, in fact, hymnals such as Rippon's precisely met the devotional and worshipping needs of the churches in that era.

What kind of theology and worship experience does the *Selection* in fact offer? Clearly people are first invited to praise God and offer thanksgiving for creation and providence. Anne Steele's hymn of praise and invitation (number 12) is typical:

> Ye humble souls, approach your God,
> With songs of sacred praise,
> For he is good, immensely good,
> And kind are all his ways.

William Cowper's famous hymn, 'God moves in a mysterious way', (number 31) was much loved by Calvinist evangelicals:

> Judge not the Lord by feeble sense,
> But trust him for his grace;
> Behind a frowning providence
> He hides a smiling face.

The next doctrine, represented by only five hymns, is the fall of humankind. In Adam, all had sinned (number 38):

> Adam, our Father and our head
> Transgress'd, and justice doom'd as dead;
> The fiery law speaks all despair,
> There's no reprieve or pardon there. (Watts)

---

95   Adey, *Class and Idol*, p. 46.

The central significance of Scripture for evangelical belief is illustrated by the several sub-headings employed. The Bible is a 'Lamp' and 'Guide' for the believer: Anne Steele's, 'Father of Mercies, in thy Word' was one notable hymn here (number 46). The familiar Calvinist emphasis on the necessity of the Law for due appreciation of the Gospel is in hymn 50 (probably by J Maxwell):[96]

> Here, Lord, my soul convicted stands
> Of breaking all thy ten commands:
> And on me justly might'st thou pour
> Thy wrath in one eternal shower.

Most of these hymns conclude on a positive note, by affirming Christ's perfect obedience to the Law.

There are 52 hymns on 'Scripture Doctrines and Blessings'. This major sub-section does demonstrate many parallels with the 1677 Confession, and Rippon clearly tried to balance the number of hymns given to each doctrine.

The characteristically Calvinist tenet of election was not given undue prominence, but is clearly present (Hymn 62, verse 1):

> How happy are we
> Our election who see,
> And venture, O Lord, for salvation on thee!
> In Jesus approv'd,
> Eternally lov'd
> Upheld by thy power we cannot be moved. (Toplady)

The Covenant of Grace (3 hymns) includes the popular hymn by the Methodist, Thomas Olivers, 'The God of Abram praise'; whilst the doctrine of Christ's substitutionary atonement is clearly taught in Hymn 74, verse 2:

> And wast thou punish'd in my stead?
> Didst thou without the city bleed,
> To expiate my stain? (Toplady)

Justification was presented in two hymns, both from the Wesleys, notably John's translation from Count Zinzendorf, 'Jesus, thy blood and righteousness' (number 84). Teaching on Pardon (6 hymns), includes Samuel Davies' popular hymn: 'Great God of wonders!' (number 85). A

---

96   J. Gadsby, *Memoirs of the Principal Hymn-Writers and Compilers of the 17th and 18th Centuries* (London: 2nd edn, 1855), p. 156.

section of four hymns on 'Communion with God in Christ' includes William Cowper's 'O for a closer walk with God' (number 98). Perseverance, another characteristic Calvinist grace, was well presented in two hymns by Doddridge, one (number 103) based on John 10: 27-29, and the other (number 104) on Noah saved in the Ark. Salvation was well summarized in Doddridge's 'Grace! 'tis a charming sound' (number 111).

The section on Scripture Invitations and Promises (15 hymns) offered clear indication of Rippon's evangelical concern, with direct appeals to the consciences of sinners. This was not solely a Methodist emphasis as the Anglican Calvinist Augustus Toplady's adaptation of Hart's 'Come, ye sinners, poor and wretched' (no. 115) indicates.[97] Verse 4 reads:

> Come, ye weary, heavy laden,
> Lost and ruin'd by the fall!
> If you tarry till you're better,
> You will never come at all:
> Not the righteous,
> Sinners Jesus came to call.

Rippon was able to employ three Baptist writers in this section, Stennett (number 114), Fawcett (number 116), and Anne Steele (numbers 117, 120), the last of which was 'The Saviour calls- let every ear'. A collection devoted to Scripture promises introduced the hymn destined to become a Baptist favourite: 'How firm a foundation' (number 128).

The strong Christocentric nature of evangelical faith is clearly suggested by 77 hymns specifically devoted to Christ, arranged in five sections:

1. Incarnation and Ministry (7 hymns). Dissenters were not concerned with the Christian Year, as we have observed, but Wesley's 'Hark, the herald Angels sing' (number 130), Robinson's 'Mighty God while angels bless thee' (number 132), Doddridge's 'Hark, the glad sound the Saviour comes' (number 134), are all well known Advent hymns. There were only three hymns on the Life and ministry of Christ.

2. Suffering and Death (4 hymns). These were to be supplemented, Rippon noted, from the hymns on Redemption and the Lord's Supper.

3. Resurrection and Ascension (7 hymns), of which the most popular still is Charles Wesley's 'Christ, the Lord is risen to-day' (no. 141).

4. Exaltation, Kingly Rule, and Intercession of Christ (9 hymns). Wesley's 'Rejoice the Lord is King' was an outstanding hymn of triumph included here.

---

97   For Joseph Hart (1712-1768), see *Julian*.

5. Characters and Representations of Christ (50 hymns). This was one subject in which Rippon thought Watts deficient. The 'characters' of Christ are all based on Biblical images or types which were held to foretell or represent Christ. Listed in alphabetical order, these included Christ as Advocate, the Brazen Serpent, a Fountain, a Kinsman, Melchizedek, the Rock ('Rock of ages', number 195). The exegesis underlying these hymns may have been eccentric at times, but it confirms a Christocentric emphasis in Baptist preaching.

The Holy Spirit (88 hymns) was another doctrine Rippon felt needed emphasis and for which he had a special concern. He provided for the first time a good section of hymns on this theme for Baptists. ('Bristol' had none.)

1. Influences of the Holy Spirit (11 hymns). These describe the work of the Spirit in Biblical images, such as the Comforter (number 206). But Rippon's adaptation of a ten-verse hymn by Toplady to produce the following poor hymn (number 212) reveals Rippon's love of expressive imagery:

> At anchor laid, remote from home,
> Toiling, I cry, SWEET SPIRIT, come!
> Celestial breeze, no longer stay,
> But swell my sails, and speed my way!
>
> Fain would I mount, fain would I glow,
> And loose my cable from below;
> But I can only spread my sail;
> THOU, THOU must breathe th'auspicious gale!

2. Graces of the Holy Spirit (77 hymns). These 'Christian Graces and Tempers' were placed alphabetically. This is, then, a list of ideal moral qualities for Christians but what is theologically significant is that Rippon should place all these hymns in the section devoted to the Holy Spirit; only the work of God can produce these virtues. Numbers in brackets indicate the number of hymns devoted to each theme: Faith (9), Fear (2), Fortitude (1), Gravity (1). This last hymn, by Watts, included the following sombre verse (229, verse 4):

> What if we wear the richest vest!
> Peacocks and flies are better drest;
> This flesh, with all its gaudy forms,
> Must drop to dust, and feed the worms.

Hope (4), Humility (4), Joy (4), Justice (1), Knowledge (3), Liberality (1), Love to God and Christ (7), Love to the Brethren (including

Fawcett's 'Blest be the tie that binds') (3), Love to Neighbour (1), Love to Enemies (2), Meekness (1), Moderation (2), Patience (2), Peace (1), Rest (1), Repentance (9). The larger number given to this last theme suggests Rippon's evangelistic note, although some, as Samuel Stennett's (270, verses 6 and 7), are excessively sentimental:

> May I round thee cling and twine,
> Call myself a child of thine,
> And presume to claim a part
> In a tender Father's heart.
>
> Yes I may, for I espy
> Pity trickling from thine eye;
> 'Tis a Father's bowels move,
> Move with pardon and with love.

Resignation (4), yet another Calvinistic theme, is encouraged (number 276, verse 4):

> What is the world with all its store?
> 'Tis but a bitter-sweet;
> When I attempt to pluck the rose,
> A pricking thorn I meet. (Beddome)

Self-Denial (2), Serenity (3), Trust (6), Wisdom (1), Zeal for Christ (2).

This section is a thoughtful link to the following collection on 'The Christian Life' (55 hymns) which moves from the more strictly doctrinal emphasis to introduce aspects of Baptist piety. Reminiscent of Wesley's 1780 book with its emphasis on 'the experience of real Christians',[98] Rippon included hymns ranging from first awakenings to faith, to times of backsliding or persecution, and to death. One hymn, by Samuel Stennett, evidences an angelology (307, verse 4):

> Hither, at his command they fly,
> To guard the beds on which we lie;
> To shield our persons, night and day;
> And scatter all our fears away.[99]

---

98   For a discussion of the arrangement of Wesley's book, see Manning, *The Hymns of Wesley and Watts*, pp. 11-12. This is the only instance of Wesley's arrangement possibly influencing Rippon's; in general, Dissenters preferred more doctrinal divisions.

99   For a discussion of Wesley's angelology, see J.E. Rattenbury, *The Evangelical Doctrines of Charles Wesley's Hymns* (London: Epworth, 1941), pp. 325-327. Similarly, for Watts' angelology, see the index to Rippon's *Watts*.

Rippon's arrangement under 'Worship' (69 hymns) reflects the various contexts for worship for Baptists.

1. Private Worship (4 hymns) designed to help the Christian in prayer and Bible reading.

2. Family Worship (5 hymns) including a hymn to be sung on moving to a new home (number 333) and two 'prayers for children'. These could be used in a way comparable to a 'Dedication' service, in which the prayer for children is specifically that they will later come to faith and baptism (number 336, verse 4):

> May they receive thy word,
> Confess the Saviour's name,
> Then follow their despised LORD
> Thro' the baptismal stream.

No hymns of this type had been included in the 'Bristol' book.

3. Public Worship (8 hymns). Rippon included three hymns suitable for the opening of a new meeting-house, one of which (number 338) was first sung at the opening of Horsley, Gloucestershire, meeting house in 1774, as Rippon noted.

4. Lord's Day (7 hymns). The spirit of this special day was thus expressed by Joseph Stennett, a Seventh Day Baptist,[100] (number 348):

> In holy duties let the day
> In holy pleasures, pass away:
> How sweet, a sabbath thus to spend,
> In hope of one that ne'er shall end!

5. Before Prayer (6 hymns) including Cowper's 'What various hindrances we meet', and a paraphrase of the Lord's Prayer by J. Straphan (no. 358) which was first published by Rippon.

6. Before Sermon (13 hymns). This and the next section emphasized the prominent part assigned to the sermon in Baptist worship. The sermon was expected to be a medium of divine power, producing conviction and conversion (hymn 360, verse 2):

---

100 For Stennett (1663-1713), see *DNB;* B.A Ramsbottom, 'The Stennetts', in Haykin (ed.), *The British Particular Baptists1638-1910,* 1, pp. 136-38.

Jesus, the work is wholly thine
To form the heart anew;
Now let thy sovereign grace divine
Each stubborn soul subdue. (adapted from Beddome.)[101]

Preaching was likened to casting the 'Gospel-net' (hymn 366). The sense
of expectancy is again illustrated in this verse by Jonathan Evans:[102]

Come, thou soul-transforming Spirit,
Bless the sower and the seed:
Let each heart thy grace inherit,
Raise the weak, thy hungry feed:
From the Gospel
Now supply thy people's need. (number 368, verse 1).

7. After sermon (21 hymns). Once the seed of the word had been
sown, only the power of God could 'make it spring and grow' (hymns
372, 373). Rippon adapted a Moravian antiphonal hymn by Cennick
(number 384) to emphasize that all glory was solely God's.[103] Fawcett's
'Lord, dismiss us with thy blessing' and paraphrases of three New
Testament benedictions concluded this section (numbers 389-392).

8. Doxologies (5 hymns, all of one verse). Services customarily
concluded with a doxology, such as Bishop Ken's 'Praise God from
whom all blessings flow' (number 395).

But worshippers eventually had to leave the sanctuary. Five hymns
reminded the devout of how they should view the world. Whilst the
characteristically negative aspect of Calvinism is not unduly prominent,
Christians are to renounce all worldly ambition:

Begone, for ever, mortal things!
Thou mighty mole-hill, earth, farewell!
Angels aspire on lofty wings,
And leave the globe for ants to dwell. (402, verse 4; Watts).

Life within the Dissenting chapel was reflected in the section entitled
'The Gospel Church' (39 hymns). There are hymns for the formation of
a church, for ordination, including one suitable for a service when a
church called one of its members to enter the ministry. The relationship
between pastors, deacons and people is seen in ten hymns that refer to

---

101 See *Julian*, pp. 567-68.
102 *Julian*, p. 358.
103 *Julian*, p. 673.

events such as the dangerous illness of a pastor or a pastor's departure from his people, which includes this solemn warning (414, verses 4, 5):

> But they who heard the word in vain,
> Tho' oft and plainly warn'd,
> Will tremble when they meet again
> The ministers they scorned.
>
> On your own heads your blood will fall,
> If any perish here;
> The preachers who have told you *all,*
> Shall stand approv'd and clear. (Olney Hymns)[104]

Then came a people's prayer for their pastor (415), and a pastor's 'wish for his people' (416). One hymn was suitable for the election of deacons, whose ministry was defined in the tradition of John Gill, (417, verse 3):

> Happy in Jesus, their own LORD,
> May they his sacred table spread,
> The table of their pastor fill,
> And fill the holy poor with bread.[105]

A few missionary hymns should be carefully noted. Hymns 419 and 420 (based on one hymn by Gibbons) evidence a longing to see the Gospel preached in every land, 'to the Jews', 'the untutor'd Indian tribes', 'Afric's sable sons'.[106] One verse, as we have seen, was something of a motto for Rippon (419, verse 7):

> Asia and Africa, resound
> From shore to shore his fame:
> And thou, America, in songs
> Redeeming love proclaim.

This was quoted in the Preface to the *Selection,* and on the cover of every issue of the *Register.* That these hymns were being sung before 1792, when the missionary society was formed, is suggestive of a global vision for the Gospel already present among key Baptists.

Associations, or 'General Meetings of Churches & Ministers', an important dimension of Baptist life at this period were provided with nine

---

104 *Olney Hymns*, Book 2, hymn 28.
105 For Gill's teaching on deacons, see above, chapter 3.
106 Gibbons, *Hymns adapted to Divine Worship*, Book 2, hymn 69.

hymns.[107] The emphasis was upon prayer for pastors, and Beddome's fine hymn 'Father of mercies, bow thine ear' (426) was introduced here. There are a few hymns which pray for revival, such as John Ryland's refrain added to a hymn by John Newton (Number 427):

Lord revive us,
All our help must come from thee!

Such hymns were doubtless sung in the area of the Northamptonshire Association, where the influential call to prayer for revival was issued in 1784. Again in this section there is a longing for the spread of the Gospel, as in William Williams' 1772 hymn (altered by Rippon): 'O'er the gloomy hills of darkness' (428, verse 2):

Let the Indian, let the Negro
Let the rude Barbarian see
That divine and glorious conquest,
Once obtain'd on Calvary;
Let the Gospel
Loud resound from pole to pole.

To what extent such hymns helped prepare for missionary advance is uncertain, but clearly when the wave of missionary enthusiasm broke over the churches these hymns helped promote its message. This section was expanded in later editions.

'Collections for Poor Churches and Poor Brethren' (5 hymns) was a regular feature of Baptist life, not least at Carter Lane Church, as we have noted. Hymn 434 is a good example:

The Lord, who rules the world's affairs,
For me a well-spread board prepares;
My grateful thanks to him shall rise,
He knows my wants, those wants supplies.

And shall I grudge to give *his* poor
A mite from all my generous store?
NO, LORD! the friends of thine and thee,
Shall always find a friend in me.

---

107 For the importance of associations, see Brown, *The English Baptists of the Eighteenth Century*, pp. 85-90.

Hymns for Church Meetings (5 hymns) provide opportunity for praise for converted sinners or regret at the backsliding of a believer, as in John Newton's hymn (number 439, verses 1,7):

> When any turn from Zion's way,
> (Alas what numbers do!)
> Methinks I hear my Saviour say,
> *Wilt thou forsake me too?*
>
> What anguish has that question stirr'd-
> *If I will also go?*
> Yet, LORD! Relying on thy word,
> I humbly answer, NO!

Central to Baptist identity is the baptism of believers and Rippon provided a good collection of baptismal hymns.[108] ('Bristol' had included only three hymns specifically linked with baptism.) There are thirteen hymns for singing before baptizing, and four afterwards, with thirteen single verses to which this note was added:

> As it is now pretty common to sing by the water-side, and as some of our brethren in the country give out a verse or two, while they are administering the ordinance, it is hoped these single verses will be acceptable.

The theology of baptism emphasized baptism as an act of obedience, of following the example of Christ (number 445, verse 3):

> Plainly here his footsteps tracing
> Follow him without delay;
> Gladly his command embracing,
> Lo! your captain leads the way:
>
> View the rite with understanding,
> Jesu's grave before you lies;
> Be interr'd at his commanding,
> After his example rise. (Fawcett)

Baptism is an 'emblem' of Christ's passion (number 449, verse 2), and there are some references to the activity of the Spirit (number 460):

---

108 Daniel Turner of Abingdon helped Rippon with this section: note to hymn 442 (in first edition only).

Eternal Spirit, heavenly Dove,
On these baptismal waters move;
That we, thro' energy divine,
May have the substance with the sign. (Beddome)

There was a clear progression from baptism to communion (number 452, verse 5):

Thus we, dear Saviour, own thy name,
Receive us rising from the stream;
Then to thy table let us come,
And dwell in Zion as our home. (J. Fellows, altered)[109]

The other sacrament or 'ordinance' among Baptists was the Lord's Supper. Rippon titled some of the nineteen hymns in this section as 'sacramental hymns', but they are mainly appropriate meditations upon the death of Christ, with little specific reference to the Table. One notable exception is Samuel Stennett's, which seems to go beyond a bare 'memorialist' emphasis (number 483, verses 1, 4, 5):

Here at thy table, Lord, we meet,
To feed on food divine:
Thy body is the bread we eat,
Thy precious blood the wine.

His body torn with rudest hands
Becomes the finest bread:
And with the blessing he commands,
Our noblest hopes are fed.

His blood, that from each op'ning vein
In purple torrents ran,
Hath fill'd this cup with glorious wine,
That cheers both God and man.

Study of subsequent collections suggests that later editors were more influenced towards a Zwinglian position than is apparent in Rippon.[110]

'Times and Seasons' (52 hymns) suggests how Baptists together celebrated their community life. There were hymns for morning and

---

109 *Hymns on Believers' Baptism*, hymn 43.

110 For a helpful analysis of Baptist theology of the Lord's Supper as found in Baptist hymnals, including Rippon's, see Walker, *Baptists at the Table*, pp. 17-30, and for the twentieth century see M. Collis, 'The Lord's Supper in British Baptist Hymnology in the Twentieth Century', *BQ* 38.6 (2000), pp. 290-304.

evening (7), and Seasons of the Year (11). Spring, a sign of God's goodness, was also a parable of the need for God's 'warmest beams' to turn 'thy winter into Spring' (Hymn 498). Summer and the harvest had an obvious spiritual application, whilst winter was a picture of the barren soul (Hymn 507). Other hymns were for: New Year's Day (3), notably Robinson's 'Come thou fount of every blessing'; Birthday (1); Wedding (1) by Berridge,[111] to which Rippon added the last verse; Welcome and Farewell of friends (3); Youth (7). (Two of these were designated for Sunday Schools in 1787, when the movement was in its early days. One was antiphonal in form, verses alternating between 'Congregation' and 'Children': Number 522); Old Age (1); Fast and Thanksgiving Days (12). These days were held either because of the spiritual condition of a local church, or more commonly, as part of a national call. One hymn prays for success in war (527, verse 4):

> With all the boasted pomp of war
> In vain we dare the hostile field;
> In vain, unless the LORD be there;
> Thy arm above is Britain's shield. (Steele)

There were hymns of thanksgiving for victory, and two to be sung on 5th November, the anniversary of the capture of Guy Fawkes and the failure of the Gunpowder Plot, (number 534, verse 3):

> When hell and Rome combin'd their power,
> And doom'd these isles their certain prey,
> Thy hand forbade the fatal hour,
> Their impious plots in ruin lay! (Steele)

'Sickness and Suffering' (6 hymns) reflected upon the brevity of life, the necessity of redeeming time, and the frailty of man. Hymn 548, verse 1, is typical:

> Eternity is just at hand;
> And shall I waste my ebbing sand,
> And careless view departing day,
> And throw my inch of time away!

'Death and Resurrection' featured 20 hymns. A pathetic feature was the need for hymns specifically referring to the death of children, or offering comfort to bereaved parents. From numerous 'dying

---

111 For John Berridge (1716-93), an Anglican, see *Julian*, p. 138.

testimonies' this section is known to have been widely used.[112] There were two hymns on the resurrection of the body, in which the Biblical statement was interpreted quite literally (as in hymn 569, verse 5):

> They leave the dust, and on the wing
> Rise to the midway air,
> In shining garments meet their King,
> And low adore him there. (Watts)

'Day of Judgment' (10 hymns) and 'Hell and Heaven' (9 hymns) were the last sections. There is, again, no undue emphasis upon the negative. Charles Wesley's 'Lo! He comers with clouds descending' is by far the best of these. Only three are about hell, in general terms, and one is simply a paraphrase of the parable of the Rich Man and Lazarus (number 582). Stennett's 'On Jordan's stormy banks I stand' (number 584) was long popular, but inevitably Isaac Watts had the honour of the last hymn, 'Earth has engross'd my love too long' (number 588).

To read these hymns gives an insight into the piety and faith of Rippon's contemporaries. To sing them together can only have reinforced their convictions and aspirations.

Editions of the Selection

Rippon's commitment to producing the best possible hymnal is evidenced by his careful attention to improving the *Selection* in successive editions, so successfully that his book was widely used for more than two generations. At the same time an analysis of these editions reveals the developing life and needs of the churches. Indeed, the *Selection* became an agent for consolidating those developments in church life in both England and America.

IN ENGLAND

Before the book was published, Rippon was assured of support 'from one End of the Kingdom to the other'.[113] Others who had been contemplating a hymnbook gave way to Rippon's project.[114] Rippon gained the support of the associations, as he wrote to Manning in 1787, 'You will be glad to hear that it has met with a respect at each of our Associations superior to any Baptist publication in my time'.[115]

---

112 *Register* 3 (1798-1801), pp. 101, 389, 409; 4 (1801-02), pp. 1144.

113 *Selection*, p. v.

114 Cf. (anon.) to Rippon, Newcastle, 28 June 1786, B.L. Add. MSS. 25389, f. 568.

115 Rippon to Manning, 29 June 1787 (original at Brown University).

Accordingly the *Selection* was advertised on association Circular Letters, and used at association meetings.[116] There are numerous orders for the *Selection* preserved among Rippon's papers, and almost every county in England, as well as Wales, Ireland and Scotland is represented. The distribution of orders must have involved Rippon and his helpers in extensive time and effort.

The first edition, of which three thousand copies were printed by June 1787,[117] had been sold out by February 1788 when Rippon prepared a second edition of three thousand. He delightedly commented to Thomas Ustick of Philadelphia, 'No book printed by a Baptist in my life time has had such a rapid sale in England - O that it may do good when I am dead & gone!'[118] For the second edition Rippon added Arabic numbers to each page (previously unnumbered), and made textual improvements to forty-one hymns. About half of these were corrections of misprints, but some were distinct alterations: two verses were deleted, and one new verse was added.

The second edition had been sold by September 1789,[119] and Rippon could claim that his book had been 'introduced into about one half of our Baptist churches all thro' England'.[120] A third edition, of three thousand five hundred, unchanged from the second, had 'nearly gone' by June 1791, and five thousand copies of a fourth edition were printed.[121] By the end of 1792 at least fifteen thousand copies had been sold.[122] For the fourth edition Rippon added suggested tunes for 126 hymns (his *Tune Book* was published *c.* 1791); only a few had been suggested for earlier editions. He included an 'Explanation of the Metres in this Volume', and made minor textual changes to twenty-four hymns. Some of these additions were suggested by Robert Hall, Senior, of Arnsby, Leicestershire,[123] and, in a later edition, suggestions from Benjamin Francis were also adopted.[124]

---

116 For example, see Northamptonshire Association Letters of 1787, 1788, 1789. See *Register* 1 (1790-93), p. 450; 2 (1794-97), pp. 33, 324, 480.

117 Rippon to J. Manning, 29 June 1787.

118 Rippon to T. Ustick, 13 February 1788 (original in possession of Dr R. Hayden of Bristol).

119 Rippon to Manning, 21 September 1789 (original at Brown University).

120 Rippon to Manning, 28 October 1788 (original at Brown University).

121 Rippon to Manning, 28 June 1791 (original at Brown University).

122 Rippon to J. Morse, 28 Feb.1793 (original at Historical Society of Pennsylvania, Philadelphia) refers to 4,000 sold in 1792. In his *Tune Book*, p. iii, Rippon claimed nearly 20, 000 copies had been sold. The preface to this was written between 1794 and 1797.

123 *Register* 1 (1790-93), p. 237, note.

124 Cf. Francis to Rippon, Horsley (Gloucs.) 28 May 1799, B.L. Add. MSS. 25387, f. 26.

For the fifth edition (1793) Rippon made a few minor alterations in the Preface, and included a suitable tune (indicated by the number from his Tune Book) for every hymn. Rippon thus made an important advance in hymnody, for this close association of words and tune does not appear to have been so fully adopted in earlier hymnals.

By this edition, Rippon had made some sixty textual changes. Editions between the fifth and tenth were not always indicated, but do not appear to have been improved or altered.[125] The first major enlargement was made for the tenth edition, for which Rippon wrote a new preface dated 10 May 1800. Gratefully he acknowledged the success of his book but admitted that some sections were inadequate. After seeking the 'advice and assistance' of his friends, he offered this enlarged edition, with sixty-two new hymns, 'the far greater part of these are entirely ORIGINALS, and are duly placed under the protection of the law'. Rippon commented:

> A few are inserted on the Trinity, on the Divinity of Christ, and on the Work of the Holy Spirit. But the greater part of the additions consist of Hymns adapted to Village Worship, to Monthly Prayer Meetings for the Spread of the Gospel, to Missionary Meetings, and to the chapter of Hymns before and after Sermon a chapter this, which there was but little danger of protracting to an undesirable length. The sections on Affliction, Death, and Judgment have also received some enlargement; and so have the Indexes, both of Scriptures and of subjects.

These additions provide an interesting commentary on the development of Baptist interest in evangelism, both in the villages of Britain and abroad. For example, five of the six hymns added to the 'Scripture' section were 'Scripture invitations', and Rippon added this note: 'As the few Hymns in the former editions of this Volume, entitled *Scripture Invitations and Promises* have been found peculiarly acceptable and encouraging, the Section is now considerably enlarged'.[126] Evidently the practice of accompanying sermons with invitation-hymns was growing, as was the evangelistic fervour of the Baptists. A further four hymns added to the 'After Sermon' section were similar in emphasis.

But the section most enlarged was 'The Church'. Indeed, one sub-section was altered from 'Church-Associations of Churches' to 'Church-Associations and Missions', and a further sub-section was entitled 'Monthly and Missionary Prayer-Meetings'. Fourteen missionary hymns

---

125 There was one 'New Edition, with eleven original hymns, not inserted in the Selection', with a new Preface, published 'circa 1799' (copy in British Library). This may have been a 'pirate' edition, since none of the additional hymns were given in subsequent editions.

126 *Selection*, (10th edn), note before hymn 114.

were added. Typical of the new attitude was Hymn 418 (4th part, verses 1 and 4):

> Go, favour'd Britons and proclaim
> The kind Redeemer you have found;
> Publish his ever-precious name
> To all the wond'ring nations round....
>
> Go, tell on India's golden shores,
> The Ganges, Tibet, and Boutan, *
> That to enrich their deathless mind
> You come - the friends of God and Man.

(* *Tibet and Boutan* - parts of Asia, Little known to Europeans, but lately mentioned by the Baptist Missionaries!)

Rippon also added nine verses to Hymn 420, noting that 'Verses 8, 9, and 10, of this Hymn in substance, were written off Margate by Mr. William Ward, one of the Baptist Missionaries, on their departure for India, May 28, 1799'.

The new hymns were added as additional 'parts' to other hymns, which avoided undue inconvenience to those who possessed earlier editions. The *Addenda* were printed separately. Most of the hymns' authors were not indicated, but several were by Baptists; as Table 2 reveals. Twelve were by Beddome, and it is of interest that his hymns helped to strengthen the missionary section (a comment on the evangelical interest of the older generation). Few of the additional hymns were of any lasting merit.

Rippon's desire that his *Selection* should be instrumental in the conversion of others was evidenced by a dedicatory 'prayer',[127] which, although unacknowledged, was freely based on a passage by Doddridge in his *Rise and Progress*.[128]

The succeeding editions were substantially unaltered, although Rippon published them in various sizes. From 1801, when his arrangement of *Watts* was published, the two were frequently bound together.

Rippon's last major expansion was for the twenty-seventh edition (1828). He was then in his seventies, but three reasons probably suggested an enlarged edition: to protect his copyright; a rival Baptist book was prepared the same year; a genuine desire to improve the book by the inclusion of hymns achieving popularity. The preface claimed that more than 200,000 copies had been sold in Britain, and a further 100,000

---

127 *Selection*, (10th edn), pp. iv-v.

128 *On the Rise and Progress of Religion in the Soul* (London: 1745), ch. 1: 'A Prayer for the success of this Work in promoting the Rise and Progress of Religion'.

in America. If this is so, taking only the British figures, between the fourth and twenty-seventh editions about 185,000 copies had been sold, an average of about 8,000 per edition.

Rippon added 118 full hymns, as well as 36 doxologies, so that he could justifiably claim to have included more than 150 new hymns. All the doxologies were placed at the end of the book, so that Rippon used hymn numbers 393 to 397 (formerly doxologies) for new hymns, but the remainder were again added as parts to earlier hymns. The Addenda were again printed separately.[129] The sections added are shown in Table 1. Two further missionary hymns were added, and two hymns suitable for 'infant-dedication', although not so described, were added.

The range of authors (see Table 2) was wide, although Beddome, the Wesleys, Doddridge, Newton, Medley and Cowper were again utilized. New authors included the youthful Henry Kirk White, Rippon's friend W.B. Collyer, Thomas Kelly, Thomas Haweis, and Bishop Heber, including his 'From Greenland's icy mountains'.[130] Baptist authors included Ryland, and Rippon's nephew, Thomas. One unusual source was Sir John Bowring's *Specimen of the Russian Poet* (1821) from which Rippon took Hymn 786, a doxology of two verses. This was originally part of the 'Izhe Kheruvimij', or 'Song of the Cherubim', the hymn chanted during the procession of the Cup.[131] Most of the original hymns, about three-quarters of the total added, were uniformly poor and none achieved lasting usage. The *Selection* now contained 803 hymns (including the doxologies).

Subsequent editions in Rippon's lifetime were substantially unaltered. (The thirtieth added a few authors' names.) The last known edition of his lifetime was the thirty-first, which the British Library dates as c.1830. Immediately after his death, John Haddon, the London printer who had issued a rival hymnbook in 1828,[132] also produced a new edition (1837) of the *Selection*. Aware that the original hymns of Rippon's 1828 edition were still under copyright, Haddon omitted 73 hymns and replaced these with others. This must have only confused the public. After the expiration of the copyright laws, an enlarged *Comprehensive Rippon*, as it became known, was published, first in 1844. The editor is not indicated, but he added some four hundred hymns, again interspersed as parts to the original Rippon edition. The total number of hymns was over a

---

129 J. Rippon, *Hymns Original and Selected; interspersed in the Twenty-seventh edition of the Selection, with Numerous Doxologies, in the Usual, the Peculiar, and in the less Common Metres* (London: 1830) A second edition appeared in 1832. So, *Julian*, p. 964.

130 For these men, see *Julian*.

131 (2nd edn, London: 1821), p. 157. For Bowring (1792-1872), see *DNB*.

132 *A New Selection of Hymns, especially adapted to Public Worship, and intended as a Supplement to Dr. Watts's Psalms and Hymns* (London: 1828).

thousand. The general arrangement was retained, but one new section for 'Dedication of Children' was added. The *Comprehensive Rippon* continued in use well into the second half of the nineteenth century, a new edition appearing in 1861.

IN THE UNITED STATES

From the beginning of his project Rippon asked leading American Baptists, like James Manning of Providence, Thomas Ustick of Philadelphia, and Richard Furman of Charleston to help distribute his *Selection*. Rippon hoped to meet the demand from England, and of the first six thousand copies printed, about eight hundred went to America. He considered printing an edition in America, but decided to supply books from England, offering a discount of 25% to any who would sell them for him.[133]

But the success of the *Selection* was so immediate, and shipments from England so delayed,[134] that two unauthorized editions were printed in 1792, one in New York by William Durell,[135] and the other in Elizabethtown by Shepard Kollock.[136] The latter was identical with the London edition, except that the preface was omitted. John Bowen, a member of Carter Lane who had migrated to America in 1799, and became a kind of agent for Rippon, reported that Kollock printed only a thousand copies which were 'principally sold to the Presbyterians for Family Use' and there were not 'Subscribers enough to defray the Expences'.[137] Rippon was so agitated about these rival editions that he wrote to Ustick in 1793 asking for 'a copy of *each* of the American editions of my Hymn book, I beg *you* to send me a copy of each & the price, *sterling*, of each in sheep & calf - and sell mine as low as they sell theirs'.[138] Eventually, even Ustick himself produced an American edition, 'printed by S. C. Ustick',[139] perhaps his son whom Rippon knew to be in the printing trade.[140] Bowen in New York described the situation in 1801:

... Mr. Ustick of Philadelphia was on a Visit here informed me that he had just printed two Thousand of your Selection of Hymns, Also offord to send me two or

---

133 Rippon to Manning, 21 September 1789 (original in Brown University).

134 The European war caused extensive dislocation of Atlantic trade in 1793, see Watson, *The Reign of George III*, p. 181.

135 C. Evans (ed.), *American Bibliography* (14 vols; Chicago: Blakely Press, 1903-59), 8, p. 348.

136 Copy in British Library.

137 Bowen to Rippon, New York, 15 August 1801, BHS *Trans* 1 (1908-9), p. 73.

138 Rippon to Ustick, 6 February 1793 (original in Brown University).

139 R.R. Shaw and R.H. Shoemaker (eds), *American Bibliography, A Preliminary Checklist* (22 vols; New York: Scarecrow Press, 1958-1966), ref. 1257.

140 Rippon to Ustick, 6 February 1793.

three Dozen & Charged me Ten for every dozen I sold; he retail's them at 87 1/2
Cents equal to 7/s N.Y. Currency, & exactly each 3s.11 d. Sterling, thus you see the
English Labors and the American enjoys the sweets of Labor with little troble... I
risfusd to take any of his Books as he could have been supplied from you what he
wanted, I told him it was not worth his while to send any of his publishing here as I
had some comeing from London of the Tenth & enlarged Edition, he was Angry
with me because, I would not let him have the Addenda, that you was so kind to send
me over...[141]

The production of these editions is expressive of the demand for the
Selection. From this time the number of local printings was
remarkable.[142] By 1828 Rippon was told that about 100,000 copies had
been sold in America.[143] There were also several editions of the
Comprehensive.

Copyright Disputes

Rippon's concern with unauthorized editions was not confined to
America. Under the first English copyright Act of 1709 the owner
(author or bookseller) had the complete monopoly of his work for a
period of fourteen years. If the owner was still living this was extended
for a further fourteen years. These privileges depended upon an entry of
the book, before publication, in the Stationers' Register.[144] Obviously
only the original hymns, about 150, in Rippon's book were subject to
this copyright. Rippon noted in his fourth edition (1792) that his book
had been 'Entered at Stationers' Hall', and specifically commented in
the Preface to his tenth edition that the originals 'were regularly assigned
to me, in my own right and as my sole property', of which Ryland,

---

141   BHS *Trans* 1 (1908-9), pp. 72-73.

142   Wilmington (1802), Baltimore (1803), Philadelphia (two different editions in
1803), Brooklyn (1803), Baltimore (1804), Philadelphia, 'the first American from the
15th London edition' (1809), Baltimore, 'the 2nd American from the 15th London', to
which William Staughton added an appendix (1813), Baltimore '-new edition' (1814),
Chillicothe (1815), Baltimore (1818), Philadelphia '4th American from the 15th
London' (1819), another edition by Staughton, with an Appendix from the *Olney Hymns*
(1826). Then several appeared in Philadelphia (1827, 1831, 1837, 1839, 1842; in New
York (1835) and Boston (1836). This list has been compiled from three sources: (1)
References in Shaw and Shoemaker, *American Bibliography*, see index 'Rippon'; (2)
Copies known to be in Brown University and the American Baptist Historical Society;
(3) Benson, *The English Hymn*, p. 201.

143   *Selection* (27th edn), p. iii.

144   H.0. Aldis, 'Book Production and Distribution', in A.W. Ward and A.R. Waller
(eds), *Cambridge History of English Literature* (15 vols; Cambridge: Cambridge
University Press, 1932), 11, pp. 313-15.

Dunscombe, and Job David of Frome (who had been in Bristol Academy with Rippon) were 'living witnesses'.[145] Rippon added, 'This statement is given to prevent all future illicit republication of the original parts of this work'. Evidently Rippon paid composers for hymns, as Francis wrote to Rippon acknowledging payment for ten hymns.[146]

There are several examples of Rippon being involved in disputes over copyright, although he does not appear to have personally taken legal action. Two at least involved fellow-Baptists. Joseph Middleton (d. 1805), formerly a Countess of Huntingdon's minister but from 1785 Baptist pastor at Lewes, Sussex, published his *Hymns* in 1793.[147] This contained 355 hymns, 104 from Watts' *Hymns and Psalms*, 150 from Rippon's *Selection*, and the rest from various sources. All the hymns from the *Selection* were given with the number in Rippon's book, for example, '105 (R.9)'. It was nowhere stated that 'R' stood for 'Rippon', although this was clearly so. These hymns were unchanged in any way, and at least 28 were first published by Rippon. In addition, Rippon's collection of single verses for Baptism was reproduced. Middleton's letters to Rippon, trying to justify his own book after he had been told of Rippon's anger, explained that he had produced his book in order to let the poor of his congregation have the best hymns available in a single volume, costing only two shillings. (Rippon's cheapest edition was three shillings). Rippon, clearly displeased with Middleton, decided not to prosecute, whereupon the latter asked that the 'goodness of my motive' would help Rippon forgive an 'unintentional offence'.[148]

Similarly, Thomas Westlake of Exeter, a friend of Rippon's, published A *Selection of hymns, from various authors, adapted to public worship* in 1796 (second edition, 1801). Again, his motive was to provide a book for the poor, indeed he told Rippon all profits would go to the Upottery church, where Rippon's father was pastor.[149] Westlake's arrangement was almost identical with Rippon's book, from which he took 104 hymns. Rippon asked that hymns by Stennett, Turner, Ryland, Beddome, Straphan, and Francis should not be used, but his request arrived too late

---

145 *Selection* (10th edn), p. iii.

146 Francis to Rippon, Horsley 2 July 1796, B.L. Add. MSS. 25387, f. 24.

147 J. Middleton, *Hymns* (London: 1793). For Middleton, see F. Buffard, *Kent and Sussex Baptist Association* (Faversham: Kent and Sussex Baptist Association, 1963), pp. 51-52.

148 19, 28 August and 18 November 1793, B.L. Add. MSS. 25388, ff. 50-54.

149 T. Westlake to Rippon, Exeter, 9 July 1796, B. L. Add. MSS. 25389, f. 442.

to prevent publication. Westlake replied that in any case those hymns were in 'Radford's'[150] and 'Lyndell's'[151] Collections.

Finally, Rippon published on the covers of his *Register* numbers 13 (August 1796) and 14 (May 1797) a caution against 'a pirated edition of his Selection of Hymns, in which the original preface is omitted, and a few pieces of trash inserted at the end'.[152] He thanked the booksellers who had undertaken legal proceedings and all 'the respectable part of the trade' who only stocked genuine *Selections*. He concluded: 'But he (Rippon) thinks it proper to assure others that if ever his right is again invaded, he shall conceive it a *duty* which he owes to himself and the public, to prosecute the offender according as the law directs.'

After this, no Baptist pastor who read the *Register* could plead ignorance as an excuse: and no evidence of copyright arguments after this date has been found. (The 1799 copy in the British Library corresponds to the description of this 'pirate' edition.)

J. Haddon suggested in 1837 that Rippon's enlargements in 1800 and 1828 were partially intended to constitute new copyrights.[153] The first enlargement was thirteen years after the first edition (one year before the expiration of the first copyright period), and the next twenty-eight years later, when the period of copyright was due to expire. Haddon claimed that by Rippon's additions in 1828 'he created a new property, for himself and his heirs, which will be enjoyed till the year 1855'.

Rippon clearly was aware of the need for copyright. After all, most of the work, and all the expense and risk of the first publications were solely Rippon's. He did publish cheap editions 'for the poor' from the beginning,[154] frequently gave away copies,[155] and even advertised that poor members would be given a copy of the addenda to the twenty-seventh edition 'gratis'.[156] Of course the obvious and important deduction from the copyright disputes was the popularity of the book - but whilst this is significant for the influence of the *Selection* it can only have brought scant comfort to Rippon. Even a dedicated pastor and loyal denominationalist could not afford to ignore commercial realities!

---

150 J. Radford, (of Ebenezer Chapel, Shadwell), *A Collection of Psalms and Hymns for Public Worship* (London:1790). Of the 353 hymns, 63 were in *Selection* but only 6 were first published there.

151 S. Lyndall, *Selection of Hymns intended as a supplement to Dr. Watts's Psalms and Hymns* (London: 4th edn, 1807). Of the 117 hymns, 45 were in *Selection*; but only 5 were first published there.

152 These unbound copies are in the Angus Library.

153 'A new and improved edition' of *Selection* (1837), preface.

154 Rippon to Ustick, 13 February 1788 (and numerous other references in letters).

155 Spurgeon, *The Metropolitan Tabernacle*, p. 51; and references in several letters preserved in Rippon's papers.

156 *Baptist Magazine* 20 (1828), p. 563.

Success of the Selection

The *Selection* was without an effective rival among British Baptists from 1787 until 1828. The earlier books retained, however, some local or personal loyalties. The 'Bristol Collection' was reprinted several times, an eighth edition in 1801, and tenth in 1827. But its use was restricted, and as late as 1803 Thomas Berry was surprised to find the Tewkesbury church still using the 'Bristol Collection', and expressed regret that reverence for the memory of Caleb Evans prompted the use of such 'a little, little thing'.[157] Again, Fawcett's book enjoyed some success in the north of England. Rippon hesitated to introduce his books there, and wrote to Sutcliff in December 1787, as he prepared his second edition, 'Are Mr. Fawcett's Hymns used much in ye churches in Yorks, I shd be sorry if mine opposed them'.[158] But Rippon's book became widely adopted in Yorkshire,[159] and, despite a few smaller books of exclusively local use, the *Selection* enjoyed a virtual monopoly - with Watts - of Baptist praise.

Similarly, the *Selection* achieved an immediate success in America. As one Kentucky pastor wrote, 'If I had a thousand copies of your Selection of Hymns, am confident I could sell them'.[160]

The *Selection* also enjoyed a measure of popular usage among non-Baptists. The main obstacle to its wider use was, of course, the group of distinctively Baptist baptismal hymns. Rippon overcame this by the following procedure which he explained to Jedidiah Morse, a Congregationalist of Boston: 'We have so modified the Sheet on Baptism that by a neat cancel which is accounted for in a note, the book may be had, with only such Hymns on that ordinance as were composed by Paedobaps.'[161] This surprised some of Rippon's Baptist friends,[162] but how many adapted versions were sold is unknown, and none has been located. However, T.G. Crippen, in a review of Congregational hymnody, described Rippon's book as 'probably the most important' of all the supplements to Watts, and added: 'The compiler was a Baptist, but the

---

157 Berry to Rippon, Tewkesbury, 4 January 1803, B.L. Add. MSS. 25386, f. 80.

158 Rippon to Sutcliff, 28 December 1787 (original at Pennsylvania Historical Society, Philadelphia).

159 For examples, see: B.L. Add. MSS. 25386, ff. 193, 307; 25387, f. 454.

160 *Register* 1 (1790-93), p. 117.

161 Rippon to Morse, 28 February 1793 (original at Pennsylvania Historical Society).

162 Cf. J.C. Sprague to Rippon, Bovey Tracey, 5 January 1799, B.L. Add. MSS. 25389, f. 148.

book was used in many paedobaptist congregations - in some within the memory of the present writer'.[163]

The first serious rival to the *Selection* was *A New Selection of Hymns, especially adapted to Public Worship, and intended as a Supplement to Dr. Watts's Psalms and Hymns* (1828), published by John Haddon, a London printer. The *Baptist Magazine* gave this new venture a most unsympathetic welcome.[164] The reviewer noted that 260 out of its 581 hymns were already in Rippon, and that Rippon's book, especially after its recent enlargement, was far superior in every way. But the new book made way, it was slightly cheaper, and all profits were designated for the widows of Baptist pastors. By 1833 over £400 had been given to this charity, and by 1837 over 60,000 copies had been sold.[165] The charitable aims led to the formation, in 1860, of the Psalms and Hymns Trust which has devoted all the profits of official Baptist hymn-books to the same ends.[166] But the *Comprehensive Rippon*, it has been noted, continued to be widely used well into the second half of the nineteenth century.

The reasons for the long monopoly by the *Selection* may be summarized.[167] The Selection was comprehensive, offering a wide range of subjects, and more hymns, than its rivals. It was nicely calculated to meet the homiletical and devotional needs of the Baptist congregations. A variety of metres was used. The indices were more detailed, and often more accurate, than others. This was invaluable for preachers seeking hymns relevant to their sermons. Universally available, at reasonable prices, the *Selection* was offered at a discount to ministers, who would be encouraged to introduce it into their churches. Rippon was aware of the need to be doctrinally orthodox. Rippon's literary taste and judgment of what the churches needed - especially with the new missionary hymns - were vital factors in its long success. Rippon was statedly concerned with the quality of hymns, not their origins, and so evidenced a catholicity in his choices. Hence by 1828 he included not only Wesleyan hymns but even a translation of a small part of the liturgy of the Russian Orthodox Church. Moreover, by linking hymns with suggested tunes, Rippon helped improve Baptist singing.

In short, the *Selection* fully met specific theological, pastoral and devotional needs of the Baptists: this was the main secret of its success. In addition, the *Tune Book* and Rippon's arrangement of *Watts*, both

---

163 T.G. Crippen, 'Congregational Hymnody', *Transactions* of Congregational Historical Society, 7 (1916-18), p. 227.

164 *Baptist Magazine* 20 (1828), pp. 468-69.

165 *Baptist Magazine* 25 (1833), p. 331; 29 (1837), p. 412.

166 R.W. Thomson, *The Psalms and Hymns Trust* (London: Psalms and Hymns Trust, 1960).

167 The first four reasons were suggested in the *Comprehensive Rippon*, (1844), preface.

successful in their own right, helped promoted the *Selection* with which they were both directly connected.

Tune Book[168]

Whilst hymns can profitably be read for private meditation and prayer, they are composed to be sung.[169] The singer is caught up in a group experience so that tune and metre are of critical importance. Writers often composed their hymns to be sung to a specific tune. Frequently it is the tune that arouses the emotional commitment of the singer and helps the hymn to be recalled long after it has been sung.[170] As J.R. Watson helpfully observes:

> The music changes the nature of the words: it makes them 'sound'. Not just in the normal way in which words make a sound, but in resonance with the music, creating a musical and verbal texture. The music has its own way of imposing pauses, fluidity, emphasis, structure upon the words: the mind has to combine an appreciation of syntax and sentence with another appreciation of movement through the musical notation... A hymn exists, not just on the page, but in sound.[171]

However, when Rippon began his ministry, singing among Dissenters was uniformly poor. Hymns were normally 'lined' or 'parcelled' out by the clerk, or precentor, usually without any aid, although some used a pitchpipe or tuning fork. Organs were not introduced until the nineteenth century, and then only with considerable opposition. One disgruntled correspondent of the *Baptist Magazine* complained about the organs in Baptist churches in London in 1835.[172] Violins, cellos and double basses were perhaps introduced earlier, but not widely adopted until the

---

168 Detailed discussion of the *Tune Book* would require specialist musical knowledge. Hence, although the editions of the *Tune Book* have been carefully examined, the musical aspects of the following discussion are indebted to previous studies: see especially 0.A. Mansfield, 'Rippon's Tunes', *BQ* 8.1 (1936-37), pp. 36-43; Young, 'The History of Baptist Hymnody', pp. 108-116.

169 For a general review of the development of hymn tunes, see E. Routley, *The Music of Christian Hymnody. A Study of the development of the hymn tune since the Reformation, with special reference to English Protestantism* (London: Independent Press, 1957).

170 Watts, *The Dissenters*, 2, p. 181.

171 Watson, *The English Hymn*, pp. 22-23.

172 *Baptist Magazine* 27 (1835), p. 58.

nineteenth century.[173] Choirs were not common, but gradually appeared as public interest in choral singing grew.

The need for the careful selection of tunes was well stated by Rippon:

Any tune, by any *incompetent person*, is sung with but very little regard to the subject of the Hymn. This inattention is extremely mischievous in tunes which have a repeat. By a misapplication of these the congregation may be forced not only to stop in the midst of a line, and to go back, before they have pronounced any distinct idea; but also to stop in the very midst of a word, and to retreat, leaving a syllable or two behind, till they advance again, and perhaps oftener than once, to meet the forlorn termination. Circumstances of this description amuse the trifling, pain the sensible and serious, and rob whole auditories of their devotion.[174]

Rippon felt strongly about the poor quality of contemporary hymn singing by Dissenters. He disapproved of lining-out of hymns, and quoted from Isaac Watts against this and other evils, such as lack of pauses, and poor pronunciation.[175] Lining-out was continued by many poorer and partly illiterate congregations well into the second half of the nineteenth century,[176] although Rippon noted that the removal of lining-out was 'gaining Ground in some Congregations of the first Note in London, at Bristol, and elsewhere'.[177] Rippon lamented that although most congregations were sensitive to 'seriousness in *prayer*, and soundness in *preaching*' few were concerned about good hymn singing, which was 'often most shamefully prostituted'.[178] Rippon also favoured '*responsive* singing', although very few hymns were so arranged in the *Selection*. To stand whilst singing was preferred: this was the practice Rippon knew as a boy in Tiverton from 1761, although some there had doubted its 'decency'.[179] Rippon published a paper by John Newton which argued that to stand signified the elevation of the soul and mind in praising God.[180] Thomas Walker, who helped Rippon in his *Tune Book*, strengthened this argument by noting that standing made singing more comfortable and effective.[181] An extract from a sermon by Jonathan

---

173 For an interesting musical group in the Rossendale Valley, in the mid-18th century, see A. Buckley, 'The Deign Layrocks', *BQ*. 4 (1928), pp. 43-48. For an account of developments in hymnody during the Victorian era, see Bradley, *Abide with Me. The World of Victorian Hymns*.

174 Rippon, *Watts*, p. ix.

175 *Selection*, pp. vii –viii.

176 Watts, *The Dissenters*, 2, p. 182.

177 *Selection*, p. viii. For amusing illustrations of problems associated with lining-out, see Bradley, *Abide with Me*, pp. 2-3.

178 *Tune Book*, p. iii.

179 See above, chapter 2.

180 *Register* 3 (1798-1801), pp. 547-48.

181 *Tune Book*, p. xii.

Edwards, published by Rippon, argued that since singing God's praises was a command of God, 'those, therefore, who neglect to *learn* to sing, LIVE IN SIN': this can only have discomfitted the tone-deaf.[182]

Rippon professed his own concern for good singing: '...and were my own head bound round with weeping willows, and my harp to lie neglected on the ground, I would, nevertheless, make a single effort to glorify God, and if it were but one, it should be this - to encourage all the thousands of Israel *to sing in the ways of the Lord*'.[183]

Although it is uncertain whether Rippon originally intended to publish a *Tune Book* as companion to the *Selection*, the former was advertised as early as 1788.[184] J. Stoughton suggested that Rippon obtained many of his tunes from certain lady composers active in Lady Huntingdon's chapel at Dublin, whilst there on a preaching visit.[185]

Rippon was helped by Robert Keene and Thomas Walker.[186] Robert Keene must be carefully distinguished from the man of the same name who was a trustee of Whitefield's Tabernacles, and a close friend of the evangelist.[187] This latter Keene died on 30 January 1793.[188] The other Robert Keene, a member of Carter Lane since 1776,[189] and their precentor,[190] was suspended from communion on 22 April 1793 because of 'breach of trust and also of the sin of 'drunkenness'. Formal exclusion followed in the next month.[191] Six of Keene's tunes were included in the *Tune Book*. Keene has been suggested as possibly the mysterious 'K', author of 'How firm a foundation'.[192] But this implies

---

182 *Register* 3 (1798-1801), p. 546.

183 *Tune Book,* p. iv.

184 Advertisement in *Selection* (2nd edn.).

185 *History of Religion in England,* 7, pp. 283-84. See *Register* 4 (1801-02) p. 408, note *. B. McDowel to Rippon, Glasgow, 2 August 1792, B.L. Add. MSS. 25386, f. 407, arranges with Rippon to visit Ireland the next spring; but it is not clear if this was Rippon's first visit.

186 W.T. Whitley, 'The Tune Book of 1791', *BQ* 10.8 (1940-41), p. 434. Whitley's suggestion is confirmed by a series of advertisements for the *Tune Book* in editions of the *Selection*. The first of these, in 1788, described the projected volume as 'by John Rippon and Robert Keene'. However, in 1792, it was advertised as 'by John Rippon and Thomas Walker'. Finally, in 1793 the *Tune Book* was 'by John Rippon' as it appeared on the title page of the first edition of the *Tune Book* itself.

187 H. Martin (ed.), *Baptist Hymn Book Companion* (London: Psalms and Hymns Trust, 1962), p. 349 confused the two men.

188 *Evangelical Magazine* 4 (1796), p. 518. For Keene's association with Whitefield, see L. Tyerman, *The Life of Rev. George Whitefield* (2 vols; London: 1876-7), references in index.

189 Carter Lane Churchbook, 16 December 1776.

190 Cf. H. Roberts to Rippon, 25 February 1796, B.L. Add. MSS. 25388, f. 440.

191 Carter Lane Churchbook, 20 May 1793.

192 See above, note 58.

Rippon gave his full name in the *Tune Book* and not in the *Selection*, although this may be explained, on Rippon's stated procedure, because of extensive alterations to the original hymn. Again, the combination of a composer of both tunes and words is unusual for this time. Possibly the inclusion of his tunes suggests that Keene was not 'K'.

The assistance of Thomas Walker (1764-1827), an alto vocalist of the metropolis, is more obvious. By the fifth edition of the *Tune Book* (1808) thirty-three of the tunes were by Walker, double the number by any other composer. John Dyer thought Walker was formerly a member of the Prescott Street church, 'but his tuneful propensities proved a snare to him - his domestic life was eminently unhappy - and he died in a state of derangement!'[193] Although Rippon was responsible for the enterprise, the actual musical work seems to have been largely done by the two musicians. Whilst Rippon must have had some knowledge of the rudiments of music there is no surviving evidence of any outstanding musical ability. (The identification of him with the 'John Rippon' who composed an oratorio, *The Crucifixion*, is wrong.)[194]

The first edition of the *Tune Book* is usually dated as *circa* 1791,[195] although it may not have been published until 1792 or 1793.[196] This edition was smaller than later editions, with only 256 tunes, and had no preface and no indices but simply a few unexplained musical examples. The second edition, dated between 1794 and 1797 (probably the latter), was much improved.[197] Rippon added a preface -inaccurately described in subsequent editions as 'Preface to the first edition' - and Thomas Walker compiled a 'Brief Introduction to Psalmody'. This latter, occupying eight pages, was an elementary introduction to the rudiments of music and 'graceful singing', together with hints for 'keeping the

---

193   E.A. Payne (ed.), 'The Necrologies of John Dyer', *BQ* 13.7 (1949-50), p. 306. For Dyer (1784-1841), secretary of the BMS (1818-1841), see E.A. Payne, *The First Generation* (London: Carey Press, 1936) pp. 120-26; Stanley, *The History of the Baptist Missionary Society 1792-1992*, pp. 208-12.

194   As, for example, by Mansfield, 'Rippon's Tunes', p. 39. The oratorio (copies of which are in the British Library, the library of the Royal College of Music and the Bodleian Library) is dated as *circa* 1837 (that is, after Rippon's death), and this John Rippon was Rippon's nephew, the son of Theophilus. (Information supplied by Ms. E. Rippon.)

195   So, British Library Catalogue. Rippon is described as 'A.M.' and not 'D.D.' (received in 1792) and see *Register* 1 (1790-93) p. 326, where Rippon lists it in the publications of '1791 &c'. (This list was in fact published in May 1792, see below, chapter 5.)

196   Advertisement in fourth edition of *Selection* (1792) still described the *Tune Book* as by Rippon and Walker.

197   Advertisement for 2nd edition on cover *Register* no. 13 (August 1796), although was given in list of books for 1797 (2, p. 475); but in 1794 it was advertised in *Baptist Catechism* (1794), although perhaps only then in preparation.

Tune' and 'pitching the Tune'. He commented: 'The respect I have for Mr. Rippon induced me, with cheerfulness, to assist him in the execution of this work; and the recollection of that friendship which subsisted between him and my late father greatly increased my pleasure.'[198]

Also in this second edition were: (1) 'An Explanation of the Musical Terms which Occur in this Volume' which offered explanations of the thirty-two Italian directions; (2) 'Explanation of the Metres in this Volume', analyzing thirty-eight metres; (3) 'Verses adapted to most of the peculiar metres in this Volume', where words for twenty-seven hymns were given, seventeen were not from either the *Selection* or *Watts* a reminder that there was a wider Dissenting use of the book envisaged; (4) 'An Index of Tunes' in alphabetical order. One additional item, an index of tunes in metrical order, was added to later editions.

For the third and fourth (1802) editions additional tunes were added. These were entirely the work of Walker, as the additions were published separately with his name as editor.[199] By the fifth edition (1808) the book had expanded to 320 'tunes and odes'.[200]

Rippon's *Tune Book* ran through several more editions. It was made available in a 'Miniature Edition', and apart from the improvement of some indices was unchanged. The thirteenth edition was 'Adapted to the Piano Forte', and this is the last located edition. Clearly the demand for a *Tune Book* was more restricted than for the *Selection*, but it did fulfil a definite need. Walker claimed in 1811 that Rippon's book had met with 'universal acceptance' and that 'many thousand copies' had been sold.[201] Apparently, Rippon's *Tune Book* did not find favour in America.[202]

Evidently, whenever a composer's name was known it was printed with the tune, 178 of the 320 tunes were so indicated. These were not always accurate, as when the 'Old 100th' was attributed to Luther (rather than to Louis Bourgeois in the Genevan Psalter of 1551),[203] and 'Hanover' to

---

198 *Tune Book,* p. xii.

199 T. Walker, *Appendix to Dr. Rippon's Selection of Tunes* (London: n.d.); T. Walker, *Second Appendix to Dr. Rippon's Selection of Tunes* (London: n.d.) The first contained tunes numbered 257 to 278; the second, tunes 279 to 294. The second contained an advertisement for 'The Happy End of Mrs. Leeks', published in *Register*, 4 (1801-02), pp. 753-63 (in January 1802).

200 It is important to distinguish between these Appendices and Supplements to Rippon's book, and a separate series of Walker's which were published in 1811 and 1815, and were known as *Walker's Companion to Dr. Rippon's Tune Book.* These were quite separate, and Rippon had no connection with them. (Walker also published other musical works: see Music Catalogue of the British Library.)

201 *Walker's Companion to Dr.Rippon's Tune Book* (1811), preface.

202 Reynolds, *Companion to Baptist Hymnal,* p. 13.

203 Martin (ed), *The Baptist Hymn Book Companion,* p. 47.

Handel, rather than Croft (though this was a common mistake at this period).[204] Thomas Walker, it has been noted, had 33 tunes, but only twelve in the first edition: which indicates the extent to which he incorporated his own work in the appendices. The other two composers most used were Benjamin Milgrove (1731-1310), precentor of the Countess of Huntingdon's chapel in Bath, from whom 17 tunes were taken; and Martin Madan (1726-1790) (14 tunes) whose *Lock Hospital Collection* (1760) enjoyed a great popularity.

The tunes may conveniently be divided into four groups.[205] First were standard tunes. Prominent among these, Mansfield has noted, were 'Tallis's Canon', 'the old 100th', 'the old 113th', 'the old 104th', 'Windsor', 'St David's', 'Babylon's Streams', 'London', 'Luther's Hymn', 'St James', 'Bedford', 'Bangor', 'Carey's', 'the Easter Hymn', 'Adeste Fideles' (as 'Portugal New') and three works by Croft: 'St Anne's', 'St Matthew', and 'Hanover'. It may be noted in passing that Rippon omitted the title 'Saint' from all cited as such here. Other early composers represented by lesser works included Drs Greene, Hayes, and Randall.

Almost half the tunes in the *Tune Book* were contemporary: either recently produced, or first introduced by Rippon.[206] The majority of Walker's tunes are not worth noting, and none has achieved general use. Grigg's 'Tiverton', still in common use, was first introduced by Rippon; whilst other tunes still popular include 'Miles Lane' by Shrubsole, 'Darwall', and 'Mount Ephraim' by Milgrove.

Adaptation was a common feature of the period. Handel was a favourite source, and Walker's 'Stoel' was possibly based on an air from Handel's *Siröe*. From his opera *Alcina* 'Verdi prati' became 'Trowbridge'; 'See the conquering hero comes' from *Judas Maccabaeus* was arranged as a 7s and called 'Georgia'; 'He shall feed His flock' from the *Messiah* became 'Manning' as a Long Metre; 'I know that my Redeemer liveth' was reduced to Common Metre as 'Messiah'. Dr. Harington's setting of 'Drink to me only with thine eyes' was termed 'Prospect'; from Dr. Arne's opera *Artaxerxes* came 'Arlington' and from his *Abel* came 'Uxbridge'; whilst 'Scotland' was based on the song, 'Water parted from the sea'.

Finally, there were 'Odes' or 'Set Pieces', usually metrical anthems by Madan, Arnold, Walker and others, written in a now quite obsolete style.

Two items are of special interest. One is the inclusion of Byrd's 'Non Nobis Domine', provided with a Latin text - surely unusual in a book for Dissenters. The other was the 'Hindoo Chorus' which was linked with

204 Martin (ed), *The Baptist Hymn Book Companion*, p. 67.
205 Following Mansfield, 'Rippon's Tunes', pp. 40-42.
206 Young, 'History of Baptist Hymnody', p. 110.

Krishna Pal's hymn.[207] The original Hindu words were also given, presumably as a novelty interest. The final chorus of *Judas Maccabaeus* was adapted to form an 'Easter Ode'.

Four distinctions may be claimed for the *Tune Book*. First, it was not only the first Baptist tune-book but was the largest hymn tune-book yet compiled in England. R. H. Young calls it 'the most complete and far-reaching book of the century'.[208]

Secondly, it was the first to add, systematically, marks of expression, such as *p*, *f*, *ff*, *cresc*., and tempo indications such as 'grave', 'lively', 'solemn', 'brisk'. O.A. Mansfield complained that the expression marks are 'somewhat mechanical' and occasionally vary from modern ideas.[209] Rippon's was evidently the first to include a table explaining the Italian musical terms. This was not without its errors either, as Mansfield showed. Walker's lessons, which accompanied examples of musical notation, do not offer the best approach to sight-reading and encourage the 'pernicious practice' of 'slurring' by inserting 'grace notes' between the essential tones of a melody'.[210] Nevertheless the attempt is to be noted as a pioneer effort by Walker.

Thirdly, the *Tune Book* became the most extensive companion to one particular hymnbook. The custom of suggesting a specific tune for each hymn was an advance in Baptist hymnody, for earlier Baptist hymnbooks had been very inconsistent in this.[211]

Fourthly, the *Tune Book* is the best example of contemporary Dissenting psalmody. Rippon explained in his preface that numerous requests for suitable tunes for some hymns with peculiar measures had necessitated references to several different tune-books and thus the need for one volume became obvious:

> With this in view it appeared advisable, not only to adopt those which are allowedly the best Tunes sung in the Dissenting Meeting-houses, and other societies in the Metropolis, but also to obtain lists of such as are used in the principal congregations throughout England; paying at the same time, a due regard to others which are highly esteemed in some of the foreign churches.

---

207 Krishna Pal was the first Indian convert of the BMS in 1800. See Stanley, *The History of the Baptist Missionary Society 1792-1992*, p. 37. Pal's hymn 'O Thou my Soul', translated by Joshua Marshman, is Number 213 in *The Baptist Hymn Book* (London: Psalms and Hymns Trust, 1962).

208 Young, 'History of Baptist Hymnody', p. 110.

209 Mansfield, 'Rippon's Tunes', p. 39.

210 Mansfield, 'Rippon's Tunes', p. 40.

211 Young, 'History of Baptist Hymnody', pp. 99-100.

Thus Rippon's book 'codified the best of the tunes in nonconformist use up to that date, and added a number of new ones'.[212] With Walker's *Companions* it represents the 'normal hymnody' of the Dissenters of the period.[213]

Remembering the difficult task Rippon and his helpers set themselves it is not surprising that several mistakes occurred, and that a greater knowledge of musical history and theory has underlined these. The following may be briefly noted.[214] As above, 'the old 100th' and 'Hanover' were given with the wrong composers. 'St. Anne' was wrongly set in triple time. 'Hanover' was given twice, the second time in a somewhat embellished form as 'Ailie Street'. There is considerable evidence of tune tampering, generally with regrettable results. Much inferior material was included, and there were several printers' errors - a reminder of the difficult engraving task necessitated by such an undertaking.[215] As noted, the 'Introduction to Psalmody' contained errors, and there was a lack of any real system in arranging the book. Many of the tunes were set in three parts only, rather than four; whilst the harmonies were 'often commonplace, and occasionally ungrammatical, the modulations being extremely limited'.[216]

Opinions may differ as to the propriety of adapting 'popular airs'. Mansfield called it 'ecclesiastical inconsistency'.[217] Certain of Rippon's contemporaries thought the same:

> After a funeral sermon for a venerable and pious lady the minister gave out Dr. Watts's excellent hymn, 'There is a land of pure delight', &c. and the clerk set it to an old convivial glee, beginning 'Drink to me only with thine eyes'&c. A lady in the congregation, who had long renounced these levities, was extremely pained by the recollections this occasioned, and bitterly assailed by the ridicule of some gay acquaintances who happened to be present. The next day she stated the fact to the minister; and on complaint being made to the clerk, he pointed to the tune called

---

212 M. Frost (ed.), *Historical Companion to Hymns Ancient and Modern* (London: Hymns Ancient and Modern, 1962), p. 110.

213 Young, 'History of Baptist Hymnody', Table 2, 'Psalm and Hymn Tunes most Frequently Found in Ten leading English Tune Books of the Eighteenth Century', which shows that of 47 tunes found in 4 or more of these books, Rippon had 33; whilst he omitted none of those which were in extensive use in the second half of the century.

214 These are summarized from Mansfield, 'Rippon's Tunes', p. 43, and Young, 'History of Baptist Hymnody', p. 111.

215 There are several letters complaining about defective copies in Rippon's correspondence in the British Library.

216 Mansfield, 'Rippon's Tunes', p. 43.

217 Mansfield, 'Rippon's Tunes', p. 43.

'Prospect' in Dr Rippon's book, and pleaded that there were many more of the same class in that collection![218]

'Prospect' was set to that very hymn of Watts in Rippon's book. Walker's defence for introducing classical airs was that it was analogous to students for the ministry being required to read Homer and Virgil.[219]

In selecting names for the tunes Rippon was able to honour his own circle of friends and his regard for different places.[220]

Clearly it would be an anachronism to judge the *Tune Book* solely by modern standards. Admittedly many of the tunes were inferior, but several were noteworthy. W.T. Whitley claimed in 1941 that 97 of the tunes were still in use.[221] Well over thirty tunes appeared in both the (English) Baptist (1962) and Congregational (1953) books. There is little doubt that the progress of Baptist hymnody was advanced by the production of this substantial volume of tunes to accompany his highly acceptable *Selection*.

Rippon's Watts

Rippon's third hymn project added to the total impact of both the *Selection* and the *Tune Book*. By his arrangement of *Watts*, Rippon sought to strengthen the traditional loyalties of Dissenters to Watts. When both the *Selection* and *Watts* were bound together - and Rippon printed them in the same sizes - they comprised the complete Dissenters' hymnbook. Again, Rippon's capacity for detailed, accurate drudgery is demonstrated (although he acknowledged some assistance from Timothy Thomas of the Devonshire Square church and the 'Rev. Mr. Collins'),[222] as also is his undoubted determination to improve every aspect of Dissenting hymnody.

---

218 *Baptist Magazine* 22 (1830), p. 57. For other criticisms of the use of 'Prospect', see Bradley, *Abide with Me*, p. 29.

219 Thomson, *The Psalms and Hymns Trust*, p. 4.

220 Whitley, 'The Tune Book of 1791': Rippon's American friends 'Furman', 'Stillman', 'Manning' and 'Ustick' were all featured; whilst English Baptists included 'Evans', 'Fawcett', 'Fountain', 'Francis', 'Sprague' and 'Rippon' himself. 'America' was represented by 'Baltimore', 'Boston', 'Carolina', 'Charleston', 'Georgia', 'Kentucky', 'New York', 'Providence College', 'Richmond', 'Vermont' and 'Virginia'. From England there were numerous place-names especially from London and the West Country: 'Bampton', 'Bermondsey', 'Bourton', 'Broadmead', 'Pithay', 'Bristol', 'Carter Lane', 'Chard', 'Culmstock', 'Eagle Street', 'Exeter', 'Grange Road' (where Rippon lived), 'Leeds', 'Portsea', 'Tooley Street' (from which Carter Lane ran), 'Uffculm' and, of course, 'Tiverton'.

221 Whitley, 'The Tune Book of 1791', p. 434.

222 *Watts*, p. xii. Collins has not been identified.

Rippon noted the inferior quality of most editions of Watts, as since 'Pasham's' (1778) Rippon had made a careful study of each printing. 'Pasham's' had omitted an entire verse from one hymn, Rippon claimed, whilst 'Wayland's' was also inaccurate. Rippon doubted that an accurate text of Watts was available in any current edition, and was determined to rectify the situation.

Watts had published his *Hymns* in three books: (i) Collected from the Scriptures; (ii) Compos'd on Divine Subjects; (iii) Prepar'd for the Lord's Supper. The paraphrases of the *Psalms* were of course in Biblical order and were, perhaps, Watts' finest work. They are remarkable in linking the Old Testament with the New.[223] Rippon arranged all these hymns into sections almost identical with those in his *Selection*. He retained Watts' section on 'Solomon's Song', and grouped some Psalms in a section under 'Church' as 'The Jewish; or the History of the Israelites'. He also added a section, 'Circumcision and Baptism', which, recognizing denominational differences on this subject, was arranged by 'one of my very respectable Brethren of the Congregational denomination'.[224]

When Watts' hymns are arranged in such a systematic way, it is remarkable, as H. Escott observed, 'that the want of structure and system in Watts's hymnody is more apparent than real'.[225] Rippon suggested suitable tunes from his *Tune Book* for each hymn, added a table of first lines, an 'enlarged' index of Scriptures, and a greatly enlarged index (occupying twenty-one pages of small print) of subjects.

Rippon attempted to forestall criticisms of his arrangement, suggesting that, for some, to meddle with Watts was extremely provocative.[226] For example, when Watts produced the second edition of his *Hymns*, he had omitted fourteen hymns which he decided were better placed in his forthcoming *Psalms*, but had not altered the numbering of the *Hymns*. However, in 1786 an edition of Watts, in the preparation of which Rippon had shared, added fourteen other hymns by Watts, placing them under those numbers which were simply references to *Psalms*. This edition was so successful - about 140, 000 copies were sold - that in 1793 a rival 'enlarged' edition added fourteen different hymns. To avoid confusion, Rippon added all those to the expanded versions. Again, Rippon defended his enlarging of the indices by insisting that if an index was to be used at all it ought to be as complete as possible. As to the arranging into subjects, Rippon felt that had Watts conceived this plan 'early enough' he would have adopted it himself; for he did have a few groupings himself, such as 'Lord's Supper', 'Songs on the Trinity', etc.

---

223 See the discussion in Watson, *The English Hymn*, pp. 152-60.
224 Note before Hymn 525.
225 Escott, *Isaac Watts Hymnographer*, p. 182.
226 *Watts*, preface is source of information for this paragraph.

Once again, Rippon seems to have sensed a genuine need and worked hard to satisfy it. The idea of an arranged edition had been publicly suggested in 1796,[227] and Rippon advertised his own project as early as 1798.[228] That it did not appear until 1801 confirms what he confessed, that the task had proved far more arduous than he had expected.[229] He circularised most of the leading Dissenting ministers, and gained their official 'recommendations': in the hundred names listed in advertisements were most of the leading Baptist and Congregational figures.[230] The Bedford Union Association officially recommended it in 1802.[231] The work was reprinted several times, at least as late as 1817. One alternative version was published by Edward Williams, of Rotherham Academy, in 1805; but his arrangement was 'not in the Body of the Work, but in a Table prefixed'. (Williams had declined to recommend Rippon's edition).[232]

The production of an accurate text was of great value, and a random check has demonstrated Rippon's textual accuracy. (He appears to have based his text on one of Watts' last three editions, the fourteenth to the sixteenth).[233] In 1810 Rippon's service to Watts' lovers was concluded by publishing, *An Index ... of all the lines in Watts's Hymns and Psalms... by J. R. assisted by S. A. -, T. R. -&c*, an arduous and mammoth task.[234]

But perhaps the principal advantage to Rippon of his *Watts* was that it meant he had virtually a complete monopoly of the hymns Baptists were singing. Inevitably, the general popularity of the *Selection* was assisted by his *Watts*, as it was by the *Tune Book*.

---

227 *Protestant Dissenters' Magazine* 3 (1796), p. 146.

228 *Register* 3 (1798-1801), p. 93: Rippon advertised two editions of Watts, one an 'improved edition', and the 'arranged' edition; but only the 'arranged' appears to have been published. Profits from his editions were to be devoted to 'village preaching', 'to assist ministers of a small income, and to other benevolent purposes'.

229 *Watts*, p. xii.

230 In editions of the *Selection*.

231 *Register* 4 (1801-02), p. 941.

232 Williams to Rippon, Rotherham, 23 February 1802, B.L. Add. MSS. 25389, f. 501.

233 For a study of the editions of Watts' *Hymns*, see S.L. Bishop (ed.), *Isaac Watts Hymns and Spiritual Songs 1707-1748. A Study in Early Eighteenth Century Language Changes* (London: Faith Press, 1962).

234 S.A. and T.R. were most probably Rippon's nephews, Samuel Adams and Thomas Rippon.

Influence of Rippon's Hymnody

Erik Routley, the distinguished hymnologist, has observed: 'There's a distinction between what people, because of their social background, choose to sing, and what editors, whose background may be very different, offer them'.[235] This is an obvious difficulty in identifying the influence of Rippon's hymnody. But numerous surviving testimonies and the huge success of the *Selection*, and of the related *Tune Book* and *Watts*, suggest Rippon exerted a wide-ranging impact, both on the Baptists as a denomination and on the history of hymnody.

Various congregations were drawn together as they united in their hymn singing. Members moving from one church to another found the same book in use. The general pattern of worship and theology in the *Selection* was impressed upon the churches, an invaluable unifying influence. For nearly fifty years the *Selection* was the only Baptist book in common use.

The main use of the *Selection* was, obviously, for local church services. It was, for example, officially adopted at Tenterden in 1798[236] and Watford in 1799:[237] but few church records in fact stipulate the hymnal used. Missionary-meetings used the *Selection* and the missionaries in India sang from it. For example, when John Fountain arrived in Serampore, Carey, Thomas, and he sang in three parts a hymn from the *Selection*.[238] Again, it provided a collection of hymns suitable for translation, as when Carey told Rippon of a baptismal service: 'We sang a Bengal translation of the 451st hymn of your Selection, 'Jesus, and shall it ever be &c' after which I prayed and descended into the water'.[239] The *Selection* was used by black congregations in Jamaica and Sierra Leone,[240] and by some British prisoners in at least one centre in France during the long war.[241]

Perhaps the most important aspect of this unifying influence was its theological impact. On the one hand it preserved the orthodoxy of the 1689 Confession, indeed unlike the 'Bristol Collection' had hymns on important Calvinistic doctrines such as election and perseverance of the saints. There was a healthy Christological and Trinitarian emphasis, whilst the necessity of the Holy Spirit for regeneration and sanctification was strongly underlined. Indeed, in 1828 the *Selection* was preferred to its

---

235 Cited by Adey, *Class and Idol*, p. 71.

236 W.S. Davies, *In Pleasant Places, Story of Tenterden Baptist Church over Two Centuries* (London: 1967), p.15.

237 J. Stuart, *Beechen Grove Baptist Church, Watford* (London: 1907), p. 46.

238 *Register* 4 (1801-02), p. 948; 3 (1798-1801) p. 73.

239 *Register* 4 (1801-02), p. 900.

240 See chapter 7 for Rippon's gifts of books to these people.

241 *Baptist Magazine* 5 (1813), p. 264.

new rival because it included sections on 'Effectual Calling', 'Moral and Ceremonial Law', 'Justification' and 'other important doctrines'.[242] However, even more important was the manner in which the *Selection* embodied an evangelistic Calvinism. As T.G. Crippen wrote of the *Selection*: 'hymns embodying the Gospel Call are as clear as any Arminian could desire'.[243] Like any good hymnbook Rippon's helped to define and interpret the Christian faith for its own generation. Not the least of the influences shaping the new evangelistic Calvinism of the Baptists was the regular singing of hymns which taught this theology. As has been shown, sermons were expected, according to the hymns in the *Selection*, to be powerful means of bringing sinners to conversion. Hymns for the spread of the Gospel, especially in the work of foreign missions were included in generous numbers, whilst hymns longing for revival - such as could be sung in the monthly services - were also provided. In each of these ways, the *Selection* helped advance the general spread of 'Fullerism' and the genuine missionary and evangelistic concern of the Baptists.

Less easily defined, but still important, was the liturgical influence of the *Selection*. Any widely adopted book standardizes worship patterns within a denomination. David Music, noting Rippon's sections on 'Hymns before Prayer', etc. suggests that Rippon's hymnbook 'represents one of the earliest recognitions by a Baptist compiler that hymns can and should be chosen to fulfil a specific function in the service'. The extensive use of Rippon's book in America 'undoubtedly helped many pastors and church leaders begin to see the potential of the hymnal as a worship book'. This method of arrangement influenced, for example, the important Baptist hymnal edited by Andrew Broaddus, *Virginia Selection of Psalms, Hymns and Spiritual Songs* (1840).[244] Its arrangement reflected the desire of the ablest Baptist ministers for a proper ordering of services. But in a period when many new congregations were formed, and numerous small gatherings were held in villages, often led by untrained laymen, the influence of the *Selection* in shaping the worship of the Baptists may be assumed. There were hymns suitable for the general praise of God found in the front of the book, there were hymns suitable for before prayer, before and after sermon, and doxologies with which to conclude the services. Hymns for Baptism, especially those for before and after the service, were also provided, as were hymns for the Lord's Supper. Indeed, one of the principal uses of the *Selection* was that it catered for almost every conceivable situation in the life of a church - seeking a pastor, election of deacons, funerals, etc.

---

242 *Baptist Magazine* 20 (1828), pp. 468-69.

243 Crippen, 'Congregational Hymnody', p. 228.

244 D.W. Music, 'Baptist Hymnals as Shapers of Worship', *Baptist History and Heritage* 31.3 (1996), pp. 7-17.

The *Selection* not only reflected and stimulated the homiletical bias of Baptist worship, but also suggested an ordered sequence for the whole service.

Another related aspect was the devotional influence of the *Selection*. The piety of its generation was both represented and encouraged. As H.W. Foote observed, it is easy to select lines or verses from old hymns which amuse or appal us, and to caricature the worship it suggests.[245] But it is more important to attempt an understanding of the genuine religious emotions they represent, and to recognize the uninterrupted stream of faith and idealism which flows from generation to generation. In an age when many people possessed very few books - perhaps only a Bible and hymn-book - the devotional use of the hymn-book in both private and family prayers is perhaps far beyond much modern imagination.

The sections designed for use in sickness, for example, are known to have been widely used. Numerous obituaries refer to the comfort of its hymns. For example, Mrs. Leeks had Hymn 550 read to her:

> Ah! I shall soon be dying,
> Time swiftly glides away;
> But, on my Lord relying,
> I hail the happy day-

This brought her great comfort: 'She felt the power of these verses, and with her hands clasped, her eyes fixed upwards, the tears trickling down her cheeks, she seemed in fervent prayer, and said, Ah, that is what I want'.[246]

Andrew Fuller read over some of the hymns in the *Selection* and shed tears of joy while he sang, as he thought of his fellow-Christians in various parts of England and India.[247] Such references are invariably from Rippon's book: it had become *the* Baptist collection.

But more immediately demonstrable is the influence of the *Selection* in the history of hymnody, especially of Baptist hymnody. Four features may be noted. The *Selection* promoted the trend, begun by the 'Bristol Collection', towards a comprehensive hymnal among Baptists; it replaced the more literary or devotional writings of individuals. The *Selection* also provided a standard for Baptist hymnody. As M. Frost observed, the Independents had Watts as the basis of their hymnody, and the Methodists had the Wesleys' or Whitefield's Collection; but that only with Rippon's *Selection* did the Baptists have a 'commanding nucleus

---

245 *Three Centuries of American Hymnody*, pp. 349-50.

246 *Register* 4 (1801-02), p. 759.

247 A. Fuller to T. Steevens, Olney, 5 October 1793, *Baptist Magazine* 8 (1816), pp. 494-95.

round which to group their hymnody'.[248] Many notable hymns, such as 'How firm a foundation' were first introduced by Rippon, whose *Selection* was without doubt the single greatest factor in the extensive circulation of the best of Baptist hymnody from one of their most productive periods.

Rippon's *Selection* became an unrivalled sourcebook for succeeding editors, Baptist and other denominations, so that Rippon permanently impressed himself upon the churches as having influenced their choice of hymns.[249] This cannot be over-emphasized. For example, some 86 hymns are described by *Julian* as being first published by Rippon and as being 'in common use'. (Julian's first edition was 1892). A further 24 centos by Rippon are similarly described. In addition, other hymns, published previously, were given a wide circulation by Rippon's book. As H.W. Foote commented about the hymns of Samuel Davies, that although Gibbons first published them, they 'owe their circulation to Dr. Rippon'.[250] The *New Selection* of 1828 had 260 hymns from Rippon's book, and when C.H. Spurgeon produced *Our Own Hymn Book* in 1866, at which time Rippon's book ceased to be used in his old congregation, he included 195 hymns from Rippon's book. Changing taste has reduced the number of hymns still in use, but 34 appeared in *The Baptist Hymn Book* (1962) and 21 are in *Baptist Praise and Worship* (1991).[251]

The influence of Rippon's book was even more pronounced in America, so that one historian of American Baptist hymnody has included a section 'The Influence of John Rippon'.[252] Rival books relied heavily on the *Selection*. As we have noted, the Philadelphia Association appointed Samuel Jones and Burgis Allison to produce *A Selection of Psalms and Hymns* (1790, 4th edition in 1819), but the Psalms were by Watts and 'most of the hymns from Rippon's Selection'.[253] John Stanford's *A Collection of evangelical Hymns* (1792) again contained little that was new. Eventually publishers either resorted to printing their own editions of Rippon, as noted above, or produced supplements, such as *A Selection of evangelical Hymns supplementary to Doctor Rippon*, Burlington, N.J. (1807). Daniel Dodge, in his *A Selection of Hymns and Psalms, from the most approved authors; principally from Watts & Rippon: together with originals,* Wilmington, Del. (1808) noted that he

---

248 M. Frost (ed.), *Historical Companion to Hymns Ancient and Modern*, p. 110.

249 Benson, *The English Hymn*, p. 145.

250 *Three Centuries of American Hymnody*, p. 151.

251 *Baptist Praise and Worship* (Oxford: Oxford University Press, 1991).

252 W.J. Reynolds, *Hymns of our Faith*, pp. xvi; 'Our Heritage of Baptist Hymnody in America', *Baptist History and Heritage* 11.4 (1976), pp. 204-17; *Companion to Baptist Hymnal*, pp. 11-12.

253 Benson, *The English Hymn*, p. 200.

had attempted to combine the best of both, for the sake of those who found it inconvenient to carry both but would not dispense with either.[254]

From about 1820, Rippon's and Watts were often printed complete in one volume, and this was commended by a large number of ministers as the best hymnbook 'in use among Christians'.[255] Among Congregationalists, Nathan Strong of Hartford issued *The Hartford Selection of Hymns* (1799), and his 387 hymns were mainly taken from *Olney*, Doddridge, and Rippon.[256] A Universalist editor, George Richards, produced *Psalms, Hymns, and Spiritual Songs,* Boston, (1792), and commented in his preface that he had surveyed the whole field of Evangelical Hymnody and ended by accepting Rippon's 'beautiful collection' as the model hymn-book.[257]

L.F. Benson rightly observed that the *Selection* was also 'a link of connection between Baptist hymnody in England and America'.[258] Whilst this is true and significant, it must be noted that the influence was all one way: Rippon is not known to have included any American Baptist writers (indeed only Samuel Davies of America was used).

Rippon's importance for Baptist hymnody was notable. He demonstrated an accurate judgment and literary taste, collected numerous worthy originals, and by his editorial discretion and skill produced a book which attained an unqualified success. He secured for himself 'a permanent place in the history of hymn singing'. As they used Rippon's books, Baptists for two generations at least fulfilled his vision of 'Churchmen and Dissenters', England and the United States, singing side by side.

Rippon's name had become well known to the Baptists of both continents. He was in a unique position to exert even greater influence upon Baptists, and his readiness to serve them in a variety of ways was amply demonstrated.

---

254 Benson, *The English Hymn*, p. 201.
255 'Recommendations' in Sommers and Dagg's edition, Philadelphia, (1838).
256 Benson, *The English Hymn*, p. 373.
257 Benson, *The English Hymn*, p. 424.
258 Benson, *The English Hymn*, p. 145.

CHAPTER 5

Wider Horizons:
The Baptist Annual Register (1790-1802)

The thirteen years during which Rippon published his *Register* were among the most significant in the history of the Particular Baptists in both Britain and the United States. In Britain there was considerable expansion in many of the older churches, new churches were formed, whilst the first foreign and home missionary organizations were inaugurated. American Baptists were in the midst of 'a formative period of organization and expansion', characterized by extraordinary religious revivals, evangelistic and missionary enthusiasm, and an increasing concern for ministerial education.[1]

All these features are recorded in the *Register* which, as the first English Baptist periodical, assumes a unique historical importance.[2] The *Register* both reflected and encouraged the denomination's new maturity and optimism. As the *Register* was largely the product of Rippon's own extensive vision and labour, his personal influence was again remarkable.

The *Register* must also be seen as the climax to an increasing desire among some Baptist ministers on both sides of the Atlantic to enlarge the vision and self-awareness of their people. Rippon evidenced two dominant motives in his preface to the *Register*: he wanted to remove ignorance about Baptists, and among Baptists. Thus, he promoted the historical awareness of Baptists; this important and fundamental aspect of the *Register*'s significance is considered separately, together with his other historiographical efforts.[3] Rippon was deeply committed to expand the Baptists' knowledge of one another. Although the Methodists, Moravians, and Quakers cherished 'an universal acquaintance' among

---

1 R.G. Torbet, *A History of the Baptists* (Valley Forge, Pa: Judson Press, rev. edn, 1963), p. 253.

2 R. Taylor, 'English Baptist Periodicals, 1790-1865', *BQ* 37.2 (1977), pp. 50-82.

3 See chapter 6.

themselves, Baptists were largely ignorant of each other: 'But *we* spend half a century, and know not in Devonshire a single circumstance of the Churches in Lancashire.' Admittedly many churches shared in their local Baptist association:

> But multitudes of our *Members*, till the *Register* appeared, never so much as heard of any Association in the world, but that to which their own or some neighbouring church belongs; while more than a few of other Ministers themselves seldom saw a letter from any Association but the one with which they are united. Consequently these annual publications were beneficial only to a few individuals, instead of promoting the knowledge, purity and joy of the whole denomination, to which some of them, I think, are peculiarly adapted.[4]

There was, however, some evidence of a desire for increased contact between some associations such as had been normal in the seventeenth century associations.[5] The Western Association in 1777 resolved to open a correspondence with other associations and for a few years published news from them.[6] The Northamptonshire Association in 1790 printed statistical details from other associations,[7] but omitted them in 1791 because of the *Register*.[8] The letters, printed annually by most associations, seem to have been exchanged at least by the leaders.

At the same time, the Kent and Sussex Association had begun a regular correspondence with the Charleston Association in 1787,[9] and the Northamptonshire Association in 1789 published information about six American associations.[10] Again, personal correspondence between American and English ministers, common through much of the seventeenth and eighteenth centuries,[11] was renewed after the War of Independence.[12] Several Baptists are known to have been in correspondence by 1790. These correspondents included: James Manning of Providence, who wrote to Caleb Evans, Booth, Ryland, William Richards of Lynn, and Rippon;[13] Isaac Backus of New England, with Stennett,

---

4   *Register* 1 (1790-93), p. iii.

5   See B.R. White, 'The Organisation of the Particular Baptists, 1644-1660', *Journal of Ecclesiastical History* 17.2 (1966), pp. 209-26.

6   *Western Association Circular Letter* (1777), p. 7.

7   *Northamptonshire Association Circular Letter* (1790), p. 9.

8   *Northamptonshire Letter* (1791), p. 8.

9   *Kent and Sussex Circular Letter* (1787), pp. 9-10.

10   *Kent and Sussex Letter* (1789), pp. 15-16.

11   J.C. Fletcher, 'Interaction between English and American Baptists from 1639-1689' (ThD thesis, Southwestern Baptist Seminary, Fort Worth, Texas, 1958).

12   H. Davies, 'The American Revolution and the Baptist Atlantic', *BQ* 36.3 (1995), pp. 132-49.

13   Cf. Guild, *Early History of Brown University*, passim.

Gifford, Joshua Thomas, Timothy Thomas, and Rippon;[14] Samuel Stillman of Boston with Samuel Medley,[15] Ryland,[16] and Rippon;[17] Lewis Richards of Baltimore with Medley;[18] Richard Furman of Charleston with the Kent and Sussex Association and Rippon; whilst Rippon also was in touch with John Gano, formerly of New York but from 1787 in Kentucky;[19] and Thomas Ustick of Philadelphia. What Rippon intended in the *Register*, as Hywel Davies has observed, was 'to institutionalize the correspondence which had previously been of an accidental and personal nature'.[20]

Rippon's interest in American Baptists was first evidenced in 1780, when Benjamin Wallin showed him a letter from Boston which described a religious revival in New England with Elhanan Winchester (1751-1797) as a leading figure.[21] Rippon was so pleased that he forwarded the account to Caleb Evans, who printed extracts from it in the 1781 Western Association letter.[22] This was the first example of Rippon publicizing American religious news.

The first letter Rippon wrote to America was evidently to Manning on 1 May 1784, which began:

> I have long wished for an opportunity of introducing myself to you, & to several other brethren on your side of ye Atlantic. And as God in his providence has now put an end to ye late bloody & unrighteous war, and opened a free communication between this country & America, I take ye liberty, ...of soliciting such a Christian Correspondence as your wisdom may suggest, & your large connections & many avocations may permit...[23]

After a brief personal introduction, Rippon commented about the American War:

---

14   T.B. Maston, *Isaac Backus: Pioneer of Religious Liberty* (Rochester, N.Y.: American Baptist Historical Society, 1962), p. 140; J. Thomas, *A History of the Baptist Association in Wales* (London: 1795), p. iv; *Northamptonshire Circular Letter* (1790), p. 10. For Backus (1724-1806), see *DEB* and S. Grenz, *Isaac Backus-Puritan and Baptist* (Macon, Ga.: Mercer University Press, 1983).

15   S. Medley to Rippon, Liverpool 28 February 1789, B.L. Add. MSS. 25388, f. 36. For Stillman (1737-1807), see *DAB* and *DEB*.

16   *Northamptonshire Circular Letter* (1789), p. 15, and (1790), p. 10

17   *Register* 1 (1790-93), p. v.

18   As in note 15. For Richards (1752-1832) see *DEB*.

19   *Register* 1 (1790-93), p. v. For Gano, (1727-1804), see *DAB* and *DEB*.

20   Davies, 'The American Revolution and the Baptist Atlantic', p 141.

21   For Winchester (1751-1797), who disappointed the Baptists by becoming a Universalist and returned to England in 1787, see *DAB*.

22   *Western Association Letter* (1781), pp. 2-4.

23   Original in Brown University, Guild, *Early History of Brown University*, pp. 374-76.

I believe all our Baptist ministers in Town, except two, & most of our brethren in ye country, were on ye side of ye Americans in ye late dispute. But sorry, very sorry, were we to hear yt ye College was a Hospital, yt ye meeting houses were forsaken, & occupied for civil or martial Purposes. We wept when ye thirsty plains drank ye blood of your departed heroes, and ye shout of a king was amongst us, when your well fought battles were crowned with victory...the independence of America will for a while secure the liberty of this country; but if the continent had been reduced, Britain would not long have been free.

Rippon seems to have accurately reflected the English Baptists' support for the Revolution.[24] He forwarded several books, as a gift to Manning, and regretted that the last news he had from America was the 1779 Letter of the Warren Association.

Manning replied on 3 August 1784, 'Nothing would be more agreeable than the correspondence you propose, which I shall endeavour to keep up with the greatest punctuality'.[25] From this time Manning and Rippon, drawn together by a warm evangelical faith and similar interests, engaged in an affectionate and regular correspondence. When Rippon began preparing his *Selection* he wrote in 1786 to Manning and Thomas Ustick of Philadelphia describing his plans. The rapid sale of the *Selection* in America strengthened Rippon's interest, and his increasing absorption in everything American is confirmed by an unusual work he republished in 1788: *A Sermon at the Execution of Moses Paul, an Indian, who had been guilty of Murder, Preached at New Haven in America by Samson Occom; to which is added A Short Account of the Late Spread of the Gospel, among the Indians; also Observation on the Language of the Muhhekanew Indians,...by Jonathan Edwards, DD.* Occom, a native Indian preacher and hymn-writer, had visited England in 1766, collecting for Indian Charity Schools.[26] The *Short Account* was from the journal of Samuel Kirkland, a missionary to the Indians;[27] whilst the linguistic study was by the second son of the celebrated Jonathan Edwards who with his father had lived at Stockbridge among the Mohican Indians.[28] Samuel Medley wrote to Rippon:

---

24   For discussion of Dissenters and the American conflict, see chapter 7.

25   Guild, *Early History of Brown University,* pp. 377-81.

26   For Occom (1723-1792), see *Julian,* p. 855 and *DEB.*; W.D. Love, *Samson Occom and the Christian Indians of New England* (Boston: 1899).

27   For Kirkland, see O.W. Elsbree, *The Rise of the Missionary Spirit in America 1790-1815* (Philadelphia: Porcupine Press, 1980 [1928]), p. 22; W.P. Love, *Samson Occom,* pp. 105-18 and *DEB.*

28   For the son (1745-1801), see *DAB* and *DEB.*

But to be sure you my Dear Bro Rippon must have a most Extraordinary Predilection for America when you reprinted that most curious Paper respecting the Indian Language - what in all the world had got into your Dear Head to lead you to do it?[29]

This increasing interest, Rippon said, 'produced a pretty general wish on both sides of the *Atlantic*, of obtaining a more comprehensive knowledge of each others religious circumstances'.[30] Rippon was approached 'two or three years following' by Americans for a 'fixed and constant medium' which would give a full account of Baptist work in Great Britain, especially in London. The *Register* was clearly a transatlantic project. This desire to help his American friends was stressed in a letter to Manning.

The happiness of the American churches lies near my heart. I see my brethren have too much neglected them. There is not a public spirit enough in this country; but I have *hinted* by this conveyance to two friends, that the *Register* is intended to serve the *American* brethren particularly.[31]

Accordingly, Rippon decided to begin his task, as he wrote in the preface of the first volume (1793):

Having had a wish therefore to gratify the Brethren at home and abroad; and hoping under a Divine blessing to be the instrument in bringing so many of the churches so far acquainted, That they may have an opportunity of relieving one anothers wants, of praying for each other when the ways of Sion mourn, and of praising God in the enjoyment of prosperous circumstances - I determined in the year 1790, God Willing, to print a periodical work, which should be intitled, THE BAPTIST ANNUAL REGISTER.[32]

Plan of the *Register* and Response by the Churches

Rippon widened the initial plan of the *Register* so as to include various features which he listed in an advertisement (substantially reprinted in the Preface to the first volume).[33] These extras included: engravings of leading Baptists; an account of the origin and design of Baptist associations from 1644, with a history of each association; with each new volume, a list of all the Particular Baptist churches in England and Wales;

---

29   Medley to Rippon, Liverpool, 23 February 1789, B.L. Add. MSS. 25388, f. 36.
30   *Register* 1 (1790-93), p. iv.
31   Guild, *Early History of Brown University*, p. 486, (original undated letter in Brown University).
32   *Register* 1 (1790-93), p. v.
33   Bound with the first number (copy in Angus Library).

the yearly association letters; extracts from the Irish Letter; the American association letters together with extracts from personal correspondence from America; an annual list of the books published by Baptists, or of general evangelical usefulness; obituaries of Baptist people; historical sketches of churches in Europe and America; 'Miscellaneous' which included extracts from scarce or expensive books, accounts of the spread of the gospel, especially of 'Foreign Missions'. This last feature was planned in 1790, before the Baptists had begun their own missionary society.

The title of Rippon's periodical was probably derived from the influential *Annual Register* begun by Edmund Burke and Robert Dodsley in 1758. Despite the title, Rippon originally planned to issue his *Register* twice a year, at Christmas and Whitsun. Although he called it the *Baptist Annual Register*, Rippon noted that it was not an 'official' product of the denomination, indeed there was no Baptist organization that could have undertaken the task. Many had expressed the need for such a journal, and had promised to support it, but as Rippon observed: 'The production ... boasts of no patronage so high, as that of the whole body of Baptists; but it would be improper not to say, *It aspires towards* that honour, *nor wishes a greater'*.[34]

At the same time, Rippon had no intention of restricting the scope of the *Register* to Baptists. The full title added, 'Including Sketches of the State of Religion among different denominations of good men at home and abroad'. In the preface he penned this fine statement:

> Though I feel it an honour to rank with the Calvinists, whose system, commonly called orthodox, is peculiarly dear to me; yet conceiving That all who hate sins and love our Lord Jesus Christ in sincerity, are *good men*, if they do not think of Baptism as I do, nor embrace half my Creed, I delight in such as my brethren, and embrace them, by thousands, in the bosom of a warm affection - and with my views, it would be criminal not to do so, though no one can be farther than I am from the opinions of these amiable persons.[35]

Accordingly, he declared, 'the *Register* will be found, with *open arms*, ready to receive materials from *every Description of good Men'*. In practice, Rippon avoided theological controversy and increasingly included general Dissenting and evangelical materials.

Rippon was keenly aware that the success of the venture was directly related to the co-operation of his fellow-Baptists. The success of the *Register* was:

---

34   *Register* 1 (1790-93), p. vi.
35   *Register* 1 (1790-93), p. vi.

proportioned to the *Communications*, the *Benevolence*, and the *Candour* of his Brethren ... I hear the voice of friendship! This scheme is *too large for one man* then, Brother, grant it your assistance. Benevolence subjoins, *The plan is too limited;* then, Brother, extend it.[36]

Fortunately, the response Rippon hoped for was immediate and enthusiastic. Rippon sought the co-operation of the leading figures in all the English associations which were both sources of local information and strategic centres for advertising and distributing the *Register*. The Northamptonshire Association advertised the *Register* with its Letters for 1790 and 1791. Fuller thought it 'a good plan',[37] whilst Ryland (Junior) commented, it 'bids fair to prove a most useful and entertaining means of diffusing the knowledge of the state of religion, especially among our own denomination'.[38] William Carey, later to send missionary letters from India for Rippon to print, helped by translating some Dutch letters for Rippon.[39] Rippon naturally had support from the Western Association. Caleb Evans assured him of 'ready compliance', but offered detailed warnings and suggestions. He feared it might 'somewhat resemble Swift's Memoirs of a parish Clerk'; suggested printing only extracts from association letters; and thought, if it was a Baptist *Register* some 'general account' of the General Baptists was necessary. He concluded: 'On you it must principally depend whether it shall be a dry, dull, insipid detail of unintg events, or an instrucv pleasg performance. If you gratify everyone of yr Brethren yt may be fond of exhibiting himself to public view you'll soon disgust the intelligent.'[40]

Benjamin Francis, Samuel Rowles, and Robert Redding (with whom Rippon had been in Bristol Academy) of Chacewater in Cornwall all gave support.[41] William Atwood of the Kent and Sussex Association gave help from the first. Both the Midland Association and the Welsh Association were served by Joshua Thomas who also supplied Rippon with much historical data. John Hitchcock of Wattisham and the Norfolk and Suffolk Association, 'approved' of the *Register*,[42] as did George Hall of Ipswich: both sent much useful material. In the north of England there were two associations. Charles Whitfield of the Northern proved a faithful correspondent of Rippon's, whilst John Fawcett, leader of the Yorkshire and Lancashire Association, was 'highly pleased with the plan' and

---

36   Advertisement with first number, pp. 5 -6.

37   Fuller to Rippon, Kettering, January 1791, B.L. Add. MSS. 25387, f. 38.

38   *Salvation Finished* (funeral sermon for Robert Hall, Sr), (London: 1791), p. 21 note.

39   See below in this chapter.

40   Evans to Rippon, Bristol, n.d., B.L. Add. MSS. 25386, f. 442.

41   Redding to Rippon, Truro, 20 December 1790, B.L. Add. MSS. 25388, f. 390.

42   *Register* 1 (1790-93), pp. 61-62.

promised to do all he could to 'forward the design'.[43] Samuel Medley, of Liverpool, also helped Rippon.

Thus Rippon had responsible leaders from all the associations supporting him. Hence he could write to Manning, 'The *Register* is taking a prodigs spread thro' almost all our Churches, the country friends themselves ordering from 15 to an 100 copies each Church'.[44] In America, under Manning's influence, the Philadelphia Association in 1790 appointed eight leading ministers throughout the continent, 'to receive the news of the Brethren who might be disposed to patronise the work'.[45] Isaac Backus of New England, a leader in the struggle for religious liberty, also thought the plan 'calculated for public good, and extensive usefulness' and promised his 'mite' towards it.[46] Samuel Stillman led the Warren Association to recommend the *Register* to all its members, and requested all suitable information.[47] The Kehukee Association in North Carolina agreed to encourage 'such a laudable work', ordered fifty copies, and appointed Lemuel Burkitt as correspondent to Rippon.[48] The Charleston Association had in 1789 received English association letters sent by Rippon,[49] and Richard Furman was receiving 150 copies of each issue by April 1792.[50]

Rippon listed several suggestions he had received from his correspondents such as abbreviating the association letters, analyzing newly printed books, more frequent issues; and adopted many of them.[51] But the most encouraging result of his extensive preparations, which had necessitated his writing as many as fifty letters a week for much of 1790,[52] was that the *Register* gradually became accepted by the churches in both England and America. Once the links had been forged, Rippon found that his trouble was not in obtaining suitable materials, so much as selecting from what he had in hand. The first two numbers were reprinted, and Rippon, though still a busy pastor and publishing his

---

43   Fawcett to Rippon, 23 November 1790 (original in Angus Library).

44   Guild, *Early History of Brown University*, p. 485. (Spelling has been given in original form, although Guild 'improved' it.)

45   Advertisement for *Register*, in number 1. These men were: B. Allison of Bordertown, N.J.; Benjamin Foster of New York; Richard Furman of Charleston, S.C.; J. Manning of Providence; Lewis Richards of Baltimore; Samuel Stillman of Boston; and Thomas Ustick of Philadelphia.

46   Backus to Rippon, 10 November 1791 (original in Angus Library). Cf. A. Hovey, *A Memoir of the Life and Times of Isaac Backus* (Boston: 1859), pp.252-55.

47   *Register* 1 (1790-93), p. 292.

48   *Register* 2 (1794-97), p. 298.

49   *Register* 2 (1794-97), p. 101.

50   Rippon to Furman, 6 April 1792 (Original at Furman University, Greenville, S.C.)

51   *Register* 1 (1790-93), pp. vii-viii.

52   *Register* 1 (1790-93), pp. vi -vii.

hymnbooks, gradually learned even more about the many and varied demands made upon an editor.[53]

Rippon as Editor

The *Register* was the responsibility of Rippon alone, and involved extensive time and effort. In 1793 Rippon confessed, 'Had the difficulties and expences of the undertaking been *all* foreseen, it is probable they would never have been encountered'.[54] But there were several reasons why Rippon, though without experience as a journalist, was qualified to make a success of the task. As his *Selection* had revealed, he had a care for detail and an application to work, had experience with printers, had the confidence of Baptists in both countries, was centrally situated in London, and was theologically orthodox. His wide range of personal contacts meant that he soon received ample material from which to select.

Nevertheless, he was constantly open to new developments. He would ply any prospective correspondent with questions; former slave-preacher George Liele, for example, was given fifty detailed questions to answer.[55] He read widely for background, especially on Indian mythology, for example, to explain terms in missionary letters.[56] He recorded *verbatim* accounts of interviews with leading ministers.[57] The pastor became a journalist.

The *Register* was Rippon's own work. He selected materials, edited them, read the proofs, and arranged the distribution of each issue. He brought great care to each of these tasks. Preserved in the Angus Library, Oxford, are three boxes of proof sheets from the *Register*. These proofs, all from the second volume, demonstrate Rippon's desire for accuracy. Often an unsatisfactory sheet was returned with a caustic comment: 'So bad I shall go no farther' - (to which the printer replied, 'Consider the MSS copy which is very unfit to be composed from'). Rippon often had boys from the printer waiting for fresh copy, as several comments reveal. He insisted on prompt and careful work: 'If it be eleven o' C tonight I shall wish to see this corrected before I go to bed'. Despite this, however, there were many misprints in each volume.[58]

---

53 *Register* 1 (1790-93), 'Addenda and Corrigenda'.
54 *Register* 1 (1790-93), p. vii.
55 *Register* 1 (1790-93), p. 332. For Liele, see below.
56 *Register* 2 (1794-97), pp.141-173 (notes).
57 *Register* 1 (1790-93), p. 473; 3 (1798-1801) pp. 285, 316.
58 Volume 1: 75; 2: 38; 3: 38; 4: 72. These have been noted by the present writer. Rippon listed his own corrections for the first volume only.

The general impression is nevertheless of a desire for accuracy. There are few slips of grammar. The indices to each volume were carefully drawn up, although by modern standards they are inevitably inadequate, cryptic and even amusing: 'Ordination, one conducted so as not to be tiresome'.[59] In addition, Rippon sometimes gave in the index the author of an article, although it had not been indicated in the body of the volume. The first copy of the *Register* cost one shilling and sixpence, but the following issues were one shilling until in 1801 Rippon began a monthly publication for sixpence. The circulation is unknown, but as already noted, the first two numbers were reprinted during 1792. By January 1796 at least 3,000 were being printed, as a note upon a corrected proof sheet suggests. There were inevitable delays in the distribution of the *Register*, and especially in America, as the French wars disrupted much communication.[60]

The *Register* was issued at irregular intervals, and during the period of publication underwent a gradual change of purpose. Table 3 lists the date of each number of the volume, helpful for accurately dating various parts of each volume. There were forty-one issues, distributed with paper-covers, some of which are extant. The *Register* was issued twice yearly from 1791 to 1796 (numbers 1 to 13); then annually from 1797 to 1800 (numbers 14 to 17); and then monthly (with the exception of August 1802) from January 1801 to January 1803 (numbers 18 to 41).

Some explanation for this irregularity in the *Register*'s production is required. Evidently, Rippon did not intend to publish only once a year, and especially regretted the long delays between 14 and 15 (May 1797 and September 1798) and between 16 and 17 (January 1799 and December 1800). There were two main reasons. The first was delay in receiving materials; and the second was Rippon's health. Both these were noted on the cover of number 14 (May 1797). Rippon had delayed so as to be able to print the newly-formed Itinerant Society's plan. Then he was ill for several weeks, and prevented from 'all regular application'. He then decided to complete the second volume. Again, Rippon is also known to have been seriously ill during 1799, expected to have to resign his pastorate, and was unable 'to write any thing, but what is unavoidably

---

59   *Register* 2 (1793-97). The reference was to p. 121, where Rippon commended an ordination service which was briefer than normal, having lasted only three and a half hours, by including only one charge and not two separate charges to the church and minister. Rippon had personally suggested this procedure; 'a distinction will be made by all, but idiots, between reformation and revolution'.

60   For a detailed illustration of the difficulties, see the letters written between 1800-1802 by John Bowen to Rippon: (i) *BHS Trans* (1909), pp. 69-76; (ii) *BQ* 10.4 (1940-41), pp. 262-73; (iii) two unpublished letters in the Angus Library.

necessary'.[61] However in December 1800 when number 17 was printed, Rippon announced that the *Register* would subsequently appear monthly, and announced: 'The EDITOR of the Baptist Register has the pleasure of informing his friends, that, his health being considerably restored, he has resumed his station, and hopes to fill it with suitable *vigour, regularity,* and *dispatch.*' From this time the *Register* was often described by his correspondents as a 'monthly magazine'.

By this decision the general character of the *Register* was changed. Every month he issued forty pages for sixpence. There were probably two main reasons for this drastic change in the general design of his periodical. The first was, as Rippon himself noted, that he had many 'arrears', and hoped to print much material he had long since collected. He especially hoped to print more histories of Dissenting churches so that his *Register* would be virtually a 'Dissenters' Magazine'. This suggests the second reason: competition from other religious magazines.

Numerous religious periodicals were contemporaneous with the *Register*.[62] The pugnaciously Calvinistic *Gospel Magazine* (1774-1784) had been succeeded by the *New Spiritual Magazine* (1783-85), but was outlasted by its rival, the *Arminian Magazine*, commenced in 1778, but changed to the less provocative *Methodist Magazine* in 1798. During the *Register*'s period more serious rivals appeared. The most important was undoubtedly the *Evangelical Magazine* (1793-1904). This counted Baptists like Fuller and Ryland among its stated contributors, and it inevitably drew away much Baptist support from the *Register. The Protestant Dissenters' Magazine* was begun in 1794, but after six volumes ended in 1799. Its stated object was to be a channel of communication between Dissenters, and to demonstrate their loyalty to the Throne: 'to enforce those precepts of our holy religion, "fear God and honour the King"'.[63] Baptists shared in this work. Then there was the *Gospel Magazine and Theological Review* (1796-) which included the Baptist Joseph Jenkins amongst its supporters. The *General Baptist Magazine* (1798-1800), edited by Dan Taylor, perhaps drew away some support for the *Register*, which had included some General Baptist content.

But Rippon in 1800 faced further Baptist rivals. William Jones (1762-1846),[64] a Scotch Baptist in Liverpool, began his *New Theological Repository* in July 1800, as a monthly. Although its sale was mainly in

---

61   J. Rippon, *Discourses on the All-Sufficient Gracious Assistance of the Holy Spirit* (1800), pp. 5-7.

62   See the list of periodicals in F.W. Bateson (ed.), *Cambridge Bibliography of English Literature* (5 vols; Cambridge: Cambridge University Press, 1940), 2, pp. 656-739.

63   *Protestant Dissenters' Magazine* 1 (1794), preface.

64   See *DNB*.

Scotland, a 'goodly number of copies were sold in England'.[65] Jones included material by Fuller, Medley, Booth, and Fawcett. (This magazine lasted until December 1808). But in the first volume of the *Periodical Accounts* of the BMS there appeared an advertisement for a new 'Dissenters' Magazine', announced to begin in January 1801: possibly planned by either William Button, or J. W. Morris, of Clipston.[66] This did not eventuate, and it is significant that Rippon should at this very time begin publishing his *Register* monthly, and describe it as a 'Dissenters' Magazine'. Evidently he persuaded the publisher not to set up a rival paper. However, J.W. Morris began his *Biblical Magazine*, a bi-monthly in 1801 and then monthly. The title of this magazine is misleading, because other materials, quite similar to Rippon's *Register*, were included. The correspondents and support for this seem to have come mainly from the Midlands, with Fuller and the late Samuel Pearce prominent in the early numbers.

Some materials from the *Register* were duplicated in Morris' magazine.[67] Both the *Theological Repository* and the *Biblical Magazine* appear to have been provincial in leadership and scope, but their appearance can only have made it difficult for the success of the *Register*. In America rival publications also appeared.[68] The *Theological Magazine* was published in New York (1795-99), and in 1800 the *New York Missionary Magazine and Repository of Missionary Intelligence* commenced.

But the most obvious result of the new monthly form of the *Register* was an uneven content. New features such as original poetry, original manuscript letters, and a 'Dissenters' Register' replaced the contents of earlier volumes, such as the list of the churches, the list of Baptist books, and caused a decrease in the amount of association or missionary news. The *Register* increasingly became a Dissenters' historical and antiquarian

---

65   W. Jones, *Autobiography* (London: 1846), p. 45.

66   BMS *Periodical Accounts*, 1 (1800), advertisement in which both were named. Whitley, *Baptist Bibliography*, 2, p. 246 listed Button as the publisher, but the advertisement claimed that the proposed magazine had no connection with any bookseller (which Button was). Morris, as printer of the *Periodical Accounts*, could easily have added the advertisement himself.

67   The *Register* printed two items first, and two were published the same month. Cf. *Register* 4 (1801-02), pp. 677, 712, 1073, 957, and *Biblical Magazine* 1, pp. 400-404; 2, pp. 230, 396, 439. In 1804 this magazine merged with the *Theological Magazine and Review* (founded by Independent ministers in 1801) and became *The Theological and Biblical Magazine* (1804-7) and editorship eventually passed to the Independent, William Maurice of Fetter-lane church. See Jones, *Autobiography*, pp. 64-66; Taylor, 'English Baptist Periodicals', pp 55-56. Morris later became bankrupt; for Morris, see Haykin, *One Heart and One Soul*, pp. 279-86.

68   Elsbree, *The Rise of the Missionary Spirit in America 1790-1815*, pp. 54-56.

repository. Its general form copied the rival magazines. The amount of space devoted to each subject for each volume is indicated in Table 4. This clearly shows the changing character of the *Register*. The amount of space devoted to the associations declined from 32.9%, in Volume 1 to 6.7% in Volume 4, whilst the space for 'intelligence' and history increased. The changes in volume 4 are clearly represented on this Table.

There are several other weaknesses in Rippon's organization which require special comment. First, his arrangement of materials is often hard to understand. To a modern reader, the *Register* is at times like an antique shop: unexpected treasures jostle with rubbish. Often clearly related materials (such as association letters) were not grouped together; probably because originals did not reach him in time. But then, at other times, Rippon would delay including certain features because newer material, which he wished to publicize, had come to hand. Hence, in number 10 (April 1795) Rippon published BMS letters, with the result that matter promised for that issue was postponed.

Secondly, he published 'extras' which can only have confused his readers. Most confusing of all was the very first number. As Rippon prepared for this, he had received, quite unexpectedly, three old manuscript volumes by Stinton, and other papers. With doubtful wisdom for the first issue of a new periodical, Rippon omitted a preface, added a slip explaining his plan, and published the following historical papers: (i) The Introduction to the 1644 London Confession; (ii) An account of Baptist work in Ireland, and letters between Irish, English, and Welsh churches, in 1653; (iii) The first section of the 1689 Baptist Confession; (iv) A narrative of the General Assembly of 1689; (v) An account of the Baptist churches in England and Wales for 1689 and 1692; (vi) The beginning of the General Epistle of the Particular Baptist Assembly for 1690 (the completion of which was never published by Rippon). His explanation was that these papers, reflecting a period of intense Baptist co-operation, 'seem adapted to supply the place of other *prefatory pages*'.

These pages were all numbered separately. In succeeding numbers the 1644 and 1689 confessions were completed. Rippon hoped to include histories of all the associations, hence his separate numbering was in order that they might form a separate volume. But the only history published was *The History of the Welsh Association* by Joshua Thomas which appeared a sheet at a time, as an extra, and dragged from 1792 to 1796 (much to Thomas' annoyance).[69] These complicated page numberings and necessitated special instruction sheets for binding the volumes of the *Register*.

---

69   For Thomas (1719-1797) see *DWB, DEB*, and E.W. Hayden, 'Joshua Thomas: Welsh Baptist Historian', *BQ* 23.3 (1969), pp. 126-37.

Thirdly, Rippon had the annoying habit of failing to deliver promised contents for succeeding numbers. There are many examples of this. For example, Rippon spoke of a comprehensive history of all the older London churches, and although he had examined the records of several churches this did not appear.[70] Other promised items included a print of a medal presented to an Indian tribe;[71] the history of Rhode Island Academy,[72] and of several local churches;[73] a Register of Births of Dissenters.[74] Rippon's impetuosity, and a concern to have only the most accurate accounts printed, do not provide sufficient excuse. He is known to have had much valuable material which be never printed.[75] Fourthly, he duplicated a few materials,[76] and failed to complete others.[77]

These serious weaknesses of his work perhaps emphasize the difficulties he faced as sole editor of the *Register*. His many other interests probably account for some of his failures. And yet, although much of the contents are inferior and sometimes poorly arranged, the general value of the *Register* is obvious. It was the only regular Baptist publication of the period, and is the only source for much valuable data. An examination of the various types of material indicates its value, not only for our understanding of Baptist history, but for Rippon's own contemporaries. The specifically historical content, such as the memorials and obituaries, and the histories of churches are discussed in chapter six. Here it is proposed to outline the other contents of the *Register* and to note how these helped to draw the Baptists throughout both continents closer to each other.

---

70   *Register* 3 (1798-1801), p. 25, note 1. Rippon's notes from the Devonshire Square Churchbook are in the Dr. Williams's Library, London.

71   *Register* 3 (1798-1801), p. 55.

72   *Register* 4 (1801-02), p. 840.

73   See below, chapter 6.

74   Advertisement with number 29 (December 1801).

75   These included: a manuscript history of the Warren Association by Backus; a history of the Midland Association and of several churches by Joshua Thomas; a history of the Northern Association by Hitchcock; extracts from earlier Yorkshire and Lancashire Associations. In addition, several anecdotes were forwarded to him and are extant in his letters.

76   Minutes of associations: *Register* 3 (1798-1801), p. 489 and 4 (1801-02), pp. 811, 627, 709.

77   The extracts from Robinson's *Ecclesiastical History* and Newman's 'Theological Dictionary' (both in volume 4) were incomplete.

Contents of the *Register*

Whilst the significance of the *Register* has long been recognized by Nonconformist historians, only general summaries of its contents have been offered.[78] A more detailed analysis of Rippon's work confirms its value.

Lists of Churches

ENGLISH LISTS

Rippon published lists of all the Particular Baptist churches in England of which he had knowledge in 1790, 1794, and 1798.[79] These were arranged according to counties and are among the most valuable contents of the *Register*. Especially important are the notes which Rippon added about many churches in the 1794 and 1798 lists. As Geoffrey Nuttall observed: 'No other denomination has such a fine contemporary record of its churches and their ministers as exists for the 1790s in Rippon's *Baptist Annual Register*'.[80]

These lists were as accurate as Rippon could possibly make them. His 1790 list was based on an earlier one compiled two years before by James Smith (1728-1803), treasurer of the Baptist Fund, but was altered 'in about an hundred and fifty places'.[81] His main sources were letters from churches applying to the Fund, letters sent by the churches to the associations, and his own personal contacts.[82] When the first two numbers were reprinted Rippon made a further eleven corrections. Again, Nuttall comments:

> Rippon published the details as they came in, expanding them and correcting errors of identification, location and spelling as he went along. If his lists and annotations are thus somewhat unsystematic and demand care in interpretation, the untidiness also conveys a sense of something growing under one's hand. The important thing is that Rippon published them.[83]

---

78   For example: Brown, *The English Baptists of the Eighteenth Century*, pp. 118-19; G.F. Nuttall, 'The Baptist Churches and their Ministers in the 1790s: Rippon's Baptist Annual Register', *BQ* 30.8 (1984), pp. 383-87.

79   *Register* 1 (1790-93), pp. 1-13; 2 (1794-97), pp. 1-24; 3 (1798-1801), pp.1-43.

80   Nuttall, 'The Baptist Churches and their Ministers in the 1790s', p. 383.

81   Title-page to 1790 list (omitted in later editions); *Theological and Biblical Magazine* 4 (1804), pp. 121-25.

82   *Register* 1 (1790-93), p. 2.

83   Nuttall, 'The Baptist Churches and their Ministers in the 1790s', p. 383.

For the 1794 list Rippon made careful preparations, sending 'printed queries' to 'most of the popular ministers in England; to which an answer was requested on or before the 15th of July'. Samuel Medley of Liverpool returned a humorous response in verse which Rippon later published separately, so that the actual questions are known.[84] These questions illustrate the type of material found in the notes and Rippon's quest for accurate detail.

(1) In what county is your place of worship situated?

(2) In what Town, Parish, or Village?

(3) Is it a Church, Chapel, or Meeting?

(4) By what denomination of professing Christians is your Congregation distinguished?

(5) Will you favour us with your Christian and Surname at length, as the Minister of the place, with your Degree, or any other addition?

(6) Have you an Assistant Minister - be pleased to subjoin his name likewise? (Medley's reply was typical of his humour:

'O yes; I've one of whom I boast

His name is call'd THE HOLY GHOST!')

(7) When are your stated Times of Worship?

(8) What number of people attend?

(9) By what means was the Gospel first introduced, and what particular Providence attended its Introduction?

(10) What success has the Gospel had, and what Opposition has it met with?

(11) What is the present State of your Church, and what encouraging Prospects of future Usefulness?

(12) If a Meeting or Chapel, when or by whom was it first built?

(13) Is it encumbered with debt, &c?

(14) What are the names of the stated ministers who have laboured in your place, from its commencement to the present period?

(15) What particulars concerning all or any of them, or their writings, do you think will interest the public attention?

(16) What places in your neighbourhood do you supply, which have no stated minister?

(17) Is your neighbourhood favourable to the reception of the Gospel?

(18) What obstructs its progress? and can you suggest any method for spreading it more effectually?

(19) Have any remarkable providences taken place, &c?

(20) We will thank you for a list of the ministers and places where the Gospel is faithfully preached in your County.

---

84   *Register* 3 (1798-1801), pp. 311-12.

Rippon claimed to have taken 'incredible pains' for this 1794 list, and some corrections were added as late as 15 May 1794 (the same month the number was issued).[85] But the fullest details were given in the 1798 list, which occupied forty pages; Rippon had spared 'neither labour nor expense', and his information came from 'more than six hundred letters'.[86] Nevertheless, some churches had no comments about them: Rippon explained that he either had nothing of interest to say, or else his information was not correct enough for publication. He intentionally made no comment about the older and larger London churches, as he planned to publish a separate history of them (which was not done).[87] Clearly the three lists are as accurate as they could have been.

These lists and their accompanying notes are of value for several reasons. They are the only comprehensive source for knowledge of the churches during this period; many of them supply the only information on the beginnings of individual churches, and they provide a statistical guide to the expansion within the denomination.[88] In 1790 Rippon listed 311 churches, of which 71 were without a settled ministry, in 1794 there were 326 churches (of which 28 were new churches, and 13 were omitted from the 1790 list), and in 1798 there were 361 churches (49 new churches, whilst 14 had either dissolved or amalgamated with other churches). In 1794 only 52 churches were without a pastor, and in 1798 only 38. Rippon recorded 103 changes of pastorate between the 1794 and 1798 lists. Whilst Rippon made no attempt at estimating the total membership of the churches (about 30,000 in 1798 has been suggested)[89] there is clear evidence of expansion in the numbers of churches. This is confirmed by some general comments Rippon added to his 1798 list.[90] He noted the large number of churches supplied with a minister, and observed that most had increased in membership. Indeed, in several churches the membership had trebled in five years, whilst in one church a hundred members had been added in two years. The five churches of the Norfolk and Suffolk Association had 739 members. Rippon estimated that within the previous five years more meeting houses had been enlarged, and within the last fifteen years more built, than had been built and enlarged for the previous thirty years. Within a short period about a hundred men had been sent into the ministry. It must be emphasized that, especially in the 196 notes added to the 1798 list, there are all manner of absorbing and interesting sidelights on the churches of

85   *Register* 2 (1794-97), p. 1.

86   *Register* 3 (1798-1801), pp. 3, 40.

87   *Register* 3 (1798-1801), pp. 25, 40

88   See also the increase in membership given in the association reports. See Table 5.

89   Payne, *The Baptist Union A Short History*, p. 267.

90   *Register* 3 (1798-1801), pp. 40-41.

the period. In addition to the type of information suggested by the 1794 questionnaire, there are these details: the number of baptisms, descriptions of meeting houses, names of deacons, relations with other denominations, whether open or closed communion, number of men called to the ministry, Sunday School work, pastor's stipend and various intriguing personal comments about individual ministers. Some of the notes, obviously culled directly from letters, are amusing: such as that concerning William Crabtree (1720-1811), the old pastor of Bradford, who had to sit down once or twice during each sermon.[91]

This news of advance must have brought considerable encouragement to the churches. They could see themselves as part of the whole denomination, and all the churches were made aware of each other. Simply to list them all together was a unifying influence. Even the struggling churches could see that they were not alone, and often what was reported from one church could be adapted in another. Churches and ministers were able to communicate, because names of ministers were given.

Again, Rippon's comments reveal those various aspects of the denomination's life that he thought important. Several features emerge with clarity. To take a practical example: Rippon was able to describe the destruction in 1792 of the Guilsborough, Northamptonshire, meeting-house by incendiaries hostile to Dissenters, and commend their needy case.[92] He praised the Northampton church for its 'sacrifice' to the 'general good' when it released John Ryland to accept the post of President of Bristol Academy.[93] Other important features were recommended on every possible occasion. Village evangelism was enthusiastically commended. After describing this activity of the Leighton Buzzard, Bedfordshire, Church, Rippon added:

Query. Might not many ministers be much better employed of a Lord's day evening, than in preaching a third sermon to people who have heard two before, especially when it is considered, that there are multitudes around who seldom hear any thing of the way of salvation?[94]

Again and again, Rippon described the activity of churches engaging in this type of work. In his 'Remarks', he emphasized 'such societies have been formed at home for village and itinerant preaching as were never before heard of among the Baptists in this country'; and then added: 'Almost the whole country is open for village preaching'.[95]

91   *Register* 3 (1798-1801), p. 38, note 337.
92   *Register* 2 (1794-97), pp. 9, 32.
93   *Register* 2 (1794-97), p. 10.
94   *Register* 3 (1798-1801), p. 3, note 10.
95   *Register* 3 (1798-1801), p. 40.

Rippon at the same time enthusiastically advocated a direct evangelistic preaching. The following is a typical example: 'Our senior brother Mr. Marshman, of Westbury Leigh, has been graciously owned of God in his ministerial labours, but more abundantly so, since he has freely invited all the poor sinners who attend his labours to come to Christ as the only saviour.'[96]

Rippon was also quick to encourage a due care for their pastors by the churches, as he commented on the Chenies, Buckinghamshire, Church: 'In the year 1795, several members having been lately added to this church, the deacons and people (a fit example for others) advanced their pastor's income £10 per annum.'[97]

Rippon also noted as significant the formation of the BMS, and the growth of prayer meetings for revival, 'eminently so among the churches which are flourishing', he emphasized.[98] The fact that Bristol Academy was 'full of students' was also highlighted and Rippon suggested that a number of pastors might be able each to train two or three young men.[99] This developing interest in ministerial education foreshadowed the formation of the London Education Society (1804) and the Northern Society (1804).

Clearly, then, the lists of churches with accompanying notes promoted a greater self-awareness among the churches, and provided opportunity for Rippon to stimulate the new evangelistic fervour of the denomination.

WELSH LISTS

The 1790 list was given alphabetically (not by counties),[100] and may have been prepared for Rippon by William Williams of 'Ebenezer', Pembrokeshire, who made the General Comments on the list.[101] The 1794 list, by counties, was compiled with characteristic thoroughness by Joshua Thomas of Leominster, who in addition to the name of each minister gave for each church the year of the church's formation, the Welsh association to which it belonged, and the number of members.[102] The 1798 list was not as detailed (Thomas had died in 1797), and was possibly compiled by John Reynolds of Treglemais, who sent Rippon the Welsh materials from 1797.[103]

These lists also suggest expansion within the churches. There were 48 churches with 61 ministers listed in 1790; many Welsh churches had a

---

96   *Register* 3 (1798-1801), p. 38, note 320.
97   *Register* 3 (1798-1801), p. 5, note 27.
98   *Register* 3 (1798-1801), p. 40.
99   *Register* 3 (1798-1801), p. 40.
100   *Register* 1 (1790-93), pp. 14-16.
101   See index to volume 2, 'Williams'.
102   *Register* 2 (1794-97), pp. 17-24.
103   B.L. Add. MSS. 25388, f. 410.

number of 'branches', thus necessitating more than one minister for each. In 1794 Thomas listed 56 churches with a membership of 7,058, and in 1798 there were 84 churches with 'we think not less than NINE thousand members'. Hence in 1798, there were 446 Particular Baptist churches in England and Wales.

GENERAL BAPTISTS' NEW ASSOCIATION LIST (1790)

Rippon published full statistics, giving the number of members, increases and decreases in each church, and the representatives at the association meeting.[104] This revealed 32 churches, and 2, 843 members. The New Connexion, under the inspiration of Dan Taylor (1738-1816), had been formed in 1770 and brought new life to the General Baptist cause.[105] Rippon introduced the list, and noted that, if an accurate list of all the General Baptists was prepared by some responsible person, he would gladly publish it. He asked Stephen Lowdell (1718-1810), the treasurer of the General Baptist Fund to distribute packets (presumably of *Registers*) at the Whitsun Assembly of 1794, but the Assembly was divided about having a list of churches published.[106] Rippon was given permission to examine the original records of the association which met in White's Alley from 1697 to 1707,[107] but the only other General Baptist material published were New Association minutes, and a copy of the memorial to Thomas Grantham[108] in the Norwich General Baptist chapel, forwarded by Stephen Lowdell.[109]

English and Welsh Associations

The pattern of associations in Particular Baptist life began with the London meetings of 1644,[110] and by 1660 there was extensive co-operation between London and the associations formed in Berkshire

---

104 *Register* 1 (1790-93), pp. 174 -75.

105 Brown, *English Baptists of the Eighteenth Century*, pp. 67-70.

106 Lowdell to Rippon, Southwark, 25 August 1794, B.L. Add. MSS. 25387, f. 444.

107 *Register* 1 (1790-93), pp. 179, 402, 548.

108 *Register* 2 (1794-97), p. 50. For Grantham (1634-1692), see *DNB* and White, *The English Baptists of the Seventeenth Century*, pp. 117-19.

109 *Register* 1 (1790-93), p. 562.

110 *The Report of the Commission on the Associations* (London: Baptist Union, 1964), section 1: 'The Origin and Purpose of the Association'; White, 'The organisation of the Particular Baptists 1644-1660', pp. 209-26; White, *The English Baptists of the Seventeenth Century*, pp. 65-70.

(1652),[111] the West (1653),[112] the Midlands (1655),[113] and Wales (1650).[114] After the Restoration joint activities were necessarily restricted, but in 1677 a significant assembly was held in London which drew up the important *Baptist Confession* (based on the Westminster Confession), revised at a larger 1689 gathering.[115] Further national assemblies were held in 1690, 1691, 1692, and 1693. In 1692 it was agreed to divide and meet in both London and Bristol. The London semi-national association quickly disappeared, but the Western was reorganized in 1733 and remained a strong group. During the eighteenth century there was a growth and revival of association life, so that by 1790 the following had begun: the Western, the Midlands, the Northern (founded 1690),[116] the Yorkshire and Lancashire (1719, reorganized 1786),[117] the Northamptonshire (1764)[118], the Kent and Sussex (1779),[119] and the Norfolk and Suffolk (1769).[120] The Welsh association in 1790 divided into three smaller associations whilst the Essex Baptists formed an association in 1796.[121]

This expansion in association life was of great importance for the development of the denomination.[122] O.C. Robison suggested that the associations became the medium of breaking down ecclesiastical isolationism, thereby contributing to the weakening of the High Calvinist

---

111 Payne, *Baptists of Berkshire*. This association lapsed after 1748. In 1802 the Oxfordshire and East Gloucestershire association began, and in 1825 the Berkshire association was recommenced.

112 Nuttall, 'Baptist Western Association 1653-1658'; J. G. Fuller, *A Brief History of the Western Association* (Bristol: 1843).

113 Cf. W. Stokes, *History of Midland Baptist Association 1655-1855* (London: 1855); J.M.G. Owen (ed.), *Records of an Old Association* (Birmingham: 1905).

114 Thomas, *A History of the Baptist Association in Wales*.

115 Lumpkin, *Baptist Confessions of Faith*, pp. 241-95

116 D. Douglas, *History of the Baptist Churches in the North of England* (London: 1846).

117 W.T. Whitley, *Baptists of North-West England 1649-1913* (London: Kingsgate Press, 1913); I Sellers (ed.), *Our Heritage. The Baptists of Yorkshire, Lancashire and Cheshire 1647-1987* (Leeds: The Yorkshire Baptist Association and the Lancashire and Cheshire Baptist Association, 1987).

118 T.S.H. Elwyn, *Northamptonshire Baptist Association 1764-1964* (London: Carey Kingsgate Press, 1964).

119 F. Buffard, *Kent and Sussex Baptist Associations* (Faversham: Kent and Sussex Association, 1963).

120 Cf. A.J. Klaiber, *The Story of the Suffolk Baptists* (London: Kingsgate Press, 1931); C.B. Jewson, *The Baptists in Norfolk* (London: Carey Kingsgate Press, 1957).

121 D. Witard, *Bibles in Barrels. A History of Essex Baptists* (Southend on Sea: Essex Baptist Association, 1962).

122 Brown, *The English Baptists of the Eighteenth Century*; see index for 'Associations'.

position, and encouraged co-operative support for new or weak congregations.[123] The best illustration of all these was the Northamptonshire Association, undoubtedly the most influential of the period. Many of the strongest and most creative Baptist personalities of the day were gathered here. Here in 1779 Robert Hall (Senior) of Arnesby, Leicestershire, preached his *Helps to Zion's Travellers*, such a statement of moderate Calvinism that Joseph Ivimey felt that that year marked 'the commencement of a new era in the history of our denomination'.[124] Here Andrew Fuller preached his moderate Calvinism, here John Sutcliff in 1784 instigated the Call to Prayer. Not least of all, here William Carey relentlessly pursued his vision of a missionary society, the formation of which was to unite the Baptists as never before. Representatives to the association would come on horseback from miles around, in such large numbers that in 1794 the Leicester meeting had to be held out of doors in an orchard.[125] Small amounts, such as two guineas given to the Burton-upon-Trent church in 1790, were symptomatic of a sympathetic encouragement to smaller churches.[126]

These justifiable claims for the associations underline the significance of the *Register*. By widely publishing what one association was doing, creative forces were released upon the whole denomination. Provincial movements became national movements. If the Northamptonshire association advocated regular united prayer, then the Western, Midland, and Kent and Sussex Associations could follow.[127] If one association, the Western, voted five guineas to the Committee for the Abolition of the slave trade, then the Northamptonshire could follow.[128] But the most important movements were the BMS and village evangelism. At least one church first learned about the BMS through the *Register* and decided to give enthusiastic support. The spread of organized village evangelism was also rapid. The Midland Association formed a fund for the purpose in 1794, and by 1798 much useful work had been accomplished. The Essex Association was commenced in 1796, stating that 'the grand object of this Association is the spread of the Gospel in the different towns and villages of the county'. An itinerant preacher was appointed, and successfully fulfilled the association's hopes. In 1797 the London Baptists began their Itinerant Society, and in 1798 the Northern Association commenced the Northern Evangelical Society.[129]

---

123 O.C. Robison, 'The Particular Baptists in England, 1760-1820' (DPhil. Thesis, Oxford University, 1963), pp. 90-91.

124 Ivimey, *History of English Baptists*, 4, p. 41.

125 *Register* 2 (1794-97), p. 186.

126 *Register* 1 (1790-93), p. 36

127 *Register* 1 (1790-93), pp. 42, 60; 2 (1794-97), p. 494.

128 *Register* 1 (1790-93), pp. 60; 200.

129 *Register* 3 (1798-1801), p. 118.

Rippon clearly appreciated the central role of the associations in the denominational life. The associations during this period reflected a new desire to work together, although earlier eighteenth century activity had been minimal. The *Register* encouraged this tendency towards combined activity by publicizing the new movements. Again, one of the main reasons for commencing the *Register* was to give a wider publicity to the Associations' Annual Letters. A few historical papers relating to associations were published by Rippon, notably the 1689 *Confession* and Joshua Thomas' *History of the Welsh Association*.

Moreover, Rippon printed in December 1792, a long poem of four pages by Benjamin Francis, 'The Association, - A Poem most respectfully addressed to the Members of each Baptist Association'.[130] The poetic worth of this is perhaps negligible, but as Ernest Payne commented, it is 'clear indication of the large place which the Association and their annual gatherings had in the Baptist consciousness'.[131] Again, 'Its definitions and repudiations tell as much as its more positive ideals', as Geoffrey Nuttall has observed.[132]

> NOT the vain tribe, assembled at the ball,
> Or glittering late, like glow-worms, at Vaux-hall...
> Nor the grave synod, grave in *garb* I mean,
> Where lords of conscience, and her rights convene...
> Nor the grand senate of the British realm,
> That aids the hand ordain'd to guide the helm...

Rather, prompted by 'love of truth and purity divine, With pious zeal for the Redeemer's cause' the Baptists gathered:

> So yearly, meet from parts remote, in Thee,
> When summer smiles on every herb and tree,
> Th' associate brethren, pastors, deacons, friends,
> And the full crowd that in thy train attends:
> What pleasure springs in each fraternal breast,
> Glowing with love, caressing and carest!
> In thee, endearing fellowship imparts
> Her sacred pleasures to congenial hearts:
> A fellowship resembling that above,
> Where all is joy, perfection, praise, and love.

---

130 *Register* 1 (1790-93), unnumbered pages, usually bound between pp. 16 and 17, but issued with number 5.

131 *Fellowship of Believers*, p. 31.

132 G.F. Nuttall, 'Assembly and Association in Dissent, 1689-1831', in G.J. Cuming and D. Baker (eds.), *Councils and Assemblies* (Studies in Church History, 7; Cambridge: Cambridge University Press, 1971), p. 303.

The association 'Breviates', or brief accounts of the annual meetings, often with statistics of increase or decrease from the constituent churches, were published, more or less consistently, in the *Register*.[133] On the other hand, the number of Circular Letters reproduced gradually decreased. Five of the 1790 Letters were given fully, and only one was abbreviated; in 1791 three, of five cited, were largely abbreviated; in 1792 five, of which two were abbreviated; in 1793 only one (and another General Baptist letter); in 1794 only four brief summaries were given whilst from 1795 to 1800 inclusive none was given in any form. Two from 1801, and only one from 1802 were included. Clearly the original plan was revised. When the first abbreviation was made Rippon noted that this was 'Contrary to the original design', and the omission or postponement of 1791 letters 'pained' the editor.[134] The reasons were varied. Some letters reached Rippon too late for inclusion at the proper place.[135] Others were very long, and of inferior quality. Rippon requested that they should be abridged,[136] and at least Thomas Langdon of Leeds obliged him in this.[137] Frequently Rippon's only comment about a Letter was its length: 'It fills 11 pages octavo'[138]; it is a 'small edifying treatise'.[139] Many of the letters made heavy reading, and many correspondents suggested either omitting or abridging the Letters - but not the news from the associations. The Kent and Sussex Association, however, resented Rippon's abbreviation of their 1790 Letter and after their 1791 meeting wrote to him, 'This letter is a babe for which we all stand father... Our only wish then, Sir, is that you let it enjoy all its limbs and features.'[140]

Nevertheless, Rippon tried to ensure that the best of the Letters were published. It is significant that the two associations most represented by their Circular Letters are the Northamptonshire (7) and the Western (5): the two largest and most influential associations. In particular, it is of interest to note exactly what Rippon did include when he became more selective. Ryland's 1792 Letter on 'Godly Zeal' occupying twenty pages in the *Register*, was given in full;[141] this was nicely calculated to prepare for Carey's famous sermon and abounds in evangelistic Calvinism: 'There is therefore nothing in the doctrine of efficacious Grace, when

---

133 The Northern Association did not meet between 1784 and 1795, and then resumed with only three churches: Douglas, *History of Baptist Churches in the North of England*, p. 223.

134 *Register* 1 (1790-93), pp. 64, note; 208, note.

135 *Register* 2 (1794-97), p. 183 note.

136 *Register* 1 (1790-93), p. 208 note

137 *Register* 1 (1790-93), p. 270 note.

138 *Register* 2 (1794-97), p. 331.

139 *Register* 2 (1794-97), p. 140.

140 Buffard, *Kent and Susex Baptist Associations*, p. 52.

141 *Register* 1 (1790-93), pp. 420-39.

rightly explained, that tends to discourage us from expressing our zeal for the conversion of souls, by the most diligent use of every means that is suited to instruct, alarm, or allure the mind.'[142]

The Northamptonshire letters of 1801, and 1802 were given because of their intrinsic merit, especially Fuller's on 'The Practical Uses of Baptism'.[143] The Yorkshire and Lancashire Letter for 1794 was too long, but Rippon could not forbear to include the following summary on such a subject as 'Evangelical Repentance': 'It is needful for all men; and as preaching is the general expedient by which sinners are brought to the enjoyment of this blessing, it should be preached to *every creature*'.[144] The same year Rippon did not miss the opportunity to publish at least extracts from Samuel Pearce's appeal to the Midland churches on behalf of missionary work: 'A christian's heart ought to be as comprehensive as the universe - the *Asiatic*, the *American*, and the *African*, as well as the *European*, have a claim on your philanthropy'.[145] This is not to suggest that Rippon ever excluded any Letters because he disagreed with them. But, whenever possible, he highlighted the new moderate Calvinism, as it was increasingly evident in association letters.

The 'Breviates' of the associations provide some guide to the expansion within the churches. Table 4 indicates the new members added to the churches of the various associations, as published in the *Register*. It must be noted that these figures are not complete for each year, and do not include any of the London churches. Indeed to take the 1790 list, only 117 of the 311 English churches were linked with an association. Nevertheless, it will be observed that there was a recorded growth of over 6,000 between 1790 and 1802 in England and Wales – and, to judge from Rippon's comments in 1798, there were many additions in the other churches.

Rippon obviously had simply to reprint, or make slight alterations, to most of this material. But some of the details are unique to the *Register*. For example, the Norfolk and Suffolk Association did not print any letters before 1795, so that the *Register* is the only guide for information prior to then. Again, the Northern Association was not active again until 1795, and additional statistics of the Northamptonshire Association for 1792, and certain details from churches of the Western (1794) and the Norfolk and Suffolk associations are only found in the *Register*.

Also published were the plans of the London Monthly Meetings, largely devotional in character, from 1790 to 1803 inclusive; 'breviates' and letters of the New Connexion of General Baptists from 1790 to 1793;

142 *Register* 1 (1790-93), p. 426.
143 *Register* 4 (1801-02), pp. 1047-56.
144 *Register* 2 (1794-97), p. 140.
145 *Register* 2 (1794-97), p. 137.

of special interest is Dan Taylor's letter 'On the Utility of Associations' (1793).[146]

American Associations, and Personal Correspondence

Rippon devoted considerable space in his *Register* to publishing American religious news, as he had originally promised.[147] In his first number Rippon printed an introductory table which must have greatly impressed his British readers with the numerical strength of Baptists in America.[148] The statistics given are obviously round figures, and both their source and reliability are unknown. But this claimed that there were thirty Baptist associations, in twelve states, whilst there were altogether 564 ministers, 743 churches, and 60,970 members. The American population in 1790, as Rippon later published from official statistics, was 3,938,635.[149]

The first American association was formed in Philadelphia in 1707, with five churches: its general plan was similar to those in England, and in 1742 it adopted the 1689 London Confession as its doctrinal norm.[150] This set the pattern for subsequent American associations: the Charleston, S.C. (1751), the Sandy Creek, N.C. (1758), Ketocton, Va. (1766), Warren, R.I. (1767) and Kehuckee, N.C. (1769). These associations disclaimed authority over local churches, but acted in a voluntary capacity with an emphasis upon advice and fellowship.

From earliest days the associations exchanged their minutes and circular letters. Often preachers would travel 150 to 200 miles to attend association gatherings, preaching at various centres on their way to and from the meetings. The associations, as the *Register* accounts confirm, helped promote new preaching centres and churches, guided in matters of theology and procedure, encouraged denominational uniformity by adoption of the Philadelphia Confession of Faith of 1742 and regular

---

146 *Register* 1 (1790-93), pp. 549-54.

147 In addition to the space indicated in Table 5 as devoted to American materials, additional American references are to be found in other sections, especially in Lists of Books, Obituaries, Intelligence, 'Negro' Christian work, and histories of churches

148 *Register* 1 (1790-93), pp. 72 -73.

149 *Register* 1 (1790-93), p. 396.

150 For the American associations, see D. Benedict, *A General History of the Baptist Denomination in America* (2 vols; Boston, 1813), especially 2, pp. 497-553; A.H. Newman, *A History of the Baptist Churches in the United States*, (Philadelphia: American Baptist Publication Society, rev. edn, 1915); H.L. McBeth, *The Baptist Heritage* (Nashville: Broadman Press, 1987), pp. 239-46. Useful reviews for the Southern States will be found in *Encyclopaedia of Southern Baptists* (4 vols; Nashville: Broadman Press, 1958, 1971, 1982) (hereafter *ESB.*).

doctrinal sermons and letters, fostered seminaries (especially the Philadelphian, Charleston, and Warren Associations); and promoted missionary work among Indians, blacks, and the 'heathen' overseas.

Not all the thirty associations listed by Rippon published their Minutes or Circular Letters; fourteen of these associations had no official details published in the *Register*. It is notable that there were no records for the years 1795-1799 (inclusive) published, and reports from only five associations irregularly for the succeeding years. The amount of space devoted to specifically American reports dropped sharply after the first volume (1790-1793), as Table 4 indicates. The main reason for this was presumably the delays and interruptions with communications because of the war. This meant that although the *Register* provided a quite unique source of information and inspiration for American Baptists, the local reports were often stale news by the time Americans read them. This probably reduced active interest.

Following the movement known as the Great Awakening, the churches in New England were divided into 'Separates' who were enthusiasts and supporters of revivalist movements, and 'Regulars' who adhered to the old order and were suspicious of the new movements.[151] Many 'Separates' became 'Separate Baptists' or 'New Lights' who would not adhere to the Philadelphia Confession and claimed the Bible as their only immediate authority. Generally these 'Separate Baptists' were characterized by extravagant preaching and emotional extremes, and were suspicious of any associational authority. Much of the pioneering evangelistic work in the Southern States was undertaken by Separate Baptists.

Undoubtedly the most common feature of the American reports was, therefore, the recounting of the remarkable Revival movements. These fascinated British readers, so much so that when, because of Rippon's ill health, some exciting accounts were not published, they were printed separately by other Baptists, such as Ryland and J.W. Morris of Clipston, Northamptonshire.[152] The accounts were graphic and detailed. Some comments were discerning, as James Manning described some revivals in New England: 'This work appears much more genuine and free from enthusiasm than in some former reformations'.[153] Rippon himself, although publishing many accounts, could not refrain from offering cautionary comments. After publishing a letter which he headed 'A Peculiar Work in America' and which described phenomena associated with revivals in Kentucky, he commented:

---

151 C.C. Goen, *Revivalism and Separatism in New England 1740-1800* (New Haven: Yale University Press, 1962).

152 A. Fuller to W. Ward, London, 13 June 1800 (in BMS archives).

153 *Register* 1 (1790-93), p. 88.

It would be a more easy than it is a welcome task to make remarks on what has been so generally called *the great work of God in America*: suffice it at present to say, That if, amidst the disorder and enthusiasm which have remarkably, of late, disgraced many of the Assemblies in Kentucky, the Lord has been really sowing the good seed, nothing is more to be feared than that it will too soon appear to the sorrow of the Church of God, that Satan has been very diligently sowing tares. O that the less in-formed among the Americans were in possession of President Edwards's excellent volume on the Affections, and would most seriously read it.[154]

Rippon's suspicion of 'enthusiasm' was typical of the English Dissenters who were sceptical of the emotional and bodily extravagances accompanying the religious experiences. Nevertheless, the most frequent type of report published by Rippon spoke of revivals. What effect these had on English churches is uncertain, although they were often read to the churches as suitable items for prayer, and may have been a spur to the prayers for revival.

Another dominant feature is a concern for religious freedom. Of special importance were the activities of the Warren Association and of its leading figure, Isaac Backus, who is rightly honoured as a leading advocate of religious liberty.[155] Baptists were still liable to taxation for religious purposes in New England, and Backus wrote to Rippon about it.[156] Again, in 1792, the Warren Association formed a committee to deal with any complaints by churches or individuals 'taxed to other denominations'.[157] Rippon wrote to Dr. Richard Price (1723-1791), the leading London Unitarian minister and political philosopher. Rippon met with Price for an hour, and published Price's reply which roundly condemned the practice.[158] Rippon himself wrote about 'The Civil State of Dissenters in England 1793' for American readers.[159]

Other American information prominent in the *Register* was the account of Baptist efforts with ministerial education. For example, he published the Annual Commencement services of the Rhode Island College 1789-1801 inclusive. His friend James Manning was President of the Academy until his death in 1791. The Academy, which had been formed in 1764 by the Philadelphia Association, played a vital part in advancing the educational status of the ministry and gradually won the confidence of the Separates, through the support of men like Isaac Backus, himself an outstanding Separate.[160] The Academy honoured English Baptists,

---

154   *Register* 4 (1801-02), p. 1010.
155   Maston, *Isaac Backus;* Goen, *Revivalism and Separatism*, pp. 275-77.
156   *Register* 1 (1790-93), p. 94.
157   *Register* 1 (1790-93), p. 387.
158   *Register* 1 (1790-93), p. 388.
159   *Register* 1 (1790-93), p. 524.
160   Maston, *Isaac Backus*, p. 30.

awarding Rippon the A.M. degree in 1784,[161] and the D.D. in 1792,[162] whilst Caleb Evans (1789)[163], John Ryland (1792)[164] and Andrew Fuller (1796),[165] were also given degrees. (Fuller refused to use his.) The Warren Association formed an Education Fund in 1791,[166] as had the Philadelphia in 1790;[167] similarly, the Charleston which had contributed funds to Rhode Island College, had established its own education fund in 1789.[168] Rippon published details of all these, and also the 1791 Annual Commencement ceremony of Princeton College, although this was not a Baptist institution.[169]

Rippon was also interested in the mounting missionary concern of the Americans, and his publicizing of the BMS origins stimulated this. The principal mission interest of the Americans centred upon the Indian tribes. Accordingly, Rippon published extracts from the journal of Samuel Kirkland, to which he had referred in his 1788 publication.[170] Kirkland was a missionary supported by the Scottish Society for Propagating Christian Knowledge. But the first specifically American mission, although interdenominational at first, was associated with the New York Association (formed in 1791), and Elkanah Holmes became a missionary to the Indian tribes in 1796.[171] An account of the 'six nations of the North American Indians' by Dr. Peter Thacher, Congregational minister in Boston, was also published.[172] Rippon retained his absorbed interest in the native Indians of the continent, and all relevant materials were published.

The American letters contain references to slavery, mostly, of course, from the southern states. One letter, from Henry Toler, pastor at Nomini, Virginia, mentioned Robert Carter, Esq. 'who had been of the King's council, he possessed eight hundred slaves'.[173] Carter was a wealthy planter, owner of Nomini Hall, and became noted for his piety and

---

161 Guild, *The Early History of Brown University*, p. 380.

162 *Register* 1 (1790-93), p. 393.

163 *Register* 1 (1790-93), p. 96.

164 *Register* 1 (1790-93), p. 393.

165 *Register* 2 (1794-97), p. 458. Fuller was made A.M. of Rhode Island, and D.D. of New Jersey College.

166 *Register* 1 (1790-93), p. 292.

167 *Register* 1 (1790-93), p. 75.

168 *Register* 1 (1790-93), p. 101.

169 *Register* 1 (1790-93), pp. 219-20.

170 *Register* 2 (1794-97), pp. 233-48.

171 *Register* 3 (1798-1801), pp. 47-55, 140-44, 369-76, 421-423; 4 (1801-02), pp. 788-89, 902-904, 948-50.

172 *Register* 3 (1798-1801), pp. 529-31.

173 *Register* 1 (1790-93), pp. 107, 543.

liberality in releasing hundreds of slaves.[174] Rippon corresponded with Carter, and compiled the following note:

> I have heard from very good authorities, that Squire Carter's conduct to his negroes is distinguished by a peculiar humanity, as well as by a religious attention to their best interests; and in a letter which I had the honour of receiving from him some time since, writing of the then existing laws concerning slaves, and of the abolition of the slave trade, he concludes his paragraph with these very expressive words: *The toleration of slavery* indicates VERY GREAT DEPRAVITY *of mind.*[175]

Although some American Baptist associations expressed disapproval of slavery, the issue was to divide the Baptists in the south.[176] Little of association action in this matter appeared in the *Register*, but Rippon devoted considerable energy to the help of black churches.

These are the main items of American interest in the *Register*. There is some account of theological discussion. For example, in 1791 the Philadelphia Association was in correspondence with Abraham Booth over the validity of baptism administered by an un-baptized person.[177] Dr. Jonathan Edwards (Junior) provided a detailed statement about theological controversies in New England.[178] Rippon also published many letters which gave his English friends some conception of the dramatic contrast between the English and American way of life. The *Register* was also important in maintaining the links between American and Welsh Baptists at a time when many Welsh Baptists were migrating to the United States.[179] The frontier situation and many of the phenomena of revivalism were clearly evident in the letters.[180] The horrors of the dreadful Yellow Fever plagues in Philadelphia during the 1790s were fully described.[181] Rippon also published much factual information about America, such as the population of each state, the duties on imports and value of exports (1790),[182] the prices of provisions in America in

---

174   For Carter see Benedict, *History of the Baptist Denomination*, 2, pp. 278-80; W.M. Gewehr, *The Great Awakening in Virginia 1740-1790* (Gloucester, Mass.: P. Smith, 1965 [1930]), pp. 21, 241, 258–60.

175   *Register* 1 (1790-93), p. 107.

176   Torbet, *A History of Baptists*, pp. 282-94; McBeth, *Baptist Heritage*, pp. 382-85.

177   *Register* 1 (1790-93), p. 295.

178   *Register* 1 (1790-93), pp. 545-46.

179   H. Davies, '"Very Different Springs of Uneasiness": Emigration from Wales to the United States of America during the 1790s', *The Welsh History Review: Cylchgrawn Hanes Cymru* 15.3 (1991), p. 393.

180   For example, cf. *Register* 2 (1794-97), pp. 201-203; 4 (1801-02), pp. 805 -807, 1007-09.

181   *Register* 2 (1794-97), p. 63; 3 (1798-1801), p. 121.

182   *Register* 1 (1790-93), p. 896.

1800,[183] and a 'Polymetric Table' which gave the distances between thirty major American cities.[184] Rippon received several letters requesting additional information: he became the leading English Baptist authority on all things American.

The value of the *Register* to the American churches was that, apart from international news, it gave them a publication of national scope and provided interesting information about fellow-Baptists scattered throughout their vast continent. It was the only national American Baptist publication, and a rival but poor *Register* produced by a Swedish immigrant John Asplund evidences that Rippon's met a real need.[185]

The wide scope of the *Register*'s information is demonstrated by a brief summary of the leading associations and correspondents from the four main settled areas of North America.

NEW ENGLAND

The first ten associations listed by Rippon came from this region, but the *Register* published no details about three of these: the New Hampshire (founded 1785),[186] the Rhode Island (perhaps the Six- Principle Baptists who held a yearly meeting),[187] and the Groton (formed in 1786, of churches favouring mixed communion).[188] In addition the Meredith Association (New Hampshire) was formed in 1789,[189] and although not in Rippon's original list the 1792 Minutes were published by him.[190] The actual materials published from the other associations were: Bowdoinham, (Mass.) formed in 1787, mainly Separates;[191] Woodstock, formed 1738 (New Hanpshire and Vermont);[192] Vermont, formed 1785;[193] Warren, (Mass. and R.I.), formed 1767;[194] Stonington, (R.I. and Conn.), founded 1772 mainly of strict communion churches;[195] Danbury (Conn.), formed 1790;[196] and the Shaftsbury (Mass. and New York), formed 1781.[197]

---

183 *Register* 3 (1798-1801), p. 880.
184 *Register* 1 (1790-93), unnumbered pages bound after the Index.
185 See below in this chapter.
186 Newman, *A History of Baptist Churches*, p. 268.
187 Benedict, *History of the Baptist Denomination*, 2, p. 506.
188 Goen, *Revivalism and Separatism*, p. 266.
189 Benedict, *History of the Baptist Denomination*, 2, p. 500.
190 *Register* 1 (1790-93), p. 587.
191 Benedict, *History of the Baptist Denomination*, 2, p. 498.
192 Newman, *A History of Baptist Churches*, 1, p. 269.
193 Newman, *A History of Baptist Churches*, 1, p. 269.
194 Torbet, *A History of Baptists*, pp. 235-36.
195 Goen, *Revivalism and Separatism*, pp. 264-66.
196 *Register* 1 (1790-93), pp. 109-11.
197 Newman, *A History of Baptist Churches*, p. 268.

Leading correspondents from this area included Manning;[198] Backus;[199] Stillman;[200] William Staughton,[201] a young man whom Rippon had recommended[202] to Dr. Furman of Charleston and who had moved to New Jersey (and later to Philadelphia) where he exercised an important educational and missionary influence;[203] and non-Baptist leaders like Dr. Jonathan Edwards,[204] Dr. Peter Thacher of Boston,[205] and other Connecticut ministers.[206]

MIDDLE COLONIES

The only associations noted by Rippon were the influential Philadelphia,[207] and the Redstone (Pa.), which was formed in 1776 and was comprised of churches west of the Allegheny Mountains.[208] Typical of the pioneering pastors was John Corbly (1733-1803)[209] most of whose family had been slaughtered by Indians, and who sent accounts of the Redstone Association to Rippon. [210] The New York Association was formed in 1791, by an amicable division from the Philadelphian,[211] whilst the Warwick Association was formed the same year of churches in New York county which had been formed in the settlements on both sides of the Hudson River.[212] Both these associations figured in the *Register*. Leaders from this area, mainly in Philadelphia and New York, included Rippon's rival hymn editor Dr. Samuel Jones of the Lower Dublin church, Philadelphia; Dr. William Rogers (1751-1824),[213] lecturer in

---

198 *Register* 1 (1790-93), pp. 88, 100 (possibly by Manning), 293.

199 *Register* 1 (1790-93), pp. 93-94, 115-16, 324, 391, 394-95, 486-87, 547-48; 2 (1794-97), p. 74; 4 (1801-02), pp. 611-12.

200 *Register* 1 (1790-93), pp. 100, 154-55; 2 (1794-97), p. 75 (possibly).

201 *Register* 3 (1798-1801), pp. 121, 267.

202 Rippon did this at the suggestion of his friend Thomas Dunscombe. Cf. T. Dunscombe to R. Furman, 22 July 1793 (original at Furman Univ.); J. Rippon to Furman, 18 July 1793, in Lynd, *Memoir of the Revd. William Staughton,* pp. 27-28.

203 For Staughton, see *DEB*.

204 *Register* 1 (1790-93), pp. 108-9, 545-46; 2 (1794-97), pp. 130-31; 3 (1797-1801), p. 532.

205 *Register* 3 (1798-1801), pp. 529-531. Cf. *Register* 1 (1790-93), p. 221.

206 *Register* 1 (1790-93), pp. 88-89; 4 (1801-02), pp. 614-24.

207 Torbet, *A History of the Baptists,* pp. 211-14.

208 J.A. Davidson, 'Redstone Baptist Association of Western Pennsylvania', *The Chronicle* 5 (1942), pp. 133-40.

209 Benedict, *History of the Baptist Denomination,* 1, pp. 598-600.

210 *Register* 1 (1790-93), p. 294.

211 N.H. Maring, *Baptists in New Jersey* (Valley Forge: Judson, 1964), p. 96.

212 Benedict, *History of the Baptist Denomination,* 1, p. 545.

213 *Register* 4 (1801-02), pp. 1009-10. Cf. *Register* 1 (1790-93), pp. 112, 220; 2 (1794-97), p. 205; 3 (1798-1801), p. 581; 4 (1801-02), pp. 696, 807, 985, 1110. For Rogers (1751-1824), see *DEB*.

Rhetoric at the University of Pennsylvania, Philadelphia; Thomas Ustick; and Dr. Benjamin Foster (1750-1798), a New York pastor.[214]

MARYLAND, VIRGINIA, NORTH CAROLINA AND KENTUCKY

Kentucky was not a state until 1792, and much of this area included frontier settlements. Fifteen associations were listed by Rippon, but reports from only five of these appeared in the *Register*. These five were the Dover, formed as the Lower District in Virginia in 1783, but which became the Dover in 1788;[215] the Lower District or Kehukey (or Kehukee) (North Carolina and Virginia) was formed in 1769 as the first association in which Regular and Separate Baptists united, and although in 1775 there was a division into two, by 1789 most were reunited;[216] the Middle District (North Carolina) formed 1784;[217] the Roanoak (Roanoke) formed 1788 of churches in central Virginia;[218] and the North Kentucky (or Elkhorn) formed in 1785 of Regular Baptists.[219] Several of the other associations in this region were quite active, the Sandy Creek was an early association in North Carolina,[220] having been formed in 1758 by the efforts of Shubal Stearns (1706-1771),[221] an ardent Separate from Connecticut. In 1790, the Virginia Portsmouth Association was formed, and Rippon published reports of its activities.[222] He also noted that nine associations in 1790 sent representatives to a General Committee for Virginia.[223] This had been formed in 1784, and sought to reconcile the Regular and Separate Baptists.[224] Rippon published minutes of this committee,[225] the Address sent by them to President Washington on his appointment to the Presidency and Washington's reply.[226] Rippon was greatly helped by correspondents from this area, who included: Lemuel

214 W. Cathcart (ed.), *Baptist Encyclopaedia* (2 vols; Philadelphia: Louis H. Everts, 1881), 1, p. 406; cf. *Register* 1 (1790-93), pp. 102, 116.

215 *ESB*, 2, p. 1461; cf. *Register* 1 (1790-93), p. 385; 4 (1801-02), p. 784-86.

216 G.W. Paschal, *History of North Carolina Baptists* (2 vols; Raleigh: General Board, North Carolina Baptist State Convention, 1930), 1, chs. 18 and 20. Cf. *Register* 1 (1790-93), pp. 98-99, 296-99; 2 (1794-97), pp. 64-65, 195.

217 *ESB* 2, p. 1462; cf. *Register* 1 (1790-93), p. 290.

218 *ESB* 2, p. 1462; *Register* 1 (1790-93), pp. 89-92

219 *ESB* 2, p. 1462; cf. *Register* 1 (1790-93), pp. 116, 291-92; 2 (1794-97), pp. 67-69, 194-95; 4 (1801-02), pp. 807-08.

220 *ESB* 1, pp. 990-91.

221 Cf. C.C. Goen, *Revivalism and Separatism,* pp. 296-98. For Stearns (1706-1771) see *DEB*.

222 *Register* 1 (1790-93), p. 210.

223 *Register* 1 (1790-93), p. 72.

224 *ESB*, 2, p. 1448.

225 *Register* 1 (1790-93), pp. 534-36; 2 (1794-97), pp. 65-67; 4 (1801-02), p. 787.

226 *Register* 1 (1790-93), pp. 168-71.

Burkitt who was elected by the Kehukee Association to compile materials
for the *Register*,[227] John Williams, of the Roanoak association,[228] Lewis
Richards of Baltimore,[229] Major Goforth[230] and several unknown
correspondents from Kentucky.[231]

SOUTH CAROLINA AND GEORGIA

All three associations from this area had reports in the *Register*: the
Charleston formed 1751;[232] the Bethel, formed in 1789 comprising
churches from the north-west of South Carolina;[233] and the Georgian
Association formed in 1784 or 1785[234] in an area largely under the
influence of Daniel Marshall (1706-1784),[235] and his son Abraham (1745-
1819).[236] Rippon's correspondents in this area included: the influential
Dr. Furman of Charleston;[237] Joseph Cook,[238] who like Lewis Richards of
Baltimore had been sent to America by the Countess of Huntingdon but
had embraced Baptist views,[239] and wrote from 'Euhaw, upper Indian
land'; Edmund Botsford of Pedee River, South Carolina;[240] Abraham
Marshall;[241] a 'Lutheran minister' in Georgia;[242] Jonathan Clarke
'treasurer of the city of Savannah',[243] and some black pastors.[244]

---

227 *Register* 1 (1790-93), p. 298; 2 (1794-97), pp. 51-52, 204-205, 271.

228 *Register* 1 (1790-93), p. 86. For Williams (1747-1795), see *ESB,* 2, p. 1502.

229 *Register* 1 (1790-93), p. 101; 2 (1794-97), p. 75; 3 (1798-1801), pp. 126-27;
4 (1801-02), p. 656.

230 *Register* 1 (1790-93), p. 218.

231 Cf. *Register* 1 (1790-93), p. 116; 2 (1794-97), pp. 201-03; 4 (1801-02), pp
805, 1007.

232 *ESB*, 2, pp. 1218-20. Cf. *Register* 1 (1790-93), pp. 100-101, 112-14, 300-
301, 589-90; 2 (1794-97), pp. 78-79; 3 (1798-1801), pp. 524-28.

233 *ESB*, 2, p. 1222. Cf. *Register* 1 (1790-93), pp. 290-91, 536-37; 2 (1794-97),
p. 193.

234 *ESB*, 1, p. 532. Cf. *Register* 1 (1790-93), pp. 537-38.

235 Cf. Benedict, *History of the Baptist Denomination*, pp. 350-55; *DEB*.

236 *ESB*, 2, p. 824.

237 *Register* 2 (1793-97), pp. 281-83; 3 (1798-1801), p. 125; 4 (1801-02), pp.
1102-105.

238 *Register* 4 (1801-02), p. 934.

239 Cf. Newman, *A History of Baptist Churches*, p. 812; and memoir in *Register* 1
(1790-93), pp. 501-509.

240 *Register* 1 (1790-93), pp.104-108. See Cathcart, *Baptist Encyclopaedia*, 1, p.
110.

241 *Register* 1 (1790-93), p. 544.

242 *Register* 1 (1790-93), p. 111.

243 *Register* 1 (1790-93), pp. 339-40; 3 (1798-1801), p. 263; and see Index to vol.
1: s.v., 'Clarke'.

244 For details of these, see below in this chapter.

Clearly Rippon had a range of contacts who provided him with information from all the settled parts of the North American continent. In addition, he published reports from Newfoundland and Nova Scotia.[245]

These 'overseas' accounts comprise some of the most intriguing materials in the *Register*, and evidence Rippon's personal interest in 'the state of religion at home and abroad'.

Reports from the European Continent

These materials further confirm both Rippon's interest in all Christian activity and his initiative in obtaining first-hand accounts. The first such account was entitled 'A Sketch of the State of Religion among different denominations of good men at home and abroad',[246] although Rippon noted that this 'defective' article was merely intended 'to shew the kind of materials which are desired to fill it up'. These two pages, taken directly, although unacknowledged, from the Northamptonshire Circular Letter of 1790, were a summary of an edict by the King of Prussia in 1788 which provided for religious toleration, and a general statement welcoming the French Revolution with the typical first reaction of the Dissenters that they hoped it presaged the complete down fall of 'Papism'.

But Rippon had laid plans to receive more accurate reports.[247] During 1791 he wrote to Daniel Hovens (1735-1795),[248] a Mennonite in Rotterdam, enclosing *Registers* and seeking his assistance in procuring European religious matter. Possibly Rippon had learnt of Hovens from his friend Job David (1746-1813), since David and Hovens had earlier been in correspondence. In 1788 David had asked Hovens to help Robert Robinson of Cambridge in his researches into Baptist history, and in particular to forward a copy of T.J. Van Braght's *Looking-Glass of Martyrs* (1685), an Anabaptist martyrology. Hovens had willingly agreed, and suggested that the researches of Johannes Cuperus (1725-1777) might be made available to Robinson.[249] The correspondence between the two was interrupted about 1787, but in May 1791 Hovens had forwarded to a Holborn bookseller a book and notes about the Mennonite churches.

---

245 *Register* 2 (1794-97), pp. 93, 206; 4 (1801-02), p. 790.

246 *Register* 1 (1790-93), pp. 166-67.

247 Cf. E.A. Payne, 'Two Dutch Translations of Carey', *BQ* 11.1 (1942), pp. 33-38, and his 'Contacts between Mennonites and Baptists', *Foundations* 4.1 (1961), pp. 39-55, reprinted in E.A. Payne, *Free Churchmen, Unrepentant and Repentant* (London: Carey Kingsgate Press, 1965), pp. 75-92. Dr. Payne based this account on letters to Rippon preserved in the Angus Library.

248 *Mennonite Encyclopaedia*, 2, p. 823.

249 *Mennonite Encyclopaedia*, 1, p. 747.

After this Hovens received Rippon's letter, so he promptly replied and advised Rippon of the papers he had recently forwarded. Rippon duly collected these, and sent them with his letter from Hovens to William Carey who, as Ryland had told Rippon, could read Dutch. Carey sent the translations back to Rippon, who then published a list (of eighteen pages) in 1793 of 'Baptist' ministers and churches.[250] This was a detailed list of Mennonites not only in Holland, but in Prussia, Poland, the Palatinate, Switzerland, France and Russia. Rippon also included in his list of books for 1791 a work by Gerrard Hesselink, 'Professor of Divinity and Philosophy in the Society of Baptists in Amsterdam', probably taken from Hovens' papers.[251] No further materials from Hovens, who died in 1796 were printed by Rippon. Indeed, although the background is of interest, the actual list of strange-sounding names can have had little interest to English readers other than to have created the impression of a widespread 'Baptist' community. Rippon later published extracts from Robinson's *Ecclesiastical Researches* which included descriptions of 'Baptists' in Bohemia, Münster, and Poland.[252] Certainly these Mennonites were included in Rippon's dedication of his first volume, written in December 1798, when Rippon expressed the hope that before long representatives of all 'the Baptized Ministers and People' might gather in London.

Rippon forwarded letters and *Registers*, by an unknown hand, to four Mennonite pastors in a church at 'Dantzig' who had been named in Hovens' list.[253] The unknown traveller sent to Rippon an interesting description of the services and customs of the Mennonites. Rippon's letter had included the query, 'Whether internal piety, or the religion of the heart flourished among them, or in any part of Poland or Prussia?' which evoked 'peculiar emotions'. For their part, the Mennonites inquired about how English Baptists administered the ordinances, whether they made collections for the poor, how long the sermons of ministers were and outlined their pacifist practices. Rippon's informant reported that these Mennonites were effectively 'Calvinistic Baptists': they were 'quite clear' in this truth, 'That it is impossible for any man to be saved without a real change of heart'. Thus the historical and continuing distinctions between Mennonites and English Baptists were largely ignored in the desire to establish a world identity for all 'Baptists'. Rippon also published a letter by C.I. Latrobe,[254] the secretary of the Moravian Missions, which published reports of Moravian activities in France, Switzerland, Denmark, Sweden, Hungary, Saxony and Russia.

---

250 *Register* 1 (1790-93), pp. 305-20.
251 *Register* 1 (1790-93), p. 324
252 *Register* 4 (1801-02), pp. 871-94, 1015-22, 1039-46, 1119-26.
253 *Register* 2 (1794-97), pp. 209-10.
254 *Register* 2 (1794-97), pp. 210-215. For Latrobe (1768-1836), see *DNB*.

The other materials were letters sent by travellers who described the general and religious situation as they observed it. These included a series of seven letters (1801-2) written by 'B',[255] mainly from Paris, and two (1802) by 'S.W.' from Emden and Amsterdam.[256] Rippon also published a letter from Voltaire to the King of Prussia, forwarded by 'D', and the articles relevant to the Protestant Religion from the 1801 Concordat between Napoleon and Pius VII.[257]

Rippon's interest in the Continent continued after the *Register*. He led in the campaign to assist the persecuted French in 1815,[258] and W.H. Angas wrote to him when he was on the Continent in 1818.[259] Obviously, however, the war that raged for most of the period of the *Register* made it difficult for Rippon to gather more material about the nature of Christian work in Europe.

Missions

The *Register* was published during the period often described as including the birth of the modern missionary movement. The Society for Promoting Christian Knowledge (formed 1698-9) and the Society for Propagating the Gospel (1701) continued in their work which was mainly to British colonies. The Moravians were the first of modern times to have the vision of taking the gospel to 'heathen' throughout the world, and by 1732 the Hërnhutt community had sent its first messengers to the West Indies. The Moravians' earliest fields included the Eskimos, Greenlanders, 'blacks', Hottentots, and American Indians.[260] Again, the pioneer work of David Brainerd among North American Indians was continued, and reference has been made to some of these later activities. These were the main subjects of 'Missions' that Rippon intended to report in his first plans for the *Register*, and some of these accounts were published by him.

But naturally after 1792 the bulk of the *Register*'s missionary content was devoted to the Baptists' own society. The London Missionary Society which followed in 1795 was also given some space, as well as other enterprises discussed below. The *Register* welcomed all missionary materials.

---

255 *Register* 3 (1798-1801), pp. 465-467; 4 (1801-02), pp. 583-85, 628-30, 653-55, 670-71, 687-88, 936-39.

256 *Register* 4 (1801-02), pp. 820-23.

257 *Register* 4 (1801-02), pp. 912-16.

258 See chapter 3 and chapter 7.

259 Angas to Rippon, Rotterdam 2 April 1818, B.L. Add. MSS. 25386, f. 17.

260 A.J. Lewis, *Zinzendorf the Ecumenical Pioneer. A Study in the Moravian Contribution to Christian Mission and Unity* (London: SCM Press, 1962), pp. 78-97.

The significance of the *Register*'s support for the BMS, especially in its earliest days, can scarcely be exaggerated. The Society, with only fourteen subscribers at its commencement, soon became national and even international in its support: and the first medium of its publicity was the *Register*. John Thomas (1757-1801), the eccentric surgeon who influenced the infant society to work in India, had written to Rippon describing his experiences in India in August 1792, that is, before the BMS was formed. Rippon published Thomas' letter in December 1792 and linked it with the account of the Society's formation.[261] This was before Thomas had met Carey, and before the field had been decided upon: thus the linking of the two was presaged in the *Register*. Rippon in his funeral sermon for Ryland preached in Northampton, on 29 July 1792, (before the Society's formation), had referred to the intended society and exclaimed, 'may it be crowned with the smile of Heaven!'[262] Thus, Rippon was probably the first London Baptist to be fully aware of the new movement. With Abraham Booth, Rippon encouraged London Baptists to support the fledgling society.[263]

The report of the new society went out to all the Baptists via the *Register*, although the society also prepared a printed account of its origins. The influence of the *Register* is illustrated by the report that at Folkstone the church learned of the plan from the *Register* and immediately formed a corresponding society to help the Mission.[264] Isaac Backus wrote to tell Rippon that he supported the new scheme.[265] The society had asked in its printed account for suggestions about selecting missionary candidates. Rippon sent the *Register* with this question in it to Latrobe, secretary of the Moravian society, who wrote a thoughtful answer which Rippon later published.[266] In these ways the *Register* assisted the infant society.

Rippon continued to advance the cause of the Mission in every possible way. But from 1794 the BMS issued its own *Periodical Accounts* which naturally meant that the *Register* ceased to be of primary importance in publicizing the Mission. There was cooperation at first between Rippon and the BMS committee. Indeed, the first number of the *Periodical Accounts* republished all the BMS papers from the first volume of the *Register*, and in return Rippon printed letters from Carey and Thomas before they appeared in the second number of the

261 *Register* 1 (1790-93), pp. 353-67.

262 J. Rippon, *The Gentle Dismission of Saints from Earth to Heaven. A sermon occasioned by the decease of the Rev. John Ryland, Senior* (London: 1792), p. 22.

263 Stanley, *The History of the Baptist Missionary Society 1792-1992*, p. 17 wrongly states Booth was the one London minister to give his support.

264 *Register* 2 (1794-97), p. 29.

265 *Register* 1 (1790-93), p. 547.

266 *Register* 1 (1790-93), pp. 531-533

Accounts.[267] This was because the Committee hoped 'that their appearance in the *Register* which had obtained a good circulation, would be of *advantage to the Society.*'[268] But from this time onwards Rippon was restricted to either summarizing materials already published in the *Accounts* or to such letters as he could personally obtain from the missionaries.

Yet Rippon's friendship with the missionaries was such that he did elicit a good number of valuable personal letters which he duly published. Carey had the deepest respect for Rippon and all he was trying to do, and once wrote to him: 'I love you, I always have loved you, since the first time I was in your company; and I feel that I shall love you through eternity'.[269] Rippon had given Carey the Dutch letters to translate and Carey preached at Carter Lane on 31 March 1793 shortly before his departure.[270] Thomas similarly had a warm regard for Rippon, whom he called, 'you my patient, unavenging (unchanging?) forbearing, & inquiring brother' and offered to accommodate Benjamin, Rippon's difficult son, for whom Thomas felt a kindred regard.[271] Accordingly, both Carey and Thomas, together with later men like William Ward (1769-1823), John Fountain (1767-1800), and Samuel Powell (not sent as a missionary, but a cousin of Thomas who was baptized by Carey in India, but died in 1802)[272] all wrote letters to Rippon which were published in the *Register.*[273] The missionaries recognized in Rippon a like-minded soul, as Ward once wrote to him; 'My dear Brother - We have repeatedly said you are cut out for a Missionary & Brother Carey has frequently wished for your aptness in accommodating yourself to hearers for their good; & in bringing forward, on every occasion, something that may profit.'[274] Certainly the missionaries appreciated Rippon's letters and eagerly awaited each issue of the *Register.*[275]

Rippon was especially interested in understanding the culture of the Indian people. Carey wrote two long letters which detailed Hindu mythology, and described Rippon's letters as 'full of questions' and

---

267 *Register* 2 (1794-97), pp. 141-76.

268 Advertisement on cover of *Register*, number 9.

269 *Register* 4 (1801-02), p. 899.

270 Carey, *William Carey* , p. 119.

271 J. Thomas to Rippon, 24 November 1799, B.L. Add. MSS. 25389, f. 247.

272 Carey, *William Carey*, pp. 167, 238-39.

273 Following is all BMS material in *Register*: 1 (1790-93), pp. 353-78, 485, 525-31; 2 (1794-97), pp. 96, 141-76, 353-60, 411-12, 524-31; 3 (1798-1801), pp. 61-80, 161-78, 320-24, 397-411, 508-10; 4 (1801-02), pp. 667, 809-11, 830, 840-44, 850-53, 860, 899-901, 909-11, 945-48, 1034-35, 1071-73, 1109.

274 W. Ward to J. Rippon, Serampore, 20 November 1800, B.L. Add. MSS. 25389, f. 391.

275 *Register* 3 (1798-1801), p. 168.

'almost boundless desires'.[276] In one letter of 10 December 1796 some four pages are occupied with details of mythology.[277] Rippon engaged in considerable research, drawing especially on the work of Sir William Jones.[278] Nine different works were cited by Rippon in his notes on the subject.[279]

However, Rippon in his eagerness to give as much information as possible, occasionally printed material which embarrassed or annoyed the BMS leaders. This emerges from two letters written by Fuller. On 22 January 1795 he wrote to John Sutcliff:

> Pearce writes that he has remonstrated to Rippon and that R. is very warm. We are all offended with him & have reason to be so. He had a letter from Carey wh. he kept back from us, & yet wanted ours. In that letter too Carey's freedom about Ram Ram's treatment for Mr. Brown's friend will do us harm among the Episcopalians. We must desire both the missionaries not to write anything confidential to Rippon.[280]

Rippon perhaps did not realize the significance of this reference, and his attitude was simply that he wanted to obtain original materials for his *Register*. Again, on 19 August 1801 Fuller wrote to Carey: 'We shd certainly have sd nothing in print of bro T. being confined in a mad-house, but Dr. Rippon who heard it via America has printed it as he does whatever comes to hand.'[281] This had been a reference in a letter from William Rogers of Philadelphia to Rippon, dated 13 June 1801;[282] 'bro T.' was John Thomas, who died on 13 October 1801.[283] These disputes confirm both Rippon's independence and his difficulty in obtaining original BMS materials, and suggest a certain lack of diplomacy. Nevertheless, there are many original letters of great value to historians of the Mission, and they can only have added to the missionary awareness of the Baptists.

Rippon also published extracts from the *Periodical Accounts* of the Moravians, which had commenced in 1790.[284] He was in regular correspondence with C.I. Latrobe, secretary of the Moravians' mission, and published several letters from him which described their work.[285] In

---

276 *Register* 2 (1794-97), pp. 411-12; 3 (1798-1801), pp. 61-66.

277 *Register* 3 (1798-1801), pp. 61-66.

278 For Jones (1746-1794), see *DNB*.

279 See works cited in notes, *Register* 2 (1794-97), pp. 141-76.

280 Original in BMS.archives. For the incident referred to see *Register* 2 (1794-97), p. 163.

281 Typescript copy in Angus Library.

282 *Register* 3 (1798-1801), p. 531.

283 *Register* 4 (1801-02), p. 950.

284 *Register* 1 (1790-93), pp. 378-84.

285 *Register* 2 (1794-97), pp. 349-52; 4 (1801-02), pp. 567-68.

order to encourage the disheartened Serampore missionaries Rippon published extracts from G.H. Laskiel, *History of the Mission of the United Brethren among the Indians in North America* (1794) which recounted their early disappointments but subsequent success.[286]

Other material included accounts of missionary work among the Indians of America;[287] a sermon preached by Melvill Horne (1781-1841), Anglican chaplain in Sierra Leone;[288] an account of the formation of the London Missionary Society at the request of that society;[289] a description of Tahitian pagan customs and the Lord's Prayer in their language, sent by James Cover (1762-1834) one of the LMS missionaries sent aboard the *Duff*;[290] a letter from Richard Johnson (1755-1827), the first Anglican chaplain at Sydney;[291] reports about SPCK work in India in 1763,[292] and extracts from the SPCK accounts of 1801 which included a description of the death of Charles Friedrich Schwartz (1724-1798) the remarkable Danish missionary;[293] extracts from *An Essay on the Propagation of the Gospel in India, Africa, and America.*[294]

Thus Rippon consistently and catholically supported the cause of Christian missions.

Work among Black Christians

An extension of this missionary activity, and one of the best examples of the direct influence of Rippon and the *Register*, are the accounts of the earliest Baptist work among the blacks of Georgia, Jamaica, Nova Scotia, and Sierra Leone. Rippon displayed considerable initiative in gathering the accounts, and encouraged the Baptists of Britain to assist these fellow-Baptists.

---

286 *Register* 2 (1794-97), pp. 171-73 (note).

287 *Register* 2 (1794-97), pp. 233-48; 3 (1798-1801), pp. 47-55, 140-44, 178-79, 239-44, 328, 369-76, 421-23, 454-58, 529-631; 4 (1801-02), pp. 788-89, 856-57, 902-904, 948-50.

288 *Register* 2 (1794-97), pp. 249-56. For Horne, see E.A. Payne, *The Church Awakes. The Story of the Modern Missionary Movement* (London: Edinburgh House Press, 1942), pp. 67-69.

289 *Register* 2 (1794-97), pp. 257-63.

290 *Register* 3 (1798-1801), pp. 421-25.

291 *Register* 3 (1798-1801), p. 222

292 *Register* 3 (1798-1801), pp. 491-98.

293 *Register* 4 (1801-02), pp. 735-42, 767-68, 860-64.

294 *Register* 4 (1801-02), pp. 1069-71, 1088-93.

Central figure in the story is a black preacher named George Liele (or Lisle, or Sharp) (c. 1750-1828).[295] Rippon first heard about 'Brother George', a poor 'negro' who had 'planted' the first Baptist churches in both Savannah, Georgia and Kingston, Jamaica, from Rev. Joseph Cook, of Euhaw, S.C., in 1790.[296] Rippon then wrote letters about Liele to Cook, Jonathan Clarke of Savannah, and 'Mr. Wesley's people at Kingston',[297] and directly to Liele proposing no less than fifty questions about himself and his work.

From replies to these letters Rippon compiled a detailed and interesting account of Liele's work.[298] His character was well attested by Stephen Cooke of Kingston,[299] a Methodist member of the Assembly. Liele began his life as a slave in Virginia, and was converted whilst a slave of Henry Sharp, a deacon of the Kiokee Baptist church in Georgia. He began preaching and formed a slave church in Savannah, *circa* 1777. Sharp was killed whilst fighting on the British side during the wars but had earlier granted freedom to Liele. After various adventures, Liele was befriended by a Colonel Kirkland who took him to Jamaica, where many colonists fled in 1783. Once in Jamaica Liele again began preaching and in 1783 formed a church in Kingston. When Liele received Rippon's letter the poor congregation had begun building their first chapel.

Rippon's unexpected letter was greatly appreciated by the congregation, mostly poor illiterate slaves. The letter was read several times, 'and did create a great deal of love and warmness throughout the whole congregation ... and that such a worthy - of London, should write in so loving a manner to such poor worms as we are'.[300] Liele hoped that Rippon would be able to assist them in the building of their chapel, 'which we look upon will be the greatest undertaking, ever was in this country for the bringing of souls from darkness into the light of the Gospel'.[301] Liele later sent to Rippon a copy of *The Covenant of the Anabaptist Church, begun in America, December 1777, and in Jamaica,*

---

295 For Liele, see C. Gayle, *George Liele. Pioneer Missionary to Jamaica* (Kingston: Jamaica Baptist Union, 1982); E.A. Payne, 'Baptist Work in Jamaica before the arrival of the Missionaries', *BQ* 7.1 (1934), pp. 20-26; J.P. Gates, 'George Liele: A Pioneer Negro Preacher', *The Chronicle* 6 (1943), pp. 118-29; E.A. Holmes, 'George Liele: Negro Slavery's Prophet of Deliverance', *BQ* 20.8 (1964), pp. 340-51; G.A. Catherall, 'The Native Baptist Church', *BQ* 24.2 (1971), pp. 65-73.

296 *Register* 1 (1790-93), p. 332.

297 This work had begun in 1789, and owed much to the inspiration of Thomas Coke (1747-1814), for whom see *DNB*.

298 *Register* 1 (1790-93), pp. 332-44.

299 *Register* 1 (1790-93), pp. 338-39.

300 *Register* 1 (1790-93), p. 337.

301 *Register* 1 (1790-93), pp. 336-37.

December 1783. [302] This was read monthly at 'sacrament meetings', and consisted of seventeen rules for members. The slaves' attitude to their masters was defined from the Bible as one of subservience, and it was emphasized by Cooke that Liele was not supported financially by his congregation as this would have been criticized by the slave-owners.[303]

Rippon was evidently able to send some help, for Liele in a letter of 12 January 1793 thanked Rippon for his 'kind attention' and books.[304] In December 1792 the New Connexion of General Baptists voted to send assistance to Liele,[305] although he had written to Rippon that he believed in election and other Calvinist emphases.[306] That the General Baptists, who had also received a letter from Liele, were influenced by the *Register* account is probable. Liele was later imprisoned because of the debt on the chapel, estimated at between £400 and £600 in 1793.[307] Eventually the money was raised and Liele released.[308] Rippon published no further letters from Liele. As early as 1793 a Methodist in Kingston urged the English Baptists to send out a suitable minister, because 'I think the Baptist church is the church that will spread the Gospel among the poor negroes'.[309] Liele at this time had baptized 'near 500' in the island.[310]

Another important aspect of Liele's influence was the leadership given in various centres by his converts, not only in Georgia and, Jamaica, but also in Nova Scotia and Sierra Leone. Two leading black preachers in Jamaica were Thomas Nicholas Swigle and Moses Baker. Swigle was originally a helper to Liele,[311] but formed a church of his own which he claimed had about five hundred members in 1802.[312] Baker, a mulatto barber, was baptized by Liele about 1787, and it was evidently he who later appealed to Britain to send out missionary help.[313] In 1814 John Rowe the first BMS missionary to Jamaica made contact with Baker on his arrival. Much of the British interest in Jamaica may be traced to

---

302 *Register* 1 (1790-93), p. 343. (A copy is in the Angus library). Text in Gayle, *George Liele*, pp. 44-45.
303 *Register* 1 (1790-93), p. 338.
304 *Register* 1 (1790-93), pp. 541-42.
305 'Minutes of the Monthly Conferences', *BHS Trans.* 5 (1916-17), p. 124.
306 *Register* 1 (1790-93), p. 336
307 *Register* 1 (1790-93), p. 541.
308 Gates, 'George Liele', p. 126.
309 *Register* 1 (1790-93), p. 543.
310 *Register* 1 (1790-93), p. 542.
311 *Register* 1 (1790-93), p. 542.
312 *Register* 4 (1801-02), p. 1145.
313 Stanley, *The History of the Baptist Missionary Society 1792-1992*, p. 70.

Rippon's publication of these letters, and to his friend John Ryland who as early as 1807 was exploring the possibility of sending a missionary.[314]

In Savannah the church formed by Liele was under the leadership of Andrew Bryan, who endured serious persecution because of his pastoral efforts. Bryan's character was duly attested, and Rippon became the London representative of a fund to assist the church erect a chapel.[315]

One of the most remarkable of Liele's converts was David George (1743-1810), who had fled from a cruel master in Virginia and was converted under Liele in Georgia.[316] During the war George was in Charleston and when the British evacuated was given opportunity to travel with about five hundred whites and a number of blacks to Nova Scotia. Here George gathered a church. In 1791 a group of Evangelicals in London, notably Granville Sharp, Henry Thornton, William Wilberforce and Thomas Clarkson, formed the Sierra Leone Company. Their aim was to establish a colony where freed slaves could be settled: a positive action in their campaign against slavery. Knowing that many of the freed slaves in Nova Scotia were unhappy with the climate and their general condition, they despatched Lieutenant John Clarkson (brother of Thomas) to interest those slaves in settling in Sierra Leone.[317]

David George acted as something of a leader for the slaves, and collected the names of those willing to go. He reported that 'almost all the Baptists went'. Whilst travelling to the new colony, Clarkson agreed to help George visit England. Accordingly, Henry Thornton sent him the passage money and George duly arrived in England early in 1793. George was well-armed with testimonials from Melvill Horne, chaplain of the company, and from Clarkson, then governor of the colony, who told Rippon that 'he esteemed David George as his brother, and that be believes him to be the best man, without exception, in the colony at Sierra Leone'.[318]

Naturally, Rippon helped George in every way. He described George as 'about fifty' and recorded every detail of George's life, as told to Pearce and him. This report occupied twelve pages of the *Register*. George was enthusiastically received. Rippon and his friends promised to erect a meeting house for him, and that, if any of his members were

---

314 F.A. Cox, *History of the Baptist Missionary Society, from 1792 to 1842* (2 vols; London: 1842), 2, pp. 17-19.

315 *Register* 1 (1790-93), p. 343

316 *Register* 1 (1790-93), pp. 473-84. See G. Gordon, *From Slavery to Freedom. The Life of David George, Pioneer Black Baptist Minister* (Hantsport, Nova Scotia: 1992) and *DEB*.

317 T. Clarkson, *History of the Rise, Progress and Accomplishment of the Abolition of the African Slave Trade by the British Parliament* (London: 1839), p. 402 claimed that over 1,100 former slaves were embarked.

318 *Register* 1 (1790-93), p. 484.

inclined, he would be kept and trained in England for a year, evidently at Bristol. The following year, 1794, John Cuthbert came to London perhaps with that promise in view. Certainly he visited Bristol and Bath in the company of Rippon.[319] Plans for the chapel were drawn, and the money raised. Cuthbert, however, decided not to take the money with him because of the risk of a French attack. His fears were well grounded. On 28 September 1794 a French squadron wrought havoc in Freetown, the new settlement, causing an estimated £52,000 damage.[320] Cuthbert's ship unwittingly entered the harbour whilst the French were still there. Cuthbert was robbed of all he had, 'they even took my hat off my head'.[321] George and Cuthbert wrote to Rippon and described their plight, for most of the people were without adequate clothing.

Rippon acted promptly. His own church sent five chests of clothes, and the Wild Street and Goodman's Fields churches also donated clothing.[322] Samuel Whitbread, the brewer, gave Rippon twenty pounds for the blacks.[323] The clothing duly arrived, and was acknowledged with a grateful letter from George.[324] The Colony revived, largely due to the efforts of Zachary Macaulay, governor from 1794 to 1799. Nevertheless it was deemed wiser not to build the chapel until hostilities had ceased.

Meanwhile, Rippon's accounts and the visits of George and Cuthbert had stimulated the English Baptists. Accordingly, the BMS committee on 7 April 1795 resolved to send missionaries to Sierra Leone.[325] A young Bristol student, Jacob Grigg (1769-1835) was eager to go, and a companion in James Rodway was found by June. The same year both landed at Freetown. David George wrote enthusiastically of their arrival, accompanied by gifts of clothing and books.[326] However, the enterprise undertaken in some haste proved a dismal failure. Rodway's health was poor from the first, and after eight months he had to return home. Grigg's radical politics led him to regard the English government as the rule of 'tyrants' and meddle in the administration of the colony. After an ultimatum from Governor Macaulay, Grigg migrated to America where

---

319 *Register* 2 (1794-97), p. 216.

320 Cf. C.P. Groves, *The Planting: of Christianity in Africa* (4 vols; London: Lutterworth, 1948-58), 1, p. 188.

321 *Register* 2 (1794-97), p. 216.

322 *Register* 2 (1794-97), p. 255.

323 *Register* 2 (1794-97), p. 409, note *.

324 *Register* 2 (1794-97), pp. 255-56.

325 BMS *Periodical Accounts*, 1, p. 97. Cp Haykin, *One Heart and One Soul*, pp. 243-45.

326 *Register* 2 (1794-97), p. 409.

he engaged in pastoral service.[327] Haste and indiscretion thus cut off the hopes of Rippon and the BMS supporters in Sierra Leone.

Evidently the blacks kept in touch with Rippon, although no further reports were printed by him. In 1807 W. Francis wrote to Rippon advising him that George had been excluded from the congregation because he had brought a legal action against a fellow-member.[328] George was a man of remarkable influence among all the settlers, was loyal to the Company, and his church included 'in general sober-minded and temperate men'.[329] In 1807 the settlement became a Crown colony.

Rippon also published reports of missionary work among blacks by the Methodists in the West Indies, as supplied by Dr. Thomas Coke (1747-1814).[330]

Ireland

Baptist work in Ireland dated from Commonwealth times,[331] but after the Restoration was very weak. Rippon published some account of the churches there in an effort to encourage support from England. An interdenominational 'General Evangelical Society' was formed in Dublin in 1787,[332] and this sponsored visits from leading English preachers. Among those Baptists who visited Ireland were Samuel Medley, Benjamin Francis, Isaiah Birt (1758-1837) of Plymouth, Samuel Pearce, John Palmer (d. 1823) of Shrewsbury, and Rippon himself.[333] By 1801 there were only six Baptist churches in Ireland, mostly of less than two hundred

---

327 H.G. Hartzell, 'Jacob Grigg-Missionary and Minister', *The Chronicle* 6 (1943), pp. 83-90, 130-143; Stanley, *The History of the Baptist Missionary Society*, pp. 23-24; B. Amey, 'Baptist Missionary Society Radicals', *BQ* 26.8 (1976), pp. 368-69; K.R.M. Short, 'A Note on the Sierra Leone Mission and Religious Freedom, 1796', *BQ* 28.8 (1980), pp. 355-60; S. Jakobsson, *Am I not a Man and a Brother? British Missions and the Abolition of the Slave Trade and Slavery in West Africa and the West Indies 1786-1838* (Lund: Gleerup, 1972), pp. 84-100. Cf. *Register* 2 (1794-97), p. 531; 4 (1801-02), p. 787; BMS *Periodical Accounts*, 1, pp. 241-61.

328 W. Francis to Rippon, Freetown, 2 May 1807, B.L. Add. MSS. 25387, f. 32.

329 M.J. Knutsford, *Life and Letters of Zachary Macaulay* (London: E. Arnold, 1900), pp. 133, 137-38, 144-45, as cited by Groves, *The Planting of Christianity in Africa*, 1, p. 207.

330 *Register*, 1 (1790-93), p. 561; 3 (1798-1801), p. 368.

331 Whitley, *History of British Baptists*, p. 80. For the influence of Bristol Academy on Irish Baptist churches, see Hayden, 'Evangelical Calvinism', pp. 85-91, and more generally J. Thompson, 'Baptists in Ireland, 1792–1922: A Dimension of Protestant Dissent' (DPhil thesis, Oxford University, 1988).

332 *Register* 2 (1794-97), p. 405.

333 *Register* 2 (1794-97), p. 408, note *.

members.[334] Rippon published reports from ministers who had preached there, and commended the work of the 'General Evangelical Society'.[335]

Baptist Itinerant Society[336]

Rippon's support for the renewed Baptist emphasis on village preaching has been noted previously, for he commented on this both in connection with the lists of churches and the activity of the associations. But the move towards a national organization for village evangelism was also publicized by Rippon. In 1796 the BMS sponsored a preaching tour into Cornwall by John Saffery and William Steadman, and helped James Hinton of Oxford in local village work. Full reports were published in the BMS *Periodical Accounts*,[337] but Rippon also published letters by Steadman.[338] In 1797 the Baptist Society in London for the Encouragement and Support of Itinerant and Village Preaching was formed, and Rippon published an account of the society's formation and its rules.[339] Rippon's support for the movement was immediate and whole-hearted, he himself undertook one of the first tours sponsored by the society, but as these activities are reviewed elsewhere, it is sufficient to note here that the society and some of its sponsored tours were well publicized in the *Register*.

Lists of Books

Rippon intended to publish lists for each year, but none were given in 1796, 1799, or 1802. Although he wanted his list to be as complete as possible, he insisted that it was the responsibility of the authors or publishers to forward their publications to him. From the beginning Rippon included books by other Dissenters or Evangelicals, and not all the books were religious: such as Martin Dunsford's *Historical Memoirs of Tiverton*, (1791), J. Morse's *American Geography*, (c. 1790), and various educational works. For some books Rippon listed the full Table of Contents, and in the 1793 list reproduced several extracts from the books and discussed some of their themes.

---

334   *Register* 4 (1801-02), p. 658.
335   *Register* 2 (1794-97), pp. 208-209, 404-408; 3 (1798-1801), p. 263, 4 (1801-02), pp. 656-59.
337   See chapter 7 for details of this society.
337   *Register* 2 (1794-97), pp. 262-76.
338   *Register* 2 (1794-97), pp. 459-64; 3 (1798-1801), pp. 56-59.
339   *Register* 2 (1794-97), pp. 465-70.

The lists are of obvious value to modern bibliographers. They doubtless helped circulate many of the important books published by Baptists during this period. Writers to whose works Rippon consistently gave full emphasis were Jonathan Edwards (Junior), Andrew Fuller, and John Ryland. Among the many influential books published by Baptists during this period were: William Carey's, *Enquiry into the obligations of Christians to use Means for the Conversion of Heathen* (1792); Andrew Fuller's *Calvinistic and Socinian Systems Examined* (1793) and *Gospel its own Witness* (second edition 1800); and Robert Hall's *Apology for the Freedom of the Press* (1793). Rippon gave due prominence to his own works; for example, he devoted two whole pages to listing the tunes contained in his *Tune Book*.[340] These lists provide an interesting sidelight on the activity of Baptists at this time, and the *Register* can only have assisted in the books' wider usefulness. In total 343 books were listed and of these 35 were by American Baptists, 58 by General Baptists and 35 by non-Baptists, with the remaining 215 by British Baptists including 17 by Scotch Baptists.[341]

Miscellaneous

The various amounts of space devoted to remaining sections may be seen in Table 5. Several of these are obviously relevant for Rippon's contribution as an historian and are reviewed elsewhere. The 'Intelligence' section included: 1. Accounts of exactly one hundred ordinations, of which five related to American Baptists, one to a General Baptist, and three to Independent pastors. These offer interesting details of these services, and provide information for the biographies of individuals or the history of the churches. 2. Accounts of the opening of twelve new meeting-houses. 2. Descriptions of the formation of three new churches. These 'Intelligence' reports should be compared with the notes of the individual churches, which contained similar materials.

But then there were other materials which may be generally classified into nine sections which provided much of the lighter and entertaining reading for the original supporters of the *Register*.

1. Accounts of Religion. These included reports from other denominations, such as 'an Evangelical Episcopalian Clergyman in Wales',[342] and interdenominational activities at Hull and Bedford.[343]

---

340 *Register* 1 (1790-93), pp. 327-28, 118-27, 321-31, 469-72; *Register* 2 (1794-97), pp. 76-91, 219-22, 340-44, 471-79; *Register* 3 (1798-1801), pp. 39-95, 192-204, 264, 469, 550.

341 *Register* 1 (1790-93), pp. 118-27.

342 *Register* 1 (1790-93), p. 221.

343 *Register* 3 (1798-1801), pp. 490-91; 4 (1801-02), pp. 939-42.

2. Sermons or Letters by Baptists. These included Caleb Evans' 'Address to the Students in the Academy at Bristol, 12 April 1770',[344] sermons and letters by Samuel Stennett, Benjamin Beddome, Samuel Pearce, and Robert Robinson.[345]

3. Brief Extracts from rare or expensive books. Rippon was especially interested in reports of travellers, or histories of ancient civilizations. Some sixteen works were cited,[346] and then there were larger extracts from church histories.[347]

4. Anecdotes. These covered various topics, such as 'Manner of Beautifying a Saint in Italy',[348] 'Sinful Farmer's Repentance and Death', [349]'Parson Wise-Acre', [350]*etc.*

5. Devotional. Some seventeen items were given, mainly in the last two volumes. Those ranged from 'Rules for the Regulation of a Christian Family',[351] to 'Encouragement to Prayer' by John Ryland Senior.[352]

6. Theological. Very few materials were of this type, but there was a 'Theological Dictionary' by William Newman,[353] and a letter on Election.[354]

7. Reports of Societies, Lists of Meetings. These included statements about the Civil State of Dissenters in 1793,[355] LMS work among the French prisoners at Liverpool,[356] lists of preachers at lectures,[357] reports of the Widows' Fund, (1801),[358] Religious Tract Society (1801)[359] and the Yearly Meetings of the Friends (1802).[360]

8. Discussion of Questions. Rippon printed on the first of his monthly *Registers* a set of five questions which he hoped correspondents would discuss in his pages. The only answer he printed was to the first question, 'What is generally meant by the Dissenting interest and is that interest on

---

344 *Register* 1 (1790-93), pp. 345-51.

345 *Register* 3 (1798-1801), pp. 290-92, 415-421, 433-438, 498-502, 520-21; 4 (1801-02), pp. 721-34, 919-26.

346 For example: *Register* 2 (1794-97), pp. 400-401; 3 (1798-1801), pp. 376, 458; 4 (1801-02), pp. 688-89, 742-44, 942, 976-77, 1131-32.

347 See chapter 6.

348 *Register* 4 (1801-02), pp. 403-404.

349 *Register* 4 (1801-02), pp. 895-99.

350 *Register* 4 (1801-02), pp. 986-88.

351 *Register* 3 (1798-1801), p. 350.

352 *Register* 3 (1798-1801), pp. 363-66.

353 *Register* 3 (1798-1801), pp. 461-63; 4 (1801-02), pp. 664-66.

354 *Register* 4 (1801-02), pp. 780-83.

355 *Register* 1 (1790-93), p. 524.

356 *Register* 3 (1798-1801), pp. 251, 298.

357 *Register* 3 (1798-1801), pp. 270, 352; 4 (1801-02), p. 710

358 *Register* 4 (1801-02), pp. 426-428.

359 *Register* 3 (1798-1801), pp. 541-43.

360 *Register* 4 (1801-02), pp. 1094-96.

the increase or not?'[361] One other later question, by 'A.B.C.', on the Mediatorship of Christ, was also answered at length in the *Register*. [362]

9. Original Poetry. This became a regular feature of the monthly *Register*. Prior to that however, several poems by Benjamin Francis on: 'The Association', 'the Dying Christian', and a poem to the 'North American Indians' together with odes to Robert Day, Caleb Evans, and Joshua Thomas, were published.[363] Other authors represented in the original poetry included Beddome, Medley, Ryland, Pearce, Fountain, Fawcett, Rippon and many anonymous writers. The poems are of varied merit.

Several engravings, mainly portraits, were published in the *Register*.[364]

End of the *Register*

Rippon ceased publishing the *Register*, evidently without any explanation,[365] with Number 41 issued in January 1803. The fourth volume had been completed, and the end of the year was probably the most convenient time to terminate the periodical. Some explanation of Rippon's decision seems to be required, and four reasons suggest themselves.

First, the excessive physical demands imposed upon Rippon by the production of the *Register* must have been a constant temptation to finish. He was still a busy pastor, and was too much of an individualist to contemplate forming a committee to continue publishing the *Register* which was so closely associated with his name.

Secondly, there was increasing competition from rival magazines, especially the *Evangelical Magazine*, commenced in 1793 with strong Baptist support from people like Fuller, Ryland, Samuel Pearce and James

---

361 *Register* 3 (1798-1801), pp. 522-24.

362 *Register* 3 (1798-1801), pp. 377-80.

363 *Register* 1 (1790-93), pp. 16-17, 222-26, 247-52; 2 (1794-97), pp. 327-28; 3 (1798-1801), pp. 204-206.

364 In Volume 1: portraits of Caleb Evans, Robert Hall (Sr.), and James Manning; Volume 2: portraits of Benjamin Francis, William Clarke, and Samuel Stennett; Volume 3: portraits of Samuel Pearce, Philip Gibbs of Plymouth, John Tommas of Bristol, John Fawcett, and William Rogers; facsimiles of the writing of John Fountain (in 'Bengallee' and English) and Samuel Pearce. Volume 4: portraits of Samuel Stillman, Jonathan Purchis of Margate, Isaac Hann of Upottery (d. 1778), and John Thomas; facsimiles of the writing of George Whitefield, Philip Doddridge, and an engraving of the Providence, R. I., meeting-house.

365 Possibly some explanation was given on the covers of numbers 40 and 41, but neither is extant.

Hinton of Oxford.[366] Then there were the BMS *Periodical Accounts*, and the two new Baptist magazines already noted, *The New Theological Repository*, and the *Biblical Magazine*. From the beginning of the *Evangelical Magazine* Baptist support of the *Register* seems not unnaturally to have declined: Samuel Rumson of Exeter wrote in February 1795, 'I suppose that the slack sale of Registers is in consequence of the people having engaged in the evangelical magazine'.[367] The irregularity of the *Register* at this time also annoyed Rippon's readers. There are several duplications of 'religious intelligence' in both the *Register* and the *Evangelical Magazine*. This was especially true of Baptist ordinations, although Rippon also printed the account of the formation of the LMS (closely associated with the *Evangelical Magazine* in its origins) at their request. A detailed comparison reveals that Rippon never duplicated any features from the *Magazine*, on the contrary the latter reproduced in June 1796 the substance of Rippon's biography of William Clarke, published in October 1795.[368] What must have annoyed Rippon was the increasing amount of Baptist material sent to the *Magazine* and not to him. Not only Fuller and Ryland, but Fawcett and Hinton became regular contributors. Biographies of some leading Baptists were given to the *Magazine*, men like Joshua Thomas, Samuel Pearce, Samuel Medley.[369] Again, other Baptists who sent copy to the *Magazine* included Samuel Medley, John Kingdon, William Rogers and James Upton, many of whom had originally supported Rippon.[370] Symptomatic of the competition from the *Magazine* is that with his monthly *Register*s Rippon largely copied the general design of the *Magazine* which enjoyed a large circulation, and devoted its profits to charity.[371] Rippon in September 1801 similarly declared that all profits would be given to charity.[372] But Baptists continued to prefer the *Magazine*, and the appeal of the *Register*, which sadly deteriorated in quality during 1801-2, continued to wane.

---

366 For the impact of Baptist involvement in this magazine on other cooperative ventures, see Martin, 'English Particular Baptists and Interdenominational Cooperation', p. 235.

367 B.L. Add. MSS. 25388, f. 474.

368 Cf. *Register* 2 (1794-97), pp. 272-30; *Evangelical Magazine* 4 (1796), pp. 221-30.

369 *Evangelical Magazine* 6 (1798), pp. 89-99; 8 (1800), pp. 177-83, 11 (1801), pp. 1-9.

370 *Evangelical Magazine* 5 (1797), pp. 485; 529-32; 7 (1799), p. 477; 8 (1800), pp. 125-27; 9 (1801), pp.56-59.

371 William Jones, *Autobiography*, p. 60, said its circulation was 15,000. By 1813 it claimed 100,000 readers: cf. W.P. Owen, *Edward Williams*, p. 65, note 1.

372 Advertisement on cover of number 26.

Thirdly, and closely related to this, was the pronounced economic stringency of the war years. Between 1790 and 1814 prices doubled, and bad harvests (especially 1799-1801) were inevitably followed by stagnation of trade, falling wages, and unemployment.[373] So Rippon received many letters such as that which James Williams of Ross wrote on 15 March 1797, 'The people will not buy - and I cannot afford to give them gratis'.[374] Thomas Steevens, of Colchester, wrote on 19 December 1800, 'Two years ago some could afford a shilling who now want that shilling to buy one Days scanty supply of food'.[375] Most probably the *Register* was not paying its way.

Finally, Rippon was himself becoming absorbed in a new project: a complete history of the Bunhill Fields Burial Ground and memoirs of all the leading Nonconformists buried there. He had been working on this since about 1790, and published a prospectus with the last issue of the *Register*. There seems little doubt that Rippon decided to relinquish the *Register* and concentrate on this enormous task which proved so demanding that despite over thirty years' work his labours were never published.[376]

Rippon may have felt that the original purposes of the *Register* had been amply fulfilled - as indeed they had. Baptists had been made aware of each other, and Rippon had played an important role in one of the most productive decades in the denomination's history. His original aims had been long since achieved.

The Influence of the *Register*

To trace the independent influence of the *Register* is difficult in that it was but one source at a time when from almost every direction the Baptist churches received a fresh breath of life. Geoffrey Nuttall has, however, commented astutely about Rippon's work in the *Register:*

> He has perhaps not received the credit that he deserves. Nor are his volumes mere scaffolding. At first his lists of churches look lifeless, and the other material…appears a jumble and far from easy to follow; but as the personality of the compiler makes itself felt, the bones stir unexpectedly into life. The fact that the *Register* is, in some ways, the work of an amateur, not a professional, yields the sense that these churches, with their ministers, are neither statistics nor waxworks but human beings, alive and open to error but also stirred by new vision and new hope. Who but Rippon would compose such entries for an Index as 'Hague,

---

373   T S. Ashton, *The Industrial Revolution*, pp. 142, 145.
374   B.L. Add. MSS. 25389, f. 509.
375   B.L. Add. MSS. 25389, f. 172.
376   See chapter 6.

rev. W of Scarborough, loving and beloved; 'Crabtree rev. W, feeble but fruitful';
'Dracup, rev. John, finished well'?[377]

There are four aspects of the *Register*'s influence which may be
suggested: practical, devotional, theological, and historiographical. (The
last of these is considered in chapter six.)

1. The practical influence covered many aspects of the denomination's
life, more than can perhaps now be accurately assessed. Important among
these influences is the promotion of unity and self-awareness among
Baptists. The simple fact that reports of Baptist work in Britain, America
and India as well as of 'Baptists' on the Continent could be gathered
within one journal must have encouraged Baptist denominational
consciousness. Churches in Cornwall could read of Baptists in Nova
Scotia or Jamaica, whilst missionaries in India could read of
developments in Sierra Leone.

Of course the *Register* promoted all the Baptist enterprises. Details of
the older institutions like the Particular Baptist Fund, and the London
Case Committee were featured. But it was the new societies, especially the
BMS, which benefited from the *Register*'s support. Americans in New
York and Philadelphia formed their own missionary societies. In more
lonely situations the influence spread. In 1803, at a meeting of the
Kehukee association in North Carolina, one Martin Ross asked could not
the association 'step forward in support of that missionary spirit which
the great God is so wonderfully reviving among the different
denominations of good men in various parts of the world?'. The
historian of Baptists in that state commented that Ross had been reading
the *Register*, known to have circulated in the association, and added, 'So
much a good paper does for the advancement of religion'.[378]

Other Baptist movements were encouraged by Rippon. His support for
village evangelism has been demonstrated, whilst by his history of the
Bristol Academy and reports of the Rhode Island College services he
encouraged the growing support for an educated ministry. Not all
appreciated these reports, as one minister told Joshua Thomas that the
Rhode Island College reports 'appear'd to formal, carnal, and what
not'.[379] But at least Baptists became aware of what others were doing, and
the recitation of Baptist enterprises was a far greater encouragement and a
more powerful apology than more polemical works. Possibly the clearest
example of the *Register*'s practical influence was in the support it
engendered for the black congregations in Georgia, Jamaica, and. Sierra
Leone.

---

377 Nuttall, 'The Baptist Churches and their Ministers in the 1790s', p. 386.

378 Paschal, *History of North Carolina Baptists*, 1, p. 545.

379 Thomas to Rippon, 20 May 1795 (original in Angus Library).

The General Baptist Assemby of 1794 decided to renew correspondence with the few General Baptists of America, and W.T. Whitley thought that this was suggested by the *Register*.[380] An unusual instance of practical aid rendered by the *Register* was when Rippon published the plight of a desperately poor Independent minister.[381] On the cover of the next number Rippon reported: 'The necessities of his family have been relieved, and it is said he is furnished "with raiment enough to last him an hundred years" if he should live so long'. Generally, Rippon avoided such direct appeals, but did commend the need of the Guilsborough church following the destruction of its chapel, urged ministers asked to go to Ireland to preach to do so, and by numerous comments commended various local efforts of which he approved.

The *Register* consistently promoted a greater toleration among Christians of all denominations. Considerable space was allocated to the evangelical enterprises of paedobaptists.

Again, the *Register* was the first avenue of literary expression provided specifically for Baptists. The value of a denominational journal, even though Rippon's was ostensibly a personal responsibility, was clearly shown. Hence in 1809 the *Baptist Magazine* was begun[382] and after the Baptist correspondents of the *Evangelical Magazine* withdrew from it in 1812, the new Baptist periodical assumed a major importance in the denomination.[383]

There may be some relation between Rippon's *Register* and a smaller work of a similar kind, John Asplund's *Annual Register of the Baptist Denomination in North-America*. Asplund (c.1750-1807) was a Swede who had been pressed into the English navy whilst in England but deserted on the American coastline.[384] His *Register* was a more restricted statistical publication, issued (evidently) in 1791, 1794, and 1798.[385] His first figures were compiled from his own extensive travels of about 7,000 miles mostly on foot. He estimated that in 1790 there were in America

---

380 *Minutes of the General-Assembly of the General Baptists,* 2, p. 214, note 5.

381 *Register* 3 (1798-1801), p. 250.

382 Fuller was sceptical of this venture: 'The Baptist Magazine sells 4,000 they say, yet it disgusts most thinking people. I know of no "talents", among them, except Steadman. There is a want of modesty, and too much made of baptism'. Fuller to C. Anderson, Kettering, 21 February 1809, in H. Anderson, *The Life and Letters of Christopher Anderson* (Edinburgh: 1854), pp. 187-88. The first editor was Thomas Smith, of Tiverton.

383 Ivimey, *History of the English Baptists,* 4, pp. 118-20.

384 See Benedict, *A General History of the Baptist Denomination,* 1. p. 276; 2, p. 266.

385 Cf. E.C. Starr (ed.), *A Baptist Bibliography* (6 vols; Philadelphia, Judson Press, 1947), Section A, pp. 185-86.

887 Baptist churches; 699 ordained ministers; 457 licensed preachers; and 65,233 members in 35 associations. Rippon's figures, published perhaps earlier than Asplund's, were different and lower. There is no evidence that Rippon ever incorporated any of Asplund's statistics, although he knew of the work, and appears to have tried in vain to interest British readers in it.[386] Asplund, however, did freely republish Rippon's English lists of churches, and some other information.[387] It is possible that Asplund was influenced in his title by Rippon's.[388] As Asplund did not publish any reports or narrative accounts of religious events it is unlikely that his work detracted from the success of Rippon's. Baptists in America began the *Massachusetts Missionary Magazine* in 1803.

Finally, it may be claimed that the *Register* pointed the way to later national and international Baptist organizations. In a sense all the *Register*'s contents prepared for these, but the possible role of the *Register* in preparing for the Baptist Union of Great Britain (formed 1812) and the Baptist World Alliance (not formed until 1905) is considered separately in chapter nine.

2. The devotional influence of the *Register* is also difficult to trace, but the *Register*'s original design, it was shown, included the hope that the churches would be given an opportunity of praying for each other. There is clear evidence that English churches read and rejoiced in their prayer-meetings over the reports of revivals from America, and the wide range of materials included in the *Register* exerted a strong devotional influence.

In particular, Rippon promoted the movement of regular monthly prayer-meetings for revival. Edmund Botsford, of South Carolina wrote to thank Rippon for his suggestion that they should join in this movement. On 7 August 1790, he stated, 'I now have to inform you, that *several churches* have been prevailed on to adopt the MONTHLY MEETING OF PRAYER',[389] and on 24 August again commented:

> I cannot help flattering myself we shall see great things, especially as meetings of prayer much prevail. O my friend, my brother, you do not conceive how much we feel ourselves indebted to you, for your requesting that we would join in this *monthly service*.[390]

---

386 He advertised it on cover of number 10 (April 1795).

387 Note that pp. 56-67, which contained this material, is frequently missing from copies of Asplund's *Register* (1791): cf. Starr, *Baptist Bibliography*. Probably Asplund added these sheets to be bound into his *Register*, after he had seen Rippon's: several copies of these sheets are preserved loose in the Angus Library.

388 The preface to Asplund's *Register* was dated 14 July 1791.

389 *Register* 1 (1790-93), p. 107.

390 *Register* 1 (1790-93), p. 108.

Rippon added a note of eleven lines in which he warmly commended the practice, and again in his notes on the churches promoted the plan. E.A Payne has shown that this prayer movement for revival may be associated with the birth of the Baptist Missionary movement.[391]

Rippon did publish some stately devotional materials, such as those noted above. He encouraged catechizing of children in his pages. The numerous 'dying testimonies' contained in the obituaries, were a great stimulus to devotions in that age.

3. The theological influence of the *Register* was also subtle, for it was not intended as a theological magazine. Yet, as has been shown, Rippon consistently advocated the new evangelistic-type of Calvinism. To give another example, in his summary of the farewell sermons preached by John Ryland at Northampton, Rippon selected one passage 'as a fair specimen of the doctrine and manner, of the far greater part of Puritans, Nonconformists, and other *genuine* Calvinists'. The passage, almost a page in length, was an excellent example of the direct appeal.[392]

Of course, at the same time, Rippon was strictly orthodox. He could publish a letter on election, [393] but could also print a sermon by Beddome on 'Avoid Foolish Questions', one of which was 'Am I elected?'.[394] Rippon, it has been shown, was suspicious of the American frontier revival movements, but rejoiced in genuine works of God. Certainly he espoused a broad tolerance which can only have promoted a spiritual unity. He gave some tentative support to new interpretations of Biblical prophecy, especially in the tumultuous days of the French Revolution. This emerges clearly in his detailed if somewhat cautious review of James Bicheno's *Signs of the Times* (1794).[395] Bicheno, a protégé of Robert Robinson, became pastor at Newbury in 1793 and offered 'an intelligent appraisal of the French Revolution and its aftermath upon a framework of prophecy, and drew from it concrete and rational conclusions for social justice and foreign policy'.[396] But the principal theological influence was undoubtedly that of moderate Calvinism. The *Register* added to the growing weight of influences hastening the breakdown of High Calvinism.

Rippon generally avoided political matters in the *Register*, except for matters of common agitation by Nonconformists.

Not the least of the results of Rippon's publication was that it brought him, together with his hymnodic works, into the forefront of the denomination's awareness. It was inevitable that he assumed a responsible

---

391   Payne, *The Prayer Call of 1784*.
392   *Register* 2 (1794-97), p. 88.
393   *Register* 4 (1801-02), pp. 780-82.
394   *Register* 3 (1798-1801), p. 418.
395   *Register* 3 (1798-1801), pp. 76-77.
396   Ward, 'The Baptists and the Transformation of the Church, 1780-1830', p. 176.

leadership, not only in the metropolis, but far beyond. The clearest examples of these are the ways in which Rippon was active in the denominational societies, and became the first chairman of the Baptist Union.

CHAPTER 6

Rippon and Baptist Historiography

Rippon was in the vanguard of the vital evangelicalism of New Dissent but he was also committed to the preservation of the history of Old Dissent. Rippon's passionate interest in both Baptist and general Nonconformist history was first demonstrated in his *Baptist Annual Register*, although Rippon claimed in 1800 that as early as 1773, the year he was ordained at Carter Lane, he had begun collecting materials for histories of London Baptist churches.[1] This youthful interest was maintained throughout his life and became another significant contribution he made to the Particular Baptist movement.

Materials of a historical nature published in the *Register* will be discussed first, and then Rippon's other relevant works.

Baptist *Register*

The urgent need for the writing and preservation of Baptist history was emphasized by Rippon in the preface to his *Register*. He then reviewed what had been accomplished on both sides of the Atlantic. With understandable pride, Rippon first cited Benjamin Stinton (1640-1704), John Gill's predecessor in his own church at Carter Lane, and Thomas Crosby (c.1685-1752), for one period a deacon under Gill. Stinton was the first Baptist known to have collected Baptist historical materials, and his important manuscripts were the basis of Crosby's *History of the English Baptists* (four volumes, 1733-40), the only Baptist history published when Rippon began the *Register*: 'It is a reflection which affords me pleasure, That I have the honor of belonging to the same Church in which these respectable men were officers.'[2]

---

1   Advertisement on cover of *Register*, number 17 (December 1800).

2   *Register*, 1 (1790-93), p. ii. For the Stinton manuscripts, see *BHS Trans* 1 (1908-9), pp. 197-202; 4 (1914-15), pp. 126-27. For an analysis of Crosby and his

Rippon noted what other of his British contemporaries had achieved. First he referred to 'the laborious investigations of that great man, the late Mr. Robinson of Cambridge'.[3] When Robert Robinson had been requested in 1781 to undertake research in Baptist history, Andrew Gifford, one of the librarians of the British Museum, offered him the use of that institution. Robinson preached regularly for Rippon during this period.[4] Robinson's researches were published as *The History of Baptism* (1790) and *Ecclesiastical Researches* (1792). As Robinson was criticized by many because of his unorthodox views in his later years, it is significant that Rippon described him as 'that great man' and published extracts from his works.[5]

Rippon also noted 'the numerous collections of Mr. Thompson of Clapham'. Josiah Thompson (d. 1730) had compiled statistics for Dissenting churches that were used in preparing Dissenters' pleas for the repeal of discriminatory laws.[6]

Finally, Rippon referred to 'the indefatigable pursuits of Mr. Thomas of Leominster, a minister this, probably not inferior to any of his contemporaries in an historical acquaintance with the English Baptists, and who is thought to be the best informed person on earth, concerning the origin and progress of the present baptized churches in Wales'.[7] Rippon published materials by Thomas, and sought his advice on several issues.

Rippon also named four Americans as having undertaken research into Baptist history. The most important was Isaac Backus with *A History of New England, with particular reference to the denomination of Christians called Baptists*, three volumes, (1777-96). This was publicized by Rippon, especially the third volume (1796) and he acted as a London agent for its

---

successors, including Rippon, see 'Historians of the English Baptists' in White, *The English Baptists of the Seventeenth Century*, pp. 164-170.

3   *Register*, 1 (1790-93), p. ii.

4   B. Flower (ed), *Miscellaneous Works of Robert Robinson*, (4 vols; Harlow: 1807), 1, p. c.

5   Rippon was described as the 'esteemed friend' of Robinson: G. Dyer, *Memoirs of the Life and Writings of Robert Robinson* (London: 1796), p. 253. For criticism of Rippon in his dealings with Robinson, see below, chapter 7.

6   For Thompson, see Ivimey, *History of the English Baptists*, 4, p. 560; Wilson, *History and Antiquities*, 4, pp. 235-37. His MSS are now in Dr. Williams's Library. Cf. *BHS Trans* 5 (1911-12), pp. 205-207. For analysis of his survey see Watts, *The Dissenters*, 2, pp. 22-24.

7   *Register*, 1 (1790-93), p. ii. For the importance of Thomas' earlier history in Welsh (1778) in building a new consciousness among Welsh Baptists, see D.D.J. Morgan, 'The Development of the Baptist Movement in Wales between 1714 and 1815 with particular reference to the Evangelical Revival' (DPhil thesis, Oxford University, 1986), pp. 139-54.

sale.[8] Backus' work was detailed and accurate, with much valuable documentary matter. Morgan Edwards (1722-1795) published *Materials towards a History of the Baptists in New Jersey* (1792), which Rippon also advertised and helped distribute.[9] Also noted by Rippon were John Leland (1754-1841),[10] and John Williams (1747-1795),[11] both of whom collected information about Baptists in Virginia. By his knowledge of all these works Rippon demonstrated his own interest, but he added with prophetic insight:

> But commendable as these efforts of the few have been for the recovery of some of our memoirs, the preservation of others, and for the promotion of knowledge and affection among the denomination at large; the many have been chargeable with such a neglect of their Church History as will be for a lamentation among the wisest and best men in our posterity, through all their generations to the very end of time.[12]

This historical awareness is to Rippon's credit, and considerable useful material was preserved in his *Register*. Rippon fully realized that, in a sense, all the contents of his periodical would be of value to posterity. This is revealed by his explanation of the tardy publication of the 1793 Midlands Association Letter: '1. To show the state of the churches; and 2. To assist any historian who may in future write the history of the Baptists'.[13] Thus, although Rippon did not write a narrative history of Baptists, he deliberately collected documents which would later make such a project feasible.

Several types of historical materials were published in the *Register*. As noted, Rippon issued additional papers with the early numbers of the *Register*, and these were of a historical nature (the 1644 London Confession and other seventeenth century materials). Rippon also issued Joshua Thomas' *History of the Welsh Association* as a supplement. No further 'extras' appeared.

Rippon included obituaries or memorials for one hundred and twenty-five of his contemporaries, including thirty Americans and eight non-Baptists, and, whilst not strictly 'history' by design, these have assumed importance for later historians. Some memoirs extended over ten or more pages, others were only a few lines. The longest included those for

---

8   *Register* 3 (1798-1801), p. 471.
9   For Edwards, cf. *Register*, 2 (1794-97), pp. 308-14; *DAB*. For a list of his other works in MSS see L.T. Crismon, 'Baptists and Religious Literature', in D.C. Woolley (ed.), *Baptist Advance. The Achievements of the Baptists of North America for a Century and a Half* (Nashville: Broadman Press, 1964), pp. 416-17.
10   See *DAB*.
11   See *ESB*, 2, p. 1502.
12   *Register*, 1 (1790-93), p. ii.
13   *Register*, 2 (1794-97), p. 133.

Thomas Trinder (a Northampton deacon), Samuel Stennett, and Benjamin Beddome.[14] After the monthly *Register*s were commenced, shorter obituaries, often in smaller type, were introduced. Much valuable detail was recorded in these memoirs, for men such as Robert Hall (Senior), James Manning, Morgan Edwards, William Nash Clarke, Oliver Hart and John Thomas.[15] However, leading Baptists who died during the *Register*'s period but for whom no memoirs were published in its pages included Dr Morgan Jones (d. 1799), Dr Thomas Llewellyn (d. 1793), Samuel Medley (d. 1799), Samuel Pearce (d. 1799), John Ryland (d. 1792), Joseph Swain (d. 1796), Daniel Turner (d. 1793) and Benjamin Francis, Rippon's poet-friend, who died in 1799.[16] The reason was most probably that Rippon did not wish to detract from the effective sale of funeral sermons or memoirs which often benefited the surviving relatives. For example, Rippon had himself published separately his funeral sermon and memoir for Ryland. He had a long and bitter dispute with Dr Joseph Jenkins to gain permission to publish an abbreviated version of his memoir for Stennett.[17] In the case of Joshua Thomas the rival *Evangelical Magazine* published a memoir.[18] Obviously Rippon was dependent on authoritative accounts being forwarded to him.

However, those accounts published by him are of great value, not least for the sidelights they frequently throw upon the ordinary people of the churches. Many correspondents (at least forty have been noted) forwarded accounts of local worthies. These frequently had a theological bias, as when John Fawcett commented about Joshua Wood, of Salendine Nook, Yorkshire, that his ministry had been more successful after he had become 'convinced of the propriety and the necessity of a ministerial address to the unconverted'.[19] The evangelical attitude to death is clearly revealed, especially in the 'instructive' accounts of the deaths of young people.[20]

Some of the most detailed memoirs were prepared by Rippon himself, and these included Henry Philips, Robert Day, Jabez Dunsford (of Tiverton), Benjamin Beddome, John Tommas (1723-1800) of Bristol, William Nash Clarke and John Reynolds (1730-1792) of London, and

---

14   *Register*, 2 (1794-97), pp. 286-303, 380-93, 314-26.

15   *Register*, 1 (1790-93), pp. 226-46, 2 (1794-97), pp. 308-14, 272-80, 507-14, 4 (1801-02), pp. 1138-44.

16   All these are listed in the 'Index to Notable Baptists', in *BHS Trans* 7 (1920-21), pp. 132-239.

17   Jenkins delayed his manuscript, and tried to make Rippon advertise the rival *Gospel Magazine* with which Jenkins was concerned: see correspondence between 24 December 1795 and 2 May 1796, B.L. Add. MSS. 25387, f. 322.

18   *Evangelical Magazine* 6 (1798), pp. 39-99.

19   *Register* 2 (1794-97), p. 226.

20   For a typical example, cf. *Register* 3 (1798-1801), pp. 438-47.

Thomas Davis (d. 1796) of Reading.[21] Rippon obviously undertook
detailed research, utilizing churchbooks, personal letters, local
newspapers, and the reminiscences of reliable witnesses. In the cases of
John Tommas and Philip Gibbs of Plymouth, Rippon interviewed them
some years before their deaths, clear indication of long-range planning.[22]
Although his accounts are inevitably eulogistic, Rippon consistently
demonstrated a commendable concern for accuracy and detail.

Rippon also hoped to publish numerous histories of local churches. In
addition to those which did actually appear, Rippon possessed several
others which either he had prepared or which had been forwarded to him
but which, unfortunately, were never published. When he began his
monthly *Registers* (1801) he announced that many 'volumes' could have
been published, but he had delayed in the hope of providing accounts of
all the churches in each county, arranged in the order of the dates of
commencement.[23] He cited several as being 'most ready' for publication,
but of these the following were not published: Broadmead, Bristol;
'Hanserd Knollis's' (then meeting at Red Cross Street); Carter Lane;
Devonshire Square; Boston, Massachusetts; and 'many more by the late
Rev. Mr. Thomas of Leominster and others'. Those actually published,
however, are important.

Robert Robinson had compiled an account of the 'Origin of the
Dissenting Churches at Cambridge &c'.[24] This was mainly an account of
Francis Holcroft (c.1629-1692) from whose labours the Independents,
Presbyterians, and Baptists traced their origins in Cambridge.[25] Baptists
dated from 1726, when they separated from the Independents. Rippon
asked Robert Hall Junior, Robinson's successor at Cambridge (1791-
1806), for assistance in completing this history. Hall's reply revealed that
not all Baptists shared Rippon's concern for Baptist history:

> Dear Sir, I thank you for the Baptist *Register* you were so kind as to send me. With
> respect to my sending the church book I do not apprehend it would quite meet the
> wishes of our friends. With respect to the sketches of the History of Churches it
> does not strike me to be of any particular utility. The records of particular churches
> are made for the benefit of that church, nor do I perceive any benefit resulting from
> their being exposed to public inspection. You are pleased to request me to draw up

---

21   *Register* 1 (1790-93), pp. 128-35, 222-26; 2 (1794-97) pp. 41-44, 303-308,
314-26, 514-523; 3 (1798-1801), pp. 313-319, 4 (1801-02), pp. 272-280.

22   *Register* 3 (1798-1801), pp. 285, 316.

23   Advertisement on cover of *Register*, number 17 (December 1800).

24   *Register* 3 (1798-1801), pp.233-39. Cf. B. Nutter, *The Story of Cambridge
Baptists and the struggle for religious Liberty* (Cambridge: W. Heffer and sons, 1912).

25   See *DNB* and A.G. Matthews, *Calamv Revised, Being a revision of Edmund
Calamy's Account of the Ministers and others Ejected and Silenced, 1660-62* (Oxford:
Clarendon Press, 1988 [1934]), pp. 271-72.

the history of our church for your *Register*, but such an undertaking would be utterly inconsistent with my other avocations and designs,

I am yours &c,

R Hall.[26]

A major study was a history of the Plymouth Baptist Church, largely based on a manuscript signed by 'H. Davie'.[27] Among Plymouth's outstanding leaders were Abraham Cheare in the seventeenth century,[28] and Philip Gibbs in the eighteenth. The *Register* version was necessarily abbreviated from the original, which contained additional valuable detail about early Baptist life in the West Country.[29] Rippon added from his own resources the following details: a letter from Cheare to William Punchard, one of several originals Rippon had in his possession;[30] extracts from *Words in Season...*(1688), a posthumous collection of Cheare's discourses and letters;[31] biographical detail about Gibbs, taken 'in a parlour conversation'; details of Gibbs' death and funeral. Rippon wisely omitted the introduction from the original manuscript entitled, 'Containing a general view of the Baptist interest in Britain from 305 to 1648'.[32]

Rippon's devotion to Isaac Watts is again revealed by an extraordinary inclusion entitled: 'Records of the Transactions of the Church of Christ under the care of the Rev. Mr. Joseph Caryl, and since of the Rev. Dr. John Owen; Mr. David Clarkson; Mr. Isaac Loeffs; Dr. Isaac Chauncy;

---

26   Hall to Rippon, Cambridge 16 February 1801, in *BHS Trans* 2 (1910-11), p. 64 and see R. Hayden (ed.), *English Baptist Records. 2. Church Book: St. Andrew's Street Baptist Church, Cambridge, 1720-1832* (Didcot: Baptist Historical Society, 1991).

27   *Register* 3 (1798-1801), pp. 273-90, 380-86. Original in Angus Library. Davie has not been further identified. This extant document, of over a hundred pages, contains numerous extracts from the churchbook and letters written to and from the church which dates from c. 1640

28   For Cheare (1626-1678) see *BHS Trans* 3 (1912-13), pp. 95-103.

29   H.M. Nicholson, *Authentic Records relating to the Christian Church now meeting in George Street and Mutley Chapels, Plymouth, 1640-1870* (London: n.d.), has utilized the *Register* account and other MS. sources, but evidently not this MS. Material not in Nicholson includes: details about Caleb Jope, suggested as tutor for Bristol Academy; Benjamin Francis' preaching tour into Cornwall (1775); a letter (1774) from Joshua Toulmin of Taunton about Josiah Thompson's researches.

30   *Register* 3 (1798-1801), p. 275.

31   *Register* 3 (1798-1801), pp. 279-82.

32   Rippon does not seem to have accepted the view that 'Baptists' could be traced in the early history of the church, an idea increasingly advanced during the nineteenth century. See W. Morgan Patterson, *Baptist Successionism: A Critical View* (Valley Forge: Judson, 1969); J.E. McGoldrick, *Baptist Successionism. A crucial Question in Baptist History* (Metuchen, N.J.: Scarecrow Press, 1994).

Dr. Isaac Watts: &c'.[33] Rippon published four extracts. (1) A list of members in 1673.[34] Although this included distinguished people like Lord Charles Fleetwood, Sir John Hartopp, Colonel Desborough and other Army officers, its significance was unexplained and must have confused many *Register* readers. (2) Extracts from the churchbook, from April 1701 to February 1702, detailing Watts' call to the church and his letter of reply.[35] (3) Church records from 15 February 1702 to 5 June 1702, with particulars of Watts' ordination.[36] (4) From the churchbook, 'The Customs of this Church in the Celebration of Worship and the Exercise of Discipline as they are practised among us at present, 1723', by Watts.[37] This last is especially valuable, including details of the Sunday order of services, and the manner of observing the Lord's Supper. As the original records of the Bury Street church for this period are not extant, Rippon's extract has assumed outstanding importance.[38] Obviously Rippon's interest in this church stemmed from his deep love for Watts, but it is significant that he was granted access to the records and should devote so much space to an Independent church.

Another non-Baptist church included was the 'Congregational Church at Yarmouth, Norfolk'.[39] This historic church was founded in 1642 after enforced exiles had returned from Rotterdam.[40] There are few connections with Baptists, and no known personal links between Rippon and the church.[41] William Walford, then the pastor of the church, added the concluding paragraphs.[42] This is yet another example of Rippon's increasing interest in general Nonconformist history.

One significant regional Baptist church's history was of the Northampton Baptist Church (College Street).[43] The substance of this history was compiled by John Ryland in about 1793 and essentially was a review of interesting items, year by year, from the churchbook. George

---

33   For this church see Wilson, *History and Antiquities*, 1, pp. 251-328.

34   *Register* 3 (1798-1801), pp. 448-52. On 5 June 1673, after Caryl's death, his congregation united with another under Dr. Owen.

35   *Register* 3 (1798-1801), pp. 513-20.

36   *Register* 4 (1801-1802), pp. 553-59.

37   *Register* 4 (1801-1802), pp. 593-603.

38   The extract was reprinted from the *Register* in *Transactions* of Congregational Historical Society 6 (1913), pp. 333-42, and is the basis of the account in Davies, *Worship and Theology in England*, 3, pp. 101-104.

39   *Register* 4 (1801-02) pp. 633-46.

40   J. Browne, *History of Congregationalism in Norfolk and Suffolk* (London: 1877), pp. 208-51.

41   There are hints of Baptist sympathizers in the sister-church of Norwich: Jewson, *The Baptists in Norfolk* , pp. 17-18.

42   Browne, *History of Congregationalism in Norfolk and Suffolk,* pp. 248-49.

43   *Register* 4 (1801-1802), pp. 713-20, 769-72, 983-86.

Keeley brought the history up to date in a letter dated 17 February 1802.[44]

Providence, Rhode Island, Church is generally regarded as the oldest Baptist church in the United States, having been founded by Roger Williams in 1639.[45] The *Register* account was evidently prepared by John Stanford (1754-1834), but Manning may have added to it.[46] Rippon also published an engraving of the church-building, taken from the *Massachusetts Magazine* for August 1789, and commented to Manning that many English Baptists were 'astonished' at the high steeple.[47]

'Some Account of the Protestant Church at Dieppe, in France' was forwarded by Rippon's European correspondent, 'B'.[48] This was an account of the church, especially during the sixteenth and seventeenth centuries, presumably based on local records and traditions.

'A Short Account of the Scots Baptists' was drawn up from 'best sources of information' and dated November 1795,[49] so was probably compiled by Archibald McLean (1733-1812), leader of the Scotch Baptists.[50] Baptists had met in Scotland during the Commonwealth period, but the 'Scotch Baptists' were a later movement and this was the first printed account of their origins. In 1763 Robert Carmichael was baptized by Gill in London, and returned to Scotland to baptize McLean and others. These 'Scotch Baptists' differed from English Baptists in several points of doctrine and practice, and Andrew Fuller, in particular, engaged in controversies with them.[51]

Rippon also included in the *Register* a condensed version of his History of Bristol Academy.[52]

---

44   *Register* 4 (1801-1802), p. 986.

45   *Register* 4 (1801-1802), pp. 793-97, 833-40; McBeth, *The Baptist Heritage*, p. 136.

46   Rippon to Manning, (no date but written on an advertisement for the *Register* so probably January 1791, original at Brown University) refers to the account by Stanford, but insists his name must not be mentioned in England, and asks Manning to take it beyond 1737. Stanford was pastor at Hammersmith from 1781 (Byrt, *Rise of the Stream*, p. 16) but left for America in 1786, and for one year was pastor at Providence. See C.G. Sommers, *Memoir of the Rev. John Stanford D.D.* (New York: 1835), pp. 39-40.

47   Rippon to Manning, as in previous note.

48   *Register* 4 (1801-1802), pp. 959-72, 1060-169, 1126-31.

49   *Register* 2 (1794-97), pp. 361-80.

50   So P. Waugh, 'The New Dawn and Rise of "Scotch Baptists"' in G Yuille (ed.), *History of the Baptists in Scotland from Pre-Reformation Times* (Glasgow: Baptist Union of Scotland Publication Committee, 1926), p. 50.

51   For the 'Scotch' Baptists, see D.B. Murray, 'The Scotch Baptist Tradition in Great Britain', *BQ* 33.4 (1989), pp. 186-98; D.W. Bebbington (ed.), *The Baptists in Scotland* (Glasgow: Baptist Union of Scotland, 1988).

52   *Register* 2 (1794-97), pp. 413-55.

'Protestant Dissenters' Register' was a feature commenced in December 1800 with the monthly *Registers*, probably in opposition to a projected new Dissenters' Magazine, although this heading was only used in the three subsequent issues. This included the following materials: Addresses of the General Body of Dissenting Ministers to the Throne in 1800 and 1802; the 'present State of the Laws respecting Nonconformity'; the origin of Robert Robinson's lectures on Nonconformity; Irish Presbyterians and the *Regium Donum*; and 'A Prayer by Mr. R.(obert) P.(orter) on the Solemn Fast Day -19 June 1672'.[53]

'Ancient Manuscript Papers', was yet another feature begun with the monthly *Registers*. Rippon claimed to have in his possession: '...great numbers of original letters, many of them written in *imprisonments*, and preserved in the *very handwriting* of those who suffered and died for the truth; with MS Sermons of ejected Ministers, and multitudes of other ancient papers.'[54]

This antiquarian matter was common in the religious periodicals of the day. Rippon published letters from Herbert Palmer (1601-1647),[55] from two ministers in Ilchester gaol to the churches at Chard and Wedmore (1663),[56] from the London Baptists to Andrew Gifford (1641-1721) in 1675,[57] and to the church at Luppitt (1689);[58] and original sermons by Oliver Heywood (1630-1702)[59] and Thomas Cole (1627?-1697).[60] He also published an extract from Thomas Grantham, 'Of the Manner of Marriages among the Baptized Believers' (1689)[61] and from the Carter Lane churchbook about the marriages of Dissenters.[62]

Almost 11% of the fourth volume consisted of substantial extracts from larger Church History publications. From T. Haweis, *An Impartial and Succinct History of the Rise, Declension, and Revival of the Church of Christ* (three volumes, 1800) Rippon took studies of John Wesley, George Whitefield, Lady Huntingdon, and the Moravians.[63] From Robinson's *History of Baptism* (1790) Rippon selected 'A Review of the

---

53   *Register* 3 (1798-1801), pp. 209-12; 4 (1801-02), pp. 943-45; 3, pp. 255-57, 299, 300, 331-36. For Porter (d. 1690), see *DNB*.

54   Advertisement on cover of *Register*, number 17

55   *Register* 3 (1798-1801), pp. 258-60, 411-14, 503-504. For Palmer see *D.N.B.* which refers to the letters in the *Register*.

56   *Register* 4 (1801-02), pp. 1023-29. The signatories S. Wade and T. Willes are not noted in Matthews, *Calamy Revised*.

57   *Register* 4 (1801-02), pp. 1004-1007.

58   *Register* 3 (1798-1801), pp. 260-61.

59   *Register* 4 (1801-02), pp. 559-67. For Heywood, see *DNB*.

60   *Register* 4 (1801-02), pp. 938-93. For Cole, see *DNB*

61   *Register* 3 (1798-1801), pp. 452-53.

62   *Register* 3 (1798-1801), pp. 453-54.

63   *Register* 4 (1801-02), pp. 649-53, 634-86, 764-66, 798-805.

Apostolical Churches' (chapter xl), [64] and from Robinson's *Ecclesiastical Researches* (1792) he extracted 'History of the Baptists at Münster' (chapter xiv).[65]

Thus a considerable body of historical material, although presented in an uncritical and haphazard manner, was included in the *Register*. Other publications also evidenced Rippon's historical interests and abilities.

Other Publications

1. *A Brief Essay Towards an History of the Baptist Academy at Bristol: read before the Bristol Education Society, at their Anniversary Meeting, in Broadmead, August 26th, 1795* (1796).

This was Rippon's best historical writing. His *Essay* is an important source for knowledge of early Baptist ministerial education, as well as for the origins and early years of the Academy. Rippon traced the first Baptist efforts at ministerial training to John Tombes (1603-1676), who in 1650 gave tuition to three ministerial students.[66] From a manuscript original Rippon knew that in 1675 London Baptists had suggested some definite scheme of ministerial training should be adopted, whist in 1689 the London Assembly had established a Fund for the purpose.[67] Little resulted from this, however, and Rippon then turned to trace the origins of the Bristol Academy.

Careful preparations were made for the essay. Rippon quoted from several original letters, and had been sent personal details by Hugh and Caleb Evans. Joshua Thomas of Leominster had supplied him with a complete list of all the students known to have been educated in the Academy.[68] For the important period around 1770 when the Bristol Education Society was inaugurated Rippon of course had his own memories. His affectionate sketches of Hugh and Caleb Evans are of importance in understanding their appeal.

The importance of the Academy for the denomination has already been noted. By this careful account of its origins, and the explicit apology for an educated ministry, Rippon promoted the usefulness of the Academy. By publishing his essay in an abridged form in the *Register*, as well as separately, Rippon gave it the widest possible circulation among

---

64   *Register* 4 (1801-02), pp. 871-94. Rippon omitted all the footnotes.

65   *Register* 4 (1801-02), pp. 1015-22, 1039-46, 1119-26, abbreviated by Rippon.

66   *Brief Essay*, pp. 8-9. Rippon's authorities were W. Wall, *History of Infant Baptism* (London: 1705) and Calamy. For Tombes see *DNB*.

67   *Brief Essay*, pp. 9f.

68   J. Thomas to Rippon, 19 March and 20 May 1795. (Originals in Angus Library).

Baptists. Although inevitably somewhat effusive in tone, the essay was the result of much careful and detailed research and became a valuable contribution to Baptist historical writing.

2. *A Discourse on the Origin and Progress of the Society for Promoting Religious Knowledge among the Poor, from its Commencement in 1750, to the year 1802, including a Succinct Account of the separate publications in their catalogue with the benefit which has attended them, and of The different Modes which the Members and their Friends have adopted, in distributing the Books to Advantage: Delivered before the Society November 17, 1796, and November 17, 1802.* (1802).

The title of this *Discourse* amply summarizes its contents. A second edition, 'Much enlarged, with Letters and Notes', was sponsored by the Treasurer of the Society, Ebenezer Maitland, Esq.: this clearly suggests that the principal value of the Discourse was as an apology for the Society. The origin of the Society was traced to Benjamin Forfitt, an influential Independent layman in 1750. The bulk of the *Discourse* was devoted to a description of the various books distributed by the Society, and extracts from letters received by the Society illustrating the usefulness of their books. A further account of the work of the Society is given below, in chapter seven, in connection with Rippon's work as a Dissenter.

In effect, this *Discourse* was more an illustrated sermon than history. However, as the work of the society is comparatively unknown - the later Religious Tract Society (founded 1799) was to outweigh it in influence and importance - Rippon's outline of its activities is of value.

3. *A Brief Memoir of the Life and Writings of the late John Gill, D. D.*

This was published with the 1810 quarto edition of Gill's *Exposition of the Old Testament,*[69] and after Rippon's death was issued separately (1838). Rippon had helped distribute earlier editions of Gill's works, and as he was able to announce discounts to ministers for the 1810 edition, may well have shared in its publication.[70] An earlier and very scanty biography of Gill had been issued in 1773, but the author of this is unknown.[71] It did, however, include a fulsome tribute by A.M. Toplady, from which Rippon quoted.[72]

Rippon worked on his *Memoir* of Gill over a long period, which included a serious illness. At one point in the *Memoir* Rippon noted,

---

69   *Exposition of the Old Testament* (6 vols; London:1810 [1766]), 1, pp. ix-lxiv.

70   Rippon to Manning, 1 May 1784 (original at Brown Univ.); and several other references in extant letters. *Baptist Magazine* 1 (1809), p. 207.

71   J. Gill, *A Collection of Sermons and Tracts* (2 vols; London: 1772), 1, pp. ix-xxxv.

72   *Memoir* (1838 edn), pp. 136-39.

'Written in 1800',[73] but later noted that a section was written during 1809 in Devonshire,

> ...where Dr. *Rippon* had been recommended for the benefit of his native air; having been laid aside, almost entirely, from his pastoral work, through the four summer months; the leisure parts of which should have been employed, in preparing this sketch of the life of his *honored* predecessor for the public eye. But having been so long afflicted, and one while brought near the gates of death, he was prevented from writing such a Memoir as he wished, which might have been worthy of the name of GILL, and not in every respect unworthy of the public notice, but his state of convalescence, at length, allowing him to write an hour or more in a day, he has paid some attention to the subject.[74]

The *Memoir* is a useful biography. Rippon again used many sources, not least of which were the Carter Lane Churchbook, various manuscripts and letters of Gill's, and Gill's numerous publications. Rippon included many amusing and interesting anecdotes about Gill which lighten the more sombre details of his personal life and serious publications. Rippon estimated that if all Gill's publications were uniformly printed in folio size they would occupy 'above TEN THOUSAND' pages: yet some account of most of them was provided.[75]

The general approach of the *Memoir* conforms to Rippon's view of Gill as 'certainly one of the greatest and best of men', and his importance as a theological controversialist and Baptist apologist was recognized.[76] Yet Rippon was not above disagreeing with Gill's theology, especially when reviewing his role in the important controversies over the direct appeal to sinners. Rippon commented on this at length, and carefully outlined both the 'high' and 'low' sides.[77] His own view, not clearly elaborated, was that the matter turned on the definitions of 'believing' and 'believing in Christ'. Rippon specifically accepted the distinction made by Jonathan Edwards, and influential in the demolition of the 'high' position, between natural and moral inability of a sinner to do good. Indeed, Rippon found a quotation from Gill which supported the 'low' position,[78] and suggested that Gill's rigid insistence on the 'high' position was after the controversies between 1730 and 1740.[79] It is of interest that writing in 1809 Rippon could hold such an objective view of the controversy, and was prepared to discuss it at length.

---

73   *Memoir* (1838 edn), p. 8, note *.
74   *Memoir* (1838 edn), p. 127, note *.
75   *Memoir* (1838 edn), p. 111.
76   *Memoir* (1838 edn), p. 1.
77   *Memoir* (1838 edn), pp. 43-48
78   From Gill's exposition of John 5.40: *Memoir* (1838 edn), p. 46.
79   *Memoir* (1838 edn), pp. 47-48.

This Memoir was the fullest, and most important, of the many biographies prepared by Rippon. It reveals careful use of source materials, and still makes interesting reading.[80]

4. Funeral sermons for Andrew Gifford (1784), John Ryland (1792) and Abraham Booth (1806).

Despite the sermonic format, these contained much useful biographical data. All three were important Baptist figures, and Rippon gave considerable attention to providing detailed and reliable accounts. Possibly the most important was that for Gifford, since Rippon quoted from several manuscript sources not extant. The most recent biography of Gifford made considerable use of Rippon's account, although it is to be noted that Rippon made no mention of the dispute between Gifford and his first church at Little Wild Street, perhaps understandable in a funeral sermon.[81] For both Ryland and Booth, Rippon made extensive use of churchbooks, manuscripts, and personal reminiscences.

Rippon's Influence on Baptist Historiogaphy

One of the *Register*'s stated aims was to promote the preservation of Baptist history, and clearly much valuable material was published. Moreover, many pastors and deacons were prompted to examine with care their own local records. Rippon, although untrained as an historian, certainly appreciated the need for accuracy and detail.

But Rippon's undoubted influence on Baptist historiography is not easily traced. Clearly the standards of accuracy he aspired towards in his own memoirs, often much more detailed than contemporary efforts, can only have encouraged improved standards. In particular, his influence may be directly seen in two contemporary Baptist histories. (There is no evidence that Walter Wilson, or David Bogue and James Bennett, the contemporary Independent historians, either made use of Rippon's researches or sought his advice.) Both David Benedict in America and Joseph Ivimey in England studied Rippon's *Register* and his other works, and utilized them. The simplest way to demonstrate their indebtedness to Rippon is to show their direct use of him.

As Benedict was preparing his history, he learned of Ivimey's project and so largely (but not exclusively) confined himself to America.[82] His work, *A General history of the Baptist Denomination in America, and other parts of the World* (two volumes, 1813), is still 'an important early

---

80   Rippon, however, made no mention of the dispute surrounding Gill's call to the church.

81   Champion, *Farthing Rushlight the Story of Andrew Gifford 1700-1784.*

82   Benedict, *A General History of the Baptist Denomination,* 1, p. 4.

source on American Baptists'.[83] Benedict referred to the *Register*, which 'contains many interesting accounts of the Baptists both in England and elsewhere', and either quoted extensively or referred to the *Register* on twenty occasions.[84] Some extracts, simply duplicated from the *Register,* filled several pages: the account of Bristol Academy; the Scotch Baptists; David George and the black church at Savannah; George Liele in Jamaica; the biographies of Joseph Cook, Morgan Edwards and James Manning; the Civil State of Dissenters in England in 1793.[85] The other instances are brief, citing the statistics of the lists of churches or references in letters.[86] Two additional items, although unacknowledged, were almost certainly taken from the *Register*: the epitaph for Thomas Grantham and the Irish Letter of 1653.[87] Benedict also referred to Rippon's memoir of Gill, and made a brief quotation from it.[88]

Ivimey's *A History of the English Baptists* was published in four volumes; 1811, 1814, 1823, and 1830. In the first volume Ivimey reprinted letters given by Rippon in his *Register*,[89] and incorporated detail about Andrew (Senior) and Emanuel Gifford of Bristol which Rippon had published in his sermon for Andrew Gifford (Junior).[90] Three references from the *Register* were given in Ivimey's second volume,[91] and a further two in the third volume.[92] In addition, Ivimey's long accounts of both Gill and Gifford were largely derived, and acknowledged, from Rippon's memoirs.[93] The main use of the *Register* was naturally in Ivimey's fourth volume which covered the period 1760 to 1820. Indeed, in the long first chapter, which summarized the principal activities of Baptists during George III's reign, Ivimey noted the publication of the *Register*, and added: 'The author, who is still Living, is entitled to the grateful acknowledgements of the denomination for his labours, and for the spirit of enterprize manifested in collecting the materials, and in his extensive correspondence with foreign Baptists, especially in America.'[94]

---

83   Torbet, *A History of the Baptists*, p. 525.

84   Benedict, *A General History of the Baptist Denomination*, 1, p. 189.

85   Benedict, *A General History of the Baptist Denomination*, 1, pp. 220-23; 231-32; 287-95; 2, pp. 189-90; 194-206; 280-88; 294-301; 346-47; 493-94.

86   Benedict, *A General History of the Baptist Denomination*, 1, pp. 148-49; 199 note; 200, 224, 229, 2, pp. 167-69; 188, 193, 278, 279 note.

87   Benedict, *A General History of the Baptist Denomination*, 1, pp. 227, 230.

88   Benedict, *A General History of the Baptist Denomination*, 1, p. 216.

89   Ivimey, *History of the English Baptists*, 1, pp. 511, 478-80.

90   Ivimey, *History of the English Baptists*, 1, pp. 412-414.

91   Ivimey, *History of the English Baptists*, 2, pp. 70, 516, 540.

92   Ivimey, *History of the English Baptists,* 3, pp. 581-83, 601-03.

93   Ivimey, *History of the English Baptists*, 3, pp. 430-55, 595-605.

94   Ivimey, *History of the English Baptists*, 4, p. 62

Ivimey did not claim the personal assistance of Rippon, but made extensive use of the *Register*. In twelve instances the *Register* is quoted *verbatim*, often for several pages. The most obvious use was in the biographies, acknowledged source for the following: the Dunsfords of Tiverton, William Clarke, Thomas Davis, Benjamin Beddome, Robert Hall (Senior) and Philip Gibbs.[95] In addition, the *Register* was the unacknowledged source for the accounts of John Tommas, Robert Day, Henry Philips, and John Reynolds.[96] Other materials taken from Rippon included: the history of the Bristol Academy; the *Register*'s statistics and summary of Baptist advance in 1798 (nearly two pages of quotation), the formation of churches, and the details of the Atkins Trust.[97] Not without reason did an astute reviewer of this volume of Ivimey comment: 'Let it be remembered that if our venerable friend Dr. Rippon had not printed his *Register* many years ago, many things which now adorn this 'History of the English Baptists' would not have been seen.'[98] It must be emphasized that most of the quoted *Register* material, especially from the biographies, had been written by Rippon himself.

Ivimey remained the standard work on English Baptist history for over a century,[99] indeed until W.T. Whitley produced *A History of British Baptists* in 1923 (revised edition 1932). Whitley made extensive use of Rippon's works and the *Register* remains, as A.C. Underwood described it in the bibliography of his history, 'a mine of information'.[100] To those who trouble to quarry, its riches are immense.

B.R. White, in his balanced survey of English Baptist historians, devotes considerable space to Rippon and concludes: 'Although he was concerned to collect and publish documents rather than to write a connected history, his work was important enough to require inclusion in company with those who actually produced narrative histories'.[101]

One serious criticism must be levelled against Rippon: few of the many valuable original manuscripts which he collected have survived. His interests became exclusively antiquarian, but he did not always take proper care of materials loaned to him. For example, the church at

---

95   Ivimey, *History of the English Baptists*, 4, pp. 300-301; 394-98; 423-27; 462-69; 603-609; 298-300.

96   Ivimey, *History of the English Baptists*, 4, pp. 286-87; 295-97; 307-309; 322-24.

97   Ivimey, *History of the English Baptists*, 4, pp. 270-80; 74-76; 405-406; 408-409; 412.

98   *Baptist Magazine* 22 (1830), p. 473

99   J.C. Carlile, *The Story of the English Baptists* was a popular account, 'intended to be a story rather than a detailed history' (Preface).

100   A.C. Underwood, *A History of the English Baptists* (London: Carey Kingsgate Press, 1947) p. 275

101   White, *The English Baptists of the Seventeenth Century*, p. 166.

Upottery, Devonshire, has records from 1813 which commence with this frustrated note: 'The old Church book belonging to New House Baptist Cause, Upottery, is lost. Was lent to Rev. Mr. Rippon, D.D., for the purpose of getting its history, and was *consequently* never returned to the Church again.'[102] Similarly, records from the historic Loughwood Baptist chapel in Devonshire were lent to Rippon and, after sixteen years, the depairing leaders wrote an angry note in their new churchbook complaining that Rippon had not returned their records.[103] Another church complained that Rippon, had put their books in a barrel, exposed to the damp; and yet another book was taken to pieces and put together in the wrong order.[104] Although some of the valuable manuscripts Rippon collected have survived, it is a sad commentary on his methods that so many which are known to have been entrusted to him have perished.

'Bunhill Fields History'

This project occupied much of Rippon's leisure time during the second half of his life, as he began preparations for it in about 1790. Sadly, despite considerable labour and expense, his researches were never published as he intended, although much is extant in manuscript form. Hence, despite the interest of the undertaking, and its importance to Rippon himself, it cannot really be considered as an example of his historical influence, nor can it be claimed that in any effective way it either influenced or enhanced the Baptist cause. Accordingly, although understanding this project is relevant for appreciating Rippon's passion for his antiquarian and historical interests, only the following brief account need here be given. There are three main sources for this outline: the extant manuscripts; the 'prospectus' for the 'History' issued in 1803;[105] and the report of a memorial presented by Rippon to the Court of Common Council for the City of London in 1827, requesting that he might be permitted to dedicate the volumes to the Lord Mayor, Aldermen, and Commons of the City of London.[106]

---

102 W.T. Andress, *The History of Newhouse Upottery* (Taunton: privately published, 1932), pp. 4-5.

103 In this case the book survived and was returned to the church by 1915: J.B. Whitely, 'Loughwood Baptists in the Seventeenth Century', *BQ* 31.4 (1985), p. 149.

104 *BHS Trans* 4 (1914-16), pp. 129-30

105 Bound with *Register* 4 (1801-02).

106 *Congregational Magazine*, n.s. 3 (1827), pp. 619-21.

Bunhill Fields is the most famous Nonconformist burial ground in Britain.[107] The early history of the site is somewhat obscure, but since the seventeenth century, when it was known as 'Tindal's burial ground' (one Henry Tindal had the lease), it had been used as a burial place for Dissenters. During the eighteenth century it was the most popular and convenient place of interment for London Dissenters. Southey called it the '*Campo Santo* of the Dissenters', and those buried there included: John Bunyan, Daniel Defoe, Charles Fleetwood, Theophilus Gale, Thomas Goodwin, William Kiffin, William Jenkyn, Daniel Neal, John Owen, Vavasor Powell, Isaac Watts, Susannah Wesley and Daniel Williams. During Rippon's life-time others buried there included: William Blake, Thomas Bradbury, John Conder, John Gill, Andrew Gifford, Andrew Kippis, Richard Price, Abraham Rees, and Matthew Wilks.

Rippon's projected work was called 'The History of Bunhill Fields Burial Ground' and was to include: 'an account of whatever appears to have been interesting in the lives and deaths of the most eminent Ministers, private Christians, and other distinguished Characters, among the Nobility and Gentry whose Remains have been deposited in this renowned and capacious spot through the last two Centuries, quite down to the end of the year 1802'; a copy of all legible inscriptions on 'several thousand Tombs and gravestones'; one hundred engraved portraits and facsimiles of the handwriting of some worthies interred there. This was planned for 'six large elegant Volumes in octavo', and it was intended to issue the 'History' in periodical numbers. In addition, 'an elegant map of the whole ground', thirty-six inches by twenty-nine inches, indicating the exact site of every tomb could be had on canvas and rollers, as an extra.[108]

This prospectus was dated 1 January 1803, although Rippon had advertised the project as early as February 1801.[109] From the 1827 memorial it is learned that Rippon had formed the plan many years before. Rippon had by his own hand and at the dictation of his son John, 'then a lad', copied out from the official Register of burials the names of all those interred there between 1713 (when the records were begun) and 1790, in all 'nearly forty thousand names'. Then he 'devoted two half-days of time weekly during several summers, aided by his said son and

---

107 The most useful literature on Bunhill Fields includes: J.A. Jones, *Bunhill Memorials, Sacred Reminiscences of Three Hundred Ministers and other Persons of note who are buried in Bunhill Fields* (London: 1849); *History of the Bunhill Fields Burial Ground, with some of the Principal Inscriptions* (London: 1872); T.G. Crippen, 'The Tombs in Bunhill Fields', *Transactions* of Congregational Historical Society, 4 (1910), pp. 347-63; A.W. Light, *Bunhill Fields* (2 vols; London: C.J. Farncombe & Sons, 1918, 1933).

108 Details from the 'prospectus'.

109 Advertisement on cover of *Register*, number 19 (February 1801).

several other persons' copying out all the visible inscriptions 'for the accomplishment of which, and in the brushing, washing, cleansing, and digging up of many hundreds of them which had either become nearly obsolete or had sunk below the surface of the earth, vast labour and expense were incurred.' At the same time Rippon was busily engaged in preparing the map of the ground, collecting biographical materials, and arranged for the engravings. A contemporary description of Rippon at work is preserved in an undated extract from the diary of a lady, who, in the company of Rev. Matthew Wilks, one day walked through the Fields:

> ... There we found a worthy man known to Mr. Wilks, Mr. Rippon by name, who was laid down upon his side between two graves, and writing out the epitaphs word for word. He had an ink-horn in his button-hole, and a pen and book. He tells us that he has taken most of the old inscriptions, and that he will, if God be pleased to spare his days, do all, notwithstanding it is a grievous labour, and the writing is hard to make out by reason of the oldness of the cutting in some, and defacings of other stones. It is a labour of love to him, and when he is gathered to his fathers, I hope some one will go on with the work.[110]

Although Rippon received several subscriptions after his advertisement of 1803, nothing was printed.[111] In the memorial of 1827 Rippon explained that: '... it pleased Divine Providence sorely to afflict him in his bodily health, insomuch that he was for a long time in imminent danger, and his life was despaired of, and he was also assailed by other considerable family afflictions, which became the occasion of the said work then being laid aside and abandoned by him.'

Rippon was desperately ill in 1799 and 1809, presumably the latter date was here intended: but this was still six years after the 'prospectus'. (The 'family afflictions' which included the debts of his son John are reviewed in chapter eight.) However, it was his son who appears to have renewed the task, and by 1827 he had completed a further list of all buried there until the end of 1826 and had had six volumes of inscriptions bound. Rippon personally attended the presentation of the memorial, briefly addressed the meeting, and was described as 'of very venerable appearance, apparently on the verge of eighty'. He had been earlier introduced as 'a scholar, and an antiquarian of vast research'. Despite the evident renewed interest in 1827 nothing was ever published.

However, twelve manuscript volumes (six of registers of burials and six of inscriptions) are used for genealogical research at the College of Heralds, London. The plans for the biographies, and masses of relevant papers, are collected into fourteen volumes purchased from a 'Mrs.

---

110 *History of the Bunhill Fields Burial Ground*, pp. 22-23.
111 References in several letters to Rippon in the B.L papers.

Rippon' by the British Museum in 1870.[112] Another Baptist minister, J.A. Jones, published *Bunhill Memorials* (1849), in which he referred to Rippon's more ambitious project: 'The worthy brother grasped at too much, and went down to his grave without accomplishing anything... I have done what I could.'[113] There is no evidence that Jones was granted the use of any of Rippon's papers, but his smaller volume perhaps finally dissuaded Rippon's descendants from ever publishing his researches.

Rippon's genuine antiquarian interests led to the preservation of valuable historical records, reveal his deep commitment to the Baptist and Dissenting causes and provide another example of his willingness to give himself freely in the service of the churches.

---

112   B.L. Add. MSS. 28513 to 28523.
113   Jones, *Bunhill Memorials*, p. iii.

CHAPTER 7

'Willing Servant of all the Churches'

'I remain in everlasting bonds, the willing Servant of all the churches, JOHN RIPPON.'[1]

So Rippon concluded the preface to his *Register*. Earlier analyses of his Baptist hymnody and his *Register* have suggested the aptness of Rippon's self-description. But Rippon did even more general work for Baptist churches and individuals. Moreover, as a Baptist, he shared in several Dissenting or evangelical enterprises. Whilst several of these societies have been introduced when reviewing the influence of Rippon's congregation, his personal activity also needs to be appreciated. Rippon's contributions as a preacher and his contribution to the formation of the Baptist Union are of sufficient importance to necessitate separate studies. In fact, all his public ministry justified Rippon's designation as 'willing Servant of all the Churches'.

First, however, a review of Rippon's involvement in the leading political issues of the day will help set the scene for understanding his service to the churches.

Rippon and the Politics of Dissent

As pastor of a prestigious Dissenting London congregation in the last three decades of the eighteenth century, Rippon was inevitably and deeply aware of the political crises which so divided the nation.

Rippon had begun at London shortly before the American crisis unfolded in 1775. As James Bradley has summarised the situation: 'Nonconformity...was not a unified movement and neither was radicalism. The majority of Dissenters were clearly pro-American in orientation, but many were evidently indifferent to political matters, and a

---

1   *Register* 1 (1790-93), p. viii.

few were outspoken defenders of the government's American policy'.[2]
As previously noted, Rippon wrote to James Manning at Providence in
1784, describing the conflict as 'ye late bloody & unrighteous war' and
reporting that all the Baptist ministers in London, except two, and 'most
of our brethren in ye country' supported the Americans.[3] John Martin
(1741-1820), of the Grafton Street, Soho Church, was clearly one
London minister who supported the English government.[4] Influential
Particular Baptists who expressed themselves strongly on the side of the
Americans included Rippon's mentor Caleb Evans at Bristol and John
Collett Ryland at Northampton.[5]

Rippon was clearly a strong supporter of the American cause. Indeed,
Benjamin Flower (1755-1829), the Unitarian biographer of Robert
Robinson, claimed that Rippon's conduct during the war was 'notorious'
and that 'he distinguished himself by such strong language of
reprobation of the measures of the administration, that some of his
friends were alarmed on his account'.[6] English Baptists did not inherit
the pacifist traditions of the Mennonites, as was clearly revealed in their
1689 Confession of Faith, and the preaching of Dissenters at this period
helped shape a political ideology.[7] Study of sermons preached during the
war period identifies contrasts between Anglicans and Dissenters in their
attitude to the government.[8] Baptist preacher Rees David (d. 1788) of
Norwich was among the more outspoken critics, likening the colonists to
Naboth (1 Kings 21) and the government to his false accusers, though he
excluded any members of the Royal House from playing the role of
Jezebel! David also claimed that the bishops had encouraged the

---

2   J. Bradley, *Religion, Revolution and English Radicalism. Non-conformity in
Eighteenth-Century Politics and Society* (Cambridge: Cambridge University Press,
1990), p. 6. See also E.A. Payne, 'British Baptists and the American Revolution',
Baptist History and Heritage 11.1 (1976), pp. 3-15; C.L. Howe, Jr. 'British Evangelical
Response to the American Revolution: the Baptists', *Fides et Historia* 8 (1976), pp. 35-
49; C. Bonwick, 'English Dissenters and the American Revolution', in H.C. Allen and R.
Thompson (eds), *Contrast and Connection: Bicentennial Essays in Anglo-American
History* (Athens: Ohio University Press, 1976), pp. 88-112.

3   Guild, *Life, Times and Correspondence of James Manning*, pp. 374-76.

4   Bradley, *Religion, Revolution and English Radicalism*, p. 123.

5   Payne, 'British Baptists and the American Revolution', pp. 10-11.

6   B. Flower (ed), *Miscellaneous Works of Robert Robinson*, 1, p. lxxxvi. For
Flower, see *DNB*.

7   T. George, 'Between Pacifism and Coercion: The English Baptist Doctrine of
Religious Toleration', *Mennonite Quarterly Review* 58.1 (1984), pp. 30-49; M.A.G.
Haykin, '"Resisting Evil": Civil Retaliation, non-resistance, and the interpretation of
Matthew 5:39a among eighteenth-century Calvinistic Baptists', *BQ* 36.5 (1996), pp.
212-27.

8   H.P. Ippel, 'British Sermons and the American Revolution', *Journal of
Religious History* 12.2 (1982), pp. 191-205.

American War, that the taxation imposed upon the colonies was unjust, and that these fellow citizens were inadequately represented in parliament. His published sermons bordered on treason.[9] David was in contact with Robert Robinson of Cambridge who was another Baptist actively agitating for reform, founding the Cambridge Constitutional Society in 1783 to advocate parliamentary reform.[10]

David, like Rippon, was a Bristol student and the influence of Caleb Evans, whose sermons in defence of the colonists were 'outspoken and uncompromising', is significant.[11] Some Welsh students of Evans at Bristol, clearly stimulated by the American War, found themselves in trouble with authorities as a result of their radical opinions and activities in seeking parliamentary reform. These included William Richards (1749-1818) of Lynn[12] and Morgan John Rhys (1760-1804) of Peny-garn.[13] William Winterbotham (1763-1829) of Plymouth was another English student in difficulties.[14]

The Dissenters had a long history of discontent because of their inferior legal status in England. The Test and Corporation Acts which required all magistrates, officers of municipal corporations and those aspiring to civil or military posts to take communion in the Church of England, theoretically kept Dissenters from public office. Rippon shared fully in attempts to have these disabilities removed. His own summary of the situation in the difficult days of 1793 stressed the vulnerability of Dissenters:

> This civil incapacity makes Dissenters be looked upon by the vulgar, most unjustly, as rebels and enemies to government, and to a family which they placed on the throne; and in all seasons of alarm and tumult, they have experienced, and do experience, great evils in this way... Dissenters pay all taxes and tythes, and are obliged to serve offices in the church, which are attended only with labour and expence, as churchwarden, &c. subject to heavy penalties if they do not serve, or find, at their own expence, a proper substitute!!![15]

---

9   Bradley, *Religion, Revolution and English Radicalism,* pp. 130-31.

1 0   Watts, *The Dissenters,* 2, p. 396; J. Bradley, 'Religion and Reform at the Polls: Nonconformity in Cambridge Politics, 1774-1784', *Journal of British Studies,* 23.2 (1984), pp. 55-78.

1 1   Bradley, *Religion, Revolution and English Radicalism,* p. 128.

12   J.A. Oddy, 'The Dissidence of William Richards', *BQ* 27.3 (1977), pp. 118-27.

13   See Davies, ' "Very Different Springs of Uneasiness": Emigration from Wales to the United States of America during the 1790s', pp. 372-75; H. Davies, 'Transatlantic Brethren: A Study of English, Welsh and American Baptists with particular reference to Morgan John Rhys and his friends' (PhD thesis, University of Wales, 1984).

14   Payne, 'British Baptists and the Revolution', p. 10.

15   *Register* 1 (1790-93), p. 524.

However, James Bradley has demonstrated that in the eighteenth century many Dissenters did hold office, and not all because they practised occasional conformity (the taking of communion as required but in no other way denying their Dissenting faith): 'The myth that Dissenters were strictly excluded from offices of trust was constructed by the Dissenters themselves in the interests of reform'. Thus, 'the perceived injustices remained a potent unifying force, while the practice of occasional conformity allowed the Dissenters a large degree of participation in unreformed politics'.[16] One notable example of this would have been well known to Rippon. Wealthy sergemaker and radical political Dissenter, Martin Dunsford of Tiverton, whose literary work Rippon publicized in his *Register*, protested against the Test Act but held numerous public offices and sat on the Tiverton corporation from 1782 until his death in 1802.[17]

The American war stimulated a more radical spirit among the Dissenters. As poet and literary figure Robert Southey (1774-1843) commented, 'The American War made the Dissenters feel once more a political party in the State. New England was more the country of their hearts than the England where they had been born and bred'.[18] Rippon echoed the sentiments of other Dissenters when he observed to Manning: '...the independence of America will for a while secure the liberty of this country; but if the continent had been reduced, Britain would not long have been free'.[19]

Hysteria following the outbreak of the French Revolution destroyed any Dissenting hopes of an early repeal of the Test and Corporation Acts. Attempts to do this in 1787, 1789 and 1790 all failed and when, in the early stages of the Revolution, some Dissenters began expressing support for the revolutionaries, the religious and political establishment hardened in their attitude. The most famous sermon preached in support of the French was that by the rational Dissenter Richard Price which in turn provoked Edmund Burke's influential *Reflections on the Revolution in France* (1790). Some Baptists greeted the Revolution with enthusiasm: Joseph Kinghorn of Norwich wrote, 'I rejoice with all my heart at the destruction of that most infamous place the Bastille'.[20] Another Baptist, Mark Wilks, preached in Norwich in 1791 and declared: '...in the defeat of the officers and soldiers at Versailles, in the capture of the King and his fugitive family, the friends of freedom are bound to exclaim with the

---

16   Bradley, *Religion, Revolution and English Radicalism*, pp. 85, 89.

17   Bradley, *Religion, Revolution and English Radicalism*, p. 81.

18   Cited by A. Lincoln, *Some Political and Social Ideas of English Dissent, 1763-1800* (Cambridge: Cambridge University Press, 1938), p. 256.

19   Guild, *Early History of Brown University*, pp. 374-76.

20   C.B. Jewson, 'Norwich Baptists and the French Revolution', *BQ* 24.5 (1972), p. 209.

warmest gratitude divine goodness can produce, "what hath God wrought"'.[21] Robert Hall Junior at Cambridge, in succession to Robinson, published *Christianity consistent with a Love of Freedom* (1791) in which he exulted that 'the empire of darkness and despotism' had been smitten.[22] Robinson himself was subject to specific criticism from Burke in Parliament.[23]

But as events in France became more violent and war broke out between Britain and France in February 1793, Dissenters became increasingly divided. Some Baptists at first maintained a radical stance. William Ward, later a missionary with Carey in India, was heavily involved in the radical press in Derby and helped organize a meeting with John Thelwall in the Baptist chapel in Derby which ended in violence.[24] Baptist preacher William Winterbotham of Plymouth was imprisoned in 1793 for a sermon judged to be seditious.[25] Morgan Rhys and William Richards fled to America.[26]

Most Baptists changed in their outlook. Robert Hall who had first regarded the French Revolution as 'the most splendid event recorded in the annals of history', by 1800 was equating it with 'Modern Infidelity'. Hall had come to the view that the Christian ministry lost 'something of its energy and sanctity by embarking on the stormy element of political debate'.[27] The more common view among Evangelicals became what D. Bebbington has called a 'blend of quietism and loyalism'.[28]

Rippon became a strong supporter of the British in their war with France. Indeed, in 1803 he preached a sermon to volunteers, commanded by William Pitt, at the fort in Margate, on the day of the general fast and again in London to the volunteers of London and Southwark. The Militia Act of 1803, which provided for raising twenty-five thousand volunteers, had met with an enthusiastic response; but the government had no idea how to manage the force, no arms were provided, and the scheme was a failure.[29] Nevertheless, it gave opportunity for stirring the patriotism of the threatened country, as Rippon's sermon, which ran to four editions, clearly reveals.[30]

---

21   Jewson, 'Norwich Baptists and the French Revolution', p. 210.
22   Watts, *The Dissenters*, 1, p. 482.
23   Brown, *The English Baptists of the Eighteenth Century*, p. 133.
24   Smith, 'William Ward, Radical Reform, and Missions in the 1790s', pp. 218-44.
25   Watts, *The Dissenters*, 2, p. 354.
26   Payne, 'British Baptists and the Revolution', p. 10.
27   Watts, *The Dissenters*, 2, p. 355.
28   Bebbington, *Evangelicalism*, p. 72.
29   Watson, *The Reign of George III 1760-1820*, pp. 415-16.
30   J. Rippon, *A Discourse delivered at the Drum Head* (London: 1803).

The contrast between Rippon's opposition to the government in the American War and then his support during the war with French, though by no means unusual among Dissenters, earned him a savage personal attack from Benjamin Flower of Cambridge. Flower wrote a memoir for Robert Robinson in which he defended Robinson from charges that he had left his Calvinism and adopted a Socinian position. There seems no doubt that Robinson had moved to a heterodox view of Christ and the Trinity and the London Baptist Abraham Booth had written against these teachings.[31] In his memoir for Booth, Rippon had praised his friend for his courage in these efforts, but Flower accused Rippon of 'vile slander' in these comments. Flower, himself a Unitarian and radical, proceeded to claim that Rippon had turned against Robinson only after others had condemned him: 'His conduct as a christian minister in this instance was similar to his recent conduct as a politician'. He commented about Rippon's attitude during the American War and then added:

> But no sooner had he an opportunity of preaching before Mr. PITT'S volunteers at the *Drum-head,* than he veered about to the opposite point of the compass, congratulated the British empire on its "BEATIFIED state", during the present reign, and expressed his hope that Mr. Pitt, as he had already proved a blessing to one half of the world, might by being again called to the councils of his sovereign, prove a blessing to the other half! So much for the *consistency* and the *integrity* of this champion of orthodoxy and loyalty, this calumniator of Mr. Robinson.[32]

The reality is that Rippon at this point more accurately represented the position of the Baptists who were loyal to their country, even if they did not all support Pitt politically. A more reasonable judgment would be that Rippon was invited to preach at this public event because his views were already known to be supportive of the government.

Of Rippon's more general leadership of the Baptists, however, there can be no doubt.

---

31   Hughes, *With Freedom Fired,* pp. 97-107. In a subtle distinction, Robinson maintained that his teachings were not Socinian but more akin to the teaching of Paul of Samosata, a third century Bishop of Antioch whose Christology was condemned in the early church. Paul appears to have taught a form of Dynamic Monarchianism, by which the Word was an attribute of the Father. This emphasis on the unity of the Godhead was, of course, a strong emphasis of the Unitarians. See Flower (ed.), *Miscellaneous Works of Robert Robinson,* 1, p. cxxxix.

32   Flower, (ed.), *Miscellaneous Works of Robert Robinson,* 1, p. lxxxvi.

Baptist Activities

Baptist Board

The first London Baptist society in which Rippon shared was the Baptist Board, the eighteenth-century equivalent of a ministers' fraternal. The Board had been formed in 1724 and its membership was confined to Particular Baptist ministers of London and its immediate neighbourhood.[33] The title of 'Board' was adopted in emulation of similar societies of Independent and Presbyterian ministers. All three 'boards' united in the General Body of Protestant Dissenting Ministers of the Three Denominations, and Rippon was also active in this larger body. The Baptist Board was usually only a small meeting, at times with only half a dozen present: but it took itself very seriously and exerted an important influence, especially in its earlier years.

In broad terms, the Board appears to have assumed five functions. The most obvious purpose was as an opportunity for discussion, dining, and smoking tobacco; it was the regular meeting of the ministers. The records have many gaps, but it evidently met weekly, from 1760 to 1823 in the Jamaica Coffee House: but often no decisions worthy of recording were made. Secondly, the Board gave 'official' recognition to London ministers and churches, for not all 'Baptist' ministers automatically enjoyed the fraternity of the Board. In several instances former members were excluded for moral or theological reasons: perhaps the outstanding example was the dis-association of Andrew Gifford, and the refusal to recognize his Eagle Street church.[34] Thirdly, the Board gave advice to ministers and churches about settlements or disputes, although not all the disputes in which it shared are recorded in its own journals. Country churches also were given this advice. Another important function of the Board was to authorize appeals from country churches. With the approval of the Board, applicants could visit the wealthier London laymen begging funds for their causes. In this sense the Board exerted a powerful influence for many churches. (From 1784 the Baptist Case Committee regularized these appeals.) The Board also nominated Baptist representatives to the General Committee of the General Body of the Three Denominations.

---

33   Minutes (1724-1335) printed, with notes, in *BHS Trans* 5 (1916-17), pp. 96-114, 197-240; 6 (1918-19), pp. 72-127; 7 (1920-21), pp. 49-70. Note however that the London ministers and elders had met since c.1714: Crosby, *The History of the English Baptists*, 4, p. 108. See also A.J. Payne, 'The Baptist Board', *BQ* 1.7 (1922-23), pp. 321-26.

34   *BHS Trans* 5 (1916-17), pp. 213-16.

Rippon was admitted to the Board on 16 March 1774, and from this time entered fully into its society.[35] He thus came into weekly contact with men like Benjamin Wallin, Samuel Stennett, John Reynolds, William Clarke, and Abraham Booth. (He wrote memoirs for the last three named.) Several interesting decisions were recorded during Rippon's time, and in most of these he shared. He became familiar with the plight of many country churches, and encouraged his own church, as has been shown, to support 'approved' cases. A reflection of the domestic and political repercussions of the French Revolution is seen in the exclusion of John Martin from the Board in 1798.[36] Martin had suggested in a sermon that if the French invaded England, some Dissenters would welcome them. The Board passed a resolution deploring Martin's statement, and affirming the loyalty of Dissenters. Martin's sermon caused quite a scandal, although it was perhaps more thoughtless than seditious. In 1803 a committee of laymen tried to reconcile the Board and Martin, but Booth refused to agree and the request was denied.[37] Although the records do not mention it, most of the practical preparations for the first Baptist Union meetings were evidently arranged by the Board: certainly they were appointed as a committee to arrange the 1813 meetings.[38]

In 1820 Rippon shared in a committee that revised the rules of the Board. These affirmed that the object of the Society was 'to afford an opportunity for mutual consultation and advice on subjects of a religious nature particularly as concerned with the interests of our own denomination'.[39] The membership was defined so that any minister requesting admission had to apply by letter, and it was stipulated that once a month a set subject would be discussed at the weekly Tuesday meetings. The first list of subjects illustrates the range of themes: What steps can be taken to promote the interests of religion in our denomination at large? How far is it practicable to form an Association of the Baptist Ministers and Churches in London and its environs? Is the practice of fasting of perpetual obligation? How can we account for the differences in the theological opinions of wise and virtuous men? Was Samson's death an act of suicide? Is there reason to apprehend the 'prevalency' of Papacy in this country? What is hyper Calvinism? What is the province of reason in matters of religion?[40]

---

35   *BHS Trans* 6 (1918-19), p. 83

36   *BHS Trans* 6 (1918-19), pp. 93-94. Cf. Ivimey, *History of the English Baptists*, 4, pp. 77-83.

37   *BHS Trans* 6 (1918-19), pp. 97-99.

38   S.J. Price, 'The Early Years of the Baptist Union', *BQ* 4.2 (1928-29), pp. 53-57.

39   *BHS Trans* 6 (1918-19), p. 109.

40   *BHS Trans* 6 (1918-19), p. 112.

The second of these subjects resulted in a motion that such a London association was 'not only practicable but also desirable'.[41] Rippon was one of five appointed to a committee for drafting rules and regulations for the proposed association. This committee duly presented reports in succeeding months, but the records then have a gap of twenty-seven months - and no further mention of the proposed association was made.[42]

Rippon, after the death of Booth in 1806, was the undisputed leader of the London ministers. He was frequently the chairman of Board meetings, and in many ways his strong personality must have been an influence in the discussions. But the effectiveness of the Board for the wider life of the churches was only marginal in these last years, especially after the formation of the Baptist Union.

Baptist Case Committee

The work of this committee, formed in 1784, was noted in connection with the influence of the Carter Lane laymen on the denomination. Rippon was also an active member, and made a special contribution in two ways. First, he published lists in the *Register* of all the approved cases, indicating both the amounts requested and actually received.[43] These records provide the only knowledge of the committee's work for the period of the *Register*. It is evident that hundreds of pounds were given each year to various churches. The method was unsatisfactory. It involved the collecting church in the expense of a minister's trip to London, not to mention the degrading and physical demands made upon a minister when it was his turn to come up to London and systematically beg money from the London laymen.[44] At least the committee regularized the appeals so that not too many requests were made in any year.

Rippon helped by acting as spokesman for some churches. He is known to have presented requests from Truro (1790), Coventry (1793), and Chertsey (1817) - and probably many others.[45] The goodwill of a London minister was an invaluable asset to a country church seeking financial assistance - not only from this committee but from other societies. Rippon's share in these applications demonstrates his willingness to serve the churches.

---

41 *BHS Trans* 7 (1920-21), p. 52
42 An association was formed in 1834.
43 *Register* 2 (1794-97), pp. 92, 176, 523; 3 (1798-1801), pp. 60, 266; 4 (1801-02), p. 1151.
44 See Price, *A Popular History of the Baptist Building Fund* , pp. 40-63.
45 Cf. B. L. Add. MSS. 25386, f. 166; 25387, f. 114 and f. 390. Only Coventry is known to have received help, cf. *Register* 3 (1798-1801), p. 60.

Monthly Meetings

These were begun in 1743, and continued at least until 1823.[46] In some senses these partook of the nature of an association. They were devotional in character, conducted by the ministers of the 'recognized' churches in strict rotation. Each church sent 'messengers' who attended the services, held in the various meeting-houses. Rippon naturally shared in these, and published plans of the meetings in his *Register*.[47] Although there are no records of the meetings, some general decisions also appear to have been taken at them. For example, Carter Lane was once requested to recognize a 'sister' church by this meeting.[48] More importantly, in 1797 the Itinerant Society was formed after a 'monthly Association' meeting, and the meetings of the new Society were held on the same days as the Monthly Meetings. Whilst these were not strictly association-meetings as compared with the less frequent rural associations, they do represent the one regular general gathering of London Baptists with some measure of continuity, and the Itinerant Society was one useful enterprise to result from its activities.

The Baptist Fund

The support of Carter Lane, both in its financial giving and in the provision of leadership for the Fund, has been noted. As minister of one of the contributing churches, Rippon was automatically in a position of influence since he was able to present petitions for assistance from country ministers or churches. He is known to have been active in this, as each year he presented twenty-four requests to the Fund.[49] Some twenty letters referring to his advocacy of their requests are extant. Some are from friends of Rippon, such as Caleb Evans seeking funds for West Country churches,[50] Robert Redding of Truro,[51] William Newman,[52] Daniel Sprague of Tiverton,[53] and James Douglas.[54] The majority of those presented by Rippon were for the West Country and this may imply that Rippon was regarded as an unofficial West Country advocate to the

---

46   Whitley, *Baptists of London*, p. 53.
47   *Register* 1 (1790-93), pp. 176, 288, 466; 2 (1794-97), pp. 92, 176, 192, 334, 534; 3 (1798-1801), pp. 60, 166, 230, 272; 4 (1801-02), pp. 752, 1152.
48   Carter Lane churchbook, 19 August 1776.
49   Particular Baptist Fund minute books.
50   30 July 1783, B. L. Add. MSS. 25386, f. 441.
51   25 February 1795, B.L. Add. MSS. 25388. f. 392.
52   8 January 1796, B.L. Add. MSS. 25338, f. 130.
53   23 December 1797, B.L Add. MSS. 25389, f. 135.
54   n.d., B.L.Add. MSS. 253886, f. 397.

Fund. Rippon was often entrusted with the payment of Fund money, and in several cases was instructed by recipients to deduct money owing to him before sending the balance.[55]

Moreover, Rippon publicized the work of the Fund in his *Register*, detailing for most years the amounts received and disbursed.[56] Most of the Fund's regular income came from annual collections from eight London churches, during the *Register*'s years in excess of £600 each year. In addition several legacies were received, so that considerable sums were in fact paid to the churches. For example: 1794, £1,564; 1795, £1,612; 1796, £1,310; 1797, £1,597; 1798, £1,345; 1799, £1,495. Usually money was given, frequently five pounds, to individual ministers or churches, although books were also given. Each year the Fund also supported a 'Mission into North Wales', but the details are not clear.

Rippon encouraged the new practice of some larger country churches also contributing funds. In 1793, after noting the gift of £7.9.4. from the Norwich church, Rippon added: 'a circumstance this truly pleasing, and which furnishes an example, perhaps worthy of being copied, by Sister Churches in the several counties, many of whom are both equal in number and superior in circumstances to several of the congregations in London, which, nevertheless always contribute generously to this institution'.[57]

In 1796 Rippon recorded that the trustees of the Fund had forwarded a letter to the deacons of all the churches receiving assistance.[58] They regretted that 'they find themselves incapable of exhibiting half the assistance which they could wish, to many of those cases which come under their notice', and asked the deacons to do all they could to support their minister themselves. The trustees suspected that several churches automatically applied for an annual grant even if there was no special need. Every receiving church was expected to make at least a nominal collection for the Fund, and to indicate the amount, together with: 'a concise representation of the faith of the church, and of your pastor, particularly in regard to the person of Christ, and the doctrine of the Trinity; of your pastor's domestic circumstances, if he have a family; of his last year's salary; and of the (number) and increase or decrease of your members, &c.'

Concern with the theological orthodoxy of Fund applicants had caused a 'sensation' in 1789 when Robert Robinson of Cambridge had 'boggled' at the idea of 'a London lord over a country brother's

---

55   E.g. I. Hutton, Broughton, 20 April 1795, B.L. Add. MSS. 25387, f. 290.

56   *Register* 1 (1790-93), pp. 8, 289, 467; 2 (1794-97), pp. 8, 92, 207, 532 f.; 3 (1798-1801), pp. 59, 265-66, 4 (1801-02), p 717.

57   *Register* 2 (1794-97), p. 92

58   *Register* 2 (1794-97), pp. 532-33.

conscience'.[59] The Fund trustees, however, felt obliged to maintain the Calvinistic designs of the money entrusted to them. In 1798 the Fund wrote to one applicant requesting assurances that he was not an Antinomian.[60]

The Fund was an obvious economic and theological influence on the denomination. Anyone who helped the Fund helped the country churches. Rippon was an ardent supporter of the Fund, and his increasing prominence through the *Register* and his hymnbooks meant that he was one Londoner known to many country churches. His advocacy of their case presumably assisted its success.

The Baptist Missionary Society

The support of Rippon and his church for the Society has been outlined. It has also been shown that the *Register* consistently promoted the cause of the mission and, indeed, this was his main contribution to its success. Rippon never served on the BMS committee, but did collect money from various churches for its funds. During 1794 he also evidently undertook a preaching tour, commending its plans and collecting funds.[61] His active support, if not leadership, was demonstrated by his recorded participation in the public meetings of the Mission in London in 1820 and 1825.[62] But his early and prompt contribution to the acceptance of the Mission in London cannot be over-emphasized.

Village Preaching[63]

One common reaction to the formation of the foreign mission societies was what J. Stoughton later called 'the cuckoo-note objection, that there is enough work to do at home without going far abroad'.[64] On the other hand, it is clear that the promotion of foreign missions provided a direct stimulus to home missions, what has been called 'the reflex action'. Leading contemporary Baptist preacher Robert Hall insisted that the

---

59   Ivimey, *History of the English Baptists*, 4, pp. 50-53; Hughes, *With Freedom Fired*, p. 57.

60   Hughes, *With Freedom Fired*, pp. 76-77.

61   J. Giles to Rippon, London, 4 July 1794, B.L. Add. MSS. 25387, f. 90, refers to a preaching tour, evidently for the Mission; but no further details are known.

62   *Baptist Magazine* 12 (1820), p. 301; 15 (1825), p. 305.

63   See especially D.W. Lovegrove, 'Particular Baptist Itinerant Preachers during the late 18th and early 19th Centuries', *BQ* 28.3 (1979), pp. 127-141 and his *Established Church, Sectarian People*.

64   *History of Religion in England*, 6, p. 370.

foreign missions movement was 'the true source' of the increase in village preaching.[65] Indeed, W.R. Ward has claimed that: 'In the short run the missionary enterprise had a more powerful impact at home than in the mission field, and it intensified the solvents at work on the old denominational order'.[66] More extensively, S. Piggin summarized:

> ...missionary enthusiasm appears to have increased lay giving for home missions as well as foreign missions; it probably stimulated interest in home missions and increased the number of candidates for the ministry; it almost certainly reinforced the already existing tendency to express piety in activity rather than quiescence; it helped to bury fatalistic and deterministic theological systems; it appears to have appealed, like the later temperance movement, to all classes of society; and...it declared war on denominational bigotry.[67]

As W. Willey of Dartmouth wrote to Rippon in 1795, 'I have tho't on ye late Mission to ye Hindoos - what swarms of White Heathen cover our land! What can be done?'[68] The BMS leaders, whilst denying that the home needs reduced responsibility for overseas missions, published in the second number (1795) of their *Periodical Account*, 'A Proposal for extending the Assistance of the Society, For the encouragement of Village Preaching in England'.[69] This proposal noted that village preaching could be conducted either by 'itinerant' or 'stationary' ministers: but the latter seemed more suited to the Baptist 'mode of church government'. This comment alerts us to the changes that were coming in the traditional Baptist way of being church as the Revival influence grew.

Theoretically, Baptists, as with other Dissenters, were supposed only to hold religious services in buildings duly registered for the purpose.[70] Early Methodists, as members of the Church of England, were not bound by such legalities. The laws can only have reinforced the Calvinistic Baptists in their understanding of the church as a 'garden enclosed', to use a popular image derived from Song of Solomon.[71] Notwithstanding this, many Baptists influenced by the Evangelical Revival began to preach

---

65   O. Gregory (ed.), *The Works of Robert Hall* (6 vols; London: 1833), 3, p. 334.

66   Ward, *Religion and Society in England 1790-1850*, p. 45. Compare Watts, *The Dissenters*, 2, pp. 20-22.

67   S. Piggin, 'Sectarianism versus Ecumenism: The Impact on British Churches of the Missionary Movement to India, c.1800-1860', *Journal of Ecclesiastical History* 27.4 (1976), pp. 387-88.

68   16 September 1795, B.L. Add. MSS. 25389, f. 405.

69   *Periodical Accounts*, 1 (1800), pp. 153-56.

70   For a useful analysis of problems for Dissenters, see R.E. Richey, 'Effects of Toleration on Eighteenth-Century Dissent', *Journal of Religious History* 8.4 (1975), pp. 350-63.

71   Haykin, *One Heart and One Soul*, p. 20.

in villages around their churches. Robert Robinson of Cambridge preached in about fifteen neighbouring villages from the 1760s.[72] The Western Association had encouraged itinerant preaching from 1775 as had the Northamptonshire from 1779.[73] Striking statistical evidence confirms the impact of village preaching. Between 1781 and 1790 Baptists registered 89 temporary places for worship, and 30 as permanent (that is, chapels or meeting houses), but from 1791 to 1800 these figures were 170 and 74, and in the next decade 216 and 98 respectively.[74]

In a perceptive analysis of the changes among Baptists from 1780 to 1830, W.R. Ward has stressed the influence of this preaching movement: 'Their denomination was being altered out of all recognition by itinerant evangelism which found no clear doctrinal or institutional expression in their inherited view of the church.'[75] The gathered church became a mission agency. 'A new empiricism was grafted on to the older churchmanship.'[76] A pastor was not only to be a shepherd for his 'flock' but also to be an evangelist to those outside. The old view, that the office of an evangelist had existed only in the New Testament era and had lapsed, was revised. This transformation of the Baptist church involved a new view of history. Accounts such as those in Rippon's *Register* were reporting that, whatever the doctrinal hesitations of high Calvinists might suggest, 'offers of grace were being made, accepted and blessed on an unheard-of scale all around the globe'.[77]

Under the influence of these movements, the BMS agreed in May 1796 to support two settled ministers to travel as itinerant preachers during the summer; their congregations were supplied by Bristol students.[78] Accordingly, William Steadman of Broughton and John Saffery of Salisbury spent all July and August preaching in all the major towns and numerous villages in Cornwall.[79] The preachers reported great interest among the locals, and specifically attributed this to the 'labors and

---

72   Brown, *English Baptists of the Eighteenth Century*, p. 123.

73   Lovegrove, *Established Church, Sectarian People*, p. 32.

74   Gilbert, *Religion and Society in Industrial England*, p. 34.

75   Ward, 'The Baptists and the Transformation of the Church, 1780-1830', pp. 173-74.

76   C. Binfield, *So Down to Prayers. Studies in English Nonconformity 1780-1920* (London: J.M. Dent & Sons, 1977), p. 24. For the changes that the Revival brought to Baptist ecclesiology and practices, see also Briggs, *English Baptists of the Nineteenth Century*, pp. 15-20.

77   Ward, 'The Baptists and the Transformation of the Church, 1780-1830', pp. 170-71.

78   *Periodical Accounts*, 1, p. 262.

79   *Periodical Accounts*, 1, pp. 264-274. For Steadman's experience and commitment to village preaching, see S. James, 'Revival and Renewal in Baptist Life: The Contribution of William Steadman (1764-1837)', *BQ* 37.6 (1998), pp. 264-66.

success of Mr. Wesley', who reproved the indolence of Dissenters and served as an example to them.[80] Again, in 1797 the Mission Society supported a tour of ten weeks by Steadman and Francis Franklin, a Bristol student, again in Cornwall.[81] In both reports the itinerants advised on the advantages of establishing a permanent ministry.[82] At the same time the BMS paid small sums to encourage local pastors in village-preaching, such as James Hinton at Oxford,[83] and others in Warwickshire and Hampshire.[84] Many others were inspired to undertake similar work.[85]

It must not be supposed that these were the first Baptist efforts at itinerant preaching, either by local pastors or on a preaching tour. Vavasor Powell, for example, is a striking example of Baptist itinerant preaching tours in Commonwealth times.[86] However, regular work of this kind, and especially of a preaching 'tour', must have been an unusual concept for many Baptists. The few tours of which we have knowledge appear to have been either privately conducted or little publicized. Philip Gibbs, pastor (1749-1800) of Plymouth, undertook regular preaching tours into Cornwall, evidently from the 1750s, and preached in the southern areas of the county.[87] Churches were formed at Chacewater and Truro. Again, in 1770 the Bristol Education Society sponsored a 'Mission' into Cornwall by Benjamin Francis, who went again in 1775.[88] Francis was a committed itinerant, and during his pastorate at Horsley undertook monthly preaching tours through 'the most uninstructed parts of Gloucestershire, Worcestershire and Wiltshire' and was 'the first means of introducing evangelical religion into many dark towns and villages in all the neighbourhood round'.[89] The Baptist Fund, it will be recalled, sponsored a 'Mission' into North Wales. Henry Philips of Salisbury is

---

80   *Periodical Accounts*, 1, p. 272.

81   *Periodical Accounts*, 1, pp. 358-60. Cf. *Register* 3 (1798-1801), pp. 56-59.

82   *Periodical Accounts*, 1, pp. 273, 360

83   *Periodical Accounts*, 1, pp. 274-276, 360. Hinton had suffered violence and abuse as a 'Jacobin rascal' on one notable occasion when preaching at Woodstock in 1794: J.H. Hinton, *A Biographical Portaiture of the late Rev. James Hinton, M.A.* (Oxford: 1824), pp. 255-62.

84   *Periodical Accounts*, 1, p. 360.

85   For examples, see Brown, *English Baptists of the Eighteenth Century*, pp. 123-24.

86   See C. Hill, 'Propagating the Gospel', in H.E. Bell and R.L. Bollard (eds), *Historical Essays, 1600-1750 presented to David Ogg* (London: A. & C. Black, 1964), pp. 35-59.

87   *Register* 3 (1798-1801), pp. 383-84.

88   See above, chapter 2.

89   For details of areas and villages preached in by Francis, see G.F. Nuttall, 'Questions and Answers; an Eighteenth-century Correspondence', *BQ* 27. 2 (1977), p. 89.

known to have travelled in Wales preaching and distributing Bibles, supplied by the philanthropist John Thornton.[90]

Thus the BMS sponsored efforts, whilst probably more extensive and given a wider publicity, were not unique. But they were undoubtedly the greatest influence determining the formation of 'The Baptist Society in London for the Encouragement and Support of Itinerant Preaching' early in 1797. There were other influences. The example of the Methodists was acknowledged by the B.MS itinerants. Again, in 1776 the *Societas Evangelica* had been formed, with funds to foster evangelism by any orthodox denomination.[91] Several similar societies were formed and organized preaching-campaigns.[92] The most significant and the most successful was the interdenominational Bedfordshire Union of Christians, founded also in 1797 and in which Baptists were most active.[93] This led to other similar interdenominational agencies in other regions.[94] Once the Baptists began emphasizing this evangelistic method, the churches widely adopted it, as was shown in chapter five. The Essex Association was formed in 1796 with the purpose of encouraging village evangelism, in 1798 the Northern Evangelical Society and in 1809 the Northern Baptist Itinerant Society were begun, and much later, in 1824, the Bristol Baptist Itinerant Society.[95]

Rippon, as has been shown, welcomed this movement in his *Register*. This enthusiasm is reflected in the leading role he played in the London Society, whose records (with some serious omissions) from 1797 to 1812 have survived and a general picture of its activities may be drawn.[96] In particular, Rippon's leadership of the Society in its early years is evident.

The Itinerant Society was formed in connection with the London Monthly Meeting, or 'Association' as it is described in the records of the Society. On 19 January 1797, 'The following Question being proposed whether it be desirable to form a Society for the Encouragement of Itinerant Preaching in this Country? It was unanimously voted in the Affirmative.' A committee of seven (not named) was appointed to

---

90   *Register* 1 (1790-93), p. 130.

91   *Evangelical Magazine* 3 (1790), p. 119. This society was revitalized in 1796: Lovegrove, *Established Church, Sectarian People*, p. 195, note 91.

92   For an Independent London Society also formed in 1797, see *Transactions* of Congregational Historical Society 7 (1916-18), pp. 310-23, 350-62. Rippon knew of this Society, see B.L. Add. MSS. 25383, f. 288.

93   Watts, *The Dissenters*, 2, p. 21; Martin, 'English Particular Baptists and Interdenominational Cooperation', pp. 236-37.

94   See the complete list of more than seventy societies (1780-1830), in chronological order, in Lovegrove, *Established Church, Sectarian People*, pp. 182-184.

95   A.G. Hamlin, 'Bristol Baptist Itinerant Society', *BQ* 21.7 (1966), pp. 321-24.

96   In BMS archives; references in the following account are given by dates of meetings. There are no entries between 21 October 1802 and 10 April 1804.

prepare a plan for the next month's meeting. One visitor at the January meeting, and possibly the one who provoked the discussion, was John Palmer, pastor at Shrewsbury, active in village evangelism and one greatly helped by the new Society. He wrote to Rippon, from a London address, on 21 January, 'I know the subject considered after dinner at the Monthly Meeting could not fail giving you and every Lover of our dr Lord great pleasure,' and commented on Rippon having taken down in shorthand his account of preaching in the Shrewsbury district.[97] Thus Rippon was present at the January meeting, was obviously sympathetic to the suggestion, and as he was chairman of the February meeting, was probably on the committee of seven.[98] The plan was not finally adopted until the March meeting, and by April this had been printed together with an address commending the scheme 'To the Friends of Evangelical Truth, in General; and To the Calvinistic Baptist churches, in Particular.'[99]

Both the Address and Plan were published in full in the *Register*, Rippon printing with it a long letter from Steadman describing his 1796 tour and with general comments on itinerant preaching.[100] The 'Address and Plan' naturally argued at length for the propriety of preaching the Gospel to all: '*Preach the gospel to every creature*, was the high command of our sovereign Lord just before he ascended the throne of universal dominion. This divine order is yet in force; and its obligation extends to all that are invested with the ministerial character.'[101]

'Private Christians' were involved, since without their 'pecuniary assistance' ministers would not be free to itinerate 'in the darker parts of any country'. Moreover, 'private brethren' could visit outlying villages to pray, read the Bible, and 'converse on sacred subjects'. There was no suggestion that other than duly recognized men should preach, although obviously there was every possibility that the 'conversation' would become a sermon. The 'Address' insisted that the times were urgent, and that the aims of the Society were not to propagate any theological or political tenet but 'to warn sinners of the *wrath to come* - to *preach the unsearchable riches of Christ* - and to render their ungodly fellow-creatures truly wise, holy, and happy.'[102]

The Rules of the new Society detailed that the Committee of the Society should consist of nine London ministers (including Rippon), together with one member from each of their churches, and eleven other subscribers. This committee met 'in the afternoon of the day of each

---

97   B.L. Add. MSS. 25388, f. 182.
98   Itinerant Society minutes, 23 February 1797.
99   Itinerant Society minutes, 23 March 1797; 20 April 1797.
100   *Register* 2 (1794-97), pp. 465-70.
101   *Register* 2 (1794-97), p. 465
102   *Register* 2 (1794-97), p. 468

monthly association'. The committee was: (1) to 'provide and send out' such Calvinistic Baptist ministers as appeared qualified for itinerant preaching; (2) to give assistance to 'settled Ministers' for village preaching; (3) to furnish their itinerants with such tracts as seemed necessary. In addition: 'This Society, though formed under the countenance of the Baptist Monthly Association, is at liberty to permit its itinerant Ministers, whenever expediency calls, to unite with Paedobaptist Ministers of evangelical principles, who may be engaged in the same general design.'[103] William Fox, of Booth's church, was appointed treasurer, whilst Samuel Gale of Carter Lane became secretary.

The Society made an enthusiastic commencement. On 1 June 1797 inquiries were commenced about finding a suitable itinerant, and on 16 June Rippon himself was invited to undertake a tour in north Devon and Somerset in the company of any person deemed suitable by him. Rippon agreed, and invited both Zenas Trivett, of Langham, Essex, and Thomas Symmons, of Wotton-under-edge, Gloucestershire, to accompany him but both regretted they were not free to come.[104] Eventually Daniel Sprague of Tiverton went with his 'bosom friend' Rippon,[105] and John Sharp, of the Pithay church, Bristol, came for part of the way.[106] The tour lasted several weeks, and began at Bridgwater. Although Rippon presented a report to the Society, the details were not recorded. The strenuous nature of the tour, however, is suggested by Rippon's comment about Sprague: 'His preaching fourteen or fifteen sermons a week strengthened his body, and invigorated his mind; so that when he resumed his pastoral work at Tiverton, he encouraged new meetings for prayer and exhortation at the extreme ends of the town, and began to preach in villages where he had never laboured before.'[107]

Rippon's report was so encouraging that the Society hoped to send others on the same general route, 'which appeared desirable as well from the recommendation of Mr. Rippon as by the request of several persons to whom he had preached, they having expressed desires and with tears besought that he and his friends should either come again or send other Gospel preachers to them directly.'[108] Rippon's expenses were £36,[109] and this was the only time that a London minister undertook such a trip, although Sprague and his nephew covered the same general region the next year.[110]

---

103 *Register* 2 (1794-97), pp. 469-70.
104 Itinerant Society minutes, 22 June 1797.
105 *Register* 3 (1798-1801), p. 10, note 68.
106 *Register* 3 (1798-1801), p. 31, note 257.
107 *Register* 3 (1798-1801), p. 10, note 68.
108 Itinerant Society minutes, 19 October 1797.
109 Itinerant Society minutes, 8 October 1797.
110 *Register* 3 (1798-1801), p. 10, note 68.

Rippon's practical experience 'in the field' meant that he had a clearer awareness of the possibilities. His intimate knowledge of the churches of the area is revealed in his comments in the 1798 list of churches. For the next few years Rippon was the guiding influence in the Society. He and Booth were charged 'to prepare an Address for the use of such Ministers as may Itinerate for this Society.'[111] Rippon received letters from several churches requesting help, and was often asked to write letters on behalf of the Society. In February 1798 Booth, Dore, and Rippon were elected to a correspondence committee: but it was Rippon who normally presented information and letters to the meetings. He was present at most meetings, until 1799 when his serious illness accounted for his absences.

However, the work of the Society in terms of immediate and obvious results must be judged only a moderate success. For example, no regular permanent itinerant was found at first, although some were considered for the appointment, but rejected. Consequently, when churches asked for an itinerant to be sent to them no one was available. Related to this were the inadequate funds raised. From the cases recorded in the period 1797 to 1812 well over £1,200 was distributed for village evangelism. Whilst this was useful, the appeal of the BMS work was far greater and incomes in excess of that sum were received annually. A fresh effort was made in 1804, by appointing a subscription collector, but this produced only a temporary improvement.[112]

In general, the Society devoted its money to assisting resident ministers itinerate in surrounding areas. One exception was in 1793 when the Society, at the suggestion of the BMS who subsequently relinquished home evangelism, supported another tour into Cornwall by Saffery and Franklin.[113] The same year local work was undertaken in Devonshire, Gloucestershire, and Shropshire. The succeeding years found similar work encouraged in most other counties of England. Some concept of the nature of this work is illustrated by John Palmer's report given in 1801, that in one month he had ridden more than 500 miles, preached 64 times to more than 11,600 hearers in 10 counties, and twice conducted baptisms.[114] The enthusiasm of the itinerants is suggested by this extract from the report sent by Samuel Norman of Bampton, Devonshire: 'It is a Work in which I much delight, & as long as my Health & Strength are continued I shall not be discouraged by any obstacles in the way animated by the Promises of the first Baptist Itinerant Preacher who is saying to all his Followers Lo I am with you always even to the End.'[115]

---

111 Itinerant Society minutes, 22 Sept. 1797.
112 Itinerant Society minutes, 19 April 1804.
113 Itinerant Society minutes, 6 April 1798. No report of this tour was printed.
114 Itinerant Society minutes 22 January 1801.
115 Itinerant Society minutes, 23 January 1800.

But from 1804 the Society decided to grant only £5 *per annum* to any individual minister, so that the work of the Society from this time was widely diffused. The committee of the Society offered helpful advice to the itinerants. The wisdom of using only buildings duly licensed for worship was commended,[116] and one minister was warned about itinerating so much that his own church was neglected.[117] One preacher inquired about the ethics of raising baptism in his sermons, and was advised: 'This Committee do not think it advisable to say much upon that Subject at present to Persons unacquainted with the Gospel but that he must be left to his own Judgment taking into Consideration the Congregations he may be preaching to'.[118]

In an effort to discover how widely village preaching was being adopted throughout the country, the Society decided in 1805 to send a list of questions to a hundred ministers.[119] The result indicated great exertions were taking place, but no detailed analysis was undertaken: several churches were, however, sent tracts to assist them in their efforts. This is a reminder that between 1803 and 1808 (inclusive) Baptists had no *Register* or *Magazine* to publicize their efforts, or to provide a basis of accurate information. A suggestion from William Newman in 1809, that a Society of Baptist Itinerant Preachers, (designed to help supply churches near London and improve the preachers' gifts), should be formed, was judged to be beyond the Society's interests: and no further reference to the suggestion was made.[120]

Rippon, as indeed most of the ministers, attended irregularly after about 1808. (It will be recalled that Rippon was critically ill during 1809). Indeed, in 1810 the Rules were revised so that the committee consisted of nine laymen and three ministers, although the meetings were open to any minister.[121] The laymen obviously maintained the drudgery of committee work. The comparative ignorance of the denomination about the Society is revealed by the fact that no reports of its activities were given in the *Baptist Magazine* between 1809 and 1812. One of the objects of the proposed Baptist Union in 1812 was to support the Itinerant Society. Accordingly, in 1813 the *Magazine* outlined the functions of the Society, suggesting that its existence 'may be information to some' but that the Society 'has for many years been doing much good in a very silent and unostentatious manner... But the funds of the Society being small, its operation has been comparatively

---

116 Itinerant Society minutes, 9 March 1798. For problems associated with this, see Lovegrove, 'Particular Baptist itinerant preachers', pp. 136-39.

117 Itinerant Society minutes, 22 July 1802.

118 Itinerant Society minutes, 1 October 1799.

119 Itinerant Society minutes, 8 January 1805.

120 Itinerant Society minutes, 14 November 1809.

121 Itinerant Society minutes, 19 July 1810.

limited'.[122] After this year, regular reports of the Society were given at the London annual meetings in June, and published in the *Magazine*.

In 1821 the Society became known as the Home Missionary Society, but still emphasized the support of village preaching.[123] By this time the Society supported eight 'missionaries', and assisted sixty ministers in 'itinerant labours.'[124] Rippon's effective leadership had, not unnaturally, long since ceased. But his continued interest is recorded by his moving the adoption of the 1821 report of the Society. His venerable authority on the subject is suggested by his speech:

> One of my brethren, a beloved friend at my right hand, has just said to me, 'Sir, if you begin to speak, you know so much of missionary business both at home and abroad, that you will hold on till midnight.' Now I shall be very far from doing so, though I think he is one of the best of all the prophets that I am acquainted with. It is true I feel much for this cause; for I happened to be one of the first, if not the very first that engaged in the work of Home Missions; all the ground in the West of England I have gone over in the operation of village preaching, and I could detail some circumstances with great pleasure; but I forbear...[125]

The widespread adoption of village evangelism owed as much to the advocacy and example of Rippon as to any other contemporary Baptist.

Baptist Academies

Rippon's main interest was, naturally, with Bristol, his *Alma Mater*. He subscribed a guinea to the Bristol Education Society annually from 1773,[126] and in 1817, promised to give £20 for the debt on the new building of the Academy.[127] In 1776, he was requested to make an appeal in his church for the Society, but whether this was done is not apparent.[128] His most useful contribution to the Academy was, of course, the *Essay* in which he attempted its history. He was present in Bristol in 1795 to deliver this lecture, and again in 1797 (whilst on his itinerant preaching tour) to commend the application of James Douglas to the Academy.[129] He also prayed at the Annual Meeting of the Society in

---

122 *Baptist Magazine* 5 (1813), p. 279.
123 *Baptist Magazine* 13 (1821), pp. 261-64.
124 *Baptist Magazine* 13 (1821), p. 308.
125 *Baptist Magazine* 13 (1821), p. 309
126 Transactions of the Bristol Education Society (MS in Bristol College).
127 Transactions of the Bristol Education Society, 6 August 1817.
128 Transactions of the Bristol Education Society,14 August 1776.
129 Transactions of the Bristol Education Society, 31 July and 2 August 1797.

1817.[130] These references, together with his sending Carter Lane men to Bristol, confirm Rippon's continuing support of the Academy.

In London, an Education Society had been formed in 1752. This was only ever a small institution, and during Rippon's time in London did very little. Rippon certainly knew of the Society, for he obtained some support for George Keeley from its funds.[131] By 1805 only one trustee of this Society was still alive, so the capital was paid into the Particular Baptist Fund.[132]

However, a new Education Society was founded in 1804, largely under the inspiration of Abraham Booth. Rippon had in 1798 advocated the general cause of academies, and suggested increased adoption of the practice of suitable students being boarded with ministers.[133] It is clear, however, that many London pastors wanted an Academy in London. As early as 4 January 1803 William Newman wrote in his diary that such an academy had been proposed.[134] Again, on 18 October 1807 he wrote, 'We want a Baptist academy in London. Dr. Llewelyn, Dr. Stennett, Mr. Clarke [to whom students had been sent] had no great success.' These tutors had all been financed by the old Education Society. Rippon's share in these discussions is confirmed by Newman's entry for 19 May 1808, 'Dr. Rippon preached 'Give instruction to a wise man' &c. History of Baptist academies and tutors. The most animated meeting among Baptists I have ever witnessed'. Rippon was a member of the London Baptist Education Society's committee, as is revealed by a letter in which Thomas Thomas invited him to attend the meeting of 2 January 1810 at the King's Head in the Poultry.[135] That was an historic meeting, for it was announced that William Taylor of the Prescott Street church had given £3,600 so that suitable premises in Stepney Green could be purchased and an Academy begun. The Education Society was then merged with the Academy, subsequently to become Regent's Park College.[136]

Rippon did not play any effective role in the development of the new Academy. Newman, of course, had been baptized by Rippon and the two men were good friends. Rippon suggested that one of the objects of the

---

130   Transactions of the Bristol Education Society, 6 August 1817.

131   Last unnumbered page in MS records of the Society (in Angus Library).

132   G.P. Gould, *The Baptist College at Regent's Park... A Centenary Record* (London: 1910), p.16.

133   *Register* 3 (1798-1801), p. 40.

134   The earlier volumes of Newman's diary have not been located. For this, and the following entries, see *The Baptist Fund and Stepney* (London: 1876), p. 16.

135   B.L. Add. MSS. 25389, f. 255.

136   See Cooper, *From Stepney to St. Giles' The Story of Regent's Park College 1810-1960*, pp. 30-31. For a careful analysis of the links between the London societies, see A.J.H. Baynes, 'The Pre-History of Regent's Park College', *BQ* 36.4 (1995), pp. 191-201.

Baptist Union was better support for the academies. His own interest in the Stepney institution is confirmed by Newman's diary-entry for 23 January 1821, 'Dr. Rippon very affectionately inquired again, as he has often done, how things stood here'.[137] Newman was then experiencing practical problems of discipline in the Academy.

Rippon also retained a lively interest in the Rhode Island College, from which he had received his honorary degrees, the AM in 1784 and the DD in 1792.

Activities in Dissenting Societies

Rippon's genuine sympathy with all other Christian activities, whether Baptist or Calvinist or not, has been suggested in the preceding chapters. In particular, Rippon was sensitive to his responsibility as a Baptist for sharing fully in the combined activities of the Dissenters and, in some societies, with Evangelical clergy. Rippon's participation can only be traced in general ways: but all those listed certainly enjoyed his patronage and are indicative of his interest in other religious societies.

General Body of the Three Denominations

This 'Body' may be traced at least to the year 1702 when representatives of the three denominations (the Presbyterians, Congregationalists, and Baptists) joined in presenting an Address to Queen Anne on her accession.[138] The Body was the first attempt to establish close co-operation between all three groups, although Presbyterians and Congregationalists had shared in the abortive 'Happy Union' of 1690. Dissenting ministers 'residing in and about the cities of London and Westminster' composed the Body.[139] The intended instrument for political action was, however, the Dissenting Deputies, formed in 1732, with whom the General Body worked in close co-operation. Such political action was necessary, as we have noted, since even after the Toleration Act of 1689 Dissenters were only second-class citizens. After 1753 only weddings celebrated by the clergy of the Established Church were legally registered. Other issues raised by Dissenters in Rippon's time concerned the right to burial in parish churchyards, Education, Church Rates, and the recognition of Dissenters' Birth Registers. Rippon survived to see the Repeal of the Test and Corporation Acts in 1828. In an age of

---

137 Original MS in Regent's Park College.

138 G.F. Nuttall, *The General Body of the Three Denominations. A Historical Sketch* (printed privately, 1955), p. 2

139 The records from 1727 to 1836 are in Dr. Williams's Library.

intense political unrest, Rippon shared in seeking to redress the chief grievances of Dissenters through the General Body.

Rippon shared fully in the activities of the Body. He first attended a meeting on 23 March 1774 when he heard a report from a committee responsible for conducting an appeal for the repeal of the Test and Corporation Acts, but the campaign was postponed.[140] Each denomination nominated members for the general committee of the Body, and Rippon regularly accepted this representative responsibility.[141] He was often chairman of the Body's meetings.[142] It must be emphasized that Rippon did far more than any other contemporary Baptist in the work of the Body; he seems to have been the obvious Baptist representative from about 1795. Eventually, after the death of Abraham Rees in 1825, Rippon was generally recognized as the Senior London Dissenter, 'the father of the United body at Redcross Street'.[143]

The Dissenters' loyalty to the Hanoverian throne was expressed on every possible occasion. Their right of access to the Sovereign was a privilege greatly cherished and frequently exercised during Rippon's time. Addresses were presented in 1786, 1789, and 1795: but Rippon did not (evidently) share in the composition or presentation of these. In all the remainder, however, he was on the drafting committees and took part in the presentation of the addresses.[144] The full list of addresses reveals the trials and joys of the monarchy: 1800, to the King congratulating him on escaping from an assassination attempt;[145] 1802, to the King on the restoration of peace;[146] 1802, to the King after another 'escape'; 1814, to the Prince Regent on the second peace restoration; 1816, to the Prince Regent on his marriage to Princess Charlotte;[147] 1817, to the Prince Regent expressing disapproval of recent outrages;[148] 1817, to the Prince Regent, on the death of Princess Charlotte;[149] 1820, to George IV on his accession (ninety ministers were presented, Rippon being fourth in seniority); 1820, to the Duchess of Kent offering sympathy on the death of the Duke of Kent; 1830, to William IV on his accession to the

140 Minute-book of the General Body.

141 He served in at least the years 1776, 1777, 1782, 1785, 1794, 1797, 1801, 1804, 1807, 1818, 1816, and 1819: after this he was also frequently present.

142 He chaired meetings during 1797, 1803, 1805, 1814, 1816, 1817, 1819, 1820, 1821, 1828, 1827, 1830.

143 E.A. Payne, 'The Necrologies of John Dyer', *B Q* 13.7 (1949-50), p. 307.

144 From minute-books of the Body. The text of the address was normally printed in the *London Gazette*.

145 Cf. *Register* 3 (1798-1801), pp. 209-12.

146 *Register* 4 (1801-02), pp. 943-45.

147 Ivimey, *History of the English Baptists*, 4, p. 177.

148 Ivimey, *History of the English Baptists*, 4, pp.178-79.

149 Ivimey, *History of the English Baptists*, 4, pp. 188-89 (signed by Rippon).

Throne;[150] and in 1832 to the King after an attack on him. Rippon on some occasions read the Address, and clearly enjoyed sharing in the atmosphere of the Court. Spurgeon recounted that once, when reading an address to George III congratulating him upon recovery from sickness (possibly in 1803), Rippon emphasized a reference to the goodness of God by reading it to the King twice.[151] William Newman wrote in his diary describing the 1814 visit:

> ...The Prince received us very graciously; we kissed his hand... I was struck by the splendour and magnificence of the rooms exceeding by far everything I had ever seen... The Bishop of Exeter sneered and expressed his surprise that we did not appear in Court dress. He seemed to despise us because we had not on the 'Wedding garment'. We afterwards dined together at the New London and Dr. Rippon (who read the address in a very tender manner much impressed with the presence of the prince) presided with much good humour.[152]

Some brief account of the other efforts of the General Body, often in association with the Deputies, will both illustrate its interests and confirm the important role fulfilled by Rippon as the Baptist representative.[153] During 1785 Rippon was present in meetings that decided to combine with the Deputies in what proved to be the successful request to have an Act passed which extended the right of registration of burials, births, and deaths to Protestant Dissenters. Again, in 1788 the Body organized a petition for the abolition of slavery. In 1792 the ministers, in reaction to reports of the disloyalty of Dissenters, published a clear statement of their respect for 'that excellent Form of Government, by King, Lords, and Commons', and 'their abhorrence of all seditious practices'.[154]

The war years brought special problems. The Militia Bill of 1796, which proposed that the volunteers could be trained on Sundays, disturbed the ministers. Rippon, and two others, were appointed to request 'some Member or Members of the Upper House to move that the Lords Day be expressly excepted in the Militia Bill now pending in Parliament'. Rippon and his colleagues duly called on the Bishop of London, the Earl of Dartmouth, the Duke of Portland and sent a copy of the Body's declaration to the Archbishop of Canterbury.[155] The offending clause was duly removed from the Bill. In 1806 another protest against drilling of soldiers on Sunday was recorded.

---

150   *Baptist Magazine*, 22 (1830), p. 390.

151   Spurgeon, *The Metropolitan Tabernacle*, p. 51.

152   MS diary, 28 July 1814.

153   For the details of these activities, see B.L. Manning, *The Protestant Dissenting Deputies* (ed. 0. Greenwood; Cambridge: Cambridge University Press, 1952).

154   Minute book of the General Body, 20 December 1792: reports in 'daily and evening papers'.

155   Minute book of the General Body, 3 November 1796 and 10 January 1797.

Rippon was also appointed to a committee that in 1799 consulted with the Deputies as to the most efficient method of registering the births of Dissenters.[156] The Deputies had kept a general register since 1742, but as individual ministers could now keep them, some agreed pattern was advisable. Lord Sidmouth's attempt in 1811 to have all preachers licensed was defeated, largely by the prompt agitation of the Deputies and the ministers (with the Methodists) who amassed over seven hundred petitions against the proposal. This victory greatly encouraged the Dissenters.

One interesting activity of the Body's own initiative was the financial support it raised for persecuted French Protestants in 1816. (The broad details of this were given in chapter two, where Carter Lane's support was indicated). Rippon was appointed to the committee for 'Inquiry, Superintendence and Distribution' of this appeal, and was chairman of the meeting which received the official report of C. Perrot.[157] On 14 April 1813 it was announced that £6,374 had been distributed to the French people.

Rippon represented the Baptists on almost every committee set up by the Body. He was one of four who visited Lord Liverpool in 1819 about the position of Dissenters under the marriage laws.[158] Again, he was on a committee which met a group of Unitarians, for whom the use of the name of the Trinity in the marriage service was a special offence.[159] In 1820 Rippon was one who was appointed to express objections to Lord Brougham's proposed Education Bill which, in an effort to provide some comprehensive plan for education, suggested all teachers should be duly attested members of the Church of England.[160] Rippon with others stated their objections personally to Brougham and Lord Liverpool, and prepared petitions against the Bill which did not become law.

But the main object of Dissenters was the repeal of the Test and Corporation Acts. The General Body helped organize petitions for this in 1789, 1812, 1819, and 1827. Rippon was chairman of a special meeting of the Body on 13 November 1827 to discuss this object, and on 11 December an 'Address to Protestant Dissenters and the religious public in general, on the subject of the Corporation and Test Acts' was approved. Rippon signed this as chairman, and was one of a committee who had

---

156 Minute book of the General Body, 16 April 1799.

157 Minute book of the General Body, 28 November 1816.

158 Minute book of the General Body, 27 April 1819.

159 Minute book of the General Body, 5 July 1819. The Deputies did not assist in this campaign.

160 Minute book of the General Body, 14 February 1821.

prepared it.[161] The repeal of the Acts received Royal Assent on 9 May 1828, amidst considerable Dissenter jubilation.

Clearly the ministers were dependent upon the more influential Deputies, with whom they worked harmoniously, for most of their political effectiveness. But it must be recalled that the gathering of ministers also had a fraternal benefit: in 1802 Rippon and John Humphreys were asked to arrange for a room at the King's Head in the Poultry, where every Tuesday dinner and discussion were enjoyed.[162] Rippon, more active than any other Baptist and their inevitable representative, thus regularly mixed with men often of a much different theological outlook. Indeed, in 1836 eighteen Presbyterians and five General Baptists, Unitarians in principle, withdrew from the Body.

Rippon shared as fully as any London minister in the corporate life of the Dissenters, and by his willingness to accept responsibility as a Baptist representative in the service of the Body, was once again willingly serving the churches.

There were two other societies, connected with the General Body by foundation, in which Rippon was active. 'The Society for the Relief of Necessitous Widows and Children of Protestant Dissenting Ministers of the Three Denominations' was founded by the General Body in 1733. Rippon's encouragement of this charity was revealed in several ways. For example, he printed 'An Address to the Public' on behalf of the Fund in his *Register*.[163] This summarized the work of the Fund. Widows of any minister accepted and approved by his denomination at the time of death and in poor circumstances could apply for assistance. Each application had to be attested by one or more ministers, and signed by a member (that is, a subscriber) of the Society. In 1800, 154 widows were helped: ten guineas each to English widows, and eight guineas to Welsh widows. The funds were allocated by managers, twenty-four laymen, appointed annually. An annual sermon and public collection, was held every April at the Old Jewry meeting-house: Rippon preached this sermon on 11 April 1792, and was duly thanked by the Society.[164] In addition, Rippon probably encouraged two of his deacons who served as managers of the Fund: William Lepard (1800-1801) and William Burls (1812-1819, 1821-1826). In 1814 it was resolved that, in addition to the laymen, one minister of each denomination should be chosen for the committee:

---

161 The Catalogue of Dr. Williams's Library lists this as a pamphlet by Rippon, cf. Whitley, *Baptist Bibliography*, 2, ref. 29-827. This could not be located, but for the text of the address see *Monthly Repository*, n.s., 2 (1828), pp. 61-66. (I am obliged to Rev. Roger Thomas for this reference). The Minute book of the General Body indicates Rippon was one of a committee who drafted the address.

162 *Register* 4 (1801-02), p. 945.

163 *Register* 3 (1798-1801), pp. 426-428.

164 Minute-book of the Widows' Fund (in Dr. Williams's Library).

Rippon was the Baptist representative in the year 1817-18. In addition, Rippon signed requests for some Baptist widows and helped them with their applications.[165] The Widows' Fund was one of the charities suggested for the Baptist Union to support in 1813.

The other society was the Society for the Relief of Aged and Infirm Protestant Dissenting Ministers. Rippon seconded the motion that this Fund should be commenced at a meeting of the General Body on 14 April 1818, and was a member of the committee who arranged for its public inauguration.[166] Accordingly, at a public meeting in the King's Head in the Poultry on 2 June the Society was duly formed: its aims are sufficiently described by its title.[167] No further evidence of Rippon's activity for it has been found.

'Book Society'

Rippon first subscribed to this Society in 1775.[168] As previously noted, he preached the annual sermon for the 'Society for Promoting Religious Knowledge among the Poor' in 1796 and 1802, and this last sermon was a history of the Society and gave a summary of its activities. Some indication of the widespread nature of the Society's support is that the annual sermon was preached by men like George Whitefield (1767), William Romaine (1777), Henry Venn (1778), John Newton (1787) and Rowland Hill (1791).[169] In broad terms, the Society (which dated from 1750) arranged that individuals, or churches, such as Carter Lane, who subscribed to the funds could select an equivalent amount in books, tracts, or Bibles which were then distributed to those in need, usually by ministers to whom they were sent. The range of the literature was illustrated in Rippon's sermon who divided it into the following sections: 1. Books for Children and Youth, such as Watts' *Catechisms* and Janeway's *Token for Children*; 2. Books in opposition to Vice; 3. Books on the Nature and Necessity of the New Birth, including such works as Alleine's *Alarm to the Unconverted*, and Baxter's *Call to the Unconverted*; 4. Books on Family Religion; 5. Books on the Present and Future State; 6. Books on Personal and Progressive Religion, notably

---

165 Cf. B.L. Add. MSS. 25389, f. 59, f. 100; f. 504, etc.

166 Minute Book of the General Body, 14 April 1818.

167 Ivimey, *History of the English Baptists*, 4, pp. 191-92. See also R.W. Thomson, *Ministers in Need. The Story of the Society for the Relief of Aged and Infirm Protestant Dissenting Ministers 1818-1968* (London: Society for Relief of Aged Ministers, 1968).

168 *An Account of the Book Society for promoting Religious Knowledge among the Poor* (London: 1830), p. 27.

169 Rippon, *Discourse on Book Society*, pp. 69-70.

Doddridge's *Rise and Progress*; 7. Poetry, especially Watts' *Hymns and Psalms*; 8. Books on the Sacred Scriptures; and 9. Testaments and Bibles. Literally thousands of books were made available to the poor, and Rippon certainly encouraged his Baptist friends to support the Society. He received numerous letters that either requested books for the poor, or acknowledged their receipt.

Two other societies, Rippon noted, were commenced in emulation of the Book Society: one in Scotland in 1756, and the other in New York in 1794.[170] However, the rise of the Religious Tract Society, commenced in 1799, rapidly assumed the major functions of tract distribution. Rippon published the second annual report of the RTS but does not appear to have been active in it.[171] In concept this new society was not dissimilar to the older Book Society, but commanded a far greater support and seems to have been able to produce cheaper tracts. Rippon continued to support the 'Book Society', and was a listed receiver of subscriptions in 1821 and 1830.[172]

'Poor Africans Society'

Rippon's sympathy with the cause of black Christians in Jamaica, Georgia, and Sierra Leone has been noted. Not surprisingly, therefore, there are indications of Rippon's later interest in the plight of native Africans in England. There were great numbers of these in London: in 1772 it was estimated there were 14,000 slaves in England, most of them in London.[173] Many had run away from, or been deserted by their masters in England, or had come as stowaways or refugees. After the American peace of 1783 their numbers were increased when blacks who had served with British forces were sent either to Nova Scotia (as David George) or to London. Blacks became conspicuous among the beggars of London. A Committee for Relieving the Black Poor was formed with Jonas Hanway as chairman.[174]

However, one of the first efforts to help the blacks specifically in their religious worship originated from the Africans themselves. In April 1805 some of them applied to Dr. John Duncan, minister of the Peter Street, Soho, meeting-house that they might have opportunity 'to meet together for worship, as they had been rudely gazed at when they attended public ordinances individually and separately'. Duncan readily agreed, free

---

170 Rippon, *Discourse on Book Society*, pp. 64-65.

171 *Register* 3 (1798-1801), pp. 541-43.

172 *Baptist Magazine* 13 (1821), p. 170; *An Account of the Book Society for promoting Religious Knowledge among the Poor*, p. 27.

173 George, *London Life in the Eighteenth Century*, p. 140.

174 George, *London Life in the Eighteenth Century*, p. 143.

seats were provided in his chapel, and teachers were procured 'to instruct them in reading, writing, arithmetic, and especially in the principles of Christianity'. A special Sunday evening lecture was established for their benefit, and the first was held in May 1805 with Rowland Hill as preacher. Subscriptions for assisting Africans 'in poverty, sickness, and old age' were received. By 1807 ninety-two Africans had joined the Society, and many of them regularly attended services.[175]

Rippon preached at the Peter Street lectures from 1806,[176] and was a member of the committee in 1807,[177] if not from the commencement of the Society. In addition, he held a special service in Carter Lane on 27 March 1807 to commemorate the abolition of the Slave Trade.[178] He had encouraged the 'people of colour' to spend 'a day of prayer and public thanksgiving to God, in prospect of the grant of this astonishing salvation'.[179] On the day, 'between four and five hundred of these sable, grateful creatures met with us, seated principally in the gallery'. Rippon supposed that 'such a Body of Africans never before assembled for religious worship in any part of Great Britain'.[180] The sermon which Rippon preached from the text, 'Ethiopia shall soon stretch out her hands unto God,' was not published, although this was 'generally desired'. Rippon drew up a long 'Address' to those members of the Royal Family, of the Nobility, and of the gentry who had helped the cause of abolition.[181] This conveyed the gratitude of the blacks, and concluded:

> Our known friend, the Reverend John Rippon, DD, Dissenting Minister in Southwark, will at our request, place his signature to this our most humble and. grateful Address, and present it in our Name.
>
> Signed in virtue of the above Appointment,
>
> JOHN RIPPON.[182]

As already noted, Rippon later published a hymn sung at the service, and most probably composed by him.

Rippon's concern with the plight of the Africans, is reflected in his subject for the Fetter-Lane lecture on 24 December 1807: 'Compassion

---

175 *Evangelical Magazine* 15 (1807), p. 244.

176 *Evangelical Magazine* 14 (1806), p. 141.

177 *Evangelical Magazine* 15 (1807), p. 244.

178 Rippon, *Sermon...Demise of George III*, pp. 29-33; *Selection* (27th edn), note to hymn 535, part 3.

179 Rippon, *Sermon...Demise of George III*, p. 29.

180 Rippon, *Sermon...Demise of George III*, p. 33.

181 Rippon, *Sermon...Demise of George III*, pp. 30-33.

182 Rippon, *Sermon...Demise of George III*, pp. 32-33.

to Africans in England'.[183] His active sympathies with the cause of abolition were recognized by the letters F.A.A.S. placed after his name. As Rippon explained, this did not stand for Fellow of the Antiquarian Society, but Fellow of the American Abolition Society.[184]

It is not surprising that in 1815, when Baptists in the Bahamas wished to report on a religious revival and ask for funds, they should write to Rippon, whose name and reputation for care for native Christians was well known.[185]

Port of London Society

Rippon's congregation often included seamen, so that it was not surprising that he should have been present in the City of London Tavern, Bishopsgate Street, on 18 March 1818 when 'The Port of London Society for promoting Religion among Merchant Seamen' was formed.[186] The chairman was Benjamin Shaw, MP, and among those who spoke 'upon the important and interesting features of such a society' were Rippon, his younger friend the Congregationalist W. B. Collyer (1782-1854), and Joseph Ivimey. The Society purchased a vessel of nearly four hundred tons which was adapted to accommodate between seven and eight hundred hearers, so that the Gospel could be preached to sailors 'upon their own element'. Rippon's support for this society cannot be traced further, although brief reports about it were published in the *Baptist Magazine* from 1818 to 1824 inclusive.

Rippon was directly associated with these organizations. In what was essentially an age of societies for a multitude of religious and charitable purposes he was also most probably interested in others. For example, be led in prayer at the annual meeting of the London Missionary Society in 1801.[187] He was a Baptist trustee for the *Regium Donum*, the money distributed to needy Nonconformists from the Royal purse.[188] He received several letters asking for this gift, and requesting his presentation of their applications to John Martin and Timothy Thomas, the successive Baptist distributors.[189] Rippon offered the ordination prayer for two

---

183 *Evangelical Magazine* 15 (1807), p. 574.

184 *Sermon...Demise of George III*, 2nd edn, p. 34. No details of this society have been located.

185 *Baptist Magazine* 7 (1815), pp. 212-13. For the background, see P. Brewer, 'British Baptist Missionaries and Baptist work in the Bahamas', *BQ* 32.6 (1988), pp. 295-301.

186 *Baptist Magazine* 10 (1818), p. 159.

187 *Evangelical Magazine* 9 (1801), p. 246.

188 T. Rees, *A Sketch of the History of the Regium Donum* (London: 1834), p. 104.

189 Cf. B.L. Add. MSS. 25387, f. 140, f. 292, f. 349; 25389 f. 422, f. 496.

ministers designated in 1821 for evangelistic work in France, sponsored by the Continental Society, an inter-denominational group.[190] Although he is not known to have shared in the British and Foreign Bible Society, founded in 1804, he thought it in 1820 one of the glories of George III's reign and called it 'the wonder of the world! This unspeakable gift to the Universe'.[191]

Rippon clearly entered fully into the religious life of his day, and as a Baptist and a Dissenter, willingly served the churches.

Personal Activities

In addition to Rippon's representative work in various societies, he also gave valuable direct advice and assistance to individual churches and people. The evidence for this is mainly from letters written to him, and so is necessarily somewhat indefinite. As a result of his increasing prominence in the denomination he received innumerable requests of a quite extraordinary range.

One frequent service undertaken by Rippon was to help rural congregations and ministers. To find a suitable pastor was often a most frustrating and hopeless task for an isolated congregation. Similarly, if a minister felt obliged to seek another situation there was no appointed person or committee from whom he could seek advice. Consequently a man like Rippon, who probably knew more about the churches and ministers of the country than anybody else, constantly received requests for assistance. To take only those recorded in his surviving correspondence, some thirty churches or ministers sought his advice about this type of decision. Naturally, many of the churches were in the West Country, such as an assistant for Gibbs at Plymouth,[192] and ministers for Tiverton,[193] Exeter,[194] Dartmouth;[195] but Kent and the Midlands also figure frequently. The Dublin church sought his advice on several occasions.[196] Rippon's Carter Lane 'men' also looked to him for advice, as has been suggested.

Of course there were difficulties and delays in communication. An outstanding illustration of the difficulties encountered was the experience of Daniel Sprague. The Tiverton church found it increasingly difficult to support him, so in 1797 he moved to Alcester, in Warwickshire. But he

---

190 *Baptist Magazine* 13 (1821), p. 407.
191 *Sermon...Demise of George III*, p. 27.
192 Gibbs to Rippon, Plymouth, 15 April 1795, B.L. Add. MSS. 25387, f. 78.
193 Rippon recommended J. Douglas to Tiverton, and see below, for Sprague.
194 W. Moxey to Rippon, Exeter, 25 March 1815, B.L. Add. MSS. 25388, f. 107.
195 W. Willey to Rippon, Dartmouth, 17 May 1797, B.L. Add. MSS. 25389, f. 489.
196 Cf. B.L. Add. MSS. 25386, f. 335, 339; 25388, f. 354; 25389, f. 182.

found conditions there were even worse, so returned to Tiverton: the church welcomed him back quite happily.[197] Rippon appears to have shared in these plans, but the difficulties of trying to advise from a distance are apparent. There are several examples of Rippon suggesting evidently happy settlements, such as Atkinson at Margate, and J. L. Sprague at Bovey Tracey.

In addition, Rippon was often called upon to give advice to pastors or churches in dispute. For example, Benjamin Coxhead was involved in most trying circumstances at Truro in 1808: the church was divided over calling him, and the services were interrupted by the disputants. Rippon's advice was urgently sought:[198] what he suggested is unknown, but Coxhead left Truro the same year.[199] Rippon also helped to arbitrate in a dispute at the Pithay Church Bristol. One H. Perkins, evidently a paedobaptist minister baptized by Rippon in 1801,[200] was invited by some members to become assistant pastor to the aged John Sharp.[201] Others did not want him. He wrote to Rippon, 'Now I want your Advice. What shall I do? Shall I leave them ungratefully? Let them scatter? or shall I comply with their Request?'.[202] Once again, Rippon's advice is unknown, but it is significant that his opinion should be so earnestly solicited. The church at Watford (1783) also sought his help with an internal dispute.[203]

Then Rippon received numerous requests for all manner of personal assistance: to recommend churches or individuals to the various funds in which he had some influence; to help a surgeon gain a post;[204] to find lodgings or trade for friends,[205] to visit prisoners in gaol,[206] to advertise medical products,[207] etc. One interesting consequence of his interest in America was that many asked his advice about emigrating. One George Pearce, a shoemaker of Canterbury, proposed eighteen questions to Rippon, in particular whether he could be expected to make a better

---

197 Cf. *Register* 3 (1798-1801), pp. 9-10; letters from. Sprague to Rippon, 5 January, 19 May, 28 December 1797, B.L. Add. MSS. 25389, f. 131-33.

198 Coxhead to Rippon, Truro 10 February 1808, B.L. Add. MSS. 25386, f. 295.

199 See B. Coxhead, *Evangelical Advice and Encouragement. A Farewell Discourse addressed to a congregation in Ebenezer Chapel Truro, October 2d 1808* (London: 1808) and *Baptist Magazine* 1 (1809), p. 34.

200 N. Sharman to Rippon, Chenies, 11 February 1801, B.L. Add. MSS. 25389, f. 36.

201 'Copy of a letter Delivered to the Church meeting in the Pithay... 11 September 1804' (printed), B.L. Add. MSS. 25388, f. 264.

202 24 September 1804, B.L. Add. MSS. 25388, f. 265.

203 J. Stuart, *Beechen Grove Baptist Church, Watford* (London: 1907), p. 36.

204 I. Callaway to Rippon, 29 July 1817, B. L. Add. MSS. 25386, f. 176.

205 Many examples in correspondence.

206 M. Porter, Wokingham, 20 August 1797, B.L. Add. MSS. 25388, f. 307.

207 Rippon issued an advertisement for 'Perkins's metallic Tractors' with his *Register* number 25 (August 1801).

living in America.[208] Others sought his help in tracing relatives in America, or Americans asked similarly about British relatives.[209]

Thus in these more personal ways Rippon willingly served the churches. His popularity as an occasional preacher increased his influence, and yet another important activity was his leadership of the Baptist Union. He gave ample demonstration of his desire to remain 'in everlasting bonds' as 'the willing servant of the churches'.

208 Pearce to Rippon, Canterbury 26 June 1801, B.L. Add. MSS. 25388, f. 242.
209 For example, B.L. Add. MSS. 25387, f. 249.

CHAPTER 8

Rippon:
The Preacher and the Man

Whatever Rippon did as a Baptist leader was made possible because of his status as a leading London Baptist preacher. To appreciate his importance for contemporaries it is necessary to give careful attention to his success as a preacher, which inevitably reflected his own character and personality.

An estimate of Rippon's effectiveness as a preacher may be formed from three main sources. Six of his sermons were printed. Three were funeral sermons: for Andrew Gifford (1784), John Ryland (1792), and Abraham Booth (1806). That Rippon was selected to speak at the funerals for these three most significant and senior figures is strongly suggestive of his status and ability. One sermon was devoted extensively to a doctrinal theme, *Discourses on the All-Sufficient Gracious Assistance of the Spirit of Christ* (1800), although this was an expanded version of a funeral sermon for William Lepard, whose memoir was added to the sermon. The other two sermons were preached on occasions of national significance. The first, as noted in the last chapter, was preached 'at the Drum Head, on the Fort, Margate, Oct. 19, 1803, the Day of the General Fast, before the Volunteers, commanded by the Right Hon. William Pitt', and then repeated at the interdenominational East Kent Association meeting at Folkstone on 26 October, and at Carter Lane on 13 November before the volunteers of London and Southwark. The other printed sermon was preached after the death of George III (1820), and warranted a second edition.

A second source for an appreciation of Rippon's preaching is the descriptions, or reactions of those who heard him. Finally, the many demands made upon him as an occasional preacher in various parts of the country confirm the popularity and effectiveness of his preaching.

Theological   Position

A vital factor in understanding any preacher's influence is his general
theological perspective and certain emphases emerge with clarity from
Rippon's printed sermons. In particular, three facets should be noted: his
practice of a direct evangelical appeal; his Calvinistic orthodoxy; and his
tolerance of divergent Christian viewpoints. To recall his general
theological position, as previously noted, will be helpful.

The fundamental importance for Baptists of the controversy about
direct appeals to sinners was discussed in chapter one. An introduction to
the impact of Rippon's evangelistic preaching is the experience of a
young German man who attended Carter Lane in the company of a
young woman friend.[1] Although 'careless' of religion, when Rippon
announced in the sermon that he had 'an awful message in reserve for
the Sinner', the young man thought Rippon fixed his eye upon him. 'He
felt hurt at being pointed-out, as he imagined, and resolved not to attend
again'. However, the next week Rippon preached on the text, 'Let them
be ashamed that transgress without cause', and the young German, who
had come again, was deeply convicted. Shortly afterwards he became ill
and died, but not before a deathbed repentance, prompted by his
recalling Rippon's sermons. What is significant is, that, under God, as
Rippon would have insisted, his preaching had such a strong convicting
power.

His use of the direct appeal may be evidenced from most of Rippon's
published sermons. The first of these clearly reveals this. For example, he
began by confessing his 'utmost diffidence' in speaking on the occasion
(of Gifford's funeral), but his prayer was: 'O, that the dead in sin, may
hear the voice of the Son of God, in the ministry of the Word, and so hear
that they may live for ever!'.[2] During the sermon, Rippon exhorted
sinners to repent with a fervour as urgent as any nineteenth-century
revivalist. In the concluding section he renewed this appeal with a series
of rhetorical questions. There was an existential emphasis: '*And now this
very moment*, you stand between heaven and hell. See heaven on the *right*
- Behold the dreadful prison on the left!'. He continued:

> Hear it, hear it - The man who *will* not be saved by Christ Jesus, saved from all *sin*
> which is *hell* in this life, and punishment, which is one part of hell in the next
> world; that man *ought* to be damned - but his condemnation and endless misery will
> not be owing to any arbitrary or merciless decree in God - but wholly to his own bad

---

1   *Register* 3 (1798-1801), pp. 348-49.
2   *A Sermon occasioned by the death of the Reverend Andrew Gifford* (London:
1784), p. 3.

choice, and abominable conduct... Almighty Lord! turn their eyes to Calvary: help them to flee to Jesus, the sinner's friend, and, to escape the wrath to come.[3]

This was apparently a characteristic note of Rippon's sermons. At the funeral for John Collett Ryland he asked the 'professors of religion': 'You say you were born of religious parents; but have you been born again?'.[4] Similarly, addressing the volunteers, Rippon declared: 'Soldiers! hear a solemn truth, which is an essential part of the creed of King George, and of the religion of King Jesus - Except a man be born again ...'.[5] In his funeral sermon for Booth, Rippon referred to the late pastor's advocacy of the duty of sinners to believe. In the printed version Rippon added a footnote of twelve lines endorsing this position, and concluded: 'All that hear the Gospel are *welcome* to believe in Christ; may the blessed Spirit make them *willing* in the day of his power!'.[6] In his earlier sermon on the 'assistance' of the Holy Spirit, Rippon had emphasized that one must not only admit oneself to be a sinner but 'must also believe, that Christ is a Saviour, able and willing to help a coming soul, or he never will go to him for it'.[7]

Clearly Rippon consistently practised a direct appeal to the consciences of his hearers. In the theological context of the day this must have been based upon profound, deliberate belief: a conviction of great importance for all Rippon's activities, as has been suggested.

Rippon was also known for his orthodox Calvinism. Joseph Swain, as a young man recently converted, was advised by a friend who discovered Swain's sympathies were Calvinistic to go and hear Rippon, saying: 'I think his preaching would suit you'.[8] W.B. Collyer later commented of Rippon that his preaching was 'always founded on the great doctrines of the gospel'.[9] The *New Spiritual Magazine* said of him: 'His principles perfectly coincide with those of the Calvinistic Independents'.[10] Rippon's reputation for orthodoxy is justified by all his printed sermons. He was especially concerned to acknowledge the work of the Trinity in the life of the Christian. For example, speaking of God's love for the redeemed person, Rippon said:

---

3   *A Sermon occasioned by the death of the Reverend Andrew Gifford*, pp. 52-53.

4   *The Gentle Dismission of Saints from Earth* (London: 1792), p. 29.

5   *A Discourse delivered at the Drum Head* (London: 1803), p. 12

6   *A Sermon occasioned by the death of the Rev. Abraham Booth* (London: 1806), p. 63.

7   *Discourses on the All-Sufficient Gracious Assistance of the Spirit of Christ* (London: 1800), p. 26.

8   J. Swain, *Experimental Essays on Divine Subjects in Verse* (London: 1834), preface 'Memoir of the Life of the Author', p. xi.

9   *Pulpit* 29 (1837), p. 301.

10   *New Spiritual Magazine* 6 (1785), p. 1707.

The *Father* hath loved him, by giving Christ to suffering and death for him, that he might not perish. The *Son* hath loved him and redeemed him from sin and punishment. The *Spirit* hath loved him, applying the benefits of Christ's redemption to his heart, producing humiliation for sin, and sealing home the pardon of it.[11]

Rippon's one printed doctrinal sermon dealt with a theme for which he had a special regard: the Person and Work of the Holy Spirit. This theme was prominent in the *Selection* and more than one Carter Lane ministerial candidate was asked to preach upon it. In this sermon, which Rippon published as an essay of one hundred and four octavo pages, he showed that the ministry of the Spirit was sufficient for all the believers' needs: as the divisions of the sermon illustrate. The Spirit was sufficient for: 1. the direction and relief of inquiring Souls; 2. our performing, with cheerfulness, the various Duties of the Christian Life; 3. the support of his people under their most grievous temptations; 4. the mortification of sin; 5. growth in grace; 6. support and sanctify us in trouble, affliction, and old age; 7. all that is necessary to raise us at present above the fear of death, and to give us victory over the last enemy in our final conflict. Rippon insisted that many Trinitarians did not practically believe in the Spirit, and insisted that the Spirit was worthy of distinct exaltation and prayers could be addressed to Him.

Finally, Rippon's sermons evidence the spirit of toleration, previously noted in connection with his hymns and *Register*. In his sermon for Gifford, Rippon noted that the Eagle Street pastor had cherished a cordial respect for George Whitefield. Rippon thought Gifford's 'liberality' redounded to his honour, and added:

And till this spirit of catholicism prevails, not in word only, but in deed and in truth - prevails towards all who love our Lord Jesus Christ in sincerity; I fear much good will not be done, nor indeed can it be reasonably expected. Has any good been done by the contrary spirit, for the last fifty years?[12]

Again, in his address to the volunteers, Rippon remarked on the many people praying for their success and commented on the various groups:

BISHOPS of fragrant name and of exalted worth, with a far greater number of pious, laborious, and evangelical *Clergy*, than ever *any* previous age has seen illuminate and adorn the ESTABLISHED CHURCH. Hosts also of eminent and indefatigable *pastors and ministers*, among the PROTESTANT DISSENTERS, among the METHODISTS in their several classifications, and among those eminent

---

11   *A Sermon occasioned by the death of the Reverend Andrew Gifford*, p. 29.
12   *A Sermon occasioned by the death of the Reverend Andrew Gifford*, p. 47.

Missionaries, the MORAVIANS, are laying themselves out in all directions...with a view to humanize and christianize the world.[13]

Rippon warmly supported the general prayer issued by the Bishops for a recent fast day which included: 'Give us all grace to put away from us all rancour of religious dissension'.

These three elements - direct appeal to sinners, a full Trinitarian theology; and a catholic spirit - are all characteristics of his published sermons. This was not an original theology. But his preaching was a powerful advocacy of the best of Calvinism.

Preaching Method and Style

William Jay of Bath, a contemporary of Rippon, described the sermons of earlier eighteenth-century Dissenters as 'not only orthodox but studied, grammatically correct, and methodical; but, with a very few exceptions, pointless, cold, and drawled off from notes.'[14] However, the Evangelical Revival, and in particular the preaching of Whitefield, largely altered the preaching style of the evangelical Dissenters. This new style among Dissenters has been summarized by Michael Watts: 'extempore, emotional, passionate, dramatic, designed to bring the hearer to a pitch of excitement at which he would respond to the call to confess that he was a sinner and that he was in need of salvation'.[15] The effective sermon was frequently described as 'pathetic' - in its literal sense.

Rippon's preaching was emphatically of this new style, as a patronizing review of Rippon's funeral sermon for Andrew Gifford indicates:

We have no Predilection for that style of oratory for which these discourses are so singularly conspicuous. It may nevertheless have its uses... There are persons whom they may affect, and that too with more certainty, and with a deeper influence, than discourses formed on the most correct and refined model of eloquence...[16]

Rippon praised the liveliness of Gifford:

His heart was in the work, and upon some occasions particularly, it might have been said of him, as it was of one of the blessed reformers, *Vividus vultus, vividi oculi, vividae manus denique omnia vivida*. His countenance was alive, his eyes

---

13   *A Discourse delivered at the Drum Head*, pp. 37-38.
14   Quoted by Jones, *Congregationalism in England 1662-1962*, p. 165.
15   Watts, *The Dissenters*, 2, pp.177-78.
16   *Monthly Review* 72 (1785), p. 79.

were alive, his hands were alive, in short all was alive. If ever any man was all alive in the public service Dr. Gifford was the man...[17]

This same quality was found in Rippon himself, for vivacity and animation were features of his style noted by contemporaries.[18] His voice was 'manly',[19] but his sermons were also 'affectionate' and emotional. Typical was this extract from the sermon to the volunteers, admittedly an emotional occasion:

> If you are to enter an actual service, and must leave your home, we will shed the friendly tear of affection over you at parting. Our bursting hearts, as you pass our doors, will say; Each of these fine fellows had a *mother*; some of them have affectionate *wives*, and many of them have sweet and lovely *children*, dearer than cherubs. Wherever you go, our earnest intercessions to God shall follow you.[20]

Funeral sermons were occasions exploited by many preachers, not least by Rippon. He began an emotional conclusion to his sermon for Booth thus: 'We are now, in a few moments, to deposit this corpse in its dreary grave; but before we do it, cast, with me, your tearful eye once more on the coffin - pause - and then if you are able -each in his own character bid *Adieu*.' Booth's brother, children, church-members, fellow-ministers, *etc*. were all personally addressed in turn. Rippon continued: 'But we will copy thy example; we will follow thy advice; we will imbibe thy spirit; we will recollect thy sermons and prayers, we will bedew thy grave with our tears...'[21] Tears seem almost to stain the printed page.

Yet Rippon's sermons were not all sentiment. They reflected considerable thought and planning, although in general he seems to have preached either extempore or from shorthand notes. Normally he preached from a text, and for special occasions selected strikingly appropriate verses. Thus his address to the volunteers was based on Deuteronomy 23: 9, 'When the host goeth forth against thine enemies, then keep thee from every wicked thing.' The sermons were clearly divided into several sub-sections. This is illustrated in the sermon for Ryland, and at the same time his concern to investigate in full the background of his texts is shown. The text was 2 Timothy 4: 6: 'The time of my departure is at hand'. After giving the general setting of the text, Rippon began by listing the various classical allusions of 'departure' ('analusis') and derived several sub-headings. The departure was likened to a prisoner loosed from his chains, travellers departing from an inn on

---

17   *A Sermon occasioned by the death of the Reverend Andrew Gifford*, p. 44.
18   J. Stoughton, *History of Religion in England*, 7, p. 282.
19   *New Spiritual Magazine* 6 (1785), p. 1707.
20   *A Discourse delivered at the Drum Head*, p. 40.
21   *A Sermon occasioned by the death of the Rev. Abraham Booth*, pp. 95-96.

their way home, an anchor weighed from the shore, the soul leaving the body. The lessons of the text were that Christians should moderate their joys and sorrows respecting all terrestrial things, look back and enquire how they had filled the stations they were about to leave, ask themselves where they were going, and pay an immediate attention to the concerns of their souls and eternity.

Rippon's published sermons contained several footnotes giving references or extracts, from various commentators. In his sermon on the Holy Spirit ten different authorities were quoted, but most frequently Owen, Goodwin, and Gill were used.

Many common rhetorical devices are evident in Rippon's sermons. When applying a point directly to his hearers he often employed a long series of rhetorical questions. For example, in his sermon for Booth, Rippon listed various qualities of the deceased pastor. After each one he asked his listeners how they had responded to it: 'It is certain that he preached as a *dying* man to dying men: Did *I* certainly hear as a dying man? and then go away, and think, and speak, and live accordingly - live for eternity.' [22]

Alliteration was often used. He 'dropped', on one occasion, 'a word of caution, of counsel, and of congratulation'.[23] He addressed the volunteers: 'instead of dismay, defeat, and death, we contemplate glory and renown'.[24] Rippon also excelled in the anecdote that led to some pithy saying. For example, he told a story of an encounter between the famous actor Garrick and a simple half-witted soul which climaxed in the saying, 'Heaven is a prepared place for a prepared people'.[25] Another example was: 'How evident it is that the best of men are but men at the best!'[26] The sermon for Gifford was concluded by three sentences that Rippon said summed up his message for all his hearers:

> Make much of the holy Bible!
> Make much of the holy Jesus!
> Make much of the holy Spirit![27]

Rippon loved vivid metaphors, often Biblical but more often original, and dramatic descriptions. Both the use of metaphors and alliteration appear in his description of the backsliding believer:

---

22 *A Sermon occasioned by the death of the Rev. Abraham Booth*, p. 91.
23 *Discourses on the All-Sufficient Gracious Assistance of the Spirit of Christ*, p. 103.
24 *A Discourse delivered at the Drum Head*, p. 41.
25 *The Gentle Dismission of Saints from Earth*, p. 23
26 *A Sermon occasioned by the death of the Reverend Andrew Gifford*, p. 11.
27 *A Sermon occasioned by the death of the Reverend Andrew Gifford*, p. 56.

My harp was unstrung, and all my instruments of mirth lay neglected on the ground. I found myself, as it were, in an enclosure of cypress and yew, my head bound round with weeping willows, and the winds wafted my melancholy murmurs thro' all the groves.[28]

With but a little imagination, the dramatic impact of Rippon's description of a savage American Indian, obviously informed as a result of his absorbing interest in the subject, may be appreciated:

Methinks I see that juvenile Sachem - the tufted feathers wave on his head - his hair in double tresses drops loosely on this side and on that, decorated with corals and silver rings - a piece of gold is suspended from the cartilage of his nostrils, and the lappits of his ears are hung with pearls, with flowers, and with silver crosses. - This part of his face is streaked with blue, the emblem of peace among Indians; and that part of it with vermilion, the signal of readiness for war. A broad collar of violet wampum ornaments his breast, on which hangs the scalping knife - in his hand is the tomohawk *(sic)* - his hatchet is slung on his girdle, and in all the insolence of pride he says, An Indian cares not for the long-knives, meaning the Americans, nor for the God of the long-knives.[29]

Not surprisingly, Rippon also made frequent use of hymns and poems in his sermons.

His preaching was clearly dramatic, direct, interesting, emotional, and effective. His enthusiasm sometimes led him into extravagances. W.B. Collyer, himself a refined preacher with 'a marked resemblance to the Addisonian model' and thought to be 'exactly the preacher for nice young ladies,'[30] said that Rippon's preaching was 'sometimes eccentric in its manner'.[31] Timothy Thomas, in a friendly letter to Rippon, commented on 'colloquial ebullitions, which upon other occasions have escaped you'.[32]

More savage was the criticism of Rippon by Benjamin Flower. Commenting on his sermon and memoir for Booth, he accused him of 'a mass of bombastic flattery' and 'pulpit buffoonery' by taking a single word and using it as a text. In particular, he was dismissive of his chosen text for Abraham Booth: 'They which be of faith are blessed with faithful Abraham'. Flower wondered that he did not find a text with the word 'booth' in it as well. This 'farrago of bigotry and calumny' was only to be despised; he thundered. Flower, of course, was incensed by Rippon's reference to Booth's attack on the views of Robert Robinson, Flower's

---

28   *A Sermon occasioned by the death of the Reverend Andrew Gifford*, pp. 13-14.

29   *Discourse...Society for promoting Religious Knowledge among the Poor* (London: 1802), p. 24.

30   Quoted by Jones, *Congregationalism in England 1662-1962*, p. 219.

31   *Pulpit* 29 (1837), p. 301.

32   Islington, 14 November 1805, B.L. Add. MSS 25388, f. 263.

respected mentor.[33] But, of course, this criticism says as much about Flower and his views as it does about Rippon.

Undoubtedly the unexpected, the novel and the colloquial constituted a large part of Rippon's appeal to many of his regular listeners. However, to sustain such a long ministry, as Rippon did, suggests that his freshness and vigour were dependent more upon solid evangelical teaching than oratorical device.

Popularity as a Preacher

Rippon gradually came to be in great demand as a preacher for special occasions in the life of the churches. His other activities meant that he became increasingly well known. Rippon preached the special sermon at the opening of the following new meeting-houses: Chesham (1797), Bow (1801), Ilford (1801), Camberwell (1802), Eythorn (1804), Eynsford (1807), Poplar (1808), Chesham (1811, again), Hackney (1812), Deal (1814), Chatham (1814), Margate (1815), Tring (1818), Moorfields Welsh Chapel (1823), Tottenham (1824), and Uffculm, Devon (1824).[34] Doubtless there were others, not recorded in contemporary periodicals. Rippon was evidently invited on these occasions in part for his ability to prompt his hearers to give generously to the inevitable collection towards the cost of the building. William Newman wrote a grateful letter thanking him for his sermon at the opening of Bow, and suggested that Rippon should print the sermon in the *Register*:

> I sincerely wish I could see there not barely the outline of your Sermon but several full paragraphs and particularly the concluding part 'Jesus and his Sandals'. I detest Flattery while I cannot help saying I think that was one of the finest Specimens of - but I forbear - forgive me. We owe half the Collection for that one passage. I wish you could write it down exactly as you delivered it. The collection was in the morng £23 odd ...[35]

Rippon also shared in numerous ordinations, more often offering the important ordination prayer than preaching, although he preached at the ordinations of most of his Carter Lane men. He preached many funeral sermons, some of which have been noted, but also for other ministers such as John Chamberlain at Guildford in 1792.[36] Coventry invited him

---

33   Flower (ed.), *Miscellaneous Works of Robert Robinson*, 1, pp. lxxxiv-lxxxviii.

34   Compiled from various sources, but mainly from: *Register; Evangelical Magazine; Baptist Magazine*.

35   26 May 1801, B.L. Add. MSS. 25388, f. 131.

36   *Register* 3 (1798-1801),p. 34, note 286.

to preach at the Sunday School annual services in 1808 and 1816, and appreciated his services.[37] Numerous other invitations are revealed from his correspondence. Certainly he preached regularly at numerous 'lectures' associated with various London Churches. Exactly when he commenced or ceased preaching at some of these is not clear, but he is known to have shared in at least ten such regular lecture arrangements.[38]

This broad outline evidences Rippon's popularity as a preacher. He was not, of course, the outstanding Baptist preacher of the day: Robert Hall clearly deserved that reputation. But he was obviously one of the leading Baptist preachers in London, perhaps the best known in his most active years. His popularity as a preacher encouraged acceptance of his views and plans for the denomination, and so is important in consideration of his total influence upon the Baptists.

The Man

Before considering Rippon's role in the Baptist Union, which in some ways epitomized much of his life's work, some account of his family and personal life is necessary. As far as is known his private life did not enter into his public life and, consequently, only little of the former has been preserved.

Rippon married a widow, Mrs. Sarah Pyne (1738-1831), at St. Olave's, Southwark on 7 December 1773 and as Mrs. Sarah Rippon she joined the Carter Lane church on 13 February 1774. She died on 1 January 1831, aged ninety-two, older than Rippon by some twelve years.[39] Her advanced age can only have made it difficult for Rippon during the 1820s, and may perhaps help to explain some of his own temperamental attitudes to the church. Only passing references to Mrs. Rippon were made in extant letters to Rippon, but George Hall of Ipswich wrote of her: 'I have an high esteem of that worthy woman having for years thought her an excellent amiable character'.[40] Mrs. Rippon was interred in Bunhill Fields, and the funeral sermon was preached by W. B. Collyer.

---

37   F. Franklin to Rippon, Coventry, 11 March 1808 and 8 March 1816, B.L. Add. MSS. 25387, ff. 34-35.

38   The following list is mainly based on: letters to Rippon, *Register*, *Evangelical Magazine*, and *Baptist Magazine*. The year is the first in which Rippon is known to have shared in that lecture: Curriers' Hall, (Sabbatarian), (1774: see Ivimey, *A History of English Baptists*, 4, p. 326); St. Helen's (1774), Walworth (1779), Broad Street (1801), Fetter Lane (1801), Camomile Street (1802), Peter Street (1806), Dean Street (1806), Shakespeare's Walk (1809), Union Street (1809).

39   *Baptist Magazine* 23 (1831), p. 154.

40   B.L. Add. MSS. 25387, f. 154.

John and Sarah Rippon had four children, two boys named John and Benjamin, and two daughters, Martha and Mary. There are several sympathetic references in letters to Rippon, especially between 1790 and 1803, to domestic trials and afflictions. Both the sons evidently acquired considerable debts. John became a solicitor, and in 1811 published *Most Rapacious Atrocities Unmasked; or A Narrative of Unparallelled Enormities committed by Beriah Drew, attorney at Law, against John Rippon, of the Same Profession.* This candidly records that John had 'very imprudently incurred debts during my minority, to the amount of several hundred pounds', which 'pride and folly' constrained him to conceal when he began his clerkship. Consequently, he had a constant struggle against 'pecuniary embarrassment'.[41] John set up practice at 116 London Road, Southwark, but met with opposition from Mr. Drew, named in the pamphlet, who had long had an office in the area. Drew's 'unparallelled enormities' consisted of exact and prompt suing of John for debts. Evidently John was an unstable youth, and this can only have added to his parents' worries but John did help his father with the Bunhill Fields project, as was noted.

Less is known about Benjamin, evidently a somewhat wild youth. He borrowed money without repaying,[42] like John, and was described as a 'prodigal'.[43] Missionary doctor John Thomas referred to Benjamin's 'wild oats' and anticipated welcoming Benjamin in India.[44] In 1795 J. L. Sprague had asked Rippon if he would like his son to join the navy as a midshipman,[45] and in 1797 Thomas Chorlock of Exeter told Rippon that Benjamin had gone to Upottery to visit his grandfather since the ship in which he was due to sail to India was damaged.[46] Parcels for Benjamin were being delivered to vessels as late as 1806,[47] but nothing else is known of him. Rippon's public achievements were in spite of certain burdens in his family life.

Martha, who married Samuel Gale, the solicitor and a deacon of Carter Lane, had died by 1826.[48] Mary married Daniel Norton, also a solicitor.[49]

---

41   *Most Rapacious Atrocities*, p. 11.

42   I. Pike to Rippon, Newton Abbot, 9 November 1797, B.L. Add. MSS. 25388, f. 282.

45   A. Carroll to Rippon, Northampton, 12 November 1796, B.L. Add. MSS. 25386, f. 198.

44   24 November 1799, B.L. Add. MSS. 25389, f. 247.

45   Plymouth, 12 March 1795, B.L. Add. MSS. 25389, f. 141.

46   12 September 1797, B.L. Add. MSS. 25386, f. 246.

47   W. Kingsbury to Rippon, Southampton, 7 April 1804, B.L. Add. MSS. 25387, f. 402.

48   Reference in Rippon's will.

49   Reference in Rippon's will.

In his will, Rippon named John and Mary, as well as the grandchildren of Martha and Samuel Gale, and the Pyne family. Although Rippon was supposed to have received 'an estate' from the sale of his *Selection*,[50] the probate granted was for only £3,000.

Rippon can have had little time for leisure or family-life, for his commitments were numerous. There was one unusual hobby, suggested by a reference in the *New Spiritual Magazine*: 'Mr. Rippon is said to be remarkably ready at inventing coats of arms for the different denominations'.[51] One example of this is perhaps the medallion which Rippon described as suitable for Gill.[52] Clearly Rippon had a comprehensive library, and in particular an outstanding collection of Americana. The Bodleian Library (Oxford) has an 1861 'Catalogue of a very curious and interesting collection of Books and Tracts wholly relating to America (the major part of which are from the Library of the late Rev. John Rippon, D.D., eminent Baptist minister).'[53] The range of this collection of 426 items was extraordinary, as the auctioneers' summary detailed:

> Comprising very numerous examples of New England Typography during the last century; tracts of local and biographical interest, and of importance for the history of religion in America; Books in foreign languages, chiefly voyages, travels, relations, etc. also some Highly Important Manuscripts, consisting of official documents connected with the affairs of Spanish America, presenting ample particulars of matters of government, commerce, trade, finance, mines, foreign polity, ecclesiastical establishments, jurisprudence, slavery, the Indians, etc. etc.'

That this remarkable Library was dispersed is singularly unfortunate. Much of it was what would have been expected from Rippon's known contacts with America: the books of Backus, Stillman, association reports, etc. Clearly Rippon's interest in Americana continued after the finishing of the *Register*. The manuscript collections (if they were Rippon's) confirm his remarkable interest in foreign lands. They are documents chiefly relating to South America, so how Rippon could have come to possess them is a mystery for they included State papers.

Rippon was a complex character. His life was devoted to his own church and to promoting greater unity and toleration among Christian people. He was a warm and emotional person, an attractive personality who evoked life-long loyalty and friendship. His conversation was witty and informed, a colourful character who enjoyed the esteem of his fellow-ministers. Newman wrote in his diary on 24 October 1832: 'Dr.

---

50   Spurgeon, *The Metropolitan Tabernacle*, p. 51.
51   *New Spiritual Magazine* 6 (1785), p. 1708.
52   *Memoir of Gill*, pp. 12-14.
53   Mus. Bibl. III 532 (14).

Rippon, green as a plant, juvenile as ever, told us that this day 60 years ago he came to London. Next day preached his first sermon. Aspland proposed his health. His acknowledgment very serious and tender.'[54] Again, Rippon who was 'intimately acquainted' with John Ryland from 1771, made a special journey to Weston-super-Mare to visit his dying friend in 1825.[55]

Yet in his own relations, especially in his older years, Rippon could be temperamental, easily offended, and stubborn. This appeared in some of his relations with his church, and it was also true in his wider London Baptist contacts. On 1 November 1808 Newman wrote: 'At coffee-house, a violent altercation between Dr. R(ippon) and Gutteridge concerning the new Baptist Magazine.'[56] Andrew Fuller referred in several letters to Rippon's strained relations with some other London ministers between 1809 and 1811.[57] On 6 February 1809 he wrote to Ward, 'At London they are united, they say, like pebbles in a halter... Rippon & Dore are always at variance.' In May 1810 he wrote: 'Rippon has so offended his brethren that he stands aloof. I have offered to be a Mediator between them provided each declares the desire to be reconciled. They did declare it; but he will not. His best friends are greatly hurt with him, and I fear he will essentially hurt himself.' The following January, Fuller (three years younger than Rippon) wrote: 'Dr. Rippon gets old and obstinate. The other ministers wd forgive & forget all - but he will not'. Unfortunately the details of the dispute are not given. By March 1811 the situation seems to have improved,[58] and in the following year Rippon was leading the Baptists into the Baptist Union plans, evidently enjoying the respect of all his brethren.

Rippon was not, of course, the first man to advocate greater unity only to find that his own impatience and temper led him into personal disputes. He may have been domineering and proud. Indeed, his use of the title 'Doctor' was open to misunderstanding. Some of the locals in Southwark thought that Rippon had taken money from the poor to get his doctorate.[59] Some ministers, such as Fuller, would not use the title. Robert Robinson declined a DD from Edinburgh, his biographer

---

54 Original in Angus Library. For the Unitarian Robert Aspland (1782-1845) see *DNB*.

55 J. Ryland, *Pastoral Memorials: selected from the Manuscripts of the late Revd. John Ryland, D.D. of Bristol: with a Memoir of the Author* (2 vols; London: 1826), 1, p. 36.

56 For Joseph Gutteridge (1752-1844) see *BHS Trans* 7 (1920-21), p. 205. Newman had several disagreements with Gutteridge, who was treasurer of Stepney Academy.

57 Typescript collection of Fuller's letters in Angus Library.

58 A. Fuller to J. Sutcliff, 12 March 1811 seems to reflect a happier situation.

59 Watford to Rippon, January 1803, B.L. Add. MSS. 25389, f. 412.

claimed.[60] Rippon's own attitude emerges from this shrewd comment by Fuller: 'When Dr. Rippon was joked for double D, he pleaded the advantage it was to him as an author. He had rather be tho't avaricious it seems than vain'.[61] Whatever his failings of temperament and character, there can, however, be no detracting from the undoubted value of Rippon's influence on his denomination.

Rippon died on 17 December 1836, and his funeral was held on 24 December in the New Park Street chapel. For the previous eight or nine Sundays his church members, as many as could be admitted, had gathered in his bedroom to pray with him, but his decease must have been a merciful release.[62] He was interred, inevitably, in Bunhill Fields where he had spent so many of his living hours. His vault was placed, as nearly as could be reckoned, on the spot where the old archway or original entrance to the ground from Bunhill Row had been, a site selected by his son John.[63] The sermons were preached by Dr F.A. Cox (1783-1853) of Hackney, Charles Room, and on the following Sunday by Dr W.B. Collyer. Room referred to the fact that all were conscious that his decease had taken place 'amidst the decripitude of years, the decay of nature, and the eclipse of intellect',[64] but all speakers paid warm tributes to the effectiveness of his active years. The inscription on the tomb reads:

The Rev. John Rippon, D.D., for 63 years pastor of a Baptist Church in Carter-Lane, Southwark; as a man and as a minister, he was endeared to all who intimately knew him. His talents pre-eminently qualified him for the useful and acceptable discharge of his Public Duties. Affable in manner, affectionate in disposition, animated in the pulpit, in doctrine incorrupt, unwavering in principle; his preaching was attractive, and his labours were abundant and successful. Among his varied services in the cause of religion, by none was he better known, or will be longer remembered in the Churches at home and abroad, than by the judicious and comprehensive Selection of Hymns, bearing his name which has aided the devotions and inspired the praises of myriads of his fellow-Christians.

Dr. Rippon, pastor of the Baptist Church, Carter Lane, Tooley-street, Southwark, sixty-three years, died 17th December, 1836, in the 86th year of his age.

In the privacy of his diary, John Dyer recorded Rippon's death and commented: 'Dr. R. had his excellencies & his failings also, but he was doubtless a good & useful man. May I be ready to follow him. I do not wish to live so long.'[65]

---

60   B. Flower, *Miscellaneous Works of Robert Robinson*, 1, p. cxxvii.
61   Fuller to W. Ward, 12 September 1805.
62   Funeral sermon by Collyer, *Pulpit* 29 (1837), p. 301.
63   B.L. Add. MSS. 28515, f. 176.
64   *Pulpit* 29 (1837), p. 301.
65   Payne, 'The Necrologies of John Dyer', p. 301.

CHAPTER 9

Rippon and the Baptist Union

An important example of Rippon's direct leadership among the Particular Baptists was his share in the formation and early leadership of the Baptist Union. In many senses it crowned and recapitulated his lifelong interests and deepest concerns. The story of the Union has been well told,[1] but it will be helpful here to indicate in greater detail Rippon's prominence in the early years of the Union. Although the success of the Union was only moderate in Rippon's lifetime, the central functions of the modern Union are directly traced to this earliest attempt.

Rippon's *Register* was one of the most important factors that had prepared for a national union. Rippon had done more than any other living person to introduce Baptists to one another. In the preface to his *Register* he had suggested that the regular combined gatherings of the Wesleyans, the Moravians, and the Quakers should provoke Baptists to imitation.[2] Moreover, the General Baptists who held an Annual Assembly, and the New Connexion of General Baptists who met separately, also provided examples. When Rippon printed the reports of the Philadelphia Association's proposal to hold a 'General Conference' of representatives from all the American associations, he commented:

> A similar object in England has, year after year, been matter of conversation among the ministers in London; but no specific plan is *yet* laid, and perhaps cannot be without previous communications between some of the brethren in town, and in different parts of the country. - EDITOR.[3]

But nothing was done until 1812. Six years previously the Congregationalists had first considered forming a union. This happened

---

1   Payne, *The Baptist Union.*
2   *Register* 1 (1790-93), p. iii.
3   *Register* 3 (1798-1801), p. 262.

in 1808, but it met with much criticism, languished, and in 1827 was merged with a Home Missionary Society.[4]

The delay by the Baptists may be attributed to several causes. Paramount probably was the common preference for talk rather than action. The denomination had many demands made upon it by existing societies that nevertheless must have continually tended to draw the churches together: the Baptist Fund, the Academies, the BMS, and the Itinerant Society. Moreover there was no regular Baptist periodical after the *Register* ceased until the *Baptist Magazine* began in 1809.

It was within the pages of the *Magazine* that the idea of the Union began to be seriously mooted. In June 1811 a paper by Ivimey, 'Union essential to Prosperity' was published, and two months later 'B.D.' contributed a similar article.[5] In October, the North Wales Association resolved, 'That a closer union and connexion among the Baptists throughout England and Wales, Ireland and America, would be a glorious thing, and we resolve to do all in our power to promote it'.[6] A further article, 'On a general Union of the Baptists' appeared in April 1812.[7]

Clearly the discussions were becoming more intensive. The principal reason why something was eventually achieved in 1812 was probably that, for the first time, the London June BMS meeting was planned for a Wednesday. For the preceding seven years these services had been held on Sundays, and it was hoped that the change would allow more ministers and people to attend.[8] Accordingly, the *Baptist Magazine* was able to announce that the day after the missionary meetings a gathering would be held in the Carter Lane church to discuss plans for 'an annual general association of the Particular Baptist Churches'.[9] One ingenious article reminded readers that the Baptists had held such an important gathering in 1689: 'The Fathers of the Particular Baptist Churches in England, to their Sons, in the year 1812', 'signed' by William Collins, Andrew Gifford, Henry Forty, William Kiffin, Hanserd Knollys and Benjamin Keach.[10] This epistle from the celestial regions lamented the failure of the 1689 plans, and exhorted support for the latest venture. Although the records of the Baptist Board do not refer to the subject, it is most

---

4   A. Peel, *These Hundred Years. A History of the Congregational Union of England and Wales, 1831-1931* (London: Congregational Union, 1931), pp. 5-44.

5   *Baptist Magazine* 3 (1811), pp. 234-37, 326-30. Payne, *The Baptist Union*, p. 18, suggests 'BD' was B.H. Draper.

6   *Baptist Magazine* 3 (1811), p. 437.

7   *Baptist Magazine* 4 (1812), pp. 157-61.

8   *Baptist Magazine* 4 (1812), p. 352.

9   *Baptist Magazine* 4 (1812), p. 274.

10   *Baptist Magazine* 4 (1812), pp. 243-45.

probable that the actual plans for the first meeting arose out of their informal discussions.[11]

The first meeting was duly held in the vestry of Carter Lane, at 8 a.m. on Thursday, 25 June 1812. Rippon, as 'a respected elder statesman'[12] and who, with Ivimey, stood out for 'vision and patience in holding the Calvinistic Baptists together'[13] was 'the obvious chairman'.[14] At least sixty ministers were present, for this number later signed in favour of the new union. It is significant that Rippon is known to have been personally acquainted, either with the minister himself or with his church, of forty-two of these. Probably he knew most of the others. After Dr Ryland had prayed, Rippon delivered an important address that reviewed the general objects of the proposed 'United Association'. The following long extract shows just how the aims of the new Union closely corresponded with those to which Rippon had devoted so much of his life, especially in his *Register*:

That one of the first and most important duties of it would no doubt be solemn PRAYER to the God of all Grace for the eminent out-pouring of his Holy Spirit on the Churches, and the whole world - a Duty, on which neither preaching, nor business of any kind should be suffered to trench. That at such meetings our MISSION in the East Indies would necessarily present a signal object of regard; when we should be able to recommend Auxiliary Societies, or Annual Collections for its support, in the far greater part of our Congregations.

That the yearly Accounts of the state of religion transmitted from the Associated Churches, and others, would create an endless variety of claims, either on our sympathy, or gratitude, or our benevolence, and, some of them, on the united exertions of the whole body.

That our ACADEMIES, the larger and smaller, would have their demands on our attention. How can they be more effectually supported? Can any other assistance be given to such whose views are towards the ministry?

That here suitable methods might be proposed by which the talents and influence of the most valuable members of every church might be brought into action for the good of the whole.

That it would be natural to consult on the best methods of *Catechising,* and to recommend the same to our families and churches.

---

11   S.J. Price, 'The Early Years of the Baptist Union', *BQ* 4.2 (1928-29), p. 53. The Minutes of the Baptist Union (1813-1817) are printed in *BQ* 4 (1928-29), pp. 56-60, 121-31, 171-78 with notes by Price.

12   Brown, *The English Baptists of the Eighteenth Century*, p. 131.

13   Briggs, *The English Baptists of the Nineteenth Century*, p. 213.

14   Payne, *The Baptist Union*, p. 17.

That such an Assembly might deliberate on the most effectual means of supporting, all through the kingdom, aged respectable ministers, who are almost beyond their labours - and on the provision which might be made for the education of the Children of our Ministers deceased, as among the United Brethren, and other denominations of Christians.

That such an assembly would afford the best opportunities to concert plans for the encouragement and support of *Village Preaching* - of *Sunday Schools* - and for the establishment of Penny, and also of Mite Societies, resembling those of our Brethren in various parts of America.

That here an opportunity would be given of recommending interesting publications, and of selecting, and disseminating through the country, such small tracts, and pamphlets, as the general state of religion, and of our own denomination might require.

That the Brethren assembled from the various districts would be able to advise where it is proper that the New Meeting-houses should be erected; and of determining that, *henceforward*, no Case for building, enlarging, or repairing any place of worship, shall be countenanced, unless it has *previously to such erection or alteration*, obtained, in writing, the direction, encouragement, and recommendation of the principal *Ministers* of their own district.

The Chairman then took a rapid glance at the State of the Baptist Churches in foreign parts; and closed with remarking that what he had been saying presented but a few articles, out of a vast multitude, which would press themselves on the consideration of such an Assembly, in which whatever relates to the real interests of the denomination at home and abroad, would engage the general attention.[15]

The meeting approved nine resolutions.[16] The object of the Union was to be 'the promotion of the cause of Christ in general, and the interests of the denomination in particular; with a primary view to the encouragement and support of the Baptist Mission'. William Button and Joseph Ivimey were appointed secretaries, and the London ministers constituted the committee. Rippon, the expert in hymnody, gave out the following verses which were then sung:[17]

> Lord, if we meet on earth no more,
> O may we meet on Canaan's shore!
> Leave guilt, and death, and sin behind,
> And every bliss in glory find.

---

15   *Baptist Magazine* 4 (1812), pp. 356-57.
16   Minutes of the Baptist Union, *BQ* 4 (1928-29), p. 57.
17   *Baptist Magazine* 4 (1812) p. 358.

> But if we no longer here remain,
> And ever meet on earth again,
> May every heart inflamed with love
> Be fitter for Thy courts above.

The London ministers on 12 January 1813 appointed a sub-committee of five, including Rippon, to prepare a plan for the 1813 meeting of the new Union.[18] This committee met six times, Rippon attended four meetings and was Chairman on three occasions.[19] Rippon was requested, with Ivimey, to arrange a place for the next meeting; and he prepared the address of invitation to the country ministers, requesting them to attend a meeting on 23 June so that a detailed plan might be agreed.[20] The next Union meeting, on Thursday 24 June, again at Carter Lane and under Rippon's chairmanship, adopted resolutions which became the constitution of the Union. These are given in full by Payne,[21] but it may be noted again how the Union's rules reflect Rippon's hopes for his *Register*. For example, the third resolution was:

> That the formation of this Union be for the purpose of affording to the ministers and churches of the denomination the means of becoming better acquainted with each other, with a view to excite brotherly love, and to furnish a stimulus for a zealous co-operation in promoting the cause of Christ in general, and particularly in our own denomination, and especially to encourage and support our missions.

The Union naturally commended support for the other Baptist enterprises, as Rippon had suggested in 1812. The Union specifically disclaimed 'all manner of superiority and superintendence over the churches', the exact phrase used at the 1689 Assembly.[22] It also commended the 'monthly prayer meeting for the spread of the gospel' - exactly as Rippon had so often done. Rippon's influence on these resolutions, drafted by the committee on which he served, was evidently strong.

The succeeding years unfortunately found a declining interest in the work of the Union. Payne aptly characterized the years 1814 to 1831 as 'Divided Interests', and showed how the denomination's energies were diffused into various organizations.[23] The annual 'General Meeting of the Particular (or Calvinistic) Baptist Denomination', as it was known

---

18   Minutes of the Baptist Union, *BQ* 4 (1928-29), p. 59.
19   Minutes of the Baptist Union, *BQ* 4 (1928-29), pp. 59-60, 121-22.
20   Minutes of the Baptist Union, *BQ* 4 (1928-29), p. 60.
21   Payne, *The Baptist Union*, pp. 24-25.
22   'Minutes of the Baptist Union', *BQ* 4 (1928-29), p. 126; 'Narrative of proceedings of...General Assembly, 1689', *Register*, supplement, p. 48.
23   Payne, *The Baptist Union*, pp. 43-58.

from 1815,[24] appears to have degenerated into just another meeting. Nevertheless, the desire for an effective Union was maintained, until in 1831-2 substantial reorganization gave the Union virtually a fresh beginning. During the intervening years Rippon and Ivimey persevered with the Union, despite severe disappointments. Rippon during this time did not himself actively initiate any new enterprises. Spurgeon tells the story that when Rippon was once asked why he did not attend more denominational meetings and take the lead, Rippon replied: 'Why, I see the Dover coach go by my house every morning, and I notice that the leaders get most lashed'.[25] However this anecdote, cited by Payne,[26] is perhaps a better indication of Rippon's wit than of his role in the denomination. Rippon moved to New Kent Road (from where he would have seen the Dover coach) some time after 1820, that is, when he was in his seventies.[27] His significant contributions were made earlier in life, and in his last years he served as a figurehead rather than as a worker. This was a not unreasonable attitude. Even so, Rippon continually played an interested part in the Union which he had helped create.

In 1814, the meeting was again at Carter Lane with Rippon as chairman. Indeed, Rippon chaired each meeting (except 1815 when he was absent) from 1812 until 1821, after which the chairmen are unknown for several years.[28] However as the meetings were normally at Carter Lane after 1821 Rippon may well have chaired others.[29] His church provided breakfast for the delegates. After the reorganization, Rippon was chairman in 1833, when the New Park Street buildings were used for the first time.[30] The close associations between the Union and Rippon's church are confirmed by the remark of Charles Room when he replied to the thanks of the Union in 1835: '... it would always afford himself and his friends the most unfeigned pleasure to have the meeting held in that chapel: indeed they should feel somewhat hurt if it were held anywhere else.'[31] The contribution of Carter Lane men like Burls and James Low for the Union was outlined in chapter three.

---

24   'Minutes of the Baptist Union,' p. 172.

25   Spurgeon, *The Metropolitan Tabernacle*, p. 52.

26   Payne, *The Baptist Union*, p. 18.

27   On 27 June 1820 the Baptist Board compiled a list of ministers and addresses. At some time after this the original address (Grange Road) was replaced by 'No. 17 Dover Place, New Kent Road'. Cf. *BHS Trans* 7 (1920-21), p. 49.

28   The first minute book of the Union concludes with 1817. For the succeeding years the only sources of knowledge are the brief reports in the *Baptist Magazine*, but there were no reports from 1822 to 1831.

29   Although no reports were given, the meeting was announced in the *Magazine* for 1824, 1825, 1827.

30   *Baptist Magazine* 25 (1833), p. 326.

31   *Baptist Magazine* 27 (1835), p. 288.

For the 1814 meeting Rippon was one of a committee who drafted the Address to the Denomination commending the Union,[32] published in the *Baptist Magazine*.[33] Earlier that year, in April, the Baptist Society for the Propagation of the Gospel in Ireland, later known as the Baptist Irish Society, had been formed.[34] This had resulted from the reports of John Saffery after his visit to Ireland in 1813 on behalf of the BMS. Rippon had pointed to the need for assistance to the Irish churches in his *Register*.[35] Although he does not seem to have been active in the Society, he welcomed its formation and left £100 to the Irish churches in his will. The Irish Society was another channel for the evangelistic zeal of the denomination, although it also became yet another society appealing to the churches for funds. The 1814 Union meeting also requested that each association should send some report of the state of the churches to subsequent meetings. From this time, much of the Union meetings were occupied with hearing just the kinds of reports Rippon had published in his *Register*.

At the 1815 meeting a proposal for one joint-activity was 'that a place of Worship should be procured in London for the use of the denomination, sufficiently large to contain the congregation usually assembling at our annual meetings, & other purposes...'[36] The London ministers were requested to make plans for this. Rippon chaired the 1816 meeting, at Fetter Lane, which resolved to ask the churches to hold a collection for the new building.[37] However, such a scheme was in advance of the times. The following reply, written to Rippon, reflects both the vision held by Rippon and what was perhaps a typical Baptist reaction:

...but permit me to state my mind freely & humbly to you – to have Committee Rooms for ye ministers & friends of ye Baptist cause to meet & transact their business in & to have a place large enough *for all the Sunday Schools* in London & ye *Lancastrian Schools* to have an annual meeting in *similar to that of St. Pauls* & to have a *famous* Baptistery for ye use of all serious Baptists, I would humbly say savours not of ye kingdom of Xst which is not of this world Luke 17: 20,21, but of Antichrist.[38]

The scheme was not referred to again, and not until 1903 when Baptist Church House was built did the Baptist Union have a permanent base.

---

32   Minutes of the Baptist Union, *BQ* 4 (1928-29), p. 127.

33   *Baptist Magazine* 6 (1814), pp. 260-62.

34   Payne, *The Baptist Union*, pp. 46-47.

35   *Register* 2 (1794-97), pp. 218-19.

36   Minutes of the Baptist Union, *BQ* 4 (1928-29), p. 172

37   Minutes of the Baptist Union, *BQ* 4 (1928-29), p. 173.

38   N. Curtis to Rippon, Wrestlingworth, Bedfordshire, 17 July 1816, B.L. Add. MSS. 25386, f. 326.

In 1816 the Union prepared a plan for compiling an account of the churches detailing the number of members, of gifted brethren, of villages supplied, of schools formed, etc.[39] Although no detailed list was published, once again the value of the work done by Rippon in the *Register* lists of churches was apparent.

In 1820 he introduced another definite project to the Union, and it was agreed 'to encourage the printing and cheap circulation of popular approved tracts written upon the subject of baptism, and the more general subject of nonconformity'.[40] In order to assist this, Rippon personally donated the paper for the printing of ten thousand copies of John Collett Ryland's *Six Views of Believers Baptism* (first published in 1774).[41] These were distributed at cost price, but no further tracts were prepared.

Yet another scheme first suggested by Rippon was begun in 1830. This was to provide funds for the education of the children of poor Baptist ministers. The Congregationalists had begun such a project in 1811,[42] and in 1812 Rippon had suggested that the Baptists might adopt this as one of the objectives of the Union. Although it was suggested for adoption in the resolutions of 1813 (probably by Rippon), it had not then been accepted.[43] The project languished for support until in 1830 Rippon and thirteen others were appointed to a committee for the purpose.[44] Rippon gave ten pounds to the new fund,[45] but although the Education Fund continued for several years, its aid 'never reached large proportions'.[46]

It was fitting that Rippon should have lived to see the Union revitalized. In 1832 a revised constitution was adopted,[47] and the re-defined objects still bore a remarkable resemblance to Rippon's work begun over forty years before:

1st. To extend brotherly love and union among the Baptist ministers and churches who agree in the sentiments usually denominated evangelical.

2nd. To promote unity of exertion in whatever may best serve the cause of Christ in general, and the interests of the Baptist denomination in particular.

---

39   *Baptist Magazine* 8 (1816), p. 301.
40   *Baptist Magazine* 12 (1820), p. 285.
41   Cf. 'Baptist Board Minutes' (11 July 1820), *BHS Trans* 7 (1920-21), p. 53.
42   Jones, *Congregationalism in England 1662-1962*, p. 239.
43   'Minutes of the Baptist Union', p. 122.
44   *Baptist Magazine* 22 (1830), p. 294.
45   *Baptist Magazine* 22 (1830), p. 294.
46   Payne, *The Baptist Union*, p. 8.
47   *Baptist Magazine* 24 (1832), pp. 303-308.

3rd. To obtain accurate statistical information relative to Baptist churches, societies, institutions, colleges, etc., throughout the kingdom and the world at large.

4th. To prepare for circulation an annual report of the proceedings of the Union, and of the state of the denomination.

Prior to this the Union's achievements had been only moderate. Ivimey, writing in 1830, recognized that the 'grand design' of the Union 'was never fully realized', and commented that 'The society soon ceased; but an annual meeting has been held at the vestry of Carter Lane meeting ever since'.[48] The few positive joint-activities attempted quickly failed. Its objects were too general, and the annual meeting had simply been a gathering to hear reports from the churches. Yet the denomination had expanded, and the various societies, individually, had flourished. In preparation for the 1832 Union meeting Joseph Belcher, of Chelsea, compiled a statistical report, published in the *Baptist Magazine*.[49] Between 1790 and 1832, he estimated, there had been a threefold increase in the number of churches: it is instructive that the only facts Belcher had for comparative purposes were Rippon's. From this time the Union regularly and systematically gathered this kind of information, continuing what Rippon had done forty years before.

Rippon, now an old man of eighty-two, was recalled to be chairman of the Union in 1833. Not inappropriately, one matter considered was the possibility of drawing up an address to be sent to the Triennial Convention of American Baptists in 1835. In fact, although Rippon perhaps was too old to know much about it, two British Baptists, James Hoby and F.A. Cox, were sent to America to convey personal greetings. Unfortunately, controversies over the slavery issue marred the harmony of this visit.[50]

Rippon must have felt considerable satisfaction to see the Union becoming actively engaged in many of those functions he had striven to promote over forty years before. The importance of the Union to the life of the denomination has increased with the years, in ways perhaps beyond Rippon's wildest dreams. Yet it is to Rippon, and a few of his contemporaries, that the vision of greater co-operation in a Baptist Union may be directly traced.

---

48   *History of English Baptists*, 4, p. 382.
49   *Baptist Magazine* 24 (1832), pp. 304-308.
50   F.A. Cox and J. Hoby, *The Baptists in America; a Narrative of the Deputation from the Baptist Union in England, to the United States of America.* (London: 1836). See Briggs, *The English Baptists of the Nineteenth Century*, pp. 296-97, 388.

Furthermore, Rippon advanced the seminal suggestion that a world gathering of Baptists should be held in London. This was clearly contained in the dedication to his *Register*:

THIS INFANT PUBLICATION
UNDER THE FOSTERING HAND
OF ITS BENEVOLENT PATRONS
IS MOST AFFECTIONATELY DEDICATED
TO ALL
THE BAPTIZED MINISTERS AND PEOPLE
IN AMERICA
ENGLAND IRELAND
SCOTLAND WALES
THE UNITED NETHERLANDS
FRANCE SWITZERLAND
POLAND RUSSIA PRUSSIA
AND ELSEWHERE
ESPECIALLY TO THOSE
WHOSE NAMES ADORN THE FOLLOWING PAGES
WITH A DESIRE OF PROMOTING
AN UNIVERSAL EXCHANGE
OF KIND OFFICES AMONG THEM
AND IN SERIOUS EXPECTATION
THAT BEFORE MANY YEARS ELAPSE
(IN IMITATION OF OTHER WISE MEN)
A DEPUTATION FROM ALL THESE CLIMES
WILL MEET PROBABLY IN LONDON
TO CONSULT
THE ECCLESIASTICAL GOOD OF THE WHOLE
WHICH IS NOW FIRST OF ALL
SUBMITTED TO THEIR SUPERIOR WISDOM
BY THE UNWORTHIEST
OF ALL THEIR BRETHREN
THE AUTHOR

There is little doubt that the idea for such a gathering came from the example of the Methodists, Moravians and Quakers, as previously noted. It is significant that Rippon included the Mennonites in his vision. Political events soon made the possibility of such a gathering very remote.

Eventually in 1905 what was called the Baptist World Alliance (BWA) was formed in London. The aims of the Alliance were later described by one of its leaders as embracing three great purposes for Baptists: '(1) to express and promote unity and fellowship among them; (2) to secure and defend religious freedom; (3) to proclaim the great principles of our common faith'.[51] Obviously these are the very ideals that Rippon desired to advance in his *Register*, and would have been the purpose of the world gathering he envisaged. No reference to Rippon's dedication appears to have been made at the first Alliance meeting, but since then it has been repeatedly claimed that the BWA was the delayed fulfilment of his vision. As F.T. Lord, the first historian of the Alliance, wrote: 'For the idea of a world gathering of Baptists it would seem that we must give the credit to John Rippon'.[52] It may be added that, not inappropriately, it has become the tradition of each Alliance Congress gathering (held every five years) to commence with the singing of Rippon's improved version of the hymn, 'All hail the power of Jesu's name'. Although he did not live to see it, the BWA gatherings symbolize the fulfilment of Rippon's dream of the day when the Baptists would be 'a people whose sentiments it is expected will in the ages to come, *cover the whole earth.*'[53]

---

51   J.H. Rushbrooke, 'The Baptist World Alliance: Origin: Constitution: Achievements: Objects', *BQ* 9.2 (1938-39), p. 69.

52   F.T. Lord, *Baptist World Fellowship* (London: Carey Kingsgate Press, 1955), pp. 1-2. Cf. Whitley, *History of British Baptists*, p. 241; Underwood, *A History of the English Baptists*, pp. 178-79; Payne, *Baptist Union*, pp. 165-66; *Baptist World* (Journal of the BWA), June 1965, p. 5.

53   *Register* 1 (1790-93), p. viii.

Conclusion

This account of the life and work of John Rippon has suggested his outstanding significance for the Particular Baptist denomination. Nothing of note happened in the Baptist world during his active years with which he was not closely connected: and much happened. He was not a man of powerful intellect or profound scholarship but of his widespread influence there can be no doubt. He did not often initiate, but with intense application often carried out the suggestions of others; both his hymnbooks and *Register* suggest this. Central to all his life was the vision of the verses he so often quoted:

> From East to West, from North to South,
> Now be his name ador'd!
> EUROPE, with all thy millions shout,
> Hosannahs to thy Lord!
>
> ASIA and AFRICA resound
> From shore to shore his fame;
> And thou, AMERICA, in songs
> Redeeming love proclaim!

Primarily, however, Rippon sought to proclaim that redeeming love as a faithful pastor. After all, the local churches, both ministers and people, constituted the denomination. In every age it is the people who are the primary material of Church History. Understandably the eminent or eccentric receive prominence in the narrative, but essentially the story of the Church must also be concerned with the ordinary people involved in the realities of sin and redemption. The community life of the Church, continuous in every generation, is basic. No apology is therefore made for the attempt to detail this work of Rippon as he served his church long and well. His sermons were earnest and eloquent, sound in doctrine and clear in application. Evangelism was the dominant motive behind not only Rippon's pastoral activities, but all he did. His evangelistic success is of importance, for he served as an excellent example to many pastors of lesser ability shackled by the High Calvinist theology.

Moreover, his hymn publications grew out of both his pastoral experiences and evangelistic concern. The patient thoroughness Rippon brought to this task was largely responsible for the phenomenal success of his *Selection*, the first Baptist book to achieve almost universal acceptance in the denomination. Certainly, it ought to be noted, it was as a hymn-publisher that his own contemporaries most frequently honoured him. Typical was the description by Charles Room in his funeral sermon for Rippon:

> ...We have a WATTS, who was the sweet singer in our British Israel, and who has enabled myriads like our venerated and deceased friend, though in another way, to sing the praises of God, throughout not only our British Zion, but throughout the empire of Britain, in its length, in its breadth, and in its extent, and the vast continent of America besides.[1]

To be described as the Baptists' 'Watts' would have delighted Rippon. His *Selection* made a deep impression on the devotional life of his denomination - and others - for more than two generations, and this may still be traced in the denomination's hymnbooks. His hymnological work, it has been claimed, was thus of basic significance for the denomination: as a theologically unifying force, both reflecting and shaping the theology and worship of the churches.

Rippon did more than any other contemporary to draw the Baptists of the world together. By his *Register* he informed and encouraged the Baptists. The rapid expansion and increasing maturity of the denomination found a 'willing servant'. Rippon's services for the American Baptists were unique and greatly appreciated. By his pioneer efforts in Baptist periodical publication, Rippon disseminated widely the schemes and hopes of his contemporaries. At the same time he promoted, even if somewhat haphazardly, the new interest in Baptist historiography.

Although he demonstrated the faults of one who was primarily a man of action, Rippon's zeal and tireless devotion to even the most routine of tasks were perhaps his greatest gifts to his denomination. In a variety of ways he helped local churches and ministers, and brought a certain distinction to the Baptist cause by his willing work in interdenominational organizations. The respect in which he was held by Baptists was demonstrated by his appointment as the chairman of the first Baptist Union meetings. Rippon thus exerted an important influence on what proved to be the formative years of the denomination's organization. The most common description of Rippon, and a quality he often referred to as worthy in others, was 'usefulness'. Rippon's supreme concern for 'usefulness', to be useful to God, and useful to his fellows, was amply fulfilled.

Moreover, Rippon dreamed dreams and saw visions. He evidently held a deeper ambition for the Baptist Union than he saw accomplished in his lifetime. Yet in the modern Union the dream of a central body

---

1   *Pulpit*, 29 (1837), p. 291.

representing and serving the churches in every conceivable way is realized.

Again, Rippon envisaged a world gathering of Baptists: now fulfilled in the Baptist World Alliance. Indeed, it could perhaps be claimed that Rippon was an ecumenical pioneer - in the most literal sense of the word. Obviously it is an anachronism to suggest that he anticipated all that the modern ecumenical movement has come to imply. Yet in his hope for a worldwide fellowship of Christians, and in his oft-evidenced toleration of Christians of all denominations, Rippon perhaps pointed the way to deeper harmony and co-operation, necessary preludes to true unity. At the very least he offers a striking example of what W.R. Ward has called 'the outpouring of undenominational religion' at the end of the eighteenth century.[2]

Rippon's life-story not only articulates his claim to a worthy place in the history of his denomination, but also casts a light upon the age in which he lived and the circle in which he moved. In particular, it illuminates the complexities of denominational life in a formative era. Rippon was not without his faults: but neither was the denomination. He was eager and enthusiastic; but also impetuous, impatient, and independent. In this he epitomized the growing pains of the denomination. During the remainder of the nineteenth century the Baptists consolidated the advances made during Rippon's time. Under the leadership of outstanding figures like Charles Haddon Spurgeon, Alexander Maclaren, John Clifford and others the churches grew, and the denomination achieved genuine national significance. Calvinism declined further and became increasingly remote from the life of the churches of the Baptist Union. Under the guidance of Samuel Booth (1824- 1902), secretary of the Baptist Union from 1877 to 1879, and from 1883 to 1898, denominational unity became increasingly strong. Many of the progressive factors had been traced by Rippon: evangelistic preaching, a strong central organization to assist weaker churches, awareness of denominational traditions and history, an evangelical hymnody. Later Baptists, more sophisticated and more aware of their denominational status, have perhaps too easily forgotten the pains of their early growth and the significance of men like Rippon.

Measured by his permanent contribution to the Baptist denomination, Rippon emerges as one of the more important figures in its history. Spurgeon's assessment of Rippon offers a suitable epitaph: 'Beloved at home, respected abroad, and useful everywhere'.[3] 'Redeeming love proclaim!' This purpose sustained the long life of John Rippon.

---

2   Ward, *Religion and Society in England 1790-1850*, p. 2.
3   Spurgeon, *The Metropolitan Tabernacle*, p. 50.

APPENDIX 1

Earlier Studies on Rippon

In 1849 the first significant biographical account of Rippon was given in *Bunhill Memorials* by J. Andrew Jones, a Baptist minister.[1] Jones included relevant extracts from Rippon's churchbook, especially the tribute recorded by the church at his death. For the first time it was suggested, quite wrongly, that Rippon's father had been minister at Tiverton. This error has been often repeated.

Earlier Nonconformist historians, such as Stoughton,[2] and Skeats and Miall,[3] clearly recognized Rippon's importance and gave brief accounts of him. C.H. Spurgeon (1834-1892) offered some review of his pastoral work in *The Metropolitan Tabernacle: its History and Work* (1876). This was valuable in that Spurgeon was able to draw on the personal reminiscences of some of his older members.[4]

Some details of Rippon's early years were given for the first time by H.B. Case in *The History of the Baptist Church in Tiverton 1607 to 1907* (1907), especially in the chapter, 'The Rippons, Father and Son'. Case failed to notice that there were three John Rippons in the church at the same time. Confusion between Rippon and his father meant that Case suggested (implicitly) that Rippon was baptized at the age of eight, a procedure quite unknown in English Baptist churches.[5]

The first attempt at an inclusive biography was by Thomas Seccombe in the *Dictionary of National Biography* (1896). Unfortunately, this contained several errors.[6] Earlier Baptist historians have, therefore, been

---

1   Jones, *Bunhill Memorials*, pp. 232-34. For Jones (1779-1863), see *DNB*.

2.   Stoughton, *History of Religion in England*, 7, pp. 282-84.

3   H.S. Skeats and C.S. Miall, *History of the Free Churches of England 1688-1891* (London: n. d.), pp. 432-33.

4   *The Metropolitan Tabernacle*, pp. 48-54.

5   Case, *The History of the Baptist Church in Tiverton 1607 to 1907*, p. 88.

6   Rippon's father was not minister at Tiverton; Rippon was not educated at the British Academy (a misprint for Bristol); the date of his *Selection of Hymns* was 1787 (not 1827); to describe J. Andrew Jones, *Bunhill Memorials* as the fulfilment of

somewhat restricted in assessing Rippon's role in the history of the denomination. W.T. Whitley recognized the importance of his *Baptist Annual Register* and placed Rippon prominently in his account of the Baptists in their age of great expansion.[7] He also appreciated Rippon's contribution to hymnody.[8] E.A. Payne later demonstrated Rippon's central role in the early Baptist Union.[9] O.C. Robison in his review of English Baptists from 1760 to 1820 noted Rippon's strategic place in the denomination but perhaps did not fully realize Rippon's influence.[10] Some recognition of Rippon's importance to hymnody was made in J. Julian's *Dictionary of Hymnology* (1892, revised 1907),[11] and in subsequent smaller studies.[12] Among others, Robert H. Young had noted Rippon's significant place in Baptist hymnody, although his account offered little analysis of Rippon's editorial work.[13] Happily, more recent Baptist historians have a clearer appreciation of his contributions.[14]

Rippon's aims regarding a history of that site is misleading; the bibliography of Rippon's works is incomplete. The main value of Seccombe's account was to note the collection of Rippon's papers deposited in the British Library.

7   *A History of British Baptists*, see index; 'The Baptist Annual Register', pp. 122-26.

8   'The Tune Book of 1791', pp. 434-43.

9   *The Baptist Union*, pp. 15-18.

10   'The Particular Baptists in England, 1760-1820'. For example, although Dr Robison stressed the importance of village preaching in the denomination's expansion, the records of the Itinerant Society demonstrate Rippon's prominence in that Society.

11   *Julian*, pp. 963-64; but see also the index.

12   Mansfield, 'Rippon's Tunes', pp. 36-43.

13   'The History of Baptist Hymnody in England from 1612 to 1800'.

14   Brown, *The English Baptists of the Eighteenth Century*; Briggs, *The English Baptists of the Nineteenth Century*; Watts, *The Dissenters* 2; S. James, 'John Rippon (1751-1836): Willing Servant of all the churches', *Reformation Today*, 179 (January-February 2001), pp. 15-24; S. James, 'John Rippon (1751-1836)' in Haykin (ed.) *The British Particular Baptists 1638-1910*, 2, pp. 57-75; have all utilized the Oxford 1967 thesis of the present writer. See also the writer's entries on Rippon for *DEB*, in T. Larsen (ed.), *Biographical Dictionary of Evangelicals* (Leicester: InterVarsity Press, 2003), pp. 552-54, and the *New DNB* (Oxford University Press).

APPENDIX 2

Rippon's Version of
'All Hail the power of Jesu's name'

The original version by Edward Perronet (1726-92) was published in the *Gospel Magazine* 7 (April, 1780, p. 185), and was included by the author in his *Occasional Verses, moral and Sacred* (London: 1785), where it was entitled 'On the Resurrection'.

> All hail! the pow'r of Jesu's Name;
>   Let angels prostrate fall;
> Bring forth the Royal Diadem,
>   To crown him Lord of all.
>
> Let highborn seraphs tune the lyre,
>   And as they tune it, fall
> Before His face who tunes their choir,
>   And crown Him Lord of all.
>
> Crown Him ye morning stars of light,
>   Who fix'd this floating ball;
> Now hail the strength of Israel's might,
>   And crown Him Lord of all.
>
> Crown Him, ye martyrs of your God,
>   Who from His altar call;
> Extol the stem of Jesse's rod,
>   And crown Him Lord of all.
>
> Ye seed of Israel's chosen race,
>   Ye ransom'd of the fall,
> Hail Him Who saves you by His grace,
>   And crown Him Lord of all.

Hail Him, ye heirs of David's line,
　　Whom David Lord did call;
The God incarnate, man Divine,
　　And crown Him Lord of all.

Sinners! whose love can ne'er forget
　　The wormwood and the gall,
Go - spread your trophies at His feet,
　　And crown Him Lord of all.

Let every tribe and every tongue
　　That bound creation's call,
Now shout in universal song,
　　The crowned Lord of all.

Rippon's version was published as Hymn 177 in his *Selection*. Rippon's alterations are in italics; he also added the general title and the headings for each verse.

The Spiritual Coronation. Cant. iii. II.

ANGELS

1. All-hail the power of Jesu's name!
　　Let angels prostrate fall:
Bring forth the royal diadem,
　　And crown him Lord of all..

MARTYRS

2. (Crown him, ye martyrs of *our* God,
　　Who from his altar call;
Extol the stem of Jesse's rod.
　　And crown him Lord of all.)

CONVERTED JEWS

3. (*Ye chosen seed of Israel's race,*
　　A remnant weak and small!
Hail him who saves you by his grace;
　　And crown him Lord of all.)

BELIEVING GENTILES

4. *Ye Gentile sinners* ne'er forget
　　The wormwood and the gall;
Go - spread your trophies at his feet,
　　And crown him Lord of all.

SINNERS OF EVERY AGE

5. *(Babes, men, and sires, who know his love,*
      Who feel your sin and thrall,
   Now joy with all the hosts above,
      And crown him Lord of all.)

SINNERS OF EVERY NATION

6. *Let every kindred, every tribe*
      On this terrestrial ball,
   To him all majesty ascribe,
      And crown him Lord of all.

OURSELVES

7. *0 that, with yonder sacred throng,*
      We at his feet may fall;
   We'll join the everlasting song,
      And crown him Lord of all.

APPENDIX 3

Examples of Hymns by Rippon

Rippon published one poem in his *Register*, signed with his name, but evidence for hymns by him is indefinite. However, five hymns from the *Selection* may be cited as possibly by him.

1. 'There's joy in heaven, and joy on earth' (No. 438)

2. 'Amid the splendors of thy state' (No. 12, 2nd part)

(Both these were suggested as Rippon's by W. R. Stevenson in *Julian* although no evidence was cited.[1])

3. '0 God, before whose radiant throne' (No. 338, 2nd part)

Rippon noted that this hymn was sung at Uffculm on 22 July 1810 when he preached there at the first communion service after the chapel had been rebuilt. Thus it is probably one composed by him for the occasion.[2]

4. 'The day has dawn'd, Jehovah comes' (No. 535, 3rd part)

This was sung at a special service to mark the abolition of slavery, held at Carter Lane on 27 March 1807; quite possibly Rippon wrote the occasional hymn.

5. 'A century now has roll'd away' (No. 435, 2nd part)

As this was sung at the centenary services of the Horsleydown (1815) and Bartholomew-Close (1817) charity schools and Rippon was the special preacher, again it is likely he composed the appropriate hymn.

---

1   *Julian*, p. 964
2   See Spurgeon, *Our Own Hymn Book*, hymn 1022.

The following three examples will illustrate his ability.

1.

'Prayer for Deliverance from the Fear of Death'.[3]

O God of Hope! with cheering ray
Gild my expiring streak of day;
Thy love, through each revolving year,
Has wip'd away affliction's tear.

Free me from death's terrific gloom,
And all the guilt which shrouds the tomb!
Heighten my joys, support my head,
Before I sink among the dead.

May death conclude my toils and tears!
May death destroy my sins and fears!
May death, through Jesus, be my friend!
May death be life when life shall end!

Crown my *last* moment with thy pow'r-
The *latest* in my latest hour;
Then to the raptur'd heights I soar
Where fears and death are known no more.
J. RIPPON

2. *Selection.* Hymn 338 (2nd Part)

'Re-building, or re-opening a Place of Worship'

1   0 God, before whose radiant throne
The heav'nly armies bend,
Now graciously incline thine ear,
And to our suit attend.

2. Where our forefathers join'd in praise,
We meet to praise thee too,
For us and others here they pray'd,
We now their work renew.

---

3   *Register* 3 (1798-1801), p. 312.

3. This house, these walls, re-edify'd, *
   Are raised, Lord, for thee,
   In all the plenitude of grace,
   Let this thy temple be.

4. By pious crowds of new-born souls
   Let countless proofs be giv'n,
   This surely is the house of God,
   The very gate of heav'n.

5. Here may the dead be made alive,
   Backsliding souls return;
   More grace by gracious souls be felt,
   And saints like seraphs burn.

6. Here build thy Church, maintain thy Cause,
   Nor let it e'er decline;
   But flourish when the trumpet sounds -
   The Kingdoms, Lord are thine.

7. And on each flock around this hill
   Show'r mercy, grace, and love;
   Thus meeten us and millions more
   For the bless'd Church above.

*Or, new beaut ify'd.

3.   *Selection.* Hymn 535 (3rd Part)

   'A Song in prospect of the Abolition of the Slave-Trade –
   Detested crime! of vices first,
   Most infamous, and most accurs'd!'

1. The day has dawn'd, Jehovah comes
   To crush oppression's rod;
   Now Ethiopia soon shall stretch
   Her hands to thee, 0 God!

2. Where'er the sun doth rise or set,
   Or spread his beauteous ray,
   May freedom, with her glorious train,
   Hurl slavery away!

3. Let charity, benevolence,
   And ev'ry smiling grace,
   In golden links of brotherhood
   Unite the human race.

4. Then, brilliant as the mid-day sun,
   And as the ocean wide,
   Christ in the chariot of his grace
   Triumphantly shall ride.

5. Tyrants no more shall lift the scourge,
   Nor captives drag the chain;
   Millions, beautified, shall bless
   The dear Redeemer's reign.

6. Then every colour, every clime
   Shall in his worship meet;
   And bring their prayers, their praise, their All,
   An offering at his feet.

7. 'Lord, for those days we wait; those days
   Are in thy word foretold;
   Fly swifter, sun and stars, and bring
   This promis'd age of gold.

8. Amen, with joys divine, let earth's
   Unnumber'd myriads cry;
   Amen, with joy divine, let heav'ns
   Unnumber'd choirs reply.'

The following plain verse to be sung first by the people of colour, and then by the whole congregation.

9. Free us from sin and all its chains,
   The worst of *slavery*;
   Bind us to Christ in holy bonds,
   The sweetest *liberty*.

(Verses 7 and 8 were not sung at the service in Carter Lane on 27 March 1807).

Table 1:

An analysis of the number of hymns allocated to each topic in the *Selection*, showing the numbers added in later editions

Number	Subject	Hymn Numbers	Total in edn 1	Added in edn 10	Added in edn 27	Total
1	God	1-26	26	2		28
2	Creation and Providence	27-37	11			11
3	Fall of Man	38-42	5			5
4	Scripture	43-128	86	6	13	105
5	Christ	129-205	77	2	12	91
6	Spirit	206-293	88	14	12	114
7	Christian Life	294-328	35	8	11	54
8	Worship	329-397	69	7	70*	146
9	The World	398-402	5			5
10	The Church	403-441	39	16	11	66
11	Baptism	442-471	30		2	32
12	Lord's Supper	472-490	19			19
13	Times and Seasons	491-542	52	3	10	65
14	Time and Eternity	543-549	7			7
15	Death and the Resurrection	550-569	20	3	3	26
16	Judgment	570-579	10	1	2	13
17	Hell and Heaven	580-588	9		7	16
Total			**588**	**62**	**153**	**803**

* This figure includes 36 short doxologies.

Table 2:

An analysis of hymn writers in the *Selection*, showing, where known, denominational allegiances

No.	Name	Denom.	Edn 1A	Edn 1B	Edn 10A	Edn 10B	Edn 27A	Edn 27B	Total
1	John Adams	Bap		1					1
2	Joseph Addison	CoE	1						1
3	James Allen	Ind		1					1
4	John Bakewell	Meth		1					1
5	Benjamin Beddome	Bap	39	3		12	4	4	62
6	John Berridge	CoE		1					1
7	Thomas Blacklock	Presb	1						1
8	Richard Blackmore	CoE		1					1
9	James Boden	Ind	1						1
10	John Bowring (tr)	Unit					1		1
11	David Bradberry	Ind	1						1
12	Jehoida Brewer	Ind					1		1
13	Simon Browne	Ind		4					4
14	John Cennick	Mor	5	3					8
15	Thomas Coles	Bap				1			1
16	S. Collett		1						1
17	William Collyer	Ind					2		2
18	Josiah Conder	Ind					1		1
19	William Cowper	CoE	9		1			1	11
20	Robert Cruttenden	Ind	2	1					3
21	Samuel Davies	Presb	7						7
22	Philip Doddridge	Ind	89	12			2	2	105
23	John Dryden (tr)	RC					1		1
24	James Edmeston	CoE						2	2
25	Jonathan Evans	Ind		2					2
26	James Fanch	Bap					1		1
27	John Fawcett	Bap	19	3		1			23
28	John Fellows	Bap		7					7
29	Miss Fitsherbert		3						3
30	John Fountain	Bap			1		1		2

31	Benjamin Francis	Bap	5						5
32	Thomas Gibbons	Ind	10	15					25
33	Ann Gilbert	Ind					1		1
34	John Glas	Glass						1	1
35	James Grant	Presb?				1			1
36	Thomas Greene	Ind	1						1
37	Joseph Grigg	Presb	1				1		2
38	William Hammond	Mor		2					2
39	Susanna Harrison	Ind						1	1
40	Joseph Hart	Ind	2	3		1			6
41	Thomas Haweis	CoE					1		1
42	? Hayward							1	1
43	Reginald Heber	CoE					1		1
44	Rowland Hill	CoE	1	1					2
45	George Horne	CoE					1		1
46	Joseph Humphreys	Ind	1	1					2
47	W. Jesse		1						1
48	Edmund Jones	Bap	1						1
49	Thomas Kelly	'Ind'						2	2
50	Thomas Ken	CoE	1						2
51	John Lawson	Bap					1		1
52	? Leech		1						1
53	John Mason	CoE		1					1
54	Mary Masters					1			1
55	James Maxwell	Meth		1					1
56	Samuel Medley	Bap	1	1			2		4
57	James Merrick	CoE	3						3
58	Henry Moore	Unit				1			1
59	John Needham	Bap	10	7			2		19
60	James Newton	Bap	1						1
61	John Newton	CoE	12	7			2		21
62	John Norman	Bap	1						1
63	Thomas Olivers	Meth	1						1
64	Krishna Pal	Bap					1		1
65	Samuel Pearce	Bap			3		1		4
66	Edward Perronet	Ind		1					1
67	Thomas Rippon	Bap					1		1
68	Robert Robinson	Bap	2						2
69	John Ryland	Bap	4			2	5		11
70	Maria Saffery	Bap					1	1	2
71	Elizabeth Scott	Ind	4	2					6
72	Thomas Scott	Ind		1		1			2

Table 2 289

73	Robert Seagrave	CoE		1					1
74	Sarah Slinn			1					1
75	Anne Steele	Bap	45	8					53
76	Joseph Stennett	Bap	9						9
77	Samuel Stennett	Bap	38						38
78	John Stocker			1					1
79	? Stogdon		1						1
80	Joseph Straphan		3						3
81	Nahum Tate	CoE	1						1
82	Augustus Toplady	CoE	9						9
83	Daniel Turner	Bap	8				1		9
84	Mrs Vokes					3			3
85	Benjamin Wallin	Bap		2					2
86	Isaac Watts	Ind	38	1	1				40
87	John and Charles Wesley	Meth	6	18			2	3	29
88	Henry White	CoE					2	1	3
89	William Williams	CoE	2						2

This table reveals the following numbers for those whose name and denomination are known:

Anglican (CoE): 18 writers with 62 hymns.

Baptist (Bap): 25 writers with 263 hymns.

Glassite (Glass): 1 writer with 1 hymn.

Independent (Ind): 20 writers with 206 hymns.

Methodist (Meth): 5 writers with 32 hymns.

Moravian (Mor): 2 writers with 10 hymns.

Presbyterian (Presb): 4 writers with 11 hymns.

Roman Catholic (RC): 1 writer (as translator [tr]) with 1 hymn.

Unitarian (Unit): 2 writers with 2 hymns.

Table 3:
An analysis of the contents of each number of the *Register*

Register No.	Date	Page Nos	Extras
VOLUME 1			
1*	'1791'[1]	1-96	17th century papers
2	c.August 1791[1]	97-?[2]	
3	c.December 1791		
4	c.May 1792	-344	
5*	December 1792	345-420	H.W.A. PP. 17-32
6	c.May 1793	421-500	
7*	December 1793	501-563	Index, Polymetric Table, Title-page for Volume, Dedication & Preface
VOLUME 2			
8*	May 1794	1-96 (not 17-24)[3]	
9*	November 1794	97-106	
10*	April 1795	177-232	H.W.A. pp. 49-64
11*	October 1795	233-296	H.W.A. pp. 65-80
12	January 1796	297-368	
13	August 1796	369-440	H.W.A.; Address to reader
14*	May 1797	441-534	Index, Title-page
VOLUME 3			
15	September 1798	1-112 (Not 13-40)	
16	January 1799	113-160 (+13-40)	
17*	December 1800	161-232	
18*	January 1801	233-272	
19*	February 1801	273-312	
20*	March 1801	313-352	
21*	April 1801	353-392	

---

1   This date is taken from an advertisement for the second part of the *Register*, found in a separate issue of the 1689 Baptist Confession of Faith (Angus Library).

2   Page 150 was in Number 2, cf. *Register* 2 (1794-97), p. 444.

3   This was the list of Welsh churches, see no. 10.

Table 3   291

22*	May 1801	393-432	
23	June 1801	433-472	
24*	July 1801	473-512	
25*	August 1801	513-552	No Index

VOLUME 4

Note. No title pages or Index for Vol. 3 were issued at this time, and possibly not until the whole work was concluded. Page numbers were carried over into Vol. 4.

26*	September 1801	553-592
27*	October 1801	593-632
28	November 1801	633-672
29*	December 1801	673-712
30	January 1802	713-776
31	February 1802	777-824
32	March 1802	825-848
33	April 1802	849-873
34	May 1802	874-918
35	June 1802	919-958
36	July 1802	959-998
37	September 1802	999-1038
38	October 1802	1039-1078
39	November 1802	1079-1118
40	December 1802	1119-1152
41	January 1803	(probably contained Indices and Title-pages for Vols 3 and 4)

* = an original cover is extant (Angus Library).
H.W.A. = History of Welsh Association.

Table 4:

Showing the increase in members of the churches, as reported to the Particular Baptist Associations (1790-1802) and printed in the *Register*. Where no figures are given, either the Association did not give them, or the *Register* did not publish the records for that year

Association	1790	1791	1792	1793	1794	1795
Yorks & Lancs		11	22		7	-6
Northampton	51	38	31	42	21	75
Midland	54	65	45	55	56	22
Kent & Sussex	21	25	82	41	3	13
Western	119	113	64	26	64	-1
Norfolk & Suffolk						28
Northern						
Essex						
Total	245	252	244	164	151	131
Welsh (all 3)	407	220	355	139	586	903

Table 4 293

1796	1797	1798	1799	1800	1801	1802	Total
41	31	31			-10	20	147
97	76	8	19		39	8	505
	54	85			26	66	528
1		4		28	-8		210
50	102	121	58	137	136	150	1139
90	97	181	48	35	68	108	655
		20					20
					3		3
279	360	450	125	200	254	352	3207
413							3023

Table 5:
An analysis of *Register* contents

Subjects	Vol. 1 = 564pp		Vol. 2 = 634pp		Vol. 3 = 554pp		Vol. 4 = 600pp	
	pp	%	pp	%	pp	%	pp	%
1. List of churches	18	3.2	24	4.5	42	7.7	0	0
2. Associations*	186	32.9	71	13.5	36	6.6	40	6.7
3. American association and correspondence	106	18.6	26	4.9	25	4.6	50	8.6
4. List of books	25	4.5	33	6.4	23.	4.2	0	0
5. Obituaries, memorials	116	20.6	156	29.2	100	18.2	57	9.7
6. Intelligence (i.e. ordination,new meeting-houses, church formations)	6	1.2	24	4.5	27	4.9	49	8.4
7. Missions	42	7.5	79	14.9	104	19.0	56	9.6
8. America (general)	6	1.3	11	2.2	3	0.6	0	0
9. Negro work	26	4.6	16	2.9	5	1.0	4	0.7
10. Europe	20	3.5	6	1.3	3	0.6	50	8.6
11. Miscellaneous (i.e. devotional, anecdotes)	11	2.1	5	1.1	89	16.1	110	18.4
12. Histories of churches	0	0	62	11.6	46	8.4	63	9.9
13. Ireland	0	0	4	0.8	1	0.1	3	0.6
14. Itinerant Society	0	0	12	2.2	7	1.2	0	0
15. Dissenters' *Register*	0	0	0	0	8	1.4	2	0.6
16. Ancient MS papers	0	0	0	0	17	3.1	20	3.6
17. Original poetry	0	0	0	0	13	2.3	22	3.7
18. History (extracts)	0	0	0	0	0	0	65	10.9

*Not including materials published in No. 1 and the History of the Welsh Association.

Bibliography

Bibliography of John Rippon's Publications

The following list has been arranged as far as is possible in chronological order. Dating some editions of the *Selection* and *Tune Book* is difficult, as they were often not indicated. The place of publication is London in each case.

1784 *A Sermon occasioned by the death of the Reverend Andrew Gifford, D.D. With an Address delivered at his interment by John Ryland, A M.*

1787 *A Selection of Hymns, from the best authors, Intended to be An Appendix to Dr. Watts's Psalms and Hymns.*

1788 *Selection.* 2nd edn

1788 (ed.) *A Sermon at the Execution of Moses Paul, an Indian, who had been guilty of Murder, preached at New Haven in America by Samson Occom; to which is added A Short Account of the Late Spread of the Gospel, among the Indians; also Observations on the Language of the Muhhekanew Indians; by Jonathan Edwards, D.D.*

1789(?) *Selection.* 3rd edn

1790-1802 *The Baptist Annual Register, Including Sketches of the State of Religion among Different Denominations of Good Men at Home and Abroad.* (Published in 41 periodical issues).

1791 (ed.) *A Confession of Faith put forth by the Elders and Brethren of many Congregations of Christians (baptized upon profession of their faith) in London and the Country. Printed at London in 1688, now reprinted with a list of the thirty-seven Ministers who recommended it in 1689; to which this edition adds, what was never before given, the places where they all laboured in the Ministry.*

1791(?) *A Selection of Psalm and Hymn Tunes from the best authors, in three and four parts; adapted principally to Dr. Watts's Hymns, & Psalms, & to Dr. Rippon's Selection of Hymns; containing in a greater variety than any other volume extant, the most approved compositions which are used in London and in the different congregations throughout England; also many original tunes never before printed. The whole forming a publication of above two hundred hymn tunes.*

1792 *Selection.* 4th edn

1792 *The Gentle Dismission of Saints from Earth to Heaven. A sermon occasioned by the decease of the Rev. John Ryland, Senior.*

1793 (ed.) S. Wilson, *A Scripture Manual or a Plain Representation of the Ordinance of Baptism.*

1793 *Selection.* 5th edn

1794 *The Baptist Catechism, commonly called Keach's Catechism. Compared with the Early Editions, and revised by John Rippon, D.D.*

1796 *A Brief Essay towards an History of the Baptist Academy at Bristol; read before the Bristol Education Society, at their Anniversary Meeting, in Broadmead, August 26th, 1795.*

1797(?) *Tune Book* 2nd enlarged edn

1800 *Discourses on The All-Sufficient Gracious Assistance of the Spirit of Christ. To which are added Memoirs of the late Mr. William Lepard, one of the Deacons of the Baptist Church in Carter Lane, Southwark, who died in the 99th year of his Age.*

1800 *Selection* 10th enlarged edn

1800 *Addenda to the Selection of Hymns.*

1801 *An Arrangement of the Psalms, Hymns, and Spiritual Songs of the Rev. Isaac Watts, D.D. including (what no other Volume contains) all his Hymns, with which the Vacancies in the First Book were filled up in 1788; and also those in 1793: now collated, with each of the Doctor's own Editions. To which are subjoined, Indexes very much enlarged, both of Scriptures and of Subjects.*

1801 *Tables and enlarged indexes to the Psalms and Hymns of I. Watts.*

1802 *Watts* 3rd edn

1802 *Tune Book* 4th edn

1802 *A Discourse on the Origin and Progress of the Society for Promoting Religious Knowledge among the Poor, From its Commencement in 1750, to the Year 1802; including A Succinct Account of the separate publications in their catalogue with the benefit which has attended them; and of The different Modes which the Members and their Friends have adopted in distributing the Books to Advantage: Delivered before the Society November 17, 1796, and November 17, 1802. To which is added A Complete List of the Treasurers and other Officers as well as of the Ministers who have preached the Annual Sermons, and of the Gentlemen who have served the Office of Stewards.* Two editions.

1803 *A Discourse delivered at the Drum Head, on the Fort, Margate, Oct. 19, 1803, The Day of the General Fast, before the Volunteers, commanded by The Right Hon. William Pitt; and also Before the Ministers and Members of the Different Denominations of Protestant Dissenters who form The East Kent Association, at Folkstone, Oct. 26. and then addressed to The Volunteers of London and Southwark, Assembled with the Author's own Congregation in Carter Lane, near London Bridge, Nov. 13, 1803.* Four editions.

1803 *Selection* 15th edn

Selection 16th (?) edn

1805 *Watts* 4th (?) edn

1806 *A Sermon occasioned by the death of the Rev. Abraham Booth, preached in Little Prescot Street, Goodman's Fields, by James Dore: and A Short Memoir of the Deceased, incorporated with The Address delivered at his interment, in Maze Pond, by John Rippon.*

1808 *Tune Book* 5th edn

1810 *An Index of all the lines in Watts's Hymns and Psalms by J. R. assisted by S. A-, T. R-, &c.*

1810 *A Brief Memoir of the Life and Writings of the late John Gill, D.D.* (Published in Gill's *Exposition of the Old Testament*).

1812(?) *Selection* 18th edn

1813(?) *Selection* 19th edn. (American Baptist Historical Society Library).

1814(?) *Selection* 21st edn

1815 *Watts* 5th(?) edn

1816 *Selection* 23rd edn. (See *Baptist Magazine* 8 (1816), p. 257.)

1817 *Watts*, 6th(?) edn

1818(?) *Selection*, 24th edn

1819(?) Selection, 25th edn

1820 *A Sermon occasioned by the Demise of our Late Venerable Sovereign, King George the Third, and by the Accession of King George the Fourth, preached at Carter Lane, Southwark, Feb. 16, 1820. With supplementary papers, not given in the Discourse.* Two editions.

1828 *Selection* 27th enlarged edn

1828 *Selection* 28th edn

1828 *Hymns, Original and Selected, interspersed in the Twenty-seventh edition of the Selection with Numerous Doxologies, in the Usual, the Peculiar, and in the less common metres.*

1830(?) *Selection* 30th edn

1831(?) *Selection*, 31st edn

1837 *Selection*, 'New and enlarged' edn (Prepared by J. Haddon).

1838 *Memoir of Gill* (Published separately)

1840 *Selection*, 'New and enlarged' edn

1844 *Comprehensive Rippon*. (Further editions appeared in 1851, 1861.)

1844 *Memoir of Mr. William Lepard*

1860 *Memoir of Mr. William Lepard* (Angus Library).

List of Portraits and Engravings of Rippon

1. Showing Rippon in pulpit, preaching, directed and looking to left, in bands, left hand on open book.
Published by 0. Paterson, 1775, Mezzotinto, 12" by 9". Painter and engraver is R. Dunkarton.
(See F. O'Donoghue, *Catalogue of Engraved British Portraits preserved in the Department of Prints and Drawings in the British Museum*, 3 (1912), p. 586).

2. Showing Rippon, directed and looking to right, in bands.
Published by R. Bowyer, 1786. 3" by 3".
Painter: R. Bowyer; Engraver: J. Fittler.
Published in *Selection* (2nd ed., 1788); *Christians' Magazine*, 1 (1790), opposite p. 435.

3. Original oil portrait, showing Rippon in old age, half length, directed and looking to right, in bands.
Artist unknown. Hanging in 'Heritage Room' of Metropolitan Tabernacle Baptist church.

4. Engraving of the last-named by W. J. Alais. (See F. O'Donaghue, *Catalogue*)

5. Small wax cameo, by C. Andras. In Regent's Park College, Oxford.

Manuscripts

Churches

METROPOLITAN TABERNACLE BAPTIST CHURCH, LONDON

1. Churchbooks (1719-1854)
2. 'Rough Minutes' for Churchbook (1829-1834) and (1834-1836).
3. Cash Books (1798-1799), (1800-1801), (1814-1833).
4. Subscription Books (1814-1827) and (1824-1825).
5. Large Envelope, containing letters and documents relating to the move from the Carter Lane to New Park Street sites.
6. List of Members (1837-1856).
7. Communion Attendances (1838-1846).

TIVERTON BAPTIST CHURCH
Churchbook 1687-1844.

TIVERTON, ST. PETER'S CHURCH OF ENGLAND
Parish Registers.

British Libraries
Angus Library, Regent's Park College, Oxford

1. Papers, collected by, or relating to Rippon, including:
   a. Letter from D. Hovens to Rippon, Rotterdam, 26 November 1791.
   b. History of Baptists at Haarlem by E. Hovens written in 1740.
   c. Translations, by William Carey, of the above.
   d. History of Baptist Church at Plymouth.
   e. Abingdon Baptist Church Covenant (1728).
   f. Letters from constituent churches to Berkshire Association, 1707-8.
   g. Letters from Joshua Thomas, of Leominster, to Rippon: 13 October 1794; 6 February; 10 February; 19 March; 2, May 1795.
   h. Extracts from letters, churchbooks, trust deeds, etc. from Baptist churches (mainly in the West Country), some original 17th Century Manuscripts.
   i. Letters from John Bowen to Rippon, New York, 5 February and 23 May 1802.
2. Volume: 'Rough Schemes of Scriptural Subjects' by J. Rippon.
3. Proof-sheets, with MS corrections, of *Register* 1794-1796 only.
4. Volume: 'Sermons Preached at the Baptist Meeting in Tiverton Anno Dom: 1765'.
5. Letter, J. Rippon to S. Gale, 10 July 1829 (bound in a copy of *Register*, volume 2 (catalogue reference 3d.15).
6. 'Letters written to Wainsgate Church from Yorkshire and Lancashire Baptist Association 1762-1770'. Letters loose inside this:
   a. J. Stutterd to Rippon, Coln, 11 September 1790.
   b. J. Fawcett to Rippon, Brearley Hall, Halifax, 23 November 1790; 24 June 1791.
7. 'History of the Warren Association' including letter, Backus to Rippon, 10 November 1791.
8. Sermons preached at Broadmead, Bristol, by B. Foskett and H. Evans (1756).
9. Diary of William Newman (1808-1814, 1820-1834).
10. Records of the London Education Society (1752-1799).
11. Typescript: Correspondence of Andrew Fuller.
12. Churchbook of Unicorn Yard Church (1719-1820).
13. Minutes of the Particular Baptist Fund.

Baptist Missionary Society Archives (at Regent's Park College)

'Minutes of the Proceedings of the Baptist Society in London for the Encouragement and Support of Itinerant Preaching' (1797-1812).

Bristol Baptist College

'Transactions of the Bristol Education Society'.

British Library

1. Additional Manuscripts 25386 to 25389. Papers relating to Rippon, mainly letters to him, arranged in alphabetical order. (Microfilm copies are held by the Angus Library, Bristol Baptist College, the American Baptist Historical Society, the author.)
2. Additional Manuscripts 28513 to 28523 (14 volumes, numbered as 11). Papers relating to Rippon's preparations for the Bunhill Fields project. Includes biographical notes on persons buried in Bunhill Fields, alphabetical list of tombs and monuments, etc.

College of Arms, Queen Victoria Street, London

Six Volumes, containing 'Bunhill Fields Register of Burials (1713-1826)' in alphabetical order; and 6 volumes containing 'Bunhill Fields Monument and Grave Stone Inscriptions' in alphabetical order.

Dr. Williams's Library, 14 Gordon Square, London

1. Minute Books of the Body of Protestant Dissenting Ministers of the Three Denominations in and about the Cities of London and Westminster.
2. General Meeting Book of the Society for the Relief of the Widows and children of Poor Protestant Dissenting Ministers Deceased.

Congregational Library at the Dr. Williams's Library

1. 'A Brief Account of ye workings of the Spirit of God on my soul' by John Rippon (Senior).
2. 'Papers, Historical, Biographical and Various. Found in the study of JOHN RIPPON, D.D.' Assorted MS.letters and papers, similar to the collection in British Museum.

Family Records Centre, 1 Myddelton Street, London

Tiverton Baptist Birth Register
Copies of wills of John Rippon, Thomas Rippon, Robert Bowyer.

American Libraries

American Baptist Historical Society, Rochester, New York

1. Letters Rippon to T. Ustick: 8 August 1786; 25 March 1794.
2. Letters Rippon to S. Williams (of New York): 14 June 1804; 16 January 1828.

Andover Newton Theological School, Newton Centre, Massachusetts

1. Letter, I. Backus to Rippon, 1791.
2. Letter, Rippon to Backus, 5 October 1798.

Brown University, Providence, Rhode Island

1. Letters Rippon to J. Manning: 1 May, 24 December 1784; 23 February, 22 June 1785; 19 September and another, 1786; 29 June 1787; 9 August, 28 October 1788; 21 September 1789; 28 June, 14 August, and another, 1791.
2. Letters, Rippon to T. Ustick: 1 March 1790; 23 August 1791; 6 February, 26 July 1793.
3. (Draft of letter), S. Drowne to Rippon, 29 July 1791.

Furman University, Greenville, South Carolina

1. Letters, Rippon to R. Furman: 6 April 1792; 30 January 1819.
2. Letter: T. Dunscombe to Furman, 22 July 1793.

Historical Society of Pennsylvania, Philadelphia, Pennsylvania

1. Letters J. Rippon to J. Sutcliff: 26 July 1773; 28 December 1787.
2. Letters J. Rippon to J. Morse: 30 June 1791; 28 February 1793.
3. Letter (incomplete), J. Rippon to W. Rogers (1796).

Private Sources

Letter, Rippon to T. Ustick, 13 Feb.1788 (in possession of Dr Roger Hayden, of Bristol, who kindly supplied a copy).

Unpublished Theses

H. Davies, 'Transatlantic Brethren: A Study of English, Welsh and American Baptists with particular reference to Morgan John Rhys and his friends' (PhD thesis, University of Wales, 1984).

J.C. Fletcher, 'Interaction between English and American Baptists from 1639-1689' (ThD thesis, Southwestern Baptist Seminary, Fort Worth, Texas, 1958).

R. Hayden 'Evangelical Calvinism among eighteenth-century British Baptists with particular reference to Bernard Foskett, Hugh and Caleb Evans and the Bristol Baptist Academy, 1690-1791' (PhD thesis, University of Keele, 1991).

M.D. McDonald, 'London Calvinistic Baptists 1698-1727: Tensions within a Dissenting Community under Toleration' (DPhil thesis, Oxford University, 1982).

D.D.J. Morgan, 'The Development of the Baptist Movement in Wales between 1714 and 1815 with particular reference to the Evangelical Revival' (DPhil thesis, Oxford University, 1986).

O.C. Robison, 'The Particular Baptists in England, 1760-1820' (DPhil Thesis, Oxford University, 1963).

K.E. Smith, 'The Community and the Believer: A Study of Calvinistic Baptist Spirituality in some towns and villages of Hampshire and the borders of Wiltshire, c.1730-1830' (DPhil thesis, Oxford University, 1986).

J. Thompson, 'Baptists in Ireland, 1792-1922: A dimension of Protestant Dissent' (DPhil thesis, Oxford University, 1988).

R.H. Young, 'The History of Baptist Hymnody in England from 1612 to 1800' (DMus thesis, Southern California University, 1959).

Periodicals

The Annual Register (1758-).

J. Asplund (ed), *The Annual Register of the Baptist Denomination in North America* (Richmond, Va.: 1791, 1794, 1796).

Baptist Magazine (1809-1908).

Baptist Quarterly (1922-).

Baptist World (Journal of Baptist World Alliance, Washington, 1954-).

Biblical Magazine (Clipstone, 1801-1803).
Christian's Magazine; or Gospel Repository (1790-92).
The Chronicle (Chester, Pa.: 1938-67).
Congregational Magazine (1818-1845).
Evangelical Magazine (1793-1904).
General Baptist Magazine (1798-1800).
Gentleman's Magazine (1731-1907).
Gospel Magazine, or Treasury of Divine Knowledge (1774-1784).
Gospel Magazine and Theological Review (1796-).
The Jewish Repository, or monthly communication respecting the Jews, and the proceedings of the London Society (1813-14).
Monthly Repository and Review of Theology and General Literature (1806-1836).
Monthly Review (1749-1845).
New Spiritual Magazine (1783-85).
New Theological Repository, consisting of original essays upon the evidences, excellency, and doctrines of Christianity (Liverpool: 1800-1803).
Notes and Queries, 6th series, 11 (1855).
Periodical Accounts relative to the Baptist Missionary Society (1794-1818).
Protestant Dissenters' Magazine (1794-99).
The Pulpit (1824-71).
Theological and Biblical Magazine (1804-1808).
Transactions of the Baptist Historical Society (1908-21).
Transactions of the Congregational Historical Society (1901-64).

Books and Articles

C.J. Abbey, and J.H. Overton, *The English Church in the Eighteenth Century* (London: 1887).
L. Adey, *Class and Idol in the English Hymn* (Vancouver: University of British Columbia, 1988).
B. Amey, 'Baptist Missionary Society Radicals', *BQ* 26.8 (1976), pp. 363-76.
An Account of the Book Society for promoting Religious Knowledge among the Poor (London: 1830).
Accounts of the Bristol Education Society (Bristol: 1770-1817).
W. Marston Acres, 'A former Chief Cashier', *The Old Lady of Threadneedle Street* (Staff Journal Bank of England, 3. 22, June 1926).
H. Anderson, *The Life and Letters of Christopher Anderson* (Edinburgh: 1854).

W.T. Andress, *History of Newhouse Upottery* (Taunton: privately published, 1932).

J. Ash and C. Evans, *A Collection of Hymns adapted to Public Worship* (Bristol: 1769).

T.S. Ashton, *The Industrial Revolution 1760-1830* (London: Oxford University Press, 1962).

W.P. Authers, *The Tiverton Congregational Church 1660-1960* (Tiverton: Tiverton Congregational Church, 1960).

I. Backus, *A History of New England with Particular Reference to the Denomination of Christians called Baptists* (3 vols; Boston: 1777, 1784, 1796).

'Baptist Board Minutes', *BHS Trans.* 5 (1916-17), pp. 96-114, 197-240; 6 (1918-19), pp. 72-127.

Baptist Building Fund. Formation and rules of the Society (London: 1824).

The Baptist Fund and Stepney (London: 1876).

The Baptist Hymn Book (London: Psalms and Hymns Trust, 1962).

Baptist Praise and Worship (Oxford: Oxford University Press, 1991).

F.W. Bateson (ed.), *Cambridge Bibliography of English Literature* (5 vols; Cambridge: Cambridge University Press, 1940-57).

A.J.H. Baynes, 'The Pre-History of Regent's Park College', *BQ* 36.4 (1995), pp. 191-201.

E.D. Bebb, *Nonconformity and Social and Economic Life 1660-1800* (London: Epworth Press, 1935).

D.W. Bebbington (ed.), *The Baptists in Scotland* (Glasgow: Baptist Union of Scotland, 1988).

– *Evangelicalism in Modern Britain. A history from the 1730s to the 1980s* (London: Unwin Hyman, 1989).

– *Holiness in Nineteenth-Century England* (Carlisle: Paternoster, 2000).

B. Beddome, *Hymns adapted to Public Worship or Family Devotion, now first published from the Manuscripts of the late Rev. B. Beddome* (London: 1817).

J.C. Beckett, *Protestant Dissent in Ireland 1687-1780* (London: Faber and Faber, 1948).

J. Belcher, *Historical Sketches of Hymns, their Writers, and their Influence* (Philadelphia: 1859).

H.S. Bender, C.H. Smith, C.J. Dyck, D.D. Martin (eds.), *The Mennonite Encyclopedia* (5 vols; Scottdale, Pa.: Mennonite Publishing House, 1956,1990).

D. Benedict, *A General History of the Baptist Denomination in America, and Other Parts of the World* (2 vols; Boston: 1813).

J. Bennett, *The History of the Dissenters during the last Thirty Years* (London: 1839).

L.F. Benson, *The English Hymn. Its development and use in Worship* (New York: 1915; Richmond, Va., John Knox Press, 1962.)

J. Berridge, *Sion's Songs, or Hymns: Composed for the Use of them that love and follow the Lord Jesus Christ in Sincerity* (London: 1785).

C. Binfield, *So Down to Prayers. Studies in English Nonconformity 1780-1920* (London: J.M. Dent & Sons, 1977).

S.L. Bishop, *Isaac Watts Hymns and Spiritual Songs 1707-1748. A Study in Early Eighteenth Century Language Changes* (London: Faith Press, 1962).

J. Boden and E. Williams, *A Collection of above Six Hundred Hymns Designed as a New Supplement to Dr. Watts's Psalms and Hymns* (Doncaster: 1801).

D. Bogue and J. Bennett, *The History of Dissenters from the Revolution to the Year 1808* (4 vols; London: 1810-12).

C. Bonner and W.T. Whitley, *Handbook to the Baptist Church Hymnal Revised* (London: Psalms and Hymns Trust, 1935).

C. Bonwick, 'English Dissenters and the American Revolution', in H.C. Allen and R. Thompson (eds.), *Contrast and Connection: Bicentennial Essays in Anglo-American History* (Athens: Ohio University Press, 1976), pp. 88-112.

A. Booth, *Paedobaptism Examined* (2 vols; London: 1787).

J. Bowring, *Specimens of the Russian Poets, translated with preliminary remarks and biographical notices* (2 vols; London: 1821-1823).

W.H. Brackney, P.S.Fiddes, J.H.Y. Briggs (eds.), *Pilgrim Pathways: Essays in Baptist History in Honour of B.R. White* (Macon, Ga.: Mercer University Press, 1999).

I. Bradley, *Abide with Me, The World of Victorian Hymns* (London: S.C.M., 1997).

J.E. Bradley, 'Religion and Reform at the Polls: Nonconformity in Cambridge Politics, 1774-1784', *Journal of British Studies* 23.2 (1984), pp. 55-78.

– *Religion, Revolution and English Radicalism: Nonconformity in Eighteenth-Century Politics and Society* (Cambridge: Cambridge University Press, 1990).

P. Brewer, 'British Baptist Missionaries and Baptist work in the Bahamas', *BQ* 32.6 (1988), pp. 295-301.

Brief History of the Baptist Church of Christ, Assembling at Upottery, Devon (n.d.).

Brief Sketch of the Life and Character of the Rev. John Giles (n.d.).

J.H.Y. Briggs, *The English Baptists of the Nineteenth Century* (Didcot: Baptist Historical Society, 1994).

W.C. Bronson, *The History of Brown University 1764-1914* (Providence: Brown University, 1914).

F.K. Brown, *Fathers of the Victorians. The Age of Wilberforce* (Cambridge: Cambridge University Press, 1961).

K.D. Brown, *A Social History of the Nonconformist Ministry in England and Wales 1800-1930* (Oxford: Clarendon Press, 1988).

R. Brown, *The English Baptists of the eighteenth Century* (London: Baptist Historical Society, 1986).

J. Browne, *History of Congregationalism in Norfolk and Suffolk* (London: 1877).

S. Browne, *Hymns and Spiritual Songs, in Three Books, designed as a Supplement to Dr. Watts* (London: 1720).

F. Buffard, *Kent and Sussex Baptist Associations* (Faversham: Kent and Sussex Baptist Association, 1963).

J. Bull, *John Newton of Olney and St. Mary Woolnoth* (London: 1868).

G. Burder, *Collection of Hymns from various Authors, intended as a Supplement to Dr. Watts* (London: 1784).

C. Burrage, *Early English Dissenters* (2 vols; Cambridge: Cambridge University Press, 1912).

H.S. Burrage, *Baptist Hymn Writers and their Hymns* (Portland: 1888).

W. Button, *Remarks on a Treatise, entitled, The Gospel of Christ worthy of all Acceptation by Andrew Fuller* (London: 1785).

G.W. Byrt, *Stream of the River. (An attempt to tell the Story of a Free Church - West End Baptist Church, Hammersmith, on the background of its Place and Period, 1793-1943)* (London: Kingsgate Press, 1944).

J.P. Carey, *Planting of the Baptist Church in Tiverton, being Extracts from Ancient Documents and Arguments Deduced therefrom* (Tiverton: 1876).

S.P. Carey, *William Carey* (London: Hodder and Stoughton, 1923).

J.C. Carlile, *The Story of the English Baptists* (London: J. Clarke & Co., 1905).

H.B. Case, *The History of the Baptist Church in Tiverton 1607 to 1907* (Tiverton: 1907).

Catalogue of a very curious and interesting collection of Books and Tracts wholly relating to America (the major part of which are from the Library of the late Rev. John Rippon, D. D., eminent Baptist Minister) (1861). (Copy in Bodleian Library, Oxford.)

W. Cathcart (ed.), *Baptist Encyclopaedia* (2 vols; Philadelphia: Louis H. Everts, 1881).

G.A. Catherall, 'The Native Baptist Church', *BQ* 24.2 (1971), pp. 65-73.

J. Cennick, *Sacred Hymns for the use of religious societies* (London: 1770)

L.G. Champion, *Farthing Rushlight. The Story of Andrew Gifford 1700–1784* (London: Carey Kingsgate Press, 1961).

– 'Evangelical Calvinism and the Structures of Baptist Church Life', *BQ* 28.5 (1980), pp. 196-208.
– 'Robert Robinson. A Pastor in Cambridge', *BQ* 31.5 (1986), pp. 241-46.
Christian Songs: To which is prefixed the Evidence and Import of Christ's Resurrection versified for the help of the Memory (8th edn, Perth: 1794).
T. Clarkson, *History of the Rise, Progress and Accomplishment of the Abolition of the African Slave Trade by the British Parliament* (London: 1839).
E.F. Clipsham, 'Fuller and Fullerism', *BQ* 20 (1983), pp. 99-114, 146-54, 214-26, 288-76.
M. Collis, 'The Lord's Supper in British Baptist Hymnology in the Twentieth Century', *BQ* 38.6 (2000), pp. 290-304.
Commencement, Constitution and Use, of the Particular Baptist Fund, in London: in an Address to the Churches in the Country (1771). (Copy in Angus Library.)
Congregational Praise (London: Independent Press, 1951).
R. Conyers, *A Collection of Psalms and Hymns from Various Authors: For the use of Serious and Devout Christians of every Denomination* (London: 1767).
W.B. Collyer, *Hymns partly collected and partly original; designed as a supplement to Dr. Watts's Psalms and Hymns* (London; 1812).
J. Conder, *Star in the East; and other Poems* (London: 1824).
R.E. Cooper, 'Selections from the Diary of William Newman', *BQ* 18 (1959-60), pp. 77-87, 275-82.
– *From Stepney to St. Giles'. The Story of Regent's Park College 1810-1960* (London: Carey Kingsgate Press, 1960).
L. Coughlain, *A Select Collection of Psalms and Hymns, extracted from several authors, and published for the use of the congregation of Cumberland-Street Chapel* (London: 3rd edn, 1775).
Covenant of the Anabaptist Church Begun in America December 1777. In Jamaica, December 1783 (Jamaica: 1796). (Copy in Angus Library.)
F.A. Cox, *Memoirs of the Rev. William Henry Angas, ordained a 'Missionary to Seafaring Men, May 11, 1822'* (London: 1834).
– and J. Hoby, *The Baptists in America; a Narrative of the Deputation from the Baptist Union in England, to the United States of America* (London: 1836).
– *History of the Baptist Missionary Society from 1792 to 1842* (2 vols; London: 1842).
B. Coxhead, *Evangelical Advice and Encouragement. A Farewell Discourse, Addressed to a Congregation in Ebenezer Chapel, Truro, October 2d 1808* (London: 1808).

T.G. Crippen, 'The Tombs in Bunhill Fields', *Transactions* of Congregational Historical Society 4 (1909-10), pp. 347-63.

– 'Congregational Hymnody', *Transactions* of Congregational Historical Society 7 (1916-18), pp. 224-34, 288-99.

T. Crosby, *The History of the English Baptists, from the Reformation to the Beginning of the Reign of King George I* (4 vols; London: 1738-40).

R. Cruttenden, *Experience of Robert Cruttenden. also several Psalms, Hymns &c composed by him* (London: 1742).

J. Culross, *The Three Rylands: A Hundred Years of various Christian Service* (London: 1897).

(A. Dakin), *Bristol Baptist College 250 Years 1679-1929* (Bristol: 1929).

J.A. Davidson, 'Redstone Baptist Association of Western Pennsylvania', *The Chronicle* 5 (1942), pp. 133-40.

D. Davie, *A Gathered Church. The Literature of the English Dissenting Interest, 1700-1930* (London: Routledge & Kegan Paul, 1978).

– *The Eighteenth-Century Hymn in England* (Cambridge: Cambridge University Press, 1993).

Horton Davies, *From Watts and Wesley to Maurice 1690-1850, Worship and Theology in England* (5 vols; Princeton: Princeton University Press, 1961-75).

H. Davies, 'The American Revolution and the Baptist Atlantic', *BQ* 36.3 (1995), pp. 132-49.

– '"Very Different Springs of Uneasiness": Emigration from Wales to the United States of America during the 1790s', *The Welsh History Review: Cylchgrawn Hanes Cymru* 15.3 (1991), pp. 368-98.

R. Davies and G. Rupp (eds.), *A History of the Methodist Church in Great Britain* (4 vols; London: Epworth, 1965-88).

W.S. Davies, *In pleasant places. The Story of Tenterden Baptist Church over Two Centuries* (London: 1967).

A.P. Davis, *Isaac Watts His Life and Works* (London: Independent Press, 1948).

Distributions of the Baptist Fund (1789-1836). (Set in Angus Library.)

K. Dix, *Strict and Particular. English Strict and Particular Baptists in the nineteenth century* (Didcot: Baptist Historical Society, 2001).

J. Dobell, *New Selection of More than Seven Hundred Evangelical Hymns* (London: 1806).

P. Doddridge, *On the Rise and Progress of Religion in the Soul* (London: 1745).

– *Hymns founded on Various Texts in the Holy Scriptures* (ed. J. Orton; London: 1755).

D. Douglas, *History of the Baptist Churches in the North of England from 1648 to 1845* (London: 1846).

L. Drummond, *Spurgeon Prince of Preachers* (Grand Rapids: Kregel, 1992).

T. Dunscombe, *The tribute of affection to the memory of the late Dr. Evans* (Oxford: 1792).

M. Dunsford, *Historical Memoirs of the town and parish of TIVERTON, in the county of Devon* (Exeter: 1790).

G. Dyer, *Memoirs of the Life and Writings of Robert Robinson* (London: 1796).

J. Dyer, *Collection of Psalms and Hymns* (2 parts; London: 1767).

J. Edmeston, *The Cottage Minstrel; or Hymns for the Assistance of Cottagers in their Domestic Worship* (London: 1821).

J. Edwards, *A Humble Attempt to Promote Explicit Agreement and Visible Union of God's People in Extraordinary Prayer for the Revival of Religion and the advancement of Christ's Kingdom on Earth* (Boston: 1747).

– *A Careful and strict Enquiry into The modern prevailing Notions of that Freedom of Will which is supposed to be essential to moral Agency, Vertue and Vice, Reward and Punishment, Praise and Blame* (Boston: 1754).

M. Edwards, *Material towards a history of the Baptists in New Jersey* (Philadelphia: 1792).

G.M. Ella, 'John Gill and the Charge of Hyper-Calvinism', *BQ* 36.4 (1995), pp. 160-77.

O.W. Elsbree, *The Rise of the Missionary Spirit in America 1790-1815* (Philadelphia: Porcupine Press, 1980 [1928]).

T.S.H. Elwyn, *The Northamptonshire Baptist Association A Short History 1764-1964* (London: Carey Kingsgate Press, 1964).

Encyclopaedia of Southern Baptists (4 vols; Nashville: Broadman Press, 1958, 1971, 1982).

W. Enfield, *Collection of Psalms proper for Christian Worship, with additions* (Liverpool: 1787).

H. Escott, *Isaac Watts Hymnographer. A Study of the Beginnings, Development, and Philosophy of the English Hymn* (London: Independent Press, 1962).

B. Evans (ed.) *The Early English Baptists* (2 vols; London: 1862-4).

Caleb Evans, *Scripture Doctrine of the Deity of the Son and Holy Spirit, represented in two sermons preached at Bristol, March 24, and April 21, 1765* (Bristol: 1766).

– *A Charge and Sermon, together with an Introductory Discourse and Confession of Faith delivered at the ordination of the Rev. Caleb Evans.* (Bristol: 1767).

– and H. Evans, *A Charge and Sermon; delivered at the ordination of the Rev. Thomas Dunscombe, at Coate, Oxon, August 4th 1774* (Bristol: 1773).

- *The Kingdom of God* (Bristol: 1775).
- *A Letter to the Rev. Mr. John Wesley, occasioned by his Calm Address to the Americans* (London: 1773).
- *Elisha's Exclamation, a Sermon occasioned by the Death of the Rev. Hugh Evans* (Bristol 1781).
- *Christ Crucified; or The Scripture Doctrine of the Atonement briefly illustrated and defended* (Bristol 1789).

Charles Evans (ed.), *American Bibliography. A Chronological Dictionary of all Books Pamphlets and Periodical Publications Printed in the United States of America from the genesis of printing in 1639 down to and including the year 1820* (14 vols; Chicago: Blakely Press, 1903-59).

H. Evans, *Ministers described, under the Characters of Fathers and Prophets* (Bristol: 1773).
- *The Able Minister* (Bristol: 1773).

J. Evans, *Memoirs of the life and Writings of the Rev. William Richards, LL.D.* (London: 1819).

J. Exall, *Sketches of the Kent and Sussex Baptist Associations, from 1779 to 1829* (London: 1829).

J. Fawcett, *Hymns adapted to the circumstances of Public Worship and Private Devotion* (Leeds: 1782).

J. Fawcett (Jr), *An Account of the Life, Ministry, and Writings of the late Rev. John Fawcett, D.D.* (London: 1818).

J. Fellows, *Hymns on Believers' Baptism* (Birmingham: 1773).

L.A. Fereday, *The Story of Falmouth Baptists. With Some account of Cornish Baptist beginnings* (London: Carey Kingsgate Press, 1950).

B.F. and L.F. Flint, *Brief Records of the Flint Family, with its Collateral Branches* (London: 1874).

B. Flower (ed.), *Miscellaneous Works of Robert Robinson* (4 vols; Harlow: 1807).

H.W. Foote, *Three Centuries of American Hymnody* (Hamden, Conn.: Shoe String Press, 1961).

H. Foreman, 'Baptists and the Charity School Movement', *BQ* 27.4 (1977-78), pp. 150-56.
- 'Baptist Provision for Ministerial Education in the 18th Century', *BQ* 27.8 (1978), pp. 358-69.

M. Frost (ed.), *Historical Companion to Hymns Ancient and Modern* (London: Hymns Ancient and Modern, 1962).

A. Fuller, *Gospel Worthy of all acceptation.* (Northampton: 1785).
- *Memoirs of the late Rev. Samuel Pearce* (Clipstone: 1800).

J.G. Fuller, *A Brief History of the Western Association from its commencement...to...1823* (Bristol: 1843).

J. Gadsby, *Memoirs of the Principal Hymn-Writers and Compilers of the 17th and 18th Centuries* (London: 1855).

F.H. Gale, *Battersea Chapel 1797-1897* (London: 1897).

J.P. Gates, 'George Liele: A Pioneer Negro Preacher', *The Chronicle* 6 (1943), pp. 118-29.

C. Gayle, *George Liele. Pioneer Missionary to Jamaica*, (Kingston: Jamaica Baptist Union, 1982).

M.D. George, *London Life in the Eighteenth Century* (Harmondsworth: Penguin, 2nd edn, 1966).

T. George, 'Between Pacifism and Coercion: The English Baptist Doctrine of Religious Toleration', *Mennonite Quarterly Review* 58.1 (1984), pp. 30-49.

– and G. Dockery (eds.), *Baptist Theologians* (Nashville: Broadman, 1990).

W.M. Gewehr, *The Great Awakening in Virginia 1740-1790* (Gloucester, Mass.: P. Smith, 1965 [1930]).

T. Gibbons, *Hymns adapted to Divine Worship in two books* (London: 1769, 1784).

W.T. Gidney, *The History of the London Society for Promoting Christianity among the Jews* (London: 1908).

A.D. Gilbert, *Religion and Society in Industrial England: Church, Chapel and Social Change, 1740-1914* (London: Longman, 1976).

J. Gill, *A Body of Doctrinal and Practical Divinity* (3 vols; London: 1769-70).

– *Collection of Sermons and Tracts* (2 vols; London: 1773).

– *Exposition of the Old Testament* (6 vols; London: 1810).

C.C. Goen, *Revivalism and Separatism in New England 1740-1800* (New Haven: Yale University Press, 1962).

G. Gordon, *From Slavery to Freedom. The Life of David George, Pioneer Black Baptist Minister*, (Hantsport, Nova Scotia: Lancelot Press, 1992).

– 'John Ryland, Jr. (1753-1825)' in M.A.G. Haykin (ed.), *The British Particular Baptists 1638-1910* (2 vols; Springfield, Mo.: Particular Baptist Press, 1998, 2000), 2, pp. 77-94.

G.P. Gould, *The Baptist College at Regent's Park. A Centenary Record* (London: 1910).

A.J. Grant, *The Huguenots* (London: Thornton Butterworth, 1934).

J. Grant, *Original Hymns and Poems, written by a Private Christian for his own use, and Published at the earnest desire of Friends* (Edinburgh: 1784).

T. Greene, *Hymns and Poems on Various Subjects, chiefly Sacred* (London: 1780).

O. Gregory (ed.), *The Works of Robert Hall* (6 vols; London: 1833).

S. Grenz, *Isaac Backus-Puritan and Baptist* (Macon, Ga.: Mercer University Press, 1983).

J. Griffin, *Selection of Missionary and Devotional Hymns* (Portsea: 1797).

C.P. Groves, *The Planting of Christianity in Africa* (4 vols; London: Lutterworth, 1948-58).

R.A. Guild, *Early History of Brown University, including the Life, Times, and Correspondence of President Manning 1756-1791* (Providence, R.I.: 1897).

C.S. Hall, and H. Mowvley, *Tradition and Challenge: The Story of Broadmead Baptist Church, Bristol from 1685 to 1991* (Bristol: Broadmead Baptist Church, 1991).

A.G. Hamlin, 'Bristol Baptist Itinerant Society', *BQ* 21.7 (1966), pp. 321-24.

S. Harrison, *Songs in the Night; by a young woman under heavy afflictions* (London: 1780).

J. Hart, *Hymns composed on Various Subjects, with the Author's Experience* (London: 1759).

H.O. Hartzell, 'Jacob Grigg - Missionary and Minister', *The Chronicle* 6 (1943), pp. 83-90, 130-43.

T. Haweis, *Carmina Christo: or Hymns to the Saviour. Designed for the Use and Comfort of Those who worship the Lamb that was slain* (Bath: 1792).

– *An Impartial and Succinct History of the Rise, declension, and Revival of the Church of Christ* (3 vols; London: 1800).

O. Hawker, *A Biographical Sketch of Francis James Blight, F.R.S.E., Publisher* (London: Elliott Stock, 1931).

E.W. Hayden, *A Centennial History of Spurgeon's Tabernacle* (London: Clifford Frost, 1962).

– 'Joshua Thomas: Welsh Baptist Historian', *BQ* 23.3 (1969), pp. 126-37.

R. Hayden (ed.), *The Records of a Church of Christ in Bristol 1640-1687* (Bristol: Bristol Record Society, 1974).

– (ed.), *English Baptist Records. 2. Church Book: St. Andrew's Street Baptist Church, Cambridge, 1720-1832* (Didcot: Baptist Historical Society, 1991).

– 'The Contribution of Bernard Foskett', in W.H. Brackney, P.S Fiddes, J.H.Y.Briggs (eds.), *Pilgrim Pathways* (Macon, Ga.: Mercer University Press, 1999), pp. 189-206.

– 'Caleb Evans and the Anti-Slavery Question', *BQ* 39.1 (2001), pp. 4-14.

M.A.G. Haykin, *One Heart and One Soul. John Sutcliff of Olney, his friends and his times*, (Darlington: Evangelical Press, 1994).

– *Kiffin, Knollys and Keach-Rediscovering our English Baptist Heritage* (Leeds: Reformation Today Trust, 1996).

– '"Resisting Evil": Civil Retaliation, non-resistance, and the interpretation of Matthew 5:39a among eighteenth-century Calvinistic Baptists', *BQ* 36.5 (1996), pp. 212-27.

- (ed.), *The Life and Thought of John Gill (1697-1771): A tercentennial Appreciation* (Leiden: E. J. Brill, 1997).
- (ed.), *The British Particular Baptists 1638-1910* (2 vols; Springfield, Mo.: Particular Baptist Press, 1998, 2000).
- 'Benjamin Beddome (1717-1795)' in *The British Particular Baptists 1638-1910*, 1, pp. 167-82.
- 'Robert Hall, Sr. (1728-1791)' in *The British Particular Baptists 1638-1910*, 1, pp. 203-210.
- 'Benjamin Francis (1734-1799)' in *The British Particular Baptists 1638-1910*, 2, pp. 17-28.
R. Heber, *Hymns written and adapted to the Weekly Church Service of the Year* (London: 1827).
C. Hill, 'Propagating the Gospel', in H.E. Bell and R.L. Bollard (eds.), *Historical Essays, 1600-1750 presented to David Ogg* (London: A. & C. Black, 1964), pp. 35-59.
R. Hill, *Collection of Psalms and Hymns, chiefly intended for Public Worship* (London: 1783).
J.H. Hinton, *A Biographical Portraiture of the late Rev. James Hinton, M.A.* (Oxford: 1824).
History of the Bunhill Fields Burial Grounds with some of the Principal Inscriptions (London: 1872).
E.A. Holmes, 'George Liele: Negro Slavery's Prophet of Deliverance', *BQ* 20.8 (1964), pp. 340-51.
W.W. Horne, *A Selection of Hymns for Public Worship; Alphabetically arranged according to their various Subjects* (Leicester: 1802).
W.G. Hoskins, *Devon (A New Survey of England)* (Newton Abbot: David & Charles, rev. edn, 1978).
A. Hovey, *Memoir of the Life and Times of the Reverend Isaac Backus* (Boston 1859).
C.L. Howe, Jr, 'British Evangelical Response to the American Revolution: the Baptists', *Fides et Historia* 8 (1976), pp. 35-49.
G. Hughes, *Robert Hall* (London: Carey Press, 1943).
- *With Freedom Fired. The Story of Robert Robinson Cambridge Nonconformist* (London: Carey Kingsgate Press, 1955).
Huntingdon, Countess of, *A Select Collection of Hymns to be universally sung in all the Countess of Huntingdon's Chapels. Collected by her Ladyship* (London: 1780).
W. Huntington, *A Letter to the Rev. Caleb Evans, M.A., containing a few remarks on a Circular Letter drawn up by him* (London: 1798).
H. P. Ippel, 'British Sermons and the American Revolution', *Journal of Religious History* 12.2 (1982), pp. 191-205.
J. Ivimey, *A History of the English Baptists* (4 vols; London: 1811-1830).

A. Jackson, *The Question Answered - whether saving Faith in Christ is a Duty required by the moral Law, of all those who live under the Gospel* (London: 1752).

S. Jakobsson, *Am I not a Man and a Brother? British Missions and the Abolition of the Slave Trade and Slavery in West Africa and the West Indies 1786-1838* (Lund: Gleerup, 1972)

P. Jalland, *Death in the Victorian Family* (Oxford: Oxford University Press, 1996).

S. James, 'Revival and Renewal in Baptist Life: The Contribution of William Steadman (1764-1837)', *BQ* 37.6 (1998), pp. 264-66.

– 'John Rippon (1751-1836): Willing Servant of all the Churches', *Reformation Today*, 179 (January-February 2001), pp. 15-24.

– 'John Rippon (1751-1836)', in M.A.G. Haykin (ed.), *The British Particular Baptists 1638-1910* (2 vols; Springfield, Mo.: Particular Baptist Press, 1998, 2000), 2, pp. 51-75.

– 'William Steadman (1764-1837)' in M.A.G. Haykin (ed.), *The British Particular Baptists 1638-1910* (2 vols; Springfield, Mo.: Particular Baptist Press, 1998, 2000), 2, pp. 163-80.

J. Jenkins, *The love of the brethren proceeding from a perception of the love of God: a sermon occasioned by the death of Samuel Stennett* (London: 1795).

R.T. Jenkins and J.E. Lloyd (eds.), *Dictionary of Welsh Biography down to 1940* (London: Cymrodorion Society, 1959).

C.B. Jewson, *The Baptists in Norfolk* (London: Carey Kingsgate Press, 1957).

– 'Norwich Baptists and the French Revolution', *BQ* 24.5 (1972), pp. 209-15.

A. Johnson *et al* (eds.), *Dictionary of American Biography* (22 vols; New York: Scribner, 1928-58).

W.C. Johnson, *Encounter London. The Story of the London Baptist Association 1865-1965* (London: Carey Kingsgate Press, 1965).

J.A. Jones, *Bunhill Memorials, Sacred Reminiscences of Three Hundred Ministers and other Persons of note who are buried in Bunhill Fields* (London: 1849).

M.G. Jones, *The Charity School Movement. A Study of Eighteenth Century Puritanism in Action* (Cambridge: Cambridge University Press, 1938).

R.T. Jones, *Congregationalism in England 1662-1962* (London: Independent Press, 1962).

W. Jones, *Autobiography.* [Edited by his Son] (London: 1846).

J. Julian (ed.), *Dictionary of Hymnology* (London: John Murray, 2nd edn, 1907).

T. Kelly, *A Collection of Psalms and Hymns extracted from Various Authors* (Dublin: 1802).

Kent and Sussex Baptist Association Circular Letters (1787-1802).

E.F. Kevan, *London's oldest Baptist Church. Wapping 1633-Walthamstow 1933* (London: Kingsgate Press, 1933).

A. Kippis, A. Rees, T. Jervis, and T. Morgan, *A Collection of Hymns and Psalms for Public and Private Worship* (London: 1795).

A.J. Klaiber, *The Story of the Suffolk Baptists* (London: Kingsgate Press, 1931).

A. Knox, *Remains* (4 vols; London: 1834-37).

Lady Knutsford (Holland, Margaret Jean), *Life and Letters of Zachary Macaulay* (London: E. Arnold, 1900).

J. Langford, *Hymns and Spiritual Songs* (London: 1776).

A.J. Lewis, *Zinzendorf the Ecumenical Pioneer. A Study in the Moravian Contribution to Christian Mission and Unity* (London: S.C.M., 1962).

D.M. Lewis (ed.), *The Blackwell Dictionary of Evangelical Biography 1730-1860* (2 vols; Oxford: Blackwell, 1995).

A.W. Light, *Bunhill Fields* (2 vols; London: C.J. Farncombe, 1913, 1933).

A.H. Lincoln, *Some Political and Social Ideas of English Dissent 1760-1800* (Cambridge: Cambridge University Press, 1935).

F.T. Lord, *Baptist World Fellowship. A Short History of the Baptist World Alliance* (London: Carey Kingsgate Press, 1955).

W.D. Love, *Samson Occom and the Christian Indians of New England* (Boston: 1899).

D.W. Lovegrove, 'Particular Baptist Itinerant Preachers during the late 18th and early 19th Centuries', *BQ* 28.3 (1979), pp. 127-41.

– *Established Church, Sectarian People. Itinerancy and the Transformation of English Dissent, 1780-1830* (Cambridge: Cambridge University Press, 1988).

W.L. Lumpkin, *Baptist Confessions of Faith* (Philadelphia: Judson Press, 1950).

S.W. Lynd, *Memoir of the Revd. William Staughton D.D.* (Boston: 1834).

S.W. Lyndall, *Selection of Hymns intended as a supplement to Dr. Watts's Psalms and Hymns* (4th edn, London: 1807).

H.L. McBeth, *The Baptist Heritage* (Nashville: Broadman, 1987).

J.E. McGoldrick, *Baptist Successionism. A crucial Question in Baptist History* (Metuchen, N.J.: Scarecrow Press, 1994).

H. McLachlan, *English Education under the Test Acts, being the history of the Nonconformist academies from 1662-1820* (Manchester: University Press, 1931).

M. Madan, *A Collection of Psalms and Hymns extracted from Various Authors, and published by the Reverend Mr. Madan* (London: 1760).

K.R. Manley, 'Robert Bowyer: Artist, Publisher and Preacher', *BQ* 23.1 (1969-70), pp. 32-46.

– 'Rippon, John', in T. Larsen (ed.), *Biographical Dictionary of Evangelicals* (leicester: InterVarsity Press, 2003), pp. 552-54.

B.L Manning, 'Congregationalism in the Eighteenth Century' in *Congregationalism through the Centuries* (London: Independent Press, 1937).

– *Essays in Orthodox Dissent* (London: Independent Press, 1939).

– *The Hymns of Wesley and Watts* (London: Epworth, 1942).

– *The Protestant Dissenting Deputies* (ed. O. Greenwood; Cambridge: Cambridge University Press, 1952).

O.A. Mansfield, 'Rippon's Tunes', *BQ* 8.1 (1936), pp. 36-43.

N.H. Maring, *Baptists in New Jersey. A Study in Transition* (Valley Forge, Pa.: Judson Press, 1964).

H. Martin (ed.), *The Baptist Hymn Book Companion* (London: Psalms and Hymns Trust, 1962).

R.H. Martin, 'English Particular Baptists and Interdenominational Cooperation', *Foundations* 22.3 (1979), pp. 233-45.

J. Mason, *Spiritual Songs, or Songs of Praise to Almighty God, upon several occasions* (London: 1859 [first edition 1683]).

M. Masters, *Familiar Letters and Poems on Several Occasions* (London: 1755).

T.B. Maston, *Isaac Backus: Pioneer of Religious Liberty* (Rochester, N.Y.: American Baptist Historical Society, 1962).

A.G. Matthews, *Calamy Revised, Being a Revision of Edmund Calamy's Account of the Ministers and others Ejected and Silenced, 1660-2* (Oxford: Clarendon Press, 1988 [1934]).

S. Medley, *Hymns on Select Portions of Scripture* (Bristol: 1785).

– *Hymns. The Public Worship and Private Devotions of True Christians assisted.* (New edn, Cambridge: 1839).

S. Medley (Jr), *Memoirs of the late Rev. Samuel Medley compiled by his Son: To which are annexed two sermons and a wide variety of miscellaneous pieces in Verse* (London: 1800).

Memoirs of Mr. John James Smith, late of Watford, Herts (London: 1821).

J. Merrick, *Psalms of David Translated or Paraphrased in English Verse* (Reading 1765).

J. Middleton, *Hymns* (London: 1793).

A.C. Miller, *Eythorne: A Village Baptist Church* (London: 1924).

N.S. Moon, 'Caleb Evans, Founder of the Bristol Education Society', *BQ* 24.4 (1971), pp. 175-90.

– *Education for Ministry: Bristol Baptist College 1679-1979* (Bristol: Bristol Baptist College, 1979).

O.A. Moore, *Brown Street Baptist Church Salisbury 1655-1955* (Salisbury: 1955).

H. Moore, *Poems, Lyrical end Miscellaneous* (London: 1806).

D.D. Morgan, 'Smoke, Fire and Light; Baptists and the Revitalisation of Welsh Dissent', *BQ* 32.5 (1988), pp. 224-32.

J.W. Morris, *Memoirs of the Life and Writings of the Rev. Andrew Fuller* (London: 1826).

A.V. Murray, 'Doddridge and Education', in G.F. Nuttall (ed.), *Philip Doddridge 1702-51. His Contribution to English Religion* (London: Independent Press, 1951), pp. 102-21.

D.B. Murray, 'The Scotch Baptist Tradition in Great Britain', *BQ* 33.4 (1989), pp. 186-98.

D.W. Music, 'Baptist Hymnals as Shapers of Worship', *Baptist History and Heritage* 31.3 (1996), pp. 7-17.

J. Needham, *Hymns Devotional and Moral on various Subjects, collected chiefly from the Holy Scriptures* (Bristol: 1768).

S. Neill, *A History of Christian Missions* (Harmondsworh: Penguin, 1964).

T. Nettles, *By His Grace and for His Glory. A Historical, Theological, and Practical Study of the Doctrines of Grace in Baptist Life* (Grand Rapids: Baker, 1968).

– 'Benjamin Keach', in M.A.G. Haykin (ed.), *The British Particular Baptists 1638-1910* (2 vols; Springfield, Mo.: Particular Baptist Press, 1998, 2000), pp. 95-130.

– 'Andrew Fuller (1754-1815)' in M.A.G. Haykin (ed.), *The British Particular Baptists 1638-1910* (2 vols; Springfield, Mo.: Particular Baptist Press, 1998, 2000), 2, pp. 97-141.

A New Selection of Hymns, especially adapted to Public Worship, and intended as a Supplement to Dr. Watts's Psalms and Hymns (London: 1828).

A.H. Newman, A *History of the Baptist Churches in the United States* (Philadelphia: American Baptist Publishing House, 1915).

H.V. Nicholson, *Authentic Records relating to the Christian Church now meeting in George Street and Mutley Chapels, Plymouth 1640 to 1870* (London: 1870).

J. Norcott, *Baptism discovered plainly and faithfully according to the Word of God* (London: 1672).

Northampton Baptist Association Circular Letters (1788-1802).

Notes, Intended as Materials for a Memoir on the Affairs of the Protestants of the Department Du Gard (London: 1816).

G.F. Nuttall (ed.), *Philip Doddridge 1702-51. His Contribution to English Religion* (London: Independent Press, 1951).

– *Richard Baxter and Philip Doddridge* (London: Oxford University Press, 1951).

– *The General Body of the Three Denominations A Historical Sketch* (printed privately, 1955).

– 'The Baptist Western Association 1653-1658', *Journal of Ecclesiastical History* 11.2 (1960), pp. 213-18.

– 'Northamptonshire and The Modern Question: A Turning-Point in Eighteenth Century Dissent', *Journal of Theological Studies*, n.s. 16.1 (1965), pp. 101-23.

– *Howel Harris 1714-1773. The Last Enthusiast* (Cardiff: University of Wales Press, 1965).

– 'Calvinism in Free Church History', *B Q* 22.8 (1968), pp. 418-28.

– 'Assembly and Association in Dissent, 1689-1831', in G.J. Cuming and D. Baker (eds.), *Councils and Assemblies* (Studies in Church History, 7; Cambridge: Cambridge University Press, 1971), pp. 289-309.

– 'Questions and Answers; an Eighteenth-century Correspondence', *BQ* 27.2 (1977), pp. 83-90.

– 'The Baptist Churches and their Ministers in the 1790s: Rippon's Baptist Annual Register', *BQ* 30.8 (1984), pp. 383-87.

B. Nutter, *Story of the Cambridge Baptists and the struggle for religious Liberty* (Cambridge: W. Heffer and sons, 1912).

J.A. Oddy, 'The Dissidence of William Richards', *BQ* 27.3 (1977), pp. 118-27.

R.W. Oliver, 'John Gill', in M.A.G. Haykin (ed.), *The British Particular Baptists 1638-1910* (2 vols; Springfield, Mo.: Particular Baptist Press, 1998, 2000), 1, pp. 145-65.

– 'Abraham Booth (1734-1806)' in M.A.G. Haykin (ed.), *The British Particular Baptists 1638-1910* (2 vols; Springfield, Mo.: Particular Baptist Press, 1998, 2000), 2, pp. 31-54.

Olney Hymns, in Three Books (London: 1779).

Origin and Design of the Particular Baptist Fund, established in London in 1717: with the Rules and orders as revised in 1817 (London: 1817).

D. Owen, *English Philanthropy 1660-1960* (London: Oxford University Press, 1965).

J.M.G. Owen, *A Memorial of the 250th Anniversary of the Midland Baptist Association 1655-1905* (Birmingham: 1905).

W.T. Owen, *Edward Williams, D.D. 1750-1813. His Life, Thought and Influence* (Cardiff: University of Wales Press, 1963).

K.L. Parry and E. Routley (eds.), *Companion to Congregational Praise* (London: Independent Press, 1953).

G.W. Paschal, *History of North Carolina Baptists* (2 vols; Raleigh: General Board, North Carolina Baptist State Convention, 1930).

W.M. Patterson, *Baptist Successionism: A Critical View* (Valley Forge: Judson, 1969).

– 'The Evangelical Revival and the Baptists', in W.H. Brackney, P.S Fiddes, J.H.Y.Briggs (eds.), *Pilgrim Pathways* (Macon, Ga.: Mercer University Press, 1999), pp. 243-61.

A.J. Payne, 'The Baptist Board', *BQ* 1.7 (1922-23), pp. 321-26.

E.A. Payne, 'Baptist Work in Jamaica before the arrival of the Missionaries', *B Q* 7.1 (1934), pp. 20-26.
- *The First Generation* (London: Carey Press, 1936).
- *The Prayer Call of 1784* (London: Baptist Laymen's Missionary Movement, 1941).
- *The Church Awakes* (London: Edinburgh House Press, 1942).
- 'Two Dutch Translations by Carey', *BQ* 11.1 (1942), pp. 33-38.
- 'The Evangelical Revival and the Beginnings of the Modern Missionary Movement', *Congregational Quarterly* 21 (July 1943), pp. 223-36.
- *The Excellent Mr. Burls* (London: Carey Press, 1943).
- *The Fellowship of Believers* (London: Carey Kingsgate Press, rev. edn, 1944).
- *Freedom in Jamaica* (London: Carey Press, 1946).
- *College Street Chapel Northampton 1697-1947* (London: Kingsgate Press, 1947).
- 'The Theology of Isaac Watts as illustrated in his Hymns', *Bulletin of the Hymn Society of Great Britain and Ireland* 2 (1948), pp. 49-58.
- 'The Necrologies of John Dyer', *BQ* 13.7 (1949-50), pp. 303-309.
- *The Baptists of Berkshire* (London: Carey Kingsgate Press, 1951).
- *The Free Church Tradition in the Life of England* (London: SCM Press, 3rd edn, 1951).
- *The Baptist Union. A Short History* (London: Carey Kingsgate Press, 1959).
- 'Contacts between Mennonites and Baptists', *Foundations* 4.1 (1961), pp. 39-55.
- *Free Churchmen Unrepentant and Repentant and other Papers* (London: Carey Kingsgate Press, 1965).
- 'Abraham Booth 1734-1806', *BQ* 26.1 (1975), pp. 28-42.
- 'British Baptists and the American Revolution', *Baptist History and Heritage* 11.1 (1976), pp. 3-15.
A. Peel, *These Hundred Years. A History of the Congregational Union of England and Wales, 1831-1931* (London: Congregational Union, 1931).
E. Perronet, *Occasional Verses, moral and Sacred* (London: 1785).
C. Perrot, *Report on the Persecution of the French Protestants presented to the Committee of Dissenting Ministers of the three denominations* (London: 1816).
S. Piggin, 'Sectarianism versus Ecumenism: The Impact on British Churches of the Missionary Movement to India, c. 1800-1860', *Journal of Ecclesiastical History* 27.4 (1976), pp. 387-402.
S.J. Price, *A Popular History of the Baptist Building Fund. The Centenary Volume 1824-1924* (London: Kingsgate Press, 1927).

– 'The early years of the Baptist Union', *BQ* 4.2 (1928-29), pp. 53-60, 121-31, 171-78.
– 'Brother Giles becomes a Recognized Minister', *BQ* 5.1 (1930-31), pp. 37-41.
– Upton. *The Story of One Hundred and Fifty Years 1785-1935* (London: 1935).
G. Pritchard, *Memoir of the Life and Writings of the Rev. Joseph Ivimey* (London: 1835).
– *Memoir of the Rev. William Newman D.D.* (London: 1837).
H.D. Rack, 'Evangelical Endings: Death-beds in Evangelical Biography', *Bulletin of the John Rylands Library University of Manchester* 74 (1992), pp. 39-56.
J. Radford, *A Collection of Psalms and Hymns for Public Worship* (London: 1790).
B.A. Ramsbottom, 'The Stennetts', in M.A.G. Haykin (ed.), *The British Particular Baptists 1638-1910* (2 vols; Springfield, Mo.: Particular Baptist Press, 1998, 2000), 1, pp. 133-43.
W. Ranwell, *Memory of the Blessed; or Biographical Sketches of Some Persons connected with the first Baptist Church at Woolwich* (London: 1837).
J.E. Rattenbury, *The Evangelical Doctrines of Charles Wesley's Hymns* (London: Epworth, 1941).
S. Redgrave, *A Dictionary of Artists of the English School: Painters Sculptors, Architects, Engravers and Ornamentists: With notices of their lives and work* (London: 1874).
T. Rees, *A Sketch of the History of the Regium Donum, and parliamentary grant to poor Dissenting ministers of England and Wales* (London: 1834).
– *History of Protestant Nonconformity in Wales* (London: 1883).
B. Reeve, *History of Maze Pond Sunday School 1801-1901* (London: 1901).
The Report of the Commission on the Associations (London: Baptist Union, 1964).
W.J. Reynolds, *Hymns of Our Faith. A Handbook for the Baptist Hymnal* (Nashville: Broadman, 1964).
– *Companion to Baptist Hymnal*, (Nashville: Broadman, 1976).
– 'Our Heritage of Baptist Hymnody in America', *Baptist History and Heritage* 11.4 (1976), pp. 204-217.
R.E. Richey, 'Effects of Toleration on Eighteenth-Century Dissent', *Journal of Religious History* 8.4 (1975), pp. 350-63.
J. Rippon (Jr), *Most rapacious Atrocities unmasked; or A Narrative of Unparallelled Enormities committed by Beriah Drew, attorney at Law, against John Rippon of the Same Profession* (London: 1811).

T. Rippon, *An elegant engraving of a geographical clock* (London: 1794). (Copy in Angus Library.)

R.P. Roberts, *Continuity and Change: London Calvinistic Baptists and the Evangelical Revival 1760-1820* (Wheaton, Ill.: Richard Owen Roberts Publishers, 1989).

R. Robinson, *History of Baptism* (London: 1790).

– *Ecclesiastical Researches* (Cambridge: 1792).

C. Room, *The Believer's Triumph over Sin and Death. A Sermon, preached October 11, 1835, in New Park Street Chapel, Southwark occasioned by the death of William Bousfield, Esq.* (London: 1835).

E. Routley, *The Music of Christian Hymnody. A Study of the development of the hymn tune since the Reformation, with special reference to English Protestantism* (London: Independent Press, 1957).

– *Hymns and Human Life* (London: John Murray, 2nd edn, 1969).

J.H. Rushbrooke, 'The Baptist World Alliance: Origin: Constitution: Achievements: Objects', *BQ* 9.2 (1938-39), pp. 67-79.

J. Ryland, *Salvation Finished ... A Funeral Sermon, occasioned by the death of the Rev. Robert Hall, Sen.* London: 1791).

– *The Presence of Christ the Source of Eternal Bliss. A Funeral Discourse, delivered December 22, 1799... occasioned by the death of the Rev. Benjamin Francis; and a Sketch of Mr. Francis's Life by Thomas Flint* (Bristol 1800).

– *The Work of Faith, the Labour of love, and the Patience of Hope illustrated in the Life and Death of the Reverend Andrew Fuller* (London: 1816).

– *Pastoral Memorials: Selected from the Manuscripts of the late Revd. John Ryland, D.D. of Bristol: with a Memoir of the Author* (2 vols; London: 1826).

– *Hymns and Verses on Sacred Subjects with a biographical sketch* (London: 1862).

P. Sangster, *Pity My Simplicity. The Evangelical Revival and the Religious Education of Children 1738-1800* (London: Epworth Press, 1963).

T. Scott, *Lyric Poems, Devotional and Moral* (London: 1773).

I. Sellers, 'Other Times, Other Ministries: John Fawcett and Alexander McLaren', *BQ* 32.4 (1987), pp. 181-99.

– (ed.), *Our Heritage. The Baptists of Yorkshire, Lancashire and Cheshire 1647-1987* (Leeds: The Yorkshire Baptist Association and the Lancashire and Cheshire Baptist Association, 1987).

A. Serle, *Horae Solitariae: or Essays upon some remarkable Names and Titles of Jesus Christ (with hymns appended)* (London: 1786).

E. Sharpe, 'Bristol Baptist College and the Church's Hymnody', *BQ* 28.1 (1979), pp. 7-16.

R.R. Shaw and R.H. Shoemaker (eds.), *American Bibliography, A Preliminary Checklist* (22 vols; New York: Scarecrow Press, 1958-66).

K.R.M. Short, 'A Note on the Sierra Leone Mission and Religious Freedom, 1796', *BQ* 28.8 (1980), pp. 355-60.

H.S. Skeats, and C. S. Miall, *History of the Free Churches of England 1688-1891* (London: 1891).

A.C. Smith, 'William Ward, Radical Reform, and Missions in the 1790s', *American Baptist Quarterly*, 10.3 (1991), pp. 218-44.

– 'William Ward (1769-1823)' in M.A.G. Haykin (ed.), *The British Particular Baptists 1638-1910* (2 vols; Springfield, Mo.: Particular Baptist Press, 1998, 2000), 2, pp. 255-71.

J. Ashley Smith, *The Birth of Modern Education. The Contribution of the Dissenting Academies 1660-1800* (London: Independent Press, 1954).

M.I. Smith, *A Short History of the First Baptist Church in Edinburgh 1765-1965* (London: 1965).

C.O. Sommers, *Memoir of the Rev. John Stanford, D.D.* (New York 1835).

C.H. Spurgeon, *Our Own Hymn Book. A Collection of Psalms and Hymns for Public, Social, and Private Worship* (London: 1866).

– *The Metropolitan Tabernacle: Its History and Work* (London: 1876).

B. Stanley, *The History of the Baptist Missionary Society 1792-1992* (Edinburgh; T. & T. Clark, 1992).

J. Stanley, *The Church in the Hop Garden* (n.d.).

A. Steele, *Poems on Subjects chiefly Devotional, by Theodosia* (2 vols; London: 1760).

E. C. Starr (ed.), *A Baptist Bibliography*: (6 vols; Philadelphia, Judson Press, 1947-66).

I. Stephen and S. Lee (eds.), *Dictionary of National Biography* (67 vols; London: Smith, Elder, 1888-1903).

J. Stennett, *Hymns for the Lord's Supper* (London: 1703).

– *Hymns composed for the celebration of the Holy Ordinance of Baptism* (London: 1712).

S. Stennett, *The Mortality of Ministers contrasted; decease of the Rev. Caleb Evans...* (London: 1791).

R. Stevenson, 'Watts in America', *Harvard Theological Review* 41 (July 1948), pp. 205-211.

P. Stock, *Foundations* (Halifax: 1933).

W. Stokes, *History of the Midland Baptist Association 1655-1855* (London: 1855).

J. Stoughton, *History of Religion in England from the opening of the Long Parliament to 1850* (8 vols; London: Hodder and Stoughton, 1901).

J. Stuart, *Beechen Grove Baptist-church, Watford* (London: 1907).

J. Swain, *Experimental Essays on Divine Subjects in Verse. With a Memoir of the Life of the Author* (London: 1834).

S.A. Swaine, *Faithful Men; or Memorials of Bristol Baptist College, and some of its most distinguished Alumni* (London: 1884).

W.W. Sweet, *The Baptists 1783-1830; A Collection of Source Material.* (Religion on the American Frontier, 1: New York: Cooper Square, 1964 [1931]).

A. Taylor, *History of the General Baptists* (2 vols; London: 1818).

J.H. Taylor, 'Some Seventeenth-Century Testimonies', *Transactions* of Congregational Historical Society, 16.2 (1949), pp. 64-66.

R. Taylor, 'English Baptist Periodicals, 1790-1865', *BQ* 37.2 (1977), pp. 50-82.

J. Thomas, *A History of the Baptist Association in Wales from the year 1650, to the year 1790* (London: 1795).

R.W. Thomson, *The Psalms and Hymns Trust: A Short History of the Trust and the Work of Publishing Baptist Hymn Books* (London: Psalms and Hymns Trust, 1960).

— *Ministers in Need. The Story of the Society for the Relief of Aged and Infirm Protestant Dissenting Ministers 1818-1968* (London: Society for Relief of Aged Ministers, 1968).

P. Toon, *The Emergence of Hyper-Calvinism in English Nonconformity 1689-1765* (London: The Olive Tree, 1967).

A.M. Toplady, *Psalms and Hymns for Public and Private Worship* (London: 1776).

R.G. Torbet, *A History of the Baptists* (Valley Forge: Judson Press, rev. edn, 1963).

F. Trestrail, *Reminiscences of College Life in Bristol* (n.d.).

E. Trivett, *Hymns and Spiritual Songs in two books* (London: 1755).

D. Turner, *Divine Songs, Hymns and other Poems* (Reading: 1747).

L. Tyerman, *The Life of Rev. George Whitefield* (2 vols; London: 1876-77).

A.C. Underwood, *A History of the English Baptists* (London: Carey Kingsgate Press, 1947).

J.B. Vaughn, 'Benjamin Keach', in T. George and G. Dockery (eds.), *Baptist Theologians* (Nashville: Broadman, 1990), pp. 49-76.

M. Walker, *Baptists at the Table* (Didcot: Baptist Historical Society, 1992).

T. Walker, *Appendix to Dr. Rippon's Selection of Tunes* (London: n.d.).

— *Second Appendix to Dr. Rippon's Selection of Tunes, consisting chiefly of Originals* (London: n.d.).

— *Companion to Dr. Rippon's Tune Book* (2 vols; London: 1811, 1815).

B. Wallin, *Evangelical Hymns and Songs* (London: 1760).

– *The Church an Habitation of God, through the Spirit: a sermon on occasion of the settlement of a people lately united in the order of the gospel (In DEAN STREET, Tooley Street, Southwark)...* (London: 1774).

J.D. Walsh, 'Methodism at the end of the Eighteenth Century', in R. Davies and G. Rupp (eds.), *A History of the Methodist Church in Great Britain* (4 vols; London: Epworth, 1965-88),1, pp. 275-315.

A.T. Ward, *Kingsgate Chapel* (London: 1912).

A.W. Ward and A.R. Waller (eds.), *Cambridge History of English Literature* (15 vols; Cambridge: Cambridge University Press, 1932).

W.R. Ward, *Religion and Society in England 1790-1850* (London: Batsford, 1972).

– 'The Baptists and the Transformation of the Church, 1780-1830', *BQ* 25.4 (1973), pp. 167-84.

J.R. Watson, *The English Hymn. A Critical and Historical Study* (Oxford: Oxford University Press, 1999).

J.S. Watson, *The Reign of George III 1760-1815* (The Oxford History of England, 12, Oxford: Oxford University Press, 1960).

I. Watts, *Hymns and Spiritual Songs* (London: 1707).

– *The Psalms of David imitated in the Language of the New Testament* (London: 1719).

– *Horae Lyricae. Poems, Chiefly of the Lyric Kind, in three books... To which is added a supplement, containing translation of all the Latin poems with notes by Thomas Gibbons* (London: 1834).

M. Watts, *The Dissenters* (2 vols; Oxford: Clarendon Press, 1978, 1995).

T. Wells, 'Samuel Pearce (1766-1799)' in M.A.G. Haykin (ed.), *The British Particular Baptists 1638-1910* (2 vols; Springfield, Mo.: Particular Baptist Press, 1998, 2000), 2, pp. 183-99.

K. Wellum, 'Caleb Evans (1737-1791)', in M.A.G. Haykin (ed.), *The British Particular Baptists 1638-1910* (2 vols; Springfield, Mo.: Particular Baptist Press, 1998, 2000), 1, pp. 213-33.

C. and J. Wesley, *The Poetical Works of John and Charles Wesley* (13 vols; ed. G. Osborn, London: 1868-72).

J. Wesley, *A Collection of Hymns, for the Use of the people called Methodists* (London: 1780).

Western Baptist Association Circular Letters (1777-1802).

T. Westlake, *A Selection of hymns, from various authors, adapted to public worship* (Bristol: 2nd edn 1801).

B.R. White, 'Thomas Crosby, Baptist Historian', *BQ* 21.4 (1965), pp. 154-68, 219-34.

– 'The Organisation of the Particular Baptists 1644-1660', *Journal of Ecclesiastical History* 17.2 (1966), pp. 209-226.

– 'John Gill in London, 1719-1729: A Biographical Fragment', *BQ* 22.2 (1967), pp. 72-91.

- *The English Baptists of the Seventeenth Century* (ed. J.F.V. Nicholson, Didcot: Baptist Historical Society, 2nd edn, 1996).
J. B. Whitely, 'Loughwood Baptists in the Seventeenth Century', *BQ* 31.4 (1985), pp. 148-58.
W.T. Whitley (ed.), *Minutes of the General Assembly of the General Baptist Churches in England* (2 vols; London: Baptist Historical Society, 1907, 1910).
- *Baptists of North-West England 1649-1913* (London: Kingsgate Press, 1913).
- *Baptist Bibliography* (2 vols; London: Kingsgate Press, 1916, 1922).
- *The Baptists of London* (London: Kingsgate Press, 1928).
- 'The Influence of Whitefield on Baptists', *BQ* 5.1 (1930-31), pp. 30-36.
- 'Bunhill Fields: the Place and the Records', *BQ* 5 (1930-31), pp. 220-26.
- *History of British Baptists* (London: Carey Kingsgate Press, rev. edn, 1932).
- (ed.), 'Calendar of Letters 1742-1831: Collected by Isaac Mann', *BQ* 6.4 (1932), pp. 173-86.
- 'The Baptist Annual Register', *BQ* 10.2 (1940), pp. 122-26.
- 'The Tune Book of 1791', *BQ* 10.8 (1941), pp. 434-43.
H.I. and S.W. Wilberforce, *The Life of William Wilberforce* (5 vols; London: 1838).
M.H. Wilkin, *Joseph Kinghorn of Norwich* (Norwich: 1855).
M. Wilks, *History of the Persecution endured by the Protestants in the South of France* (2 vols; London: 1821).
H.M. Williams, *On the Late Persecution of the Protestants in the South of France* (London: 1816).
E. Williams, *The Psalms and Hymns of the Rev. Isaac Watts D.D. A New Edition with Improved Indexes of Subjects and of Scriptures and a New Arrangement of the Whole not in the Body of the Work, but in a Table Prefixed* (Doncaster: 1805).
W. Williams, *Gloria in Excelsis: or Hymns of Praise to God the Lamb* (Carmarthen: 1772).
L. Wilson, *Constrained by Zeal; Female Spirituality amongst Nonconformists 1825-1875* (Carlisle: Paternoster Press, 2000).
W. Wilson, *The History and Antiquities of Dissenting Churches and Meeting Houses, in London, Westminster, and Southwark* (4 vols; London: 1808-14).
D. Witard, *Bibles in Barrels. A History of Essex Baptists* (Southend on Sea: Essex Baptist Association, 1962).
A.S. Wood, *Thomas Haweis 1734-1820* (London: S.P.C.K., 1957).

D.C. Woolley (ed.), *Baptist Advance, The Achievements of the Baptists of North America for a Century and a Half*, (Nashville, Tenn.: Broadman, 1964).

C. Woollacott, *Brief History of the Baptist Church in Little Wild Street, Lincoln's-Inn Fields; from 1691 to 1858* (London: n.d)

Yorkshire and Lancashire Baptist Association Circular Letters (1790-1802).

G. Yuille (ed.), *History of Baptists in Scotland* (Glasgow: Baptist Union of Scotland Publication Committee, 1926).

Index

Adams, John 92, 287
Adams, Samuel 133
Addington, S. 45, 65
Addison, Joseph 287
Adey, Lionel 99-100
Africa 107
Aged Ministers' Fund 242
Aikin, Ann 60
Aikin, William 40, 45, 51, 74
Alcester, Warwickshire 246
'All hail the power' 93-94, 273, 279-81
Alleine, Joseph 242
Allen, James 287
Allison, Burgiss 88, 137
Almshouses 60-61
Alston, Mildred 52
America 88, 107, 117-18, 137, 139-43, 150, 164-73, 186, 192-93, 247-48, 260, 271, 272, 275
American Indians 142-43, 179, 188, 256
American Revolution 21-22, 140-41, 215-20
Amiens, Treaty of 56
Angas, William Henry 49, 50, 76-77, 175
Angelology 104
Angus, Joseph 81
Anne, Queen 237
Antinomianism 13, 21, 26, 40, 63, 97, 226
Applegath, Augustus 51, 75
Applegath, Captain 51
Arianism 4
Arminian Magazine 149
Arminianism 29, 95-96
Arne, Thomas 128
Arnold, Mrs 69
Arnold, Samuel 128
Arnsby, Leicestershire 113
Asia 107, 115, 272

Ash, John 17, 22, 87
Aspland, Robert 261
Asplund, John 169, 192-93
Assurance 5
Atkins Trust 210
Atkinson, George 74, 77, 247
Atonement, doctrine of 97, 101
Atwood, William 145
Australia 179
Authers, W.P. xv

Backus, Isaac 140, 146, 166, 170, 176, 197, 260
Bahamas 243
Baker, Moses 181
Bakewell, John 287
Bampton, Devonshire 233
Bankruptcy 51, 61-62, 64
Baptism 41-42, 97-99, 109-110, 134, 163, 168, 234, 270
Baptist Annual Register 7, 9, 25, 139-205, 215, 218, 252, 257, 260, 263-65, 267, 269, 272-75
Baptist Associations 107-108, 112, 140, 143, 158-64, 222-23
-English
  Berkshire 158-59
  Essex 159-60, 230, 292-93
  Kent and Sussex 140-41, 145, 159-60, 162, 292-93
  Midlands 145, 159-60, 198, 292-93
  Norfolk and Suffolk 145, 155, 163, 292-93
  Northamptonshire 30, 32, 34, 108, 140, 145, 159-60. 162-63, 173, 228, 292-93
  Northern 145, 159-60, 292-93
  Western 11, 140-41, 145, 159-60, 162, 228, 292-93
  Yorkshire and Lancashire 145, 159, 163, 192-93

-Welsh 145, 151, 159-60, 264, 292-93
-American
    Bethel 172
    Bowdoinham 169
    Charleston 140, 146, 164, 167, 172
    Danbury 169
    Dover 171
    Elkhorn 171
    Georgian 172
    Groton 169
    Kehukee 146, 164, 171-72, 191
    Ketocton 164
    Meredith 169
    Middle District 171
    New Hampshire 169
    New York 167, 170
    Philadelphia 88, 137, 146, 164, 166-68, 170, 263
    Redstone 170
    Rhode Island 169
    Roanoke 171
    Sandy Creek 164, 171
    Shaftsbury 169
    Stonington 169
    Vermont 169
    Virginia Portsmouth 171
    Warren 142, 146, 164, 166-67, 169
    Warwick 170
    Woodstock 169
Baptist Board 38, 67, 221-23, 264
Baptist Case Committee 67, 191, 221, 223
Baptist Confession (1644) 151, 198
Baptist Confession (1689) 2, 99, 134, 151, 159-60, 216
Baptist Continental Society 70
Baptist Fund 33, 66, 68, 153, 191, 224-26, 229, 236, 264
Baptist Home Missionary Society 7, 70, 235
Baptist Itinerant Society 70, 160, 185, 224, 230-35, 264
Baptist Irish Society 70, 269
Baptist Magazine 192, 234-35, 245, 261, 264, 269, 271

Baptist Missionary Society 7, 50, 69, 72, 74-76, 81, 115, 134, 150-51, 157, 167, 175-78, 181, 185, 226, 228-30, 233, 264
Baptist Monthly Meetings (London) 224, 230
Baptist Union 7, 70, 193, 195, 222, 237, 242, 263-71
Baptist World Alliance 193, 272-73, 276
Baptistery 41, 65, 269
Barber, Chapman 54, 68-70, 72
Barnoldswick, Yorkshire 30
Bartholomew Close Dissenters' School 50, 71
Bath 128, 183, 253
Baxter, Richard 5, 83, 242
Bebbington, D. 5, 31, 219
Beddome, Benjamin 17, 30, 46, 83, 86-87, 91-93, 106, 108, 110, 115-16, 119, 187-88, 194, 199. 210, 287
Bedford 186
Bedford Union Association 133, 230
Belcher, Joseph 271
Benedict, David 208-209
Bennett, James 208
Benson, L. F. 84, 138
Berkshire, W. xvi
Berridge, John 111, 287
Berry, Thomas 120
Bhutan 115
Biblical Magazine 150, 189
Bicheno, James 194
Biggs, James 50
Birmingham 75
Birt, Isaiah 184
Births of Dissenters 152, 240
Blake, William 212
Black Christians 179-84, 243-45
Blacklock, Thomas 287
Blackmore, Richard 287
Blight, Gilbert 49, 54, 68-70, 72, 79
Boden, James 287
Bogue, David 208
Bohemia 174
Book Lists 185
Book Society 72, 206, 242-43

Booth, Abraham 32, 42, 45-46, 53, 68, 140, 150, 168, 176, 208, 220, 222-23, 232-33, 236, 249, 251, 254-56
Booth, Samuel 276
Boston, Massachusetts 121, 200
Botsford, Edmund 172, 193
Bourgeois, Loius 127
Bousfield, John 49, 70
Bousfield, William 51
Bovey Tracey 247
Bow, 257
Bowen, John 117
Bowring, Sir John 116, 287
Bowyer, Harriet 43-44
Bowyer, Robert 44, 49, 69, 75
Bradberry, David 287
Bradbury, Thomas 212
Bradford, Wiltshire 12
Bradford, Yorkshire 156
Bradley, Ian 85
Bradley, James 215, 218
Brainerd, David 175
Bramley. Yorkshire 53
Brewer, Jehoida, 287
Bricknell, Somerset 67
Bridgwater 232
Brine, John 24, 30
Bristol 183, 232, 247
Bristol Academy 2, 5, 12, 17-29, 74, 76-77, 119, 156-57, 187, 191, 203, 205-206, 209-210, 217, 228-29, 235-36
Bristol Baptist Itinerant Society 230
'Bristol Collection' 22, 87, 90-91, 97-98, 103, 109, 121, 134, 136
British and Foreign Bible Society 72, 75, 246
British and Foreign School Society 50, 71
Broaddus, Andrew 135
Broadmead, Bristol 17, 26, 200
Brooksbank, 'Sister' 58
Broughton 228
Browne, Simon 287
Brussels 50
Bryan, Andrew 182
Bunhill Fields 190, 211-14, 258-59, 262, 277

Bunyan, John 4, 55, 83, 212
Burder, G. 89-90
Burke, Edmund 218
Burkitt, Lemuel 146, 171-72
Burls, William 49, 54, 69-70, 72, 241, 268
Burton-upon-Trent 160
Button, William 32, 37, 150, 266
Byrd, William 128

Calcutta 53
Calldee, H. 40
Calvin, John 29, 62
Calvinism, High 1-2, 29-31, 78, 207
Calvinism, Moderate 26, 29-32, 160, 162-63, 194, 199, 207, 250-51
Camberwell 257
Cambridge 34, 200, 225
Canterbury 247
Carey, William 5, 8, 27, 69, 134, 145, 160, 162, 174. 176-78, 186
Carmichael, Robert 203
Carroll, Joseph 54, 68
Carter Lane Baptist Church 6, 28, 32, 33-81, 196, 200, 204, 224, 236, 240, 242, 249-50, 257-58, 265, 271
Carter, Robert 167-68
Caryl, Joseph 201
Case, H.B. 277
Catechizing 46, 194
Cennick, John 92, 106, 287
Chacewater, Cornwall 145, 229
Chamberlain, John 69
Chamberlain, John 257
Champion. L. xv
Chard 204
Charleston 88
Charlotte, Princess 238
Charnock, Stephen 24
Chatham 257
Chauncey, Isaac 201
Cheare, Abraham 201
Chelsea 271
Cheltenham, 12
Chenies, Buckinghamshire 157
Chertsey 223
Chesham 257
Children 45

Chorlock, Thomas 259
Christ, Doctrine of 99, 102-103
Christian life 99, 104
Church Discipline 61-65
Church, Doctrine of 99, 106, 114, 227-28
Church finances 65-67
Church of England 227, 289
Churches, lists of
  -English, Particular Baptists 153-57
  -English, General Baptists 158
  -Welsh Baptists 157-58
Clarke, Jonathan 172, 180
Clarke, William Nash 19, 189, 199, 210, 222, 236
Clarkson, David 201
Clarkson, John 182
Clarkson, Thomas 182
Clifford, John 276
Clipston 150
Coate 28
Coke, Thomas 184
Colchester 190
Cole, Thomas 204
Coles, Thomas 287
Colebrook, Mrs 50
Collett, S. 287
Collier, Thomas 11
Collins, Rev. 131
Collins, William 46, 264
Collyer, W.B. 116, 245, 251, 256, 258, 262, 287
Communion, terms of 53
Conder, John 212, 287
Congregationalists – see Independents
Continental Society 246
Conyers, R. 90
Cook, Joseph 172, 180, 209
Cooke, Stephen 180
Cooper, John 68
Copyright 114, 116, 118-20
Corbly, John 170
Cornwall, 27, 185, 228-29, 233
Coventry, 11, 223, 257
Cover, James 179
Cowell, Jeremiah 69, 77
Cowper, William 83, 92, 100-102, 105,116, 287

Cox, F.A. 262, 271
Coxhead, Benjamin 43, 45-46, 59, 74, 77, 247
Crabtree, William 156, 191
Creation and Providence 99-100
Crippen, T.G. 121, 135
Croft, William 128
Crosby, Thomas 196
Cross, A. xvi
Cruttenden, Robert 287
Cuperus, Johannes 173
Cuthbert, John 183

Dartmouth 227, 246
David, Job 119, 173
David, Rees 216-17
Davie, Donald 85-86
Davie, H. 201
Davies Horton 76, 84
Davies, Hywel 141
Davies, Robert 49, 51, 69
Davies, Samuel 90, 92, 101, 137-38, 287
Davis, Thomas 200, 210
Day, Robert 15, 188, 199, 210
Deacons 53-55, 107
Deal 257
Dean Street Church 36, 39, 54, 79
Dearmer, Percy 94
Death and dying 43-45, 111-12, 136, 188, 199, 283
'Death and Resurrection' 99, 112
Defoe, Daniel 212
Denham, S. 41
Denmark 174
Derby 219
Desborough, Colonel 202
Devonshire 232-33
Devonshire Square Church, 131, 200
Dissenters, Civil State of 187, 209, 237-41
Dissenting Deputies 34, 71, 237, 240
Doddridge, Philip 5-6, 18, 23-24, 32, 83, 91-93, 99, 102, 115-16, 242, 287
Dodge, Daniel 137
Dore, James 233, 261
Douglas, James 50, 74, 78, 224, 235

Dracup, John 191
Draper, B. H. 264
Drew, Beriah 259
Drunkenness 64
Dryden, John 287
Dublin, 125, 184, 246
Duncan, John 243
Dunscombe, Samuel 12
Dunscombe, Thomas 20, 23-25, 28, 93, 119
Dunsford, Jabez 16, 199, 210
Dunsford, Martin 16, 185, 218
Durell, William 117
Dyer, John 126, 262

Eagle Street Church 39, 252
East India Company 69, 75
East Kent Association 249
Edinburgh 76-77
Edinburgh Missionary Society 72
Edmeston, James 287
Education, Ministerial 166-67
Edwards, Jonathan 5, 24, 30-32, 56, 124-25, 166, 207
Edwards, Jonathan (Jr) 142, 168, 170, 186
Edwards, Morgan 198-99, 209
Election, doctrine of 96, 101, 187, 194
Escott, H. 132
Europe 173
Evangelical Magazine 149, 189, 192
Evangelical Revival 3-4, 227, 253
Evangelism 114, 135, 157, 228, 230, 250
Evans, Caleb 10, 18-19, 21-29, 87, 121, 140-41, 145, 167, 187-88, 205, 216, 224
Evans, Hugh 10, 12, 16, 18, 20-22, 25-26, 35, 205
Evans, Jonathan 106, 287
Evans, Thomas 54, 79
Exeter 12, 14, 119, 189, 246, 259
Eynsford 257
Eythorn 74, 257

Facy, Wiliam 11
'Fall of Man' 99-100
Falmouth 25

Family Worship 105
Fanch, James 287
Faringdon, Berkshire 25
Fawcett, John 10, 30, 32, 35, 83, 87, 102, 106, 109, 121, 145, 150, 188-89, 199, 287
Fellows, John 87, 110
Fetter Lane Church 46
Fitsherbert, Miss 287
Fleetwood, Lord Charles 202, 212
Flower, Benjamin 216, 220, 256
Folkstone 176, 249
Foote, H.W. 136-37
Forfitt, Benjamin 206
Forty, Henry 264
Foskett, Bernard 17-18
Foster, Benjamin 171
Fountain, John 134, 177, 188, 287
Fox, Joseph 50, 71
Fox, William 68, 232
France, 71, 134, 174-75, 183, 187, 203, 219, 240, 246, 272
Francis, Benjamin 18, 27, 30, 32, 35, 83, 91, 93, 113, 119, 145, 161, 184, 188, 199, 229, 288
Francis, W. 184
Franklin, Francis 229, 233
French Revolution 173, 194, 218, 222
Friendly Societies 57
Frost. M. 136
Fuller, Andrew 4-6, 8, 24, 26-27, 31, 34, 40, 53, 69, 75, 136, 145, 149-50, 160, 163, 167, 178, 186, 189, 203, 261-62
Fullerism 4, 27
Furman, Richard 88, 117, 141, 146, 170, 172

Gale, Martha (Rippon) 49
Gale, Samuel 49, 54, 67-70, 232, 259
Gale, Theophilus 212
Gano, John 141
General Assembly (1689) 151
General Baptist Magazine 149
General Baptists 4, 11, 92, 145, 158, 163-64, 181, 186, 192, 241, 263

General Body of the Three
  Denominations 71, 204, 221, 237-
  42
George III , King 238-39, 246, 249
George IV, King 238
George, David 182-83, 209, 243
George, M.D. 48
Georgia 172, 179, 191, 243
Germany, 71
Gibbons, Thomas 90-93, 97, 107, 137,
  288
Gibbs, Philip 200-201, 210, 229, 246
Gifford, Andrew (Sr) 204, 209, 264
Gifford, Andrew (Jr) 10, 30, 141, 197,
  208, 212, 221, 249-50, 252-53, 255
Gifford, Emmanuel 209
Gilbert, Ann 288
Giles, John 51, 54, 74, 77
Gill, John   1-2, 6, 19, 24, 30,
  35-37, 39, 43, 52-54, 71, 78, 85,
  107, 195, 203, 206-209, 212, 255,
  260
Glas, John 288
Glassite, 289
Gloucestershire 229-30
God, Doctrine of 99
Goforth, Major 172
Goodman's Fields Church 183
Goodwin, Ann 50
Goodwin, Thomas 24, 212, 255
Gospel Magazine 149
*Gospel Magazine and Theological
  Review* 149
Gough, Thomas 76
Grant, James 288
Grantham, Thomas 158, 204, 209
Great Awakening 165
Greene, Dr 128
Greene, Thomas 288
Grigg, Jacob 183-84
Grigg, Joseph 128, 288
Guildford 257
Guilsborough, Northamptonshire 156,
  192
'Gunpowder Plot' 111
Gutteridge, Joseph 68, 261

Hackney 257, 262

Haddon, John 116, 120, 122
Hague, W 190-91
Hall, George 145, 258
Hall, Richard 37
Hall, Robert (Sr) 31, 113, 160, 199,
  210
Hall, Robert (Jr) 8, 10, 25, 53, 186,
  200-201, 219, 226-27, 258
Hammond, William 288
Hampshire 229
Handel, G.F. 128
Hanway, Jonas 243
Harington, Henry 128
Harris, Howel 15, 32
Harrison, Susanna 288
Hart, Joseph 102, 288
Hart, Oliver 199
Hartop, Sir John 202
Harwood, E. 21
Haweis, Thomas 116, 204, 288
Hayden, R. xvi, 2
Hayes, Dr. 128
Haykin, M. 2
Hayward, Mr 288
'Heaven and Hell' 99, 112
Heber, Reginald 116, 288
Herbert, George 83
Hesselink, Gerrard 174
Heywood, Oliver 204
Hill, Rowland 90, 242, 244, 288
Hinduism 177
Hinton, James 185. 188, 229
Hitchcock, John 145
Hoby, James 271
Holcroft, Francis 200
Holland 76, 145, 173-75, 202, 272
Holmes, Elkanah 167
Holy Spirit, doctrine of 77, 99, 103-
  104, 249, 252
Horne, Melvill 179
Horne, George 288
Horsley, Gloucestershire 105, 229
Hovens, Daniel 173
Hudson, David 54
Hull 50, 186
Humphreys, John 241
Humphreys, Joseph 288
Hungary 174

Hunter, William 52
Huntingdon, Countess of 90, 119, 125, 128, 172, 204
Huntington, William 21
Hymnody 41, 82-138
Hymn Singing 2, 16, 41, 82, 123-24

Ilchester 204
Ilford, 257
Illidge, Thomas 74, 77
India 75, 136,147
Independents 3-4, 121, 136, 167, 192, 200, 208, 221, 237, 251, 263, 270, 289
Infant Dedication 45-46, 105, 117
Ipswich 145, 258
Ireland 70, 113, 125, 144, 151, 184-85, 192, 204, 209, 269, 272
Ivimey, Joseph 8, 15, 53, 160, 208-210, 245, 264-66, 268

Jackson, Alverey 30
Jamaica, 134, 179-80, 191, 243
Janeway, James 242
Jay, William 253
Jenkins, Joseph 149, 199
Jenkyn, William 212
Jesse, W. 288
Jews, London Society for promoting Christianity among 72
Johns, William 50, 69, 75
Johnson, Richard 179
Jones, Edmund 288
Jones, J.A. 214, 277
Jones, Morgan 199
Jones, Samuel 88, 137, 170
Jones, William 149-50
Jones, Sir William 178
Jope, Caleb 17
Judgment 99, 112
Julian, J. 93, 137, 278, 282

'K' 91, 125
Keach, Benjamin 34, 46, 264
Keeley, George 74, 203, 236
Keene, Robert 41, 125
Keith, George 37
Kelly, Thomas 116, 288

Ken, Thomas 83, 106, 288
Kent 246
Kent, Duchess of 238
Kentucky 121, 165, 171
Kiffin, William 212, 264
Kingdon, John 189
Kinghorn, Joseph 20, 22, 53, 218
Kippis, Andrew 212
Kirkland, Colonel 180
Kirkland, Samuel 142, 167
Knolding, William 61
Knollys, Hanserd 264
Knox, Alexander 92
Kollock, Shepard 117

Lambeth Church 39, 60
Lancaster, Joseph 50
Langdon, Thomas 162
Langham Essex 232
Laskiel, G.H. 179
Latrobe, C.I. 174, 176, 178
Lawson, John 288
Lectures at churches 55
Leech, - 288
Leeds, 162
Leeks, Mrs 136
Leicester 160
Leighton Buzzard, Bedfordshire 156
Leland, John 198
Lepard, Benjamin 48, 54, 68-70, 72
Lepard, William(Sr) 44, 47-48, 51, 54, 249
Lepard, William (Jr) 48, 54, 59, 68, 70, 72, 241
Lewes, Sussex 119
Lewis, Thomas 12, 14
Liele, George 147, 180-82, 209
Lincoln, 11
Little Wild Street Church 38-39, 74, 183
Liverpool 145, 149
Liverpool, Lord 240
Llewellyn, Thomas 17-18, 199, 236
Loeffs, Isaac 201
London, Baptists 2, 11, 32-35, 40, 152, 155, 158, 176, 195, 205, 221-24, 261
London Baptist Building Fund 67

London Education Society 157, 236
London Missionary Society 74, 175,
   179, 189, 245
London Monthly Meetings 163
Lord, F.T. 273
Lord's Supper 42-43, 97, 99, 110
Loughwood 211
Lovegrove, D.W. 6
Low, James 49, 54-55, 69-70, 268
Lowdell, Stephen 158
Luppitt 204
Luther, Martin 127
Lutherans 172
Lynall, Sarah 60
Lyndall, S. 120

Mabbott, Thomas 50
Maclaren, Alexander 276
Macaulay, Zachary 183
Madan, Martin 128
Maitland, Ebenezer 206
Manning, B.L. 4, 84
Manning, James 23, 88, 112, 117,
   140-43, 146, 165-66, 170, 199,
   203, 209, 216, 218
Mansfield, O.A. 129-30
Margate 74, 115, 219, 247, 249, 257
Marriages among Dissenters 204, 240
Marshall, Abraham 172
Marshall, Daniel 172
Marshman, Robert 157
Martin, John 70, 216, 220, 245
Mason, John 288
Massachusetts Missionary Magazine
   193
Masters, Mary 288
Maurice, Matthias 29
Maxwell, J. 101, 288
Maze Pond Church 38, 57, 70
McGregor, Robert 74
McLean, Archibald 203
Medley, Samuel (Sr) 83, 116, 142-43,
   146, 150, 154, 184, 188-89, 199,
   288
Medley, Samuel (Jr) 49, 69
Mennonites 76, 173-74, 216, 272
Merrick, James 288

Methodism 3-5, 43, 136, 139, 180-81,
   184, 227, 230, 263, 272, 289
Methodist Magazine 149
Miall, C.S. 277
Middleton, Joseph 119
Miles's Lane Church 79
Milgrove, Benjamin 128
Militia 219, 239
Mills, S. xvi
Misnard, Stephen 54, 68
Missions 107, 115, 144, 167, 175-79,
   227
Moore, Henry 288
Moore, Mark 62, 75
Moorfields Welsh Chapel 257
Moravians, 5, 106, 139, 174-76, 178-
   79, 204, 253, 263, 272, 289
Morris, J.W. 150, 165
Morse, Jedidiah 121, 185
Mudditt, J. xvi
Münster 174, 205
Music, David 135

Napoleon 57, 175
Neal, Daniel 212
Needham, John 87, 288
New England 165-66, 169-70
New London Bridge 67, 78
New Park Street 57, 79-80, 262, 268
New Spiritual Magazine 149, 251, 260
New Theological Repository 149-50,
   189
New York 53, 243
New York Magazine 150
Newbury 194
Newfoundland 173
Newman, William 42, 187, 224, 234,
   236-37, 239, 257, 260-61
Newport, Rhode Island 88
Newton, James 22, 288
Newton, John 83, 92-93, 108-
   109,116, 124, 242, 288
Norman, John 288
Norman, Samuel 233
North Carolina 171
Northampton 53, 67, 74, 156, 176,
   199, 202-203
Northern Baptist Itinerant Society 230

Northern Education Society 157
Northern Evangelical Society 160, 230
Norton, Daniel 259
Norton, James 49, 54, 68-70, 72
Norwich 158, 216, 218, 225
Nova Scotia 173, 179, 181-82, 243
Nuttall, G. xv, 5, 153, 190

Oakham 74
Occom, Samson 142
Olivers, Thomas 101, 288
Olney Hymns 83, 91
Olney, Thomas 45, 55
Ordination 186, 257
Owen John 24, 201, 212, 253
Oxford 185, 229

Pal, Krishna 129, 288
Page, John 59
Palatinate 174
Palmer, Herbert 204
Palmer, John 184, 231, 233
Particular Baptist Assembly (1690) 151
Pasham's *Watts* 132
Pastoral visitation 43
Patterson, W.M. xv
Paul, Moses 142
Payne, E.A. xv, 84, 194, 267, 278
Pearce, Samuel 27, 150, 163, 182, 184,
    187-89, 199, 288
Peck, John 50
Pelagianism 29
Periodical Accounts (BMS) 150, 176,
    185, 189, 227
Perkins, H. 247
Perronet, Edward 93, 279, 288
Perrot, C. 240
Philadelphia 88, 113, 164, 168
Philadelphian Confession of Faith 164-
    65
Philips, Henry 15, 32, 199, 210, 229
Piggin, S. 227
Pithay, Bristol 22, 53
Pitt, William 219-20, 249
Pius VII 175
Plymouth 184, 200-201, 217, 229,
    246
Poetry 188

Poland 174, 272
Politics of Dissent 215-20
Poor Africans' Society 243
Poor, help for 58-61, 108
Poplar, 257
Port of London Society 245
Portsea 74
Portsmouth 44
Powell, Samuel 177
Powell, Vavasor 212, 229
Prayer meetings 56-57, 193
Preaching 105, 253-57
Preaching, Testing for gift 73
Presbyterians 117, 200, 204, 221,
    237, 241, 289
Prescott Street Church 39, 68, 126, 236
Price, Richard 166, 212, 218
Priestley, Joseph 26
Prince Regent 238
Princeton College 167
Prior, Alexander and Elizabeth 62
Prophecy 194
'Protestant Dissenters' Register' 204
Protestant Dissenters' Magazine 149
Providence, Rhode Island 88, 203
Prussia 173-75, 272
Psalms and Hymns Trust 122
Punchard, William 201
Pyne, Sarah (later, Rippon) 258

Quakers 139, 187, 263, 272

Rack, H. D. 43
Radford, J. 120
Randall, Dr 128
Ravish, John 63
Reading, Berkshire 53, 200
Redding, Robert 145, 224
Rees, Abraham 212, 238
Regent's Park College 236
'Regular Baptists' 165, 171
Relief of Aged and Infirm Protestant
    Dissenting Ministers, Society for 72
Relief of Poor Africans in London 72
Religious Freedom 166
Religious Tract Society 187, 206, 243
Regium Donum 70, 204, 245

Revival 56, 108, 141, 157, 165-66, 168, 193
Reynolds, John 157, 199, 210, 222
Rhode Island Academy 152, 166-67, 191, 237
Rhys, Morgan 217, 219
Richards, George 138
Richards, Lewis 141, 172
Richards, William 25, 140, 217, 219
Rippon, Benjamin 177, 259
Rippon, Evelyn xv
Rippon, Grace 11
Rippon, Jane (Hopkins) 13
Rippon, John (Dr)
  -early years at Tiverton, 11-17;
  -student at Bristol, 17-29;
  -pastor at Carter Lane, 33-81
  -and Baptist hymnody 82-138, *Tune Book*, 41, 123-31
  -alteration of Perronet's 'All Hail the Power' 279-81
  -hymns by 282-85
  -influence through *Baptist Annual Register*, 139-95
  -degrees 167, 237
  -and Baptist historiography 196-214
  -and Dissenting politics 215-220
  -and Baptist activities 221-237
  -and Baptist Union 263-73
  -and other Dissenting societies 237-46
  -personal activities for churches and individuals 246-48
  -as preacher 249-58
  -published sermons 249
  -theology of 250-53
  -family 258-60
  -character 260-62
  -death 262
Rippon, John (Senior) (d. 1772) 11
Rippon, John (Junior) (1730-1800) 12-13, 16, 119, 259, 277
Rippon, John (son of Dr Rippon) 212, 259, 262
Rippon, John (son of Theophilus) 126
Rippon, Martha (later Gale), 49, 259
Rippon, Mary 11
Rippon, Mary (later Cozins) 13

Rippon, Mary (later Norton) 259-60
Rippon, Sarah (Pyne) 258-59
Rippon, Theophilus 13-14, 126
Rippon, Thomas 13
Rippon, Thomas (1791-1825) 75-76, 116, 133, 288
Rippon, William 13
Roberts, Henry 51
Roberts, R.P. 2
Robinson, Robert 10, 34, 55, 70, 83, 87, 91, 102, 111, 173-74, 187, 194, 197, 200, 204-205, 216-17, 219-20, 225-26, 228, 256, 261, 288
Robison, O.C. 159, 278
Rodway, James 183
Rogers, William 170, 178, 189
Romaine, William 242
Roman Catholic 289
Room, Charles 55, 80-81, 262, 268, 275
Ross, 190
Ross, Martin 191
Routley, Erik 134
Rowe, John 181
Rowles, Samuel 145
Rumson, Samuel 189
Russia 174, 272
Ryland John Collett 17, 23, 176, 199, 216, 249, 251, 254, 270
Ryland, John 10, 24, 30, 32, 53, 74, 91, 108, 116, 118-19, 140-41, 145, 149, 156, 162, 165, 167, 182, 186, 188-89, 194, 202, 208, 261, 265, 288

Saffery, John 27, 185, 228, 233, 269
Saffery, Maria 288
Saffron Walden 74
Salendine Nook, Yorkshire 199
Salisbury 11, 15, 228-29
Savannah 172, 180, 182
Saxony 174
Scarborough 67
Schwartz, Charles 179
Scotch Baptists 149, 186, 203, 209
Scotland 113, 150, 243, 272
Scott, Thomas 288
Scripture, doctrine of 99, 101

Seagrave, Robert 289
Seccombe, Thomas 277
'Separate Baptists' 165, 171
Serampore 75, 134
Seventh Day Baptists 105
Sexual immorality 64
Sharp, Granville 182
Sharp, Henry 180
Sharp, John 232, 247
Sharp, Peter 49, 54, 58-59, 65, 68
Shaw, Benjamin 245
Shrewsbury 184, 231
Shropshire 233
Shrubsole, William 128
Sidmouth, Lord 240
'Sickness and Suffering' 111, 136
Sierra Leone 72, 134, 179, 181-84,
    191, 243
Six-Principles Baptists 169
Skeats, H.S. 277
Skepp, John 30
Slavery, Abolition of 160, 167-68,
    182, 239, 244, 271, 282
Slinn, Sarah 289
Smith, James 153
Societas Evangelica 230
Socinianism 4, 25-26, 220
Somerset 232
South Carolina, 172
Southerland, Helena 58
Southey, Robert 212, 218
S.P.C.K. 175, 179
S.P.G. 175
Sprague, Daniel 16, 224, 232, 246
Sprague, J.L. 247, 259
Spurgeon, C. H. 36, 47, 60-61, 80-81,
    137, 239, 268, 276-77
St Albans 75
Stanford, John 137, 203
Staughton, William 27
Steadman, William 27, 185, 228-29,
    231
Stearns, Shubal 171
Steele, Anne 83, 87, 91-93, 100-102,
    289
Steevens, Thomas 190
Stennett, Joseph 97, 105, 289

Stennett, Samuel 10, 18, 38, 84, 91-
    93, 102, 104, 110, 112, 119, 140,
    187, 199, 222, 236, 289
Stepney Academy 42, 68, 70, 77, 81,
    236-37
Stevenson, W.R. 282
Stillman, Samuel 141, 146, 170, 260
Stinton, Benjamin 71, 151, 196
Stocker, John 289
Stogdon, - 289
Stoughton, John 125, 226, 277
Straphan, J. 105, 119, 289
Strong, Nathan 138
Stuart, John 74
Sunday 105
Sunday Schools 57, 111, 258
Sunday School Society 68
Suspension from communion 61-62
Sutcliff, John 25, 27, 30, 32, 46, 121,
    160, 178
Swain, Joseph 49, 51, 74, 77, 199,
    251
Sweden 174
Swigle, Thomas 181
Switzerland 174, 272
Sydney, 179
Symmons, Thomas 232

Tahiti 179
Tate, Nahum 82, 289
Taylor, Dan 149, 158, 164
Taylor, William 68, 236
Tenterden 134
Terrill, Edward 17
Terry, Henry 14. 16
Test and Corporation Acts 217-18,
    237-38, 240-41
Tewkesbury 121
Thacher, Peter 167, 170
Thelwall, John 219
Theological Magazine 150
Thomas, John 134, 176-78, 199, 259
Thomas, Joshua 141, 145, 151, 157-
    58, 161, 188-89, 191, 197-200, 205
Thomas, Timothy 131, 141, 245, 256
Thomas, Thomas 236
Thompson, Josiah 197
Thornton, Henry 182

Thornton, John 230
Tibet 115
'Time and Eternity' 99
'Times and Seasons' 99, 110-11
Tindal, Henry 212
Tipping, Martha 65
Tiverton 6, 11-17, 20-21, 32, 74, 124, 185, 224, 232, 246-47, 277
Toler, Henry 167
Toleration Act 237
Tombes, John 205
Tommas, John 22, 199-200, 210
Toplady, Augustus 82-83, 90, 92-96, 98, 102-103, 206, 289
Tottenham 257
Transient Communion 52
Trinder, Thomas 199
Tring 257
Trivett, Zenas 232
Truro 74, 223-24, 229, 247
Turner, Daniel 83, 87, 91, 93, 119, 199, 289

Uffculm, Devonshire 68, 257, 282
Underwood, A.C. 210
Unicorn Yard Church 79
Unitarians 166, 216, 220, 240-41, 289
Universalism 138
Upottery 13, 119, 211, 259
Upton, James 39, 189
Ustick, Thomas 88, 113, 117, 141-42, 171

Van Braght, T.J. 173
Venn, Henry 242
Village Evangelism 7, 27, 156, 185, 226-35
Virginia 171
Vokes, Mrs 289
Voltaire 175
Volunteers (Militia) 219, 249, 252, 254

Waldron, Thomas 76
Wales, Baptists 17, 113, 151, 168, 225, 229-30, 272
Walford, Wiliam 202
Walker, Thomas 124-31

Wallin, Benjamin 38, 87, 141, 222, 289
Walsh, J.D. 3
Walworth 74
War 111, 141, 219
Ward, William 69, 76, 115, 177, 219, 261
Ward, W.R. 227-28, 276
Warmington, J 68
Warwickshire 229
Washington, President 171
Watford 134, 247
Watford, Ann 59
Watson, J.R. 82, 84, 92-93, 98-99, 123
Wattisham 145
Watts, Isaac 7, 43, 82-83, 86-93, 99-100, 103, 106, 112, 119, 121-22, 124, 131-33, 136, 201-202, 212, 242-43, 275, 289
Watts, Michael 55-56, 72, 253
Waugh, Alexander 72
Wayland's *Watts* 132
Webbell, Elizabeth 52
Wedmore 204
Wellington, Somerset 15
Wesley, Charles and John 21, 82, 84, 92-96, 99, 101-102, 104,112, 116, 136, 204, 229, 289
Wesley, Susannah 212
West, W.M.S. xv
West Indies 76, 175,184
Westlake, Thomas 119
Westley, Robert 49, 54, 59, 68-70
Weston-super-Mare 261
Whitbread, Samuel 183
White, B.R. xiii, xv, 210
White Henry Kirk 116, 289
Whitefield, G. 3, 10, 30, 125, 136, 204, 242, 252-53
Whitfield, Charles 145
Whitley, W.T. xv, 25, 131, 192, 210, 278
Widows' Fund 72, 187, 241-42
Wilberforce, William 34, 182
Wilkinson, Josiah 50, 74-75
Wilks, Matthew 212-13, 218
Willey, W 227

William IV, King 238-39
Williams, Daniel 212
Williams, Edward 4, 133
Williams, James 190
Williams, John 172, 198
Williams, Roger 203
Williams, William 108, 289
Williams, William 157
Wilson, Samuel 42
Wilson, Walter 38, 208
Wiltshire 229
Winchester 74
Winchester, Elhanan 141
Winterbotham, William 217, 219

Wood, Joshua 199
Woolwich 74
Worcestershire 229
Worship 40-41, 99, 105-106, 135, 202
'World' 99, 106
Wotton-under-edge, Gloucestershire 232

Yarmouth 74, 78, 202
Young, R.H. 93, 99, 129, 278

Zinzendorf, Count 101
Zwingli, U. 110

Studies in Baptist History and Thought

(All titles uniform with this volume)
Dates in bold are of projected publication
Volumes in this series are not always published in sequence

David Bebbington and Anthony R. Cross (eds)
Global Baptist History
(SBHT vol. 14)

This book brings together studies from the Second International Conference on Baptist Studies which explore different facets of Baptist life and work especially during the twentieth century.

2006 / 1-84227-214-4 / approx. 350pp

David Bebbington (ed.)
The Gospel in the World
International Baptist Studies
(SBHT vol. 1)

This volume of essays from the First International Conference on Baptist Studies deals with a range of subjects spanning Britain, North America, Europe, Asia and the Antipodes. Topics include studies on religious tolerance, the communion controversy and the development of the international Baptist community, and concludes with two important essays on the future of Baptist life that pay special attention to the United States.

2002 / 1-84227-118-0 / xiv + 362pp

John H.Y. Briggs (ed.)
Pulpit and People
Studies in Eighteenth-Century English Baptist Life and Thought
(SBHT vol. 28)

The eighteenth century was a crucial time in Baptist history. The denomination had its roots in seventeenth-century English Puritanism and Separatism and the persecution of the Stuart kings with only a limited measure of freedom after 1689. Worse, however, was to follow for with toleration came doctrinal conflict, a move away from central Christian understandings and a loss of evangelistic urgency. Both spiritual and numerical decline ensued, to the extent that the denomination was virtually reborn as rather belatedly it came to benefit from the Evangelical Revival which brought new life to both Arminian and Calvinistic Baptists. The papers in this volume study a denomination in transition, and relate to theology, their views of the church and its mission, Baptist spirituality, and engagements with radical politics.

2007 / 1-84227-403-1 / approx. 350pp

July 2005

Damian Brot
Church of the Baptized or Church of Believers?
A Contribution to the Dialogue between the Catholic Church and the Free Churches with Special Reference to Baptists
(SBHT vol. 26)

The dialogue between the Catholic Church and the Free Churches in Europe has hardly taken place. This book pleads for a commencement of such a conversation. It offers, among other things, an introduction to the American and the international dialogues between Baptists and the Catholic Church and strives to allow these conversations to become fruitful in the European context as well.

2006 / 1-84227-334-5 / approx. 364pp

Dennis Bustin
Paradox and Perseverence
Hanserd Knollys, Particular Baptist Pioneer in Seventeenth-Century England
(SBHT vol. 23)

The seventeenth century was a significant period in English history during which the people of England experienced unprecedented change and tumult in all spheres of life. At the same time, the importance of order and the traditional institutions of society were being reinforced. Hanserd Knollys, born during this pivotal period, personified in his life the ambiguity, tension and paradox of it, openly seeking change while at the same time cautiously embracing order. As a founder and leader of the Particular Baptists in London and despite persecution and personal hardship, he played a pivotal role in helping shape their identity externally in society and, internally, as they moved toward becoming more formalised by the end of the century.

2006 / 1-84227-259-4 / approx. 324pp

Anthony R. Cross
Baptism and the Baptists
Theology and Practice in Twentieth-Century Britain
(SBHT vol. 3)

At a time of renewed interest in baptism, *Baptism and the Baptists* is a detailed study of twentieth-century baptismal theology and practice and the factors which have influenced its development.

2000 / 0-85364-959-6 / xx + 530pp

Anthony R. Cross and Philip E. Thompson (eds)
Baptist Sacramentalism
(SBHT vol. 5)

This collection of essays includes biblical, historical and theological studies in the theology of the sacraments from a Baptist perspective. Subjects explored include the physical side of being spiritual, baptism, the Lord's supper, the church, ordination, preaching, worship, religious liberty and the issue of disestablishment.

2003 / 1-84227-119-9 / xvi + 278pp

Anthony R. Cross and Philip E. Thompson (eds)
Baptist Sacramentalism 2
(SBHT vol. 25)

This second collection of essays exploring various dimensions of sacramental theology from a Baptist perspective includes biblical, historical and theological studies from scholars from around the world.

2006 / 1-84227-325-6 / approx. 350pp

Paul S. Fiddes
Tracks and Traces
Baptist Identity in Church and Theology
(SBHT vol. 13)

This is a comprehensive, yet unusual, book on the faith and life of Baptist Christians. It explores the understanding of the church, ministry, sacraments and mission from a thoroughly theological perspective. In a series of interlinked essays, the author relates Baptist identity consistently to a theology of covenant and to participation in the triune communion of God.

2003 / 1-84227-120-2 / xvi + 304pp

Stanley K. Fowler
More Than a Symbol
The British Baptist Recovery of Baptismal Sacramentalism
(SBHT vol. 2)

Fowler surveys the entire scope of British Baptist literature from the seventeenth-century pioneers onwards. He shows that in the twentieth century leading British Baptist pastors and theologians recovered an understanding of baptism that connected experience with soteriology and that in doing so they were recovering what many of their forebears had taught.

2002 / 1-84227-052-4 / xvi + 276pp

Steven R. Harmon
Towards Baptist Catholicity
Essays on Tradition and the Baptist Vision
(SBHT vol. 27)

This series of essays contends that the reconstruction of the Baptist vision in the wake of modernity's dissolution requires a retrieval of the ancient ecumenical tradition that forms Christian identity through rehearsal and practice. Themes explored include catholic identity as an emerging trend in Baptist theology, tradition as a theological category in Baptist perspective, Baptist confessions and the patristic tradition, worship as a principal bearer of tradition, and the role of Baptist higher education in shaping the Christian vision.

2006 / 1-84227-362-0 / approx. 210pp

Michael A.G. Haykin (ed.)
'At the Pure Fountain of Thy Word'
Andrew Fuller as an Apologist
(SBHT vol. 6)

One of the greatest Baptist theologians of the eighteenth and early nineteenth centuries, Andrew Fuller has not had justice done to him. There is little doubt that Fuller's theology lay behind the revitalization of the Baptists in the late eighteenth century and the first few decades of the nineteenth. This collection of essays fills a much needed gap by examining a major area of Fuller's thought, his work as an apologist.

2004 / 1-84227-171-7 / xxii + 276pp

Michael A.G. Haykin
Studies in Calvinistic Baptist Spirituality
(SBHT vol. 15)

In a day when spirituality is in vogue and Christian communities are looking for guidance in this whole area, there is wisdom in looking to the past to find untapped wells. The Calvinistic Baptists, heirs of the rich ecclesial experience in the Puritan era of the seventeenth century, but, by the end of the eighteenth century, also passionately engaged in the catholicity of the Evangelical Revivals, are such a well. This collection of essays, covering such things as the Lord's Supper, friendship and hymnody, seeks to draw out the spiritual riches of this community for reflection and imitation in the present day.

2006 / 1-84227-149-0 / approx. 350pp

Brian Haymes, Anthony R. Cross and Ruth Gouldbourne
On Being the Church
Revisioning Baptist Identity
(SBHT vol. 21)

The aim of the book is to re-examine Baptist theology and practice in the light of the contemporary biblical, theological, ecumenical and missiological context drawing on historical and contemporary writings and issues. It is not a study in denominationalism but rather seeks to revision historical insights from the believers' church tradition for the sake of Baptists and other Christians in the context of the modern–postmodern context.

2006 / 1-84227-121-0 / approx. 350pp

Ken R. Manley
From Woolloomooloo to 'Eternity': A History of Australian Baptists
Volume 1: Growing an Australian Church (1831–1914)
Volume 2: A National Church in a Global Community (1914–2005)
(SBHT vols 16.1 and 16.2)

From their beginnings in Australia in 1831 with the first baptisms in Woolloomoolloo Bay in 1832, this pioneering study describes the quest of Baptists in the different colonies (states) to discover their identity as Australians and Baptists. Although institutional developments are analyzed and the roles of significant individuals traced, the major focus is on the social and theological dimensions of the Baptist movement.

2 vol. set 2006 / 1-84227-405-8 / approx. 900pp

Ken R. Manley
'Redeeming Love Proclaim'
John Rippon and the Baptists
(SBHT vol. 12)

A leading exponent of the new moderate Calvinism which brought new life to many Baptists, John Rippon (1751–1836) helped unite the Baptists at this significant time. His many writings expressed the denomination's growing maturity and mutual awareness of Baptists in Britain and America, and exerted a long-lasting influence on Baptist worship and devotion. In his various activities, Rippon helped conserve the heritage of Old Dissent and promoted the evangelicalism of the New Dissent

2004 / 1-84227-193-8 / xviii + 340pp

Peter J. Morden
Offering Christ to the World
Andrew Fuller and the Revival of English Particular Baptist Life
(SBHT vol. 8)
Andrew Fuller (1754–1815) was one of the foremost English Baptist ministers
of his day. His career as an Evangelical Baptist pastor, theologian, apologist and
missionary statesman coincided with the profound revitalization of the Particular
Baptist denomination to which he belonged. This study examines the key
aspects of the life and thought of this hugely significant figure, and gives
insights into the revival in which he played such a central part.
2003 / 1-84227-141-5 / xx + 202pp

Peter Naylor
Calvinism, Communion and the Baptists
A Study of English Calvinistic Baptists from the Late 1600s to the Early 1800s
(SBHT vol. 7)
Dr Naylor argues that the traditional link between 'high-Calvinism' and
'restricted communion' is in need of revision. He examines Baptist communion
controversies from the late 1600s to the early 1800s and also the theologies of
John Gill and Andrew Fuller.
2003 / 1-84227-142-3 / xx + 266pp

Ian M. Randall, Toivo Pilli and Anthony R. Cross (eds)
Baptist Identities
International Studies from the Seventeenth to the Twentieth Centuries
(SBHT vol. 19)
These papers represent the contributions of scholars from various parts of the
world as they consider the factors that have contributed to Baptist
distinctiveness in different countries and at different times. The volume includes
specific case studies as well as broader examinations of Baptist life in a
particular country or region. Together they represent an outstanding resource for
understanding Baptist identities.
2005 / 1-84227-215-2 / approx. 350pp

James M. Renihan
Edification and Beauty
The Practical Ecclesiology of the English Particular Baptists, 1675–1705
(SBHT vol. 17)
Edification and Beauty describes the practices of the Particular Baptist churches at the end of the seventeenth century in terms of three concentric circles: at the centre is the ecclesiological material in the Second London Confession, which is then fleshed out in the various published writings of the men associated with these churches, and, finally, expressed in the church books of the era.
2005 / 1-84227-251-9 / approx. 230pp

Frank Rinaldi
'The Tribe of Dan'
A Study of the New Connexion of General Baptists 1770–1891
(SBHT vol. 10)
'The Tribe of Dan' is a thematic study which explores the theology, organizational structure, evangelistic strategy, ministry and leadership of the New Connexion of General Baptists as it experienced the process of institutionalization in the transition from a revival movement to an established denomination.
2006 / 1-84227-143-1 / approx. 350pp

Peter Shepherd
The Making of a Modern Denomination
John Howard Shakespeare and the English Baptists 1898–1924
(SBHT vol. 4)
John Howard Shakespeare introduced revolutionary change to the Baptist denomination. The Baptist Union was transformed into a strong central institution and Baptist ministers were brought under its control. Further, Shakespeare's pursuit of church unity reveals him as one of the pioneering ecumenists of the twentieth century.
2001 / 1-84227-046-X / xviii + 220pp

Karen Smith
The Community and the Believers
*A Study of Calvinistic Baptist Spirituality in Some Towns and Villages of
Hampshire and the Borders of Wiltshire, c.1730–1830*
(SBHT vol. 22)

The period from 1730 to 1830 was one of transition for Calvinistic Baptists. Confronted by the enthusiasm of the Evangelical Revival, congregations within the denomination as a whole were challenged to find a way to take account of the revival experience. This study examines the life and devotion of Calvinistic Baptists in Hampshire and Wiltshire during this period. Among this group of Baptists was the hymn writer, Anne Steele.

2005 / 1-84227-326-4 / approx. 280pp

Martin Sutherland
Dissenters in a 'Free Land'
Baptist Thought in New Zealand 1850–2000
(SBHT vol. 24)

Baptists in New Zealand were forced to recast their identity. Conventions of communication and association, state and ecumenical relations, even historical divisions and controversies had to be revised in the face of new topographies and constraints. As Baptists formed themselves in a fluid society they drew heavily on both international movements and local dynamics. This book traces the development of ideas which shaped institutions and styles in sometimes surprising ways.

2006 / 1-84227-327-2 / approx. 230pp

Brian Talbot
The Search for a Common Identity
The Origins of the Baptist Union of Scotland 1800–1870
(SBHT vol. 9)

In the period 1800 to 1827 there were three streams of Baptists in Scotland: Scotch, Haldaneite and 'English' Baptist. A strong commitment to home evangelization brought these three bodies closer together, leading to a merger of their home missionary societies in 1827. However, the first three attempts to form a union of churches failed, but by the 1860s a common understanding of their corporate identity was attained leading to the establishment of the Baptist Union of Scotland.

2003 / 1-84227-123-7 / xviii + 402pp

Philip E. Thompson
The Freedom of God
Towards Baptist Theology in Pneumatological Perspective
(SBHT vol. 20)

This study contends that the range of theological commitments of the early Baptists are best understood in relation to their distinctive emphasis on the freedom of God. Thompson traces how this was recast anthropocentrically, leading to an emphasis upon human freedom from the nineteenth century onwards. He seeks to recover the dynamism of the early vision via a pneumatologically-oriented ecclesiology defining the church in terms of the memory of God.

2006 / 1-84227-125-3 / approx. 350pp

Philip E. Thompson and Anthony R. Cross (eds)
Recycling the Past or Researching History?
Studies in Baptist Historiography and Myths
(SBHT vol. 11)

In this volume an international group of Baptist scholars examine and re-examine areas of Baptist life and thought about which little is known or the received wisdom is in need of revision. Historiographical studies include the date Oxford Baptists joined the Abingdon Association, the death of the Fifth Monarchist John Pendarves, eighteenth-century Calvinistic Baptists and the political realm, confessional identity and denominational institutions, Baptist community, ecclesiology, the priesthood of all believers, soteriology, Baptist spirituality, Strict and Reformed Baptists, the role of women among British Baptists, while various 'myths' challenged include the nature of high-Calvinism in eighteenth-century England, baptismal anti-sacramentalism, episcopacy, and Baptists and change.

2005 / 1-84227-122-9 / approx. 330pp

Linda Wilson
Marianne Farningham
A Plain Working Woman
(SBHT vol. 18)

Marianne Farningham, of College Street Baptist Chapel, Northampton, was a household name in evangelical circles in the later nineteenth century. For over fifty years she produced comment, poetry, biography and fiction for the popular Christian press. This investigation uses her writings to explore the beliefs and behaviour of evangelical Nonconformists, including Baptists, during these years.

2006 / 1-84227-124-5 / approx. 250pp

Other Paternoster titles
relating to Baptist history and thought

George R. Beasley-Murray
Baptism in the New Testament
(Paternoster Digital Library)
This is a welcome reprint of a classic text on baptism originally published in 1962 by one of the leading Baptist New Testament scholars of the twentieth century. Dr Beasley-Murray's comprehensive study begins by investigating the antecedents of Christian baptism. It then surveys the foundation of Christian baptism in the Gospels, its emergence in the Acts of the Apostles and development in the apostolic writings. Following a section relating baptism to New Testament doctrine, a substantial discussion of the origin and significance of infant baptism leads to a briefer consideration of baptismal reform and ecumenism.

2005 / 1-84227-300-0 / x + 422pp

Paul Beasley-Murray
Fearless for Truth
A Personal Portrait of the Life of George Beasley-Murray
Without a doubt George Beasley-Murray was one of the greatest Baptists of the twentieth century. A long-standing Principal of Spurgeon's College, he wrote more than twenty books and made significant contributions in the study of areas as diverse as baptism and eschatology, as well as writing highly respected commentaries on the Book of Revelation and John's Gospel.

2002 / 1-84227-134-2 / xii + 244pp

David Bebbington
Holiness in Nineteenth-Century England
(Studies in Christian History and Thought)
David Bebbington stresses the relationship of movements of spirituality to changes in their cultural setting, especially the legacies of the Enlightenment and Romanticism. He shows that these broad shifts in ideological mood had a profound effect on the ways in which piety was conceptualized and practised. Holiness was intimately bound up with the spirit of the age.

2000 / 0-85364-981-2 / viii + 98pp

Clyde Binfield
Victorian Nonconformity in Eastern England 1840–1885
(Studies in Evangelical History and Thought)
Studies of Victorian religion and society often concentrate on cities, suburbs, and industrialisation. This study provides a contrast. Victorian Eastern England—Essex, Suffolk, Norfolk, Cambridgeshire, and Huntingdonshire—was rural, traditional, relatively unchanging. That is nonetheless a caricature which discounts the industry in Norwich and Ipswich (as well as in Haverhill, Stowmarket and Leiston) and ignores the impact of London on Essex, of railways throughout the region, and of an ancient but changing university (Cambridge) on the county town which housed it. It also entirely ignores the political implications of such changes in a region noted for the variety of its religious Dissent since the seventeenth century. This book explores Victorian Eastern England and its Nonconformity. It brings to a wider readership a pioneering thesis which has made a major contribution to a fresh evolution of English religion and society.
2006 / 1-84227-216-0 / approx. 274pp

Edward W. Burrows
'To Me To Live Is Christ'
A Biography of Peter H. Barber
This book is about a remarkably gifted and energetic man of God. Peter H. Barber was born into a Brethren family in Edinburgh in 1930. In his youth he joined Charlotte Baptist Chapel and followed the call into Baptist ministry. For eighteen years he was the pioneer minister of the new congregation in the New Town of East Kilbride, which planted two further congregations. At the age of thirty-nine he served as Centenary President of the Baptist Union of Scotland and then exercised an influential ministry for over seven years in the well-known Upton Vale Baptist Church, Torquay. From 1980 until his death in 1994 he was General Secretary of the Baptist Union of Scotland. Through his work for the European Baptist Federation and the Baptist World Alliance he became a world Baptist statesman. He was President of the EBF during the upheaval that followed the collapse of Communism.
2005 / 1-84227-324-8 / xxii + 236pp

Christopher J. Clement
Religious Radicalism in England 1535–1565
(Rutherford Studies in Historical Theology)
In this valuable study Christopher Clement draws our attention to a varied assemblage of people who sought Christian faithfulness in the underworld of mid-Tudor England. Sympathetically and yet critically he assess their place in the history of English Protestantism, and by attentive listening he gives them a voice.
1997 / 0-946068-44-5 / xxii + 426pp

Anthony R. Cross (ed.)
Ecumenism and History
Studies in Honour of John H.Y. Briggs
(Studies in Christian History and Thought)
This collection of essays examines the inter-relationships between the two fields in which Professor Briggs has contributed so much: history—particularly Baptist and Nonconformist—and the ecumenical movement. With contributions from colleagues and former research students from Britain, Europe and North America, *Ecumenism and History* provides wide-ranging studies in important aspects of Christian history, theology and ecumenical studies.
2002 / 1-84227-135-0 / xx + 362pp

Keith E. Eitel
Paradigm Wars
*The Southern Baptist International Mission Board
Faces the Third Millennium*
(Regnum Studies in Mission)
The International Mission Board of the Southern Baptist Convention is the largest denominational mission agency in North America. This volume chronicles the historic and contemporary forces that led to the IMB's recent extensive reorganization, providing the most comprehensive case study to date of a historic mission agency restructuring to continue its mission purpose into the twenty-first century more effectively.
2000 / 1-870345-12-6 / x + 140pp

Ruth Gouldbourne
The Flesh and the Feminine
Gender and Theology in the Writings of Caspar Schwenckfeld
(Studies in Christian History and Thought)
Caspar Schwenckfeld and his movement exemplify one of the radical communities of the sixteenth century. Challenging theological and liturgical norms, they also found themselves challenging social and particularly gender assumptions. In this book, the issues of the relationship between radical theology and the understanding of gender are considered.
2005 / 1-84227-048-6 / approx. 304pp

David Hilborn
The Words of our Lips
Language-Use in Free Church Worship
(Paternoster Theological Monographs)
Studies of liturgical language have tended to focus on the written canons of
Roman Catholic and Anglican communities. By contrast, David Hilborn
analyses the more extemporary approach of English Nonconformity. Drawing
on recent developments in linguistic pragmatics, he explores similarities and
differences between 'fixed' and 'free' worship, and argues for the
interdependence of each.

2006 / 0-85364-977-4

Stephen R. Holmes
Listening to the Past
The Place of Tradition in Theology
Beginning with the question 'Why can't we just read the Bible?' Stephen
Holmes considers the place of tradition in theology, showing how the doctrine
of creation leads to an account of historical location and creaturely limitations as
essential aspects of our existence. For we cannot claim unmediated access to the
Scriptures without acknowledging the place of tradition: theology is an
irreducibly communal task. *Listening to the Past* is a sustained attempt to show
what listening to tradition involves, and how it can be used to aid theological
work today.

2002 / 1-84227-155-5 / xiv + 168pp

Mark Hopkins
Nonconformity's Romantic Generation
Evangelical and Liberal Theologies in Victorian England
(Studies in Evangelical History and Thought)
A study of the theological development of key leaders of the Baptist and
Congregational denominations at their period of greatest influence, including
C.H. Spurgeon and R.W. Dale, and of the controversies in which those among
them who embraced and rejected the liberal transformation of their evangelical
heritage opposed each other.

2004 / 1-84227-150-4 / xvi + 284pp

Galen K. Johnson
Prisoner of Conscience
John Bunyan on Self, Community and Christian Faith
(Studies in Christian History and Thought)
This is an interdisciplinary study of John Bunyan's understanding of conscience across his autobiographical, theological and fictional writings, investigating whether conscience always deserves fidelity, and how Bunyan's view of conscience affects his relationship both to modern Western individualism and historic Christianity.
2003 / 1-84227- 151-2 / xvi + 236pp

R.T. Kendall
Calvin and English Calvinism to 1649
(Studies in Christian History and Thought)
The author's thesis is that those who formed the Westminster Confession of Faith, which is regarded as Calvinism, in fact departed from John Calvin on two points: (1) the extent of the atonement and (2) the ground of assurance of salvation.
1997 / 0-85364-827-1 / xii + 264pp

Timothy Larsen
Friends of Religious Equality
Nonconformist Politics in Mid-Victorian England
During the middle decades of the nineteenth century the English Nonconformist community developed a coherent political philosophy of its own, of which a central tenet was the principle of religious equality (in contrast to the stereotype of Evangelical Dissenters). The Dissenting community fought for the civil rights of Roman Catholics, non-Christians and even atheists, on an issue of principle which had its flowering in the enthusiastic and undivided support which Nonconformity gave to the campaign for Jewish emancipation. This reissued study examines the political efforts and ideas of English Nonconformists during the period, covering the whole range of national issues raised, from state education to the Crimean War. It offers a case study of a theologically conservative group defending religious pluralism in the civic sphere, showing that the concept of religious equality was a grand vision at the centre of the political philosophy of the Dissenters.
2007 / 1-84227-402-3 / x + 300pp

Donald M. Lewis
Lighten Their Darkness
The Evangelical Mission to Working-Class London, 1828–1860
(Studies in Evangelical History and Thought)
This is a comprehensive and compelling study of the Church and the complexities of nineteenth-century London. Challenging our understanding of the culture in working London at this time, Lewis presents a well-structured and illustrated work that contributes substantially to the study of evangelicalism and mission in nineteenth-century Britain.

2001 / 1-84227-074-5 / xviii + 372pp

Stanley E. Porter and Anthony R. Cross (eds)
Semper Reformandum
Studies in Honour of Clark H. Pinnock
Clark Pinnock has clearly been one of the most important evangelical theologians of the last forty years in North America. Always provocative, especially in the wide range of opinions he has held and considered, Pinnock, himself a Baptist, has recently retired after twenty-five years of teaching at McMaster Divinity College. His colleagues and associates honour him in this volume by responding to his important theological work which has dealt with the essential topics of evangelical theology. These include Christian apologetics, biblical inspiration, the Holy Spirit and, perhaps most importantly in recent years, openness theology.

2003 / 1-84227-206-3 / xiv + 414pp

Meic Pearse
The Great Restoration
The Religious Radicals of the 16th and 17th Centuries
Pearse charts the rise and progress of continental Anabaptism – both evangelical and heretical – through the sixteenth century. He then follows the story of those English people who became impatient with Puritanism and separated – first from the Church of England and then from one another – to form the antecedents of later Congregationalists, Baptists and Quakers.

1998 / 0-85364-800-X / xii + 320pp

Charles Price and Ian M. Randall
Transforming Keswick
Transforming Keswick is a thorough, readable and detailed history of the convention. It will be of interest to those who know and love Keswick, those who are only just discovering it, and serious scholars eager to learn more about the history of God's dealings with his people.

2000 / 1-85078-350-0 / 288pp

Jim Purves
The Triune God and the Charismatic Movement
A Critical Appraisal from a Scottish Perspective
(Paternoster Theological Monographs)
All emotion and no theology? Or a fundamental challenge to reappraise and realign our trinitarian theology in the light of Christian experience? This study of charismatic renewal as it found expression within Scotland at the end of the twentieth century evaluates the use of Patristic, Reformed and contemporary models (including those of the Baptist Union of Scotland) of the Trinity in explaining the workings of the Holy Spirit.
2004 / 1-84227-321-3 / xxiv + 246pp

Ian M. Randall
Evangelical Experiences
A Study in the Spirituality of English Evangelicalism 1918–1939
(Studies in Evangelical History and Thought)
This book makes a detailed historical examination of evangelical spirituality between the First and Second World Wars. It shows how patterns of devotion led to tensions and divisions. In a wide-ranging study, Anglican, Wesleyan, Reformed and Pentecostal-charismatic spiritualities are analysed.
1999 / 0-85364-919-7 / xii + 310pp

Ian M. Randall
One Body in Christ
The History and Significance of the Evangelical Alliance
In 1846 the Evangelical Alliance was founded with the aim of bringing together evangelicals for common action. This book uses material not previously utilized to examine the history and significance of the Evangelical Alliance, a movement which has remained a powerful force for unity. At a time when evangelicals are growing world-wide, this book offers insights into the past which are relevant to contemporary issues.
2001 / 1-84227-089-3 / xii + 394pp

Ian M. Randall
Spirituality and Social Change
The Contribution of F.B. Meyer (1847–1929)
(Studies in Evangelical History and Thought)
This is a fresh appraisal of F.B. Meyer (1847–1929), a leading Free Church minister. Having been deeply affected by holiness spirituality, Meyer became the Keswick Convention's foremost international speaker. He combined spirituality with effective evangelism and socio-political activity. This study shows Meyer's significant contribution to spiritual renewal and social change.
2003 / 1-84227-195-4 / xx + 184pp

Geoffrey Robson
Dark Satanic Mills?
Religion and Irreligion in Birmingham and the Black Country
(Studies in Evangelical History and Thought)
This book analyses and interprets the nature and extent of popular Christian belief and practice in Birmingham and the Black Country during the first half of the nineteenth century, with particular reference to the impact of cholera epidemics and evangelism on church extension programmes.
2002 / 1-84227-102-4 / xiv + 294pp

Alan P.F. Sell
Enlightenment, Ecumenism, Evangel
Theological Themes and Thinkers 1550–2000
(Studies in Christian History and Thought)
This book consists of papers in which such interlocking topics as the Enlightenment, the problem of authority, the development of doctrine, spirituality, ecumenism, theological method and the heart of the gospel are discussed. Issues of significance to the church at large are explored with special reference to writers from the Reformed and Dissenting traditions.
2005 / 1-84227330-2 / xviii + 422pp

Alan P.F. Sell
Hinterland Theology
Some Reformed and Dissenting Adjustments
(Studies in Christian History and Thought)
Many books have been written on theology's 'giants' and significant trends, but what of those lesser-known writers who adjusted to them? In this book some hinterland theologians of the British Reformed and Dissenting traditions, who followed in the wake of toleration, the Evangelical Revival, the rise of modern biblical criticism and Karl Barth, are allowed to have their say. They include Thomas Ridgley, Ralph Wardlaw, T.V. Tymms and N.H.G. Robinson.
2006 / 1-84227-331-0

Alan P.F. Sell and Anthony R. Cross (eds)
Protestant Nonconformity in the Twentieth Century
(Studies in Christian History and Thought)
In this collection of essays scholars representative of a number of Nonconformist traditions reflect thematically on Nonconformists' life and witness during the twentieth century. Among the subjects reviewed are biblical studies, theology, worship, evangelism and spirituality, and ecumenism. Over and above its immediate interest, this collection provides a marker to future scholars and others wishing to know how some of their forebears assessed Nonconformity's contribution to a variety of fields during the century leading up to Christianity's third millennium.

2003 / 1-84227-221-7 / x + 398pp

Mark Smith
Religion in Industrial Society
Oldham and Saddleworth 1740–1865
(Studies in Christian History and Thought)
This book analyses the way British churches sought to meet the challenge of industrialization and urbanization during the period 1740–1865. Working from a case-study of Oldham and Saddleworth, Mark Smith challenges the received view that the Anglican Church in the eighteenth century was characterized by complacency and inertia, and reveals Anglicanism's vigorous and creative response to the new conditions. He reassesses the significance of the centrally directed church reforms of the mid-nineteenth century, and emphasizes the importance of local energy and enthusiasm. Charting the growth of denominational pluralism in Oldham and Saddleworth, Dr Smith compares the strengths and weaknesses of the various Anglican and Nonconformist approaches to promoting church growth. He also demonstrates the extent to which all the churches participated in a common culture shaped by the influence of evangelicalism, and shows that active co-operation between the churches rather than denominational conflict dominated. This revised and updated edition of Dr Smith's challenging and original study makes an important contribution both to the social history of religion and to urban studies.

2006 / 1-84227-335-3 / approx. 300pp

July 2005

David M. Thompson
Baptism, Church and Society in Britain from the Evangelical Revival to
Baptism, Eucharist and Ministry
The theology and practice of baptism have not received the attention they deserve. How important is faith? What does baptismal regeneration mean? Is baptism a bond of unity between Christians? This book discusses the theology of baptism and popular belief and practice in England and Wales from the Evangelical Revival to the publication of the World Council of Churches' consensus statement on *Baptism, Eucharist and Ministry* (1982).
2005 / 1-84227-393-0 / approx. 224pp

Martin Sutherland
Peace, Toleration and Decay
The Ecclesiology of Later Stuart Dissent
(Studies in Christian History and Thought)
This fresh analysis brings to light the complexity and fragility of the later Stuart Nonconformist consensus. Recent findings on wider seventeenth-century thought are incorporated into a new picture of the dynamics of Dissent and the roots of evangelicalism.
2003 / 1-84227-152-0 / xxii + 216pp

Haddon Willmer
Evangelicalism 1785–1835: An Essay (1962) and Reflections (2004)
(Studies in Evangelical History and Thought)
Awarded the Hulsean Prize in the University of Cambridge in 1962, this interpretation of a classic period of English Evangelicalism, by a young church historian, is now supplemented by reflections on Evangelicalism from the vantage point of a retired Professor of Theology.
2006 / 1-84227-219-5

Linda Wilson
Constrained by Zeal
Female Spirituality amongst Nonconformists 1825–1875
(Studies in Evangelical History and Thought)
Constrained by Zeal investigates the neglected area of Nonconformist female spirituality. Against the background of separate spheres, it analyses the experience of women from four denominations, and argues that the churches provided a 'third sphere' in which they could find opportunities for participation.
2000 / 0-85364-972-3 / xvi + 294pp

Nigel G. Wright
Disavowing Constantine
Mission, Church and the Social Order in the Theologies of
John Howard Yoder and Jürgen Moltmann
(Paternoster Theological Monographs)
This book is a timely restatement of a radical theology of church and state in the
Anabaptist and Baptist tradition. Dr Wright constructs his argument in dialogue
and debate with Yoder and Moltmann, major contributors to a free church
perspective.

2000 / 0-85364-978-2 / xvi + 252pp

Nigel G. Wright
Free Church, Free State
The Positive Baptist Vision
Free Church, Free State is a textbook on baptist ways of being church and a
proposal for the future of baptist churches in an ecumenical context. Nigel
Wright argues that both baptist (small 'b') and catholic (small 'c') church
traditions should seek to enrich and support each other as valid expressions of
the body of Christ without sacrificing what they hold dear. Written for pastors,
church planters, evangelists and preachers, Nigel Wright offers frameworks of
thought for baptists and non-baptists in their journey together following Christ.

2005 / 1-84227-353-1 / xxviii + 292

Nigel G. Wright
New Baptists, New Agenda
New Baptists, New Agenda is a timely contribution to the growing debate about
the health, shape and future of the Baptists. It considers the steady changes that
have taken place among Baptists in the last decade – changes of mood, style,
practice and structure – and encourages us to align these current movements and
questions with God's upward and future call. He contends that the true church
has yet to come: the church that currently exists is an anticipation of the joyful
gathering of all who have been called by the Spirit through Christ to the Father.

2002 / 1-84227-157-1 / x + 162pp

P **Paternoster:**
thinking faith

Paternoster
9 Holdom Avenue,
Bletchley,
Milton Keynes MK1 1QR,
United Kingdom   July 2005
Web: www.authenticmedia.co.uk/paternoster